A New Stage of Civilization

A New Stage of Civilization: Striving for the Great Harmony

BY

SHIXIONG CAO
Retired Professor at the School of Economics, Minzu University of China

emerald PUBLISHING

United Kingdom – North America – Japan – India – Malaysia – China

Emerald Publishing Limited
Emerald Publishing, Floor 5, Northspring, 21-23 Wellington Street, Leeds LS1 4DL.

First edition 2025

British Library Cataloguing in Publication Data
A catalogue record for this book is available from the British Library

ISBN: 978-1-83708-259-9 (Print)
ISBN: 978-1-83708-258-2 (Online)
ISBN: 978-1-83708-260-5 (Epub)

Contents

About the Author

Shixiong Cao is the corresponding author. He is a retired Professor at School of Economics, Minzu University of China. His interests include ecology, economics, and politics. His research has focused on institutional economics, ecological restoration, ecological economics, development economics, and environmental policy, and he has published more than 160 papers (including 130 English and 30 Chinese papers) in journals including *PNAS*, *Science*, *Nature*, *Economic Systems*, *Future*, *Economic Modeling*, *Time and Society*, *Earth-Science Reviews*, and the *Journal of Cleaner Production*. He won the Science and Practice in Ecology and Society Award in 2014. His paper titled "Development and Testing of a Sustainable Environmental Restoration Policy on Eradicating the Poverty Trap in China's Changing County" was selected for the Faculty of 1,000 Biology award in 2009. He has taught the courses development economics, social economics, and governance economics. He has been one of the most highly cited scholars and top scientists in the world since 2018.

Acknowledgements

I thank Geoffrey Hart of Montréal, Canada, for his help in writing this book. I am also grateful for the comments and criticisms of the anonymous reviewers and my colleagues.

Introduction

Human civilization has struggled with hatred, conflict, and war since the first people tried to privately own property and protect their property and the resources it provides against other people. This phase of civilization has lasted for at least 7,000 years, and probably much longer. Since the 1970s, promoted by the Chicago School of Economics, the global economy has fallen into a development model that rejects government regulation and strives for a completely free market. The success of this approach led to the collapse of the communist movement in the former Soviet Union and reform of the economic system in socialist countries such as China. At the same time, the worldwide wealth gap between the richest and poorest people has rapidly widened. The lack of government supervision inevitably led to multiple economic crises, including the "great recession" of 2007–2009 associated with the American subprime mortgage crisis. Unfortunately, such anthropogenic disasters sometimes overlap natural disasters such as the COVID-19 pandemic that began in 2020, and these simultaneous disasters create greater difficulties for human society.

Unfortunately, due to limitations imposed by term and election limits (e.g., limits on how many years a US president can serve, statutory limits on the maximum period between elections), politicians are strongly motivated to approach issues from the perspective of their own short-term interests (e.g., getting re-elected). Although most politicians still regard their national interests as more important than their own, an unfortunately high number place national or personal interests above the interests of humanity as a whole when they judge whether an action is right or wrong. (The relationships between a state, a country, and a nation are subtle. For simplicity, I will generally refer to *countries* and *nations* in this book but will use *state* in a special context in Chapter 4.) They rarely consider the evolution of society from a truly ethical perspective that accounts for the needs of all of humanity. Without an appropriate ethical perspective, it's impossible for them to understand the evolution of society as a whole. However, if we can start from a historical perspective, based on a longer time scale and overall perspectives based on human social and economic development, these perspectives let us see political outcomes and their consequences more clearly. About 2,500 years ago, the Chinese philosopher Confucius emphasized that "all people in the world are brothers," which is true from both biological and ethical perspectives. Therefore, political concepts that distinguish humans into different races and groups appear

A New Stage of Civilization: Striving for the Great Harmony, 1–8

doi:10.1108/978-1-83708-258-220251001

childish, false, and unproductive. Rather than uniting the world, these concepts will lead to division and confrontation. How we can unite humanity so that we can jointly address natural and social challenges is an unsolved problem.

Since the 1960s, humanity has experienced several major turning points. First, Rachel Carson (1907–1964) published *Silent Spring* (Carson, 1962). Since then, environmental protection has become a widely accepted norm. Second, since the 1970s, the world's developed countries and rapidly developing countries are both showing a decreasing birth rate, and the alarm over overpopulation is easing, although it has now been replaced by growing fears of population shrinkage, which will have important demographic consequences. Third, since the 1990s, the global knowledge economy has let knowledge workers replace manual laborers as the main creators of wealth, although manual labor remains critical for any society (e.g., farming). Fourth, global climate change and the associated natural disasters have attracted more and more attention, although this has not led to the collaborative action that will be necessary to solve this problem. I ask readers to keep this last phenomenon in mind, since everything I describe in this book will be affected by the consequences of ongoing climate change.

Some politicians, such as China's leaders, emphasize that this is a once-in-a-century period of change. However, if we observe the development of human society at larger temporal and spatial scales, we see that human society is entering the kind of special period that occurs once in a millennium. In particular, the traditional private ownership system that has operated for thousands of years cannot solve the abovementioned problems, leading to political conflicts and economic crises caused by globalization, simultaneously with large-scale natural disasters caused by government willingness to ignore the climate crisis. To explore how we will transition from the present situation to the next development stage for society, we must consider how the old paradigms have begun to show their limitations, and what may replace them. In this book, I will use examples from Chinese history (because Chinese history has the world's longest continuous duration and thus provides more evidence), as well as recent social and economic changes in China, while also accounting for Western history, to interpret the driving forces that guide the development of human civilization. Based on this analysis, I will propose a series of methods and paths to achieve the "Great Harmony" proposed by Confucius from the perspectives of culture, politics, economics, and the environment. Given the negative impact of the Cold War mentality, which led to nearly a century of unproductive conflict, I will strive to avoid the harm caused by nationalist thinking and to combine the wisdom of traditional Chinese philosophy with the achievements of Western science and culture. Throughout, I will adopt the perspective of "one world, one country" to support the smooth transition of human society to a more inclusive and cooperative stage of civilization.

The Framework of This Book

This book is not only an academic work but also a reference book for students and professionals in fields such as cultural studies, political science, economics, and environmental science. Considering the rapid evolution and fast pace of modern society, readers may not have time to read this book in one go. Therefore, I have written each chapter of this book so that it can be completed independently. I explain one of the key concepts in each chapter so that readers can selectively read the chapters they are most interested in, rather than having to read the entire text.

In the first three chapters of this book, I discuss cultural topics. The first chapter criticizes the errors of the capitalist ideology of "everyone for themselves" and the communist ideology of "selfless contribution to the state," which represent two current societal extremes. Instead, I propose the construction of a "prosocial society" based on the ideology that everyone has responsibility for other members of society and must dare to accept this responsibility. This would become the starting point for more harmonious social development. Chapter 2 reviews the long-term survival of Chinese culture, with a focus on traditional values such as cultural diversity and inclusivity. My goal is to demonstrate the Confucian philosophy of harmony through diversity as a more reasonable alternative to a single cultural ideology such as capitalism or communism. This chapter will also help readers understand the difference between the Confucianism of 2,500 years ago and its main philosophical opponent, *fajia* philosophy. *Fajia* has been misleadingly translated as "legalism," but it more closely resembles what is now called authoritarianism or *realpolitik* (https://slife.org/legalism-in-chinese-philosophy). Chapter 3 specifically introduces the harm caused by the centralized politics advocated by both ancient Chinese emperors and modern Chinese governments and the problems this centralization has caused; these include China's difficulty in matching Western successes such as scientific innovation. I will propose answers to the famous question of Joseph Needham about why China has not produced science as good as Western science, and Qian Xuesen's question about why China's good basic education has failed to cultivate outstanding talents.

Chapters 4–6 discuss political topics. From an economic perspective, a country is an institutional arrangement to meet the needs of a population, particularly in the context of an insufficient resource supply. Although a large and increasingly specialized population can provide both better access to resources and economies of scale in exploitation of the resources, any attempt to expand the population and economy without limits can lead to wars and other disasters. Fortunately, Confucius proposed a solution: the *great harmony*, whose goals are to avoid war and achieve harmony by building a political system that brings together nations in the form of a federation based on economic cooperation (see Chapter 4). Unfortunately, governments have the dual and contradictory attributes of both serving the people and exploiting them. Therefore, any nation must face the challenge of developing a political system that balances these contradictory attributes (see Chapter 5). Whether in historical periods or contemporary society, achieving this balance has been jeopardized by collusion between the government and the wealthy, leading to unequal distribution of social wealth, which is the main cause of poverty and social unrest. From a certain perspective, both poverty and unrest can be seen as carefully planned "political conspiracies" (see Chapter 6).

Chapters 7–9 discuss economic development issues. China's current economic growth has been promoted by a new institution that I call the "shared property rights" regime, in which innovative knowledge workers obtain a share of the benefits created by their innovations. This solves the problem in which traditional hourly or piece-rate wages fail to capture the benefits produced by these workers by increasing their enthusiasm to innovate (see Chapter 7). This approach also protects the interests of the owners of an enterprise. Unlike traditional stock option systems, the new "knowledge" shares cannot be transferred or inherited and must be returned to the enterprise when a worker changes employment. This not only retains funds the enterprise can use to fund future innovation; it also mitigates the intergenerational transmission of wealth through inherited stock shares, which promotes poverty in those who cannot benefit from stock options. Therefore, shared property rights represents a new and more equitable system. As the number of people who rely on the new system grows, the influence of the purely capitalist system will gradually shrink, leading to coexistence of the two systems in future society (see Chapter 8).

Because such social changes can be disruptive, and therefore frightening, it's necessary to seek ways to reduce the perceived and real costs of institutional change. Scholars can motivate the public to embrace such change by communicating the benefits of the change and thereby changing public ideology. The government can also reduce the fear of change by learning from its successful implementation of innovative measures such as the creation of special economic zones (e.g., Shenzhen). In this approach, the government tests a proposed new system to confirm that it works and identify any problems that must be solved before allowing adoption of the new system elsewhere. The government can demonstrate the new approach's benefits, increase confidence by allowing modification of the approach to account for local strengths and constraints, and further decrease the fear of change by compensating anyone who will be disadvantaged by the change. By allowing the old system to continue operating in parallel with the new system, those who depend on the old system for their livelihood, power, and stability feel less fear of the system and are thus more willing to support rather than oppose the system. This approach has also been implemented on a national scale in China by allowing the political and economic systems to evolve in parallel to maintain social stability. For example, China's government has retained the institution of central planning to achieve the nation's goals, while gradually decentralizing power so that provinces and other administrative divisions have some flexibility in how they meet these goals. This reduces both the perceived costs and the actual costs of institutional change and represents an important modern Chinese contribution to world culture (see Chapter 9).

Chapters 10 and 11 discuss environmental issues from the perspective that the Earth can exist without humans, but humans cannot exist without the Earth. Governments are increasingly recognizing this reality in the context of slow-moving anthropogenic disasters such as climate change and the need to account for more dramatic and sudden natural disasters such as the earthquakes, volcanic eruptions, tsunamis, and floods that frequently threaten humanity. Therefore, humanity must unite to protect the Earth's environment but also to respond to more immediate disasters (see Chapter 10). Despite decades of fearful predictions of the consequences of overpopulation, we are now facing a potential demographic disaster due to shrinking populations (Chapter 11). With the rapid development of industrialization and a knowledge-based economy, combined with increasing education and improvement of women's status, the trend of families with fewer children is becoming a consistent trend in industrialized countries. The resulting population reduction may mitigate the long-standing damage caused by overpopulation but will lead to demographic problems such as insufficient taxpayers to cover the costs of government programs and insufficient consumers to sustain economic growth. Therefore, as populations begin to shrink, governments will need to find ways to encourage childbirth to create a population capable of sustaining future society. Mothers will gain higher social status because they have the unique power to create the scarcest resource (new humans) in future society.

In Chapter 12, I review and summarize the book's content.

Differences Between the Book and Previous Publications

Most previous scholarly research has suggested that Confucianism, Buddhism, and Taoism represent the entirety of traditional Chinese culture, but this is not the case. An important omission in previous work relates to a philosophical conflict between Confucianism, which demands that the government serve the people, and *fajia*, which demands that the people serve the government. *Fajia* has been favored by Chinese governments throughout history because it preserved their power. To make *fajia* more palatable to the people, rulers tried to disguise *fajia* as nothing more than a different form of Confucianism, promoting service to one's country on behalf of the people through government service. Today, whether in Chinese or other languages, the literature on Chinese culture is heavily influenced by the legacy of authoritarianism (with *fajia* often mistranslated as "legalism") disguised as Confucian culture.

To help readers understand modern Chinese culture, Chapter 2 explores the differences between *fajia* culture and Confucianism. *Fajia* has continued to oppress the Chinese people for more than 2,500 years, creating tragic historical events such as banning of Confucianism by Emperor Qin Shi Huang and the Cultural Revolution launched by Mao Zedong. Historically, Chinese dynasties have fallen after an average of 71 years since *fajia* culture was implemented because the people revolted when they could no longer tolerate their oppression. Unfortunately, Confucius did not provide specific strategies for building a people's political power to counterbalance the government's power. One goal of this book is to propose solutions to this omission of Confucian philosophy.

As a scholar, one of my responsibilities is to find the courage to speak truth to power. Chapters 3, 5, and 6 criticize the harm that has been done to contemporary Chinese society by excessive reliance on *fajia*. Chapters 7–9 provide a detailed introduction to Chinese institutional innovations during the more than 40 years since Deng Xiaoping opened China to the West and began reforming its economy and society. Today, China struggles against the contradiction between two goals: strong and monolithic centralized government based on the ideologies of Marx and Mao, with the goal of harmonious economic development, and the cultural diversity advocated by Confucius, which emphasizes harmony through diversity. The great harmony of Confucius, which emphasizes a shared future for all humanity, will necessarily coexist with Chinese socialism.

Political economists have constantly debated the efficiency of various forms of property ownership, including the public ownership of all resources under communism and the private property rights under capitalism. They have largely ignored the possibility of a third system that combines the best aspects of both forms of property. In this book, I have proposed a third alternative, which I call the shared property rights system, that is different from and that combines aspects of these two older systems. If this approach proves to be as successful as I believe, it will lead society into a new stage in which multiple systems coexist within an overall prosocial context.

Some scholars don't distinguish between evolution and revolution and believe that violent revolution is an effective means of social progress, but this is not necessarily the case. In thousands of years of history, many regimes have been violently overthrown, but most social progress has been a matter of gentle evolution rather than violence or bloodshed. China's peasant uprisings unquestionably provided opportunities for new dynasties to emerge but contributed little to social progress. (I will discuss this in more detail in Chapter 8.) The real process of institutional evolution (Chapter 9) is more like the growth and development of a tree, in that each new branch sprouts from the stem or older branches and is nurtured by those older structures. It is the combination of the new and old branches that contributes to the tree's growth, not the new branches alone. The appearance of new branches does not negate the importance of the old branches, particularly since the new branches cannot grow into the sunlight without support from the old branches. For example, when society developed the concept of private ownership of property, it gradually built on the foundation of an older system in which families or small communities owned most property collectively.

In the same way, when new industries emerge, new production relationships, new forms of employment, and new social groups also emerge. For example, early communities of small farmers that emphasized self-sufficient agricultural production gradually gave rise to the production of surplus food that could be sold, and wealthier farmers often became *a new social group* (e.g., merchants, landlords) who had strong incentives to privatize ownership. A similar transition occurred from small-scale domestic production of necessary items such as agricultural tools to large-scale manufacturing of such goods, accompanied by the expansion of capitalism and increased numbers of workers with the specialized skills required to focus on a single specialized activity (e.g., building specific tools) or to work in factories. Today, the information revolution depends on the innovation of knowledge workers and their development of new techniques and technologies. The rapid growth of this new social group has led to the evolution of new institutional arrangements to meet their needs, and these institutions will be a key foundation for evolution of the next stage of civilization. Just as the growth of a tree's new branches does not negate the existence of the old branches, modern institutions such as the shared property rights system will coexist with older institutions (such as private property rights) for a long time. The diversity of harmonious systems is one of the fundamental characteristics of the *great harmony*.

From a historical perspective, social progress never stops. But we must recognize that social progress is not linear and that institutional lock-in and economic reversals occur from time to time. For example, the neoliberal movement that has emerged since the 1970s has represented a regression of the economic system or a lock-in of the capitalist system, and failure to regulate the associated economic activity has led to severe economic shocks and the associated recessions. Such reversals can be political, not just economic. For example, China is moving backwards toward a system based strongly on Marxist dogma. Since 2012, China's economic growth has slowed, with disturbing similarities to the economic recession that struck Japan in the 1990s. The ideal of the *great harmony* is still a work in progress!

For more than 2,500 years, Chinese society has pursued a world based on the *great harmony*. The greatest danger to future society will not be wars caused by differences between countries in ideology and interests, but rather how to adapt to the many challenges facing the natural environment, such as destruction of ecosystems and the natural disasters associated with climate change. Building a global federal political system that overcomes the failures of existing federations such as the United Nations and transforming the mission of the global military from responding to war to responding to natural disasters will be essential if we are to survive apocalyptic disasters such as climate change. Here, I must emphasize that if we cannot abandon the old mindset of nationalism and state supremacy, society will inevitably embark on the "clash of civilizations" that American political scientist Samuel Huntington feared. For more than 20 years, I have been searching for a feasible alternative that would achieve harmonious development by recognizing our shared humanity and developing political, economic, and cultural institutions that promote the Confucian great harmony.

By integrating historical and cultural knowledge with modern political economics, I show how we may achieve the goal of "one home, one world" – a beautiful future for society and the start of a new civilization. I firmly believe that the moment has arrived for humanity to awaken and embrace the beginning of a new era!

Chapter 1

Lessons Learned from the Cold War

After the Industrial Revolution of the 18th century CE, the global economy grew rapidly as mechanized mass production flourished. At the same time, the gap between the rich and the poor in capitalist countries widened rapidly, causing increasing dissatisfaction among workers, which was exacerbated by low wages and extremely poor working conditions. Because a market economy is guided by Adam Smith's famous "invisible hand," it is blind to changing human needs. This has resulted in periodic overcapacity (when supply exceeded demand, leading to layoffs of workers) and economic crises (*market failure*), further impoverishing workers and leading to a series of strikes that affected Europe's major economies. The labor movement, most familiar to us in the form of labor unions, evolved to solve the livelihood problem for impoverished workers, and gradually expanded into a political movement whose goal was to eliminate exploitation of workers and promote the ideal of communism, under which workers would be fairly compensated for their contribution to the economy. On June 2, 1847, the world's first communist party (the "Communist League") was founded, with the goal of overthrowing the exploitative upper class and establishing a society based on equality of all citizens. In November 1847, the Second Congress of the Communist League commissioned Karl Heinrich Marx (1818–1883) and Friedrich Engels (1820–1895) to draft *The Communist Manifesto*.

In March 1917, the proletarian revolution broke out in Russia. Vladimir Lenin (1870–1924) led the left wing of the Russian Social Democratic Labor Party (the Bolsheviks) and united with other parties on the left to launch an uprising in St Petersburg. He then established the world's first communist state regime, the Soviet Federal Socialist Republic, during what has become known as the "October Revolution." On November 7, 1917, he seized power from the provisional government that had overthrown the Tsarist regime in February of that year. After the October Revolution, various ethnic groups in Russia established their own independent states or autonomous republics. During the civil war, the Soviet Federation formed military and political alliances with Ukraine, Belarus, Azerbaijan, Armenia, and Georgia to fight against what they perceived as a common enemy. On December 30, 1922, the Union of Soviet Socialist Republics held its first Congress of Soviets (councils of representatives) in Moscow and adopted the founding treaty that established the Soviet Union.

A New Stage of Civilization: Striving for the Great Harmony, 9–36

doi:10.1108/978-1-83708-258-220251002

The establishment of the Soviet Union provided a base for the global communist movement and promoted the vigorous development of an international communist cause. After World War II, the global communist federation achieved its greatest success, with 39 countries that declared themselves communist countries (Cao & Liu, 2020). In the rest of this book, I will make an important distinction for clarity: I will refer to *communism* as the approach followed by the Soviet Union before 1991 and China before Deng Xiaoping's opening to the West in 1978, and *socialism* as the approach followed by China after 1978. This is clearly simplistic but nonetheless lets me make a useful distinction between the two systems.

1.1. Lessons Learned from Communism

The international communist movement took the elimination of capitalism and the realization of global communism as its ultimate goal. This inevitably aroused the vigilance of and vigorous resistance by the capitalist countries. Because the world had just emerged from the horrors of World War II, no nation was eager to begin a new war. Instead, the competition between the communist and capitalist ideologies became what is known as the Cold War, which centered on the competition between the Soviet Union and the United States for global dominance. (Many other countries were, of course, involved. Here, I am only naming the two most powerful players.) This is perhaps one of the most important ideological wars in history. When the Soviet Union was founded, it immediately repudiated the market economy that had operated throughout most of history. The Soviet Union comprehensively implemented a single, centrally planned economic system that was designed to replace capitalism and all of the old systems by which Russia (the core of the Soviet Union) had operated.

After the Great Depression of the global economy in the 1930s, the capitalist countries recognized some of the flaws in a purely capitalist society and adopted some of the features of a centrally planned economy, in part by implementing the "Keynesianism" – proposed by economist John Maynard Keynes and his colleagues. "Keynesian economics" advocates that in times of economic crisis, the state should adopt expansionary economic policies to promote economic growth by increasing demand. That is, they should increase government spending, permit deficit financing, stimulate the economy, and thereby sustain prosperity. However, in contrast with the Soviet Union's single centrally planned economic system, the reforms implemented by capitalist countries did not try to eliminate the traditional market-based economic system but rather promoted increased government intervention using the mechanisms of the market-based economic system. This, along with other factors, allowed the capitalist countries to resolve the economic crisis and once more achieve economic growth.

The central planning adopted by communist countries didn't suffer from the global Depression but encountered an additional series of social problems unique to their system such as economic *stagflation* (i.e., inflation accompanied by stagnation of economic growth). In the 1980s, Soviet leader Mikhail Sergeyevich Gorbachev (1931–2022) admitted the problems with the Soviet system and promoted acceptance of the American model, which had been largely successful and had demonstrated that the market was a powerful economic force. As a result, the communist system collapsed throughout Eastern Europe without firing a single shot at its Western enemies. The collapse of the communist system led to dramatic changes. Former Romanian President Nicolae Ceausescu (1918–1989) was executed by firing squad in one of the series of anti-communist rebellions that led to the breakup of the former Yugoslavia, Czechoslovakia, and Soviet Union. This is perhaps the first successful example in history of subduing the enemy through ideological warfare without fighting a "hot" war (Cao, Lv, et al., 2015).

1.1.1. Lessons of the Soviet Union

Dramatic changes continued after the collapse of the communist nations of Eastern Europe. For example, Russian President Boris Nikolayevich Yeltsin (1931–2007) became convinced that only a pure market economy based on the American system could save Russia (Cao, 2012a). Without any preparation, he abandoned the planned economy and fully opened Russia to the global market. When Russia opened their foreign exchange markets, the Western world's financial giants came pouring in. Of course, this led to abuses. For example, Western financial giants such as George Soros are said to have spent US$25 million to drive down the ruble's value. Such efforts, accompanied by Yeltsin's lack of success, led to rapid and large devaluation of the ruble, by 1.7 million times compared to the US$ (Basdevant & Hall, 2002). Another problem was that Yeltsin adopted the system of owning corporate stocks (i.e., "shares" in the ownership of a company) and divided ownership of state-owned enterprises by distributing these shares among Russian citizens. Unfortunately, many immediately sold their shares, leading to the collapse of the Russian stock market and offering large financial gains to rich investors who had predicted the problem and sold their stocks first.

In the end, Russia's economy was looted by capitalists, as well as by powerful Russian individuals, and the country's socioeconomic system collapsed. Between 1990 and 2000, Russia's gross domestic product (GDP) fell by 52%, industrial output decreased by 64.5%, and agricultural output fell by 60.4% (Russia Statistics, 2019). Russia went from a large industrialized country with one private car for every four households in the 1980s to a developing country with a GDP smaller than that of China's Guangdong Province. Since 1993, Russia's population has been decreasing, and the average life expectancy has dropped from 70 years in the 1980s to 64 years in the early 2000s (World Bank, 1958–2023), setting a new record for the most rapid peacetime lifespan decrease in history (excluding plague periods). Many people don't understand why Yeltsin allowed the currency to depreciate for 10 years by holding to the capitalist ideology and allowing investors to buy and sell rubles freely. This is a remarkable feature of all ideological wars.

Ideology refers to the moral standards generally observed by a social group and that guide the group's behavior. Once a person firmly believes that a certain idea is right, they will then adhere to this standard. For example, for thousands of years, the ancient Chinese people practiced "arranged marriage," in which parents decided who their children would marry. Until Western liberalism came to China in the 20th century, few people questioned the correctness of this practice.

In March 1985, Mikhail Sergeyevich Gorbachev was elected as the general secretary of the Central Committee of the Communist Party of the Soviet Union and proposed to boldly transform the Soviet Union with "new thinking" (Cao, Lv, et al., 2015). His new thinking strongly advocated democracy and humanitarianism that were not based on class, historical practice, or ideology and instead promoted a common value standard for everyone (Zwick, 1989). After more than five years of propaganda, Gorbachev's new thinking took root in the hearts of people throughout the Soviet Union (including Eastern European countries) and became a core value (i.e., the de facto ideology of the Soviet Union at that time). Boris Yeltsin subsequently insisted on not intervening in the market for a decade because of the ideology he promoted with his colleagues, which arose from their conviction that market fluctuations were normal and that under a free-market system, the economy would eventually stabilize and rebound.

In essence, the plundering and subsequent crash of Russia's economy is yet another example of the harm caused to the free market by an *oligopoly*. An oligopoly is a market state dominated by a small number of sellers (the oligarchs). Its most prominent feature is that a few enterprises monopolize a certain industry, and their output accounts for such a high proportion of the industry's total output that they effectively control the supply of the industry's products. The dominant players may be individuals rather than enterprises. Due to decades of the constraints imposed by long-term central planning of the economy, few Russians understood international currency transactions when Russia opened its foreign exchange market, and few people used Russian currency (the ruble) in international markets. Therefore, ruble-based transactions were quickly controlled by several financial speculators, who created a typical oligopoly market. At the same time, the Russian government adopted an anarchic (unregulated) free trade policy that provided a wonderful opportunity for financial oligarchs to speculate on the ruble.

How did they achieve this? First, the financial speculators deposited a certain amount of international currency (such as US$10 million) in a Russian commercial bank and then borrowed rubles at the current exchange rate using that cash as collateral to "leverage" their original investment. For example, if we assume that the exchange rate is 1.0 ruble per US$, the speculator can typically borrow 10 times this value (i.e., US$100 million) by financially leveraging their cash deposit. If these rubles are released into the financial market in exchange for US$, this will lead to depreciation of the ruble and appreciation of the US$. If the rubles sold by the financial speculators gradually alter the initial exchange rate of 1.0 to a final exchange rate of (for example) 0.1, the gradual sale of their 100 million rubles will earn them an amount that depends on how fast they sell their rubles and how fast the ruble depreciates in response to that sale; for example, they might earn US$55 million if the mean exchange rate during the period of their loan was US$0.55 per ruble. Finally, they could exchange US$15 million for rubles at the final exchange rate of 0.1 and earn 150 million rubles that they would then use to repay their loans and interest payments with the Russian bank. Thus, they would earn a net profit of US$40 million for an investment of only US$10 million. This process can be repeated as long as the speculator believes that there will be someone willing to purchase their rubles in the exchange market. This repetition over a period of 10 years turned the ruble into a piece of waste paper.

In addition, Western financial speculators also opened their own savings banks in Russia to absorb the rubles held by the Russian people and then exchanged these rubles for dollars to earn additional profits. This speculation cost them almost nothing but further accelerated depreciation of the ruble. This is a common method used by financial oligarchs to stir up trouble in international foreign exchange markets. They used similar methods to plunder Latin America (1985), Britain (1992), Southeast Asia (1997), and others, creating financial tragedies one after another for people around the world (Arestis & Glickman, 2002; Sevilla, 1995; Weisbrod & Rojas-Suárez, 1995).

The experience of Russia tells us that the free market works best as a theoretical ideal, since it is a highly imperfect economic system in practice. After the global economic depression in the 1930s, the governments of all countries in the world intervened in the market to varying degrees with good intentions (i.e., to stabilize the global economy). However, not everyone acts with good intentions. Managing a national currency is a powerful tool for preserving a government's credibility. It is also an essential tool to resolve exchange rate disputes through reciprocal negotiations between governments, such as the Plaza Accord. (This refers to the agreement reached by the finance ministers and central bank governors of the United States, Japan, the Federal Republic of Germany, France, and the United Kingdom at the Plaza Hotel in New York on September 22, 1985, to jointly intervene in the foreign exchange market to depreciate the US$ against other major currencies and mitigate the huge trade deficits developed by the United States.) A government's control over the international exchange rate of its own currency is an important tool for managing the national economy. The abandonment of this power is no different from a loss of sovereignty.

The capitalist market-based economy maintains its rapid growth through the "invisible hand" of the market. However, it also works through intervention by states and individual actors (e.g., the abovementioned oligarchs) in ways that distort the action of that hand. Both state inaction and unwise state action lead to cyclical fluctuations of the market that can sometimes grow out of control, leading to an economic crisis. Ideological warfare has been a continuous part of the evolution of civilization. The Cold War is just a recent example. For example, the religious wars between the many different Christian denominations and between Islam and Christianity have lasted for many hundreds of years. Unlike the Cold War, these ideological conflicts frequently became "hot" wars, leading to millions of deaths. Today, similar ideological conflicts have not stopped. For example, the 9/11 terrorist attack was motivated primarily by religious ideology (this refers to the terrorist attack on the World Trade Center in New York and the Pentagon in Washington on September 11, 2001) (Cao, Lv, et al., 2015).

1.1.2. Rigidity of an Ideology

When an ideology describes the world well and provides effective tools for dealing with the world's complexity, it can serve its believers well. Unfortunately, ideologies tend to become more rigid over time, due in part to the human reluctance to change, and prevent their believers from seeing exceptions to the rules that underlie the ideology and from seeing that the world has changed enough to invalidate all or part of the ideology. For example, the Chinese people have learned from decades of state monitoring and censorship to be afraid to talk about politics, and few scholars are willing to begin that discussion for fear of reprisals. Has the world changed enough that this monitoring and censorship, originally intended to preserve stability by presenting a single consistent message from the state to the people, is no longer necessary? Ideologies are present in every moment of our lives and in the deepest depths of our souls. Wherever civilization has existed, ideology has been involved, and wherever there is ideology, there is politics. In this section, I will discuss the consequences of the relationship between ideology and politics.

1.1.2.1. What Is Politics?

In a narrow sense, *politics* refers to the behavior of the government and its component political parties in governing the country. More broadly defined, politics refers to the social and power relationships between individuals, between groups, and between individuals and groups. It can also refer to the relationships between humanity and nature, which interact with the relationships between countries, governments, groups, and individuals. Ideology is a fundamental factor that unites individuals into groups and countries, and ideological differences inevitably lead to political differences and politics. An ideology is a moral standard that is universally observed, though to a greater or lesser degree, by the members of a social group. However, an ideology can become rigid over time. This can be seen in the Chinese phrase that "when words get sour, adding more words is useless."

The first prerequisite for governance is ideological consistency, since that ideology defines how the state functions. In this context, an ideology's goal is clear: to help the citizens live in harmony and unite to meet the challenges they face. However, ideologies tend to become inflexible over time, as they represent codes of conduct that have been formed by specific groups of people in response to their natural and social challenges over a long period of time. Because they do a good job of meeting those challenges, they are stable and change only with difficulty when the conditions under which they evolved change. This rigidity means they can also be difficult to reconcile with competing ideologies.

An unfortunate consequence of ideological rigidity is that there is no motivation to seek a compromise that incorporates the best aspects of two or more ideologies. Chinese culture emphasizes the principle that everything is limited and that we shouldn't overuse something; that is, we shouldn't follow an ideology to extremes. By actively seeking a compromise strategy that tolerates and harmonizes different ideologies, thereby avoiding or mitigating conflicts, it becomes easier to achieve the *great harmony* proposed by Confucius. The wisdom of traditional Chinese culture can help us resolve ideological conflicts and provide intelligent strategies for achieving a more harmonious society.

1.1.2.2. Spiritual Power

Ray Cline, director of the Center for Strategic and International Studies at Georgetown University in the United States, proposed a formula for calculating a nation's comprehensive strength (Cline, 1975):

$$\text{National strength} = \text{material strength} \times \text{spiritual strength}$$

Here, material strength refers to the total of a country's military strength, economic strength, population, resources, and other material strengths, whereas spiritual strength represents the willingness to follow an ideology no matter how difficult this becomes (and therefore implicitly accounts for heroism). The spiritual strength is measured from 0% to 100%. Therefore, no matter how large a country's material power, its strength falls to zero when the state's spiritual power is zero.

If we compare people to computers, the human mind is equivalent to the software, and the ideology is the operating system on which the software runs. No matter how much software you put on your computer, and how high the software quality, it will be ineffective without a good operating system. The core of the spiritual power is an effective ideology. When the spiritual component of a country is destroyed, the country becomes powerless.

Consider the case of the Korean War in the 1950s. Before the war, China and the Soviet Union negotiated with the United States to divide Korea into northern and southern occupied areas, separated at 38°N, with each area governed under their occupier's political ideology (communism in the north and capitalism in the south). Warfare soon began, with the two Koreas serving as proxies for the occupiers. When the United States intervened in this war to resist the invasion of South Korea by North Korea, this should have led to a quick resolution of the invasion given the overwhelming material advantages enjoyed by the Americans. However, China intervened on the side of North Korea because the two countries shared a communist ideology.

In 1950, the year after the Chinese communist revolution, the United States produced 87.72 Mt of steel, equal to 140 times that of China. The total value of American industrial and agricultural production was US$280 billion, versus about US$10 billion in China at the exchange rate of the time, which amounts to 28 times that of China (China Statistics Agency, 1952–2021; United States Statistics, 1953). Despite this huge gap, the Chinese military was still able to keep the US military south of the 38th parallel. What explains China's success? The spirit derived from the heroic ideology that was so strongly valued by Chinese culture.

Sacrificing one's life for a righteous cause is the highest level of heroism in Chinese ideology, so it is easy to understand why so many soldiers rushed forward to participate in this war. Under Chinese ideology, those who did not rush to participate were seen as cowards and were despised. The war was seen as a threat to China, not just to North Korea, and became a national crisis that required acts of heroism to resist the Americans. The United States lacked an equally strong ideology; opposing the spread of communism had not yet become a central component of American society's ideology.

Because of how strongly ideology affects how we think, it's necessary to understand the ideologies we have accepted and how they affect key social processes such as economic development and environmental protection. Therefore, to predict the future of society, it is first necessary to understand the ideology that is sustaining the evolution of society. It's important to note that no ideology is ever truly universal; there is always some variation in what people believe and how strongly they believe it. In this book, I focus on the overall trend of the evolution of social ideology rather than individual differences.

1.1.2.3. The Political Significance of Ideology

Ideology is an important resource during a war. Sun Tzu's *Art of War*, written more than 2,000 years ago, emphasized that victory without war is the wisest approach. Adopting an effective ideology is one way to accomplish this. As I described earlier for the Cold War, ideological conflict can sometimes achieve victory without a "hot" war. After the collapse of the Soviet Union in 1991, China emerged as a major rival to the United States. However, the rivalry currently focuses more on economic power than on military power. Although the conflict appears, on the surface, to be based on the same ideology (i.e., competition within a global economic market), the true situation is more subtle. Both countries have embraced market-based capitalism, but China has learned from the fall of the Soviet Union and has adopted an ideology that has gradually evolved into what the Chinese government calls "socialism with Chinese characteristics."

"Birds of a feather flock together" represents the observation that people with the same or similar moral standards tend to become part of the same group and may even become friends. This is not because one of the friends has superior understanding or a more powerful position in society but rather because their worldviews are compatible, and this promotes agreement and cooperation. In contrast, friendship and cooperation are more difficult when two people do not agree on an ideology, since the resulting disagreements often lead to quarrels.

People in different regions or countries may, because of historical reasons, have formed different ideologies, so that there are countless contradictions in their worldviews. Because of ideological rigidity, these contradictions are often irreconcilable. Therefore, in dealing with international relations, American Secretary of State Henry Kissinger noted that "America has no permanent friends or enemies, only interests" (Kissinger, 1995). Smart politicians don't waste their time obsessing over the rights and wrongs of ideologies but instead take advantage of ideological differences for their political and economic gain.

Ideologies exist in two main forms: customs and beliefs. Both are aspects of a person's culture. From a broad perspective, a group's *culture* refers to the sum of the spiritual wealth created by the group as well as the sum of all the group's knowledge, including science, religion, customs, literature, and art. We often say that science, literature, and art know no borders; however, the religious and customary aspects of an ideology are strongly influenced by a person's country of origin.

Unlike science, in which a key goal is to form consensus among different groups or individuals, people from different ideological environments may be reluctant to seek a consensus, particularly when their ideologies differ greatly. Ideology directly constrains behavior. It not only affects an individual's judgment and behavior but also affects the judgment and behavior of a country. For example, the current competition between China and the United States seems very complicated. But at its core, it is focused on the ideological opposition between Eastern and Western culture, complicated by differences in how the two countries perceive capitalism. Dealing with the contradictory aspects of their ideologies will be essential if the goal is to reach consensus and détente.

Although an ideology that agrees with the world's characteristics can provide a powerful tool for dealing with the world's complexity, an incorrect ideology leads to ignorance and error. For example, the Chinese began to bind the feet of women from the Southern Tang Dynasty (937–975 CE), and included the empress Li Yu (937–978 CE). The empress danced with strips of cloth wrapped around her feet in the shape of the moon. This shape gradually evolved from the emperor's preference into a legal system for the mutilation of women. Girls had their feet tightly wrapped in cloth from the age of four or five to make their feet smaller, and the cloth was not untied until their adult skeletons were set; in some cases, the binding remained for the rest of the woman's life. It was not until 1949 that communist China banned this practice. The abuse of Chinese women lasted for more than 1,000 years. During this period, Emperor Zhu Yuanzhang (1328–1398 CE) of the Ming Dynasty (1368–1644 CE) prohibited domestic foot binding, but the effect was short-lived. In the Qing Dynasty (1636–1912 CE), the government also prohibited the Manchu people and women in the Imperial Palace from binding their feet. However, the preferences of the Han people remained strong, and they convinced the Manchu people of the Qing Dynasty to continue binding a woman's feet.

Confucius noted that individuals are responsible for more than their own relatives and children and must use their power to support the old and other vulnerable groups so that everyone can realize their own value and share in social welfare. This coexistence reflects what Confucius called *the great harmony*. After the Great Depression that damaged the global economy in the 1930s, the capitalist world gradually moved toward what became known as a welfare society, in which the government took measures to aid the poorest and most disadvantaged individuals. However, such efforts were constrained by nationalistic ideologies such as the American concept of self-sufficiency. Such ideological opposition slowed social progress and, in some cases, reversed the progress that had been made. One of my most important goals in writing this book is to explore the possibility of an ideology that can be accepted by most readers and that can contribute to eliminating warfare and other forms of conflict and to achieving a more harmonious coexistence for everyone.

1.2. The Economic Significance of Ideology

What is the point of having an ideology? An ideology provides a code of conduct that will motivate people to cooperate through the moral constraints imposed by the ideology and the ways it encourages prosocial behavior. Thus, an effective ideology minimizes the contradictions within groups, maintains harmony and friendliness within groups, and promotes the harmonious development of society by potentially mitigating conflicts between groups. A careful study of religious cultures reveals that most surviving religions and cultures encourage cooperation, encourage prosocial behavior, and oppose and punish antisocial behavior, thus directing the evolution of society toward harmony (Cao, 2016a).

In all stages of society, religion has played contradictory roles. On the one hand, religion has attempted, through the development of an ethical ideology, to promote social harmony. On the other hand, religious ideology has been a tool for seeking power over a nation's political structure, leading to inequity and conflict. Today, religion has been marginalized in many countries, but in some of the most powerful countries, it continues to exert a powerful political influence. Religious leaders have different titles that reveal how their ideology shapes their role in society. For example, in Judaism, the word *rabbi* for a religious leader translates as "teacher," and represents the leader's role of teaching Jews how to seek God. This is similar in some ways to how Chinese people see Confucius (551–479 BCE). The Japanese, influenced by China, have similar attitudes toward religion. In contrast, many Christian sects see their "priest" as someone who must intercede between God and worshippers, because they believe that worshippers cannot seek God successfully on their own. But in all cultures, an important role of religion is to spread knowledge, educate people, and maintain social stability.

1.2.1. The Supervisory Role of Religion

One function of religion is to monitor behavior and promote prosocial behavior, in a role that could be described as society's "third eye." To regulate behavior, most religions have created deities that are everywhere and that are always watching us. If you know that you are being watched and will be punished for bad behavior, there is strong motivation toward what your religion defines as good behavior. Conversely, good behavior is rewarded (e.g., in heaven, through reincarnation). A case study illustrates the tradeoffs between good and bad behavior.

The following study is based on a true story that happened in Taiwan. When you refuel your car at a gas station, the gas that fills the hose doesn't enter your car's fuel tank; instead, it flows back into the gas station's reservoir to reduce the risk that it will ignite and cause a fire. Although you pay for this fuel, the gas station retains it. What should gas stations do with the extra fuel?

In the Taiwanese story, a gas station's employee wondered whether they should report this problem to their boss. Doing so would be ethical, but the boss might continue to simply take all the extra money from this fuel. It would also be impractical to give the gasoline to every customer who filled their tank at the station. Finally, he came up with a solution: sell the extra gas and split the money with co-workers. Most employees were willing to accept the plan, but one refused. So what should this employee do to be "right"? The employee thought about quitting, but didn't dare because he feared his co-workers would know that he disapproved of their plan and that he might turn them in to the station's manager. So how did the employee deal with the problem?

On the advice of his teacher, he chose to remain silent and instead apply to a school. That way, he could make it clear to everyone that he was leaving his employment to improve his education, not as a protest against his co-workers. Although this might not be the most ethical behavior, it was the recommended solution in a Chinese context because it offended the fewest people, thereby avoiding social disharmony.

The case study provides an example that is characteristic of Chinese culture, which differs greatly from Western culture in this case. A Westerner would probably report the problem or resign and seek employment elsewhere. It's a very Chinese solution to neither go along with behavior they dislike nor to offend someone by engaging in conflict over the solution.

1.2.1.1. What Does a Society Look Like Without Divine Supervision?

When the Chinese Communist Party came to power in 1949, it began to promote atheism. (In this book, I will not discuss the question of whether gods exist; instead, I will focus on the fact that many believe in their religion's god.) In 1957, China's rectification movement aimed to overthrow all "ghosts and gods," and the clergy from various temples were forced to leave their temple. Then came the Great Leap Forward of 1958, which followed from the same logic. (The "Great Leap Forward" refers to the government's imposition of mass production targets from 1958 to 1960 to achieve the goal of catching up with the West in 15 years. It included the implementation of production and supply systems based on shared labor, common dining halls, free meals, and free medical treatment.) Trouble and problems soon followed.

To meet the production targets, the people responsible for meeting the targets lied about their progress. In 1958, the national news agency reported that farmers in Henan Province could produce 10 t of grain per mu (0.067 ha) of land, an annual increase to more than 20 times the yield before the Great Leap. Others followed suit, trumpeting their own higher yields. The national news media was caught up in a frenzy of fake prosperity, which had consequences I'll describe shortly.

Why did Chinese society instantly become like this? Because China's gods, and the associated moral supervision, were replaced by the Chinese government; that is, gods were no longer present to punish people for unethical behavior, and those who accepted the government's policy of atheism had no fear of punishment after death. But the atheists knew that they could be punished by their supervisors and therefore had a strong incentive to make their supervisors happy. This ideology led farmers and their managers to report clearly unrealistic results because they were rewarded for this behavior, with no fear of being punished for lying.

China's grain output in 1958 was more than 10 times that in 1957 only because local governments and the news media inflated the figures. Mao Zedong initially didn't believe these results (Wu, 2010). Then, he read an article in the *People's Daily* newspaper published by Qian Xuesen (1911–2009, a Chinese aerospace engineer and cyberneticist who made significant contributions to the field of aerodynamics and established engineering cybernetics, but he was not an agricultural expert). In the article, "How much grain per mu will there be?" Qian noted that a maximum of 30% of the solar energy captured by a plant can be converted into nourishment for the plant, and 20% of the amount captured can be converted into food for humans and animals. Yet despite this, he claimed that the yield of rice per mu was 20 times this limit imposed by the laws of physics.

Another article by Qian, *Knowledge is power, mechanical problems in agriculture – 5000 kg/mu of grain is achievable*, made a more nuanced calculation (Wu, 2010). Qian calculated that if the light-harvesting efficiency of plants could be increased to 100%, the annual production of plant biomass could reach 470 t. As an expert in rocket engineering, Qian clearly knew that the energy conversion rate of any fuel could never reach 100%, yet he calculated the grain yield based on the assumption of a 100% light energy conversion rate. In reality, the average utilization of light energy by Chinese crops in 1958 was only 0.4%.

This case is a good illustration of the importance of ideological supervision, whether by a deity or by the people. In a society such as China's society in the 1950s, this supervision was lost and was replaced by supervision by officials who had no incentive to be honest. Deception is a common strategy in human interactions when honesty may have adverse consequences and there is little penalty for dishonesty. For example, flattery is a common trick used by subordinates to please their superiors (Dugas, 2016).

Failing to detect and punish fraud has consequences. After listening to Qian, the abovementioned rocket expert, Mao Zedong, began to think about how to store so much grain. As a result, he built a large number of warehouses. Immediately after the Great Leap Forward, China experienced widespread crop failures and suffered three years of famine, resulting in a GDP loss of 17% (Cao, 2012a). If we use the average population growth rate from 1956 to 1958 to estimate China's population from 1959 to 1961, the population decreased by 25.98 million people. After subtracting the decrease in the number of babies born, the number of abnormal deaths was about 7.64 million (Table 1). Because many of the people who died were the elderly, newborns, and people with underlying medical conditions, they were counted as normal unavoidable deaths. But if food had been plentiful, many of these people could have survived. More importantly, this disaster could have been avoided if local officials had reported the actual yields and advised the government to purchase additional food from other countries or regions of China to ensure that the grain warehouses were full when the famine occurred. Because local officials hid information on the magnitude of the disaster, disaster relief was delayed. Mao Zedong immediately fired the government

Table 1. Estimation of the Number of Excess Deaths in China from 1959 to 1961 Caused by the Famine. The Predicted Population and Births Represent the Numbers Expected Based on the Birth and Death Rates from 1956 to 1958.

	Population ($\times 10^6$)	**Growth Rate (%)**	**Predicted Population ($\times 10^6$)**	**Population Reduction ($\times 10^6$)**	**Births ($\times 10^6$)**	**Birth Rate (%)**	**Predicted Births ($\times 10^6$)**	**Reduction of Births ($\times 10^6$)**	**Excess Deaths ($\times 10^6$)**
1956	627.80	2.14	627.80	0	19.61	3.12	19.61	0	0
1957	642.38	2.32	642.38	0	21.38	3.33	21.38	0	0
1958	653.46	1.72	653.46	0	18.89	2.89	18.89	0	0
1959	660.12	1.02	666.92	6.80	16.35	2.48	20.55	4.20	2.59
1960	662.07	0.30	673.71	11.64	14.02	2.12	20.61	6.59	5.05
1961	664.57	0.38	675.70	11.13	9.49	1.43	20.65	11.16	0
Total				29.58				21.94	7.64

Source: China Statistics Agency (1952–2020).

leaders in Qinghai and Henan provinces, where the famine was worst, and this punishment may have prevented similar disasters in subsequent years by encouraging other provincial leaders to be more honest.

To some extent, this disaster arose from ideological rigidity and a loss of diversity of opinion in China's social system. The result was a society in which leaders only heard what they expected to hear. Just as the loss of biodiversity increases the vulnerability of natural ecosystems to disaster, a cultural system that becomes an ideological monoculture is fragile, and this can destabilize a society (Cao, 2012a). However, it's also true that the fear of being punished for not meeting production targets was a powerful force in causing the disaster. An ideology that prioritizes obedience over truth is constantly at risk of such disasters.

1.2.2. The Redemptive Role of Religion

Humans are good at giving. Every time there is a natural disaster, not only the government but also ordinary citizens give generously to those who were affected by the disaster, and a country's temples and other places of worship unite their members to provide food and other assistance. This is how society has survived hard times again and again. With declining interest in religion, governments have increasingly begun to take responsibility for such assistance. However, research will be required to determine how well they handle this problem, and in the meantime, much of the assistance comes from the people.

After the Industrial Revolution, the division of labor in society led to increasing specialization, but as some people became specialists, their ability to survive a disaster became more and more fragile. Unlike in agricultural societies, where every household stockpiled food to get them through times of famine, few people in today's industrialized and urbanized society are willing or able to store enough food to get them through a disaster. There have also been changes in the ideology of many professions to emphasize the profit motive. For example, doctors and teachers once performed their jobs primarily because they believed they were doing good for society and were treated with respect because of this. Now, however, the desire to earn money for their services has become a powerful motivation. Commercialization of these professions has led to a society based on self-interest, and this new ideology has weakened society's strength (Shang et al., 2019). To reverse this trend, we must develop a new ideology that will support social cohesion and promote the development of civilization.

Salvation is one of the important functions of religion, and performing good deeds is one way to achieve salvation. However, clergy serve other important roles in social cohesion. For example, one important job of the Christian clergy is to accept confessions from those who have "sinned" and offer forgiveness or psychological comfort. Buddhist clergy play a similar role in China, even today, when religion is deprecated. In addition, clergy provide help, medical care, and assistance in gathering food during a crisis. For example, the city of Yushu, in Qinghai Province, lies at an elevation of nearly 4,500 m above sea level and is sparsely populated, making transportation difficult. After the 2010 Yushu earthquake, government aid was unable to reach the city quickly, making rescue work difficult. At the critical moment, more than 300 Buddhist clerics left their monastery to rescue people from the rubble and provide psychological comfort before government forces arrived (Cao, 2012a). This demonstrates that religion provides some key services unavailable from the government.

1.2.3. The Environmental Roles of Religion and Government

The Earth's environment is a common resource shared by 8 billion people and is clearly a *public good.* A public good is one whose utility affects the public as a whole, regardless of whether any individual is willing to consume the good. For example, efforts to eliminate the smallpox virus protected everyone, not just those who paid for the vaccine. In contrast, a private good (such as bread) that is consumed by one person generally cannot be consumed by others. Unfortunately, when no person or group is responsible for protecting a good, the tragedy of the commons (Hardin, 1968) is a likely outcome; this name describes a process in which a public good (the "commons") is damaged or destroyed because nobody is responsible for protecting it. Tragedies related to a failure to protect public goods affect not only individual decisions but also the state's decisions. If our goal is to improve social cohesion and stability, we must find new ways to prevent such behavior. Finding these ways will be an important challenge for economics and other areas of research.

Economics currently offers several ways to protect public goods. One common, ethical, and potentially effective approach is to offer payment for ecological services, in which people who are harmed by environmental protection efforts (e.g., eliminating grazing so that degraded grasslands can recover) receive enough compensation to replace lost income or are helped to relocate to areas where they can continue earning their livelihood. As another example, carbon trading lets rich regions pay poor regions to compensate them for the greenhouse-gas emissions by rich regions. However, because environmental protection is not controlled in the same way as markets for common commodities, these practices have often been costly and unsatisfactory (Liu et al., 2015).

If one believes that destroying the environment will be punished by a deity (i.e., a pro-environmental religious ideology), then environmental protection becomes a common goal, and the cost decreases because it will be widely shared. For example, Taoism advocates the unity of nature and man and therefore promotes environmental protection. As a result, trees that are thousands of years old are a common sight at Taoist sites (Fig. 1). No one dares to cut down such trees while they are protected by a deity. In contrast, similar trees that grow where non-religious people live are not considered sacred trees and will be cut down if local residents require the wood. From their perspective, keeping trees to provide a spiritual connection with nature and improving air quality is the government's task, not theirs.

Most religions invent evil or punitive gods to discourage unethical behavior. The aim is to encourage prosocial behavior, which is a value of continuing importance provided by religion. Although the reality of religion is constantly questioned by scientists and atheists, its cultural and economic values cannot be ignored. Therefore, humans cannot just erase it from society without providing something to replace it. Governments sometimes try to play this role, with varying degrees of success.

Fig. 1. At the Shennong Temple in Shennongjia, a 1,000-Year-old Tree Grows. Legend has it that one summer, when a tree was split in half by a lightning bolt, the temple's Taoist priest inserted a silver statue of Shennong (an ancient Chinese emperor who was worshipped as a cultural hero) into the gap and asked for heaven's blessing. As a result, the tree miraculously healed, and no one dares to harm the sacred tree. (Photograph by the author.)

1.3. Ideological Evolution

After the Spring and Autumn Period and the Warring States Period (770–221 BCE), China entered an age with an agricultural economy based on self-sufficiency. The original family-based management system of tribes and small villages was preserved, and a centralized system that was centered on the emperor was formed, with control from the top down. Ancient China's economic system was characterized by the coexistence of a self-sufficient rural agricultural economy, a market economy based on small urban workshops that produced specialized items such as tools, and a centralized government monopoly on strategic goods such as iron, salt, and the products or services of high-profit industries. After residents of each village or workshop completed their required military service and paid their taxes, the government allowed them to benefit from their hard work under the traditional family management system by retaining the remaining profits. For nearly 2,000 years during China's imperial era, the political system was a federal state (i.e., a federation) composed of tribes, villages, and larger cities. The tribal system in the countryside and the centralized politics in the cities together formed a stable, mutually dependent, political structure.

To create a unified national ideology that would increase social cohesion, the central government of Emperor Wu during the Han Dynasty (who reigned from 141 to 87 BCE) seemed to accept the Confucian philosophy of governing the state for the benefit of the people but, in reality, adopted an authoritarian philosophy (*fajia*) in which the goal was to support the emperor (rather than the people) by supporting the government. This ideology lasted, in various forms, for more than 2,000 years until 1949, when the Communist Revolution led to the founding of the People's Republic of China. Confucius advocated moral education and believed that the cultivation of moral citizens promoted the harmonious development of individuals and society. He advocated benevolence and respect (the Chinese utopian ideas that a father loves his son, a son honors his mother, brothers are harmonious with each other, and all people get along). As a result, the number of wars launched by China after Emperor Wu gradually decreased. However, the centralized and authoritarian political ideology has had serious negative impacts on China's socioeconomic development (which I will discuss in later chapters).

1.3.1. Ideology of the Ancient Chinese

Hero worship is a common phenomenon in most societies. In traditional Chinese ideology, Pangu, Tianwu, Bifang, and Nuwa were all gods who fought with harsh nature. In the early stages of Chinese civilization, the "three emperors and five sovereigns" (mythological leaders who lived from ca. 3162 to 2070 BCE) were not only the ancestors of the Chinese people but also the gods of the Chinese people. Subsequently, historical figures who made important contributions to Chinese society were canonized. Examples include Lao-Tsu (571–471 BCE), the founder of Taoism; Guan Yu (160–220 CE), the great general of the Three Kingdoms (220–280 CE); and Yue Fei (1103–1142 CE), the great general of the Southern Song Dynasty (1127–1279 CE).

As humanity advanced in knowledge and sophistication, the mysterious world of the gods gradually made room for a focus on human rather than divine concerns, thus giving birth to humanism. As early as the late Shang Dynasty (1600–1046 BCE), King Wu of the Zhou (who reigned from 1088 to 1043 BCE) adopted a humanist ideology and issued the slogan that we should respect heaven but protect the people in response to the traditional idea that royal power was conferred by heaven. Subsequently, whether during the time of Mencius (372–289 BCE), who proposed benevolent governance under which the people are more important than the monarch, or Zheng Wei (580–643 CE) in the Tang Dynasty, who proposed that "water can carry a boat or overturn it" (i.e., people can support or overthrow a government), Chinese ideology acknowledged that the people are the foundation of a country. (This aspect of the ancient ideology is preserved today in China's socialist ideology.) "Human life matters" became a key principle in Chinese ideology.

Chinese historical records from this period (1600 BC–1911 AD) have also been based on the importance of people, recording not only the deeds of the emperors but also the deeds of lower-class people such as sages, famous scholars, craftsmen, and artists. The ancient government set up shrines for those who made outstanding contributions to Chinese society so that future generations would remember their contributions. The idea that "the world is for the common people" is deeply rooted in Chinese history and culture. This is reflected in several principles.

1.3.1.1. Public Power Is Greater Than Private Rights

The evolution of China's culture has not always been clear. However, throughout Chinese history, there has been a common thread: the importance of family ties and friendships. When taken together, these relationships represented strong social power that could outweigh that of individuals. China still recognizes the importance of family relationships, which date back to the earliest period of private ownership of resources, and the old family structure and family culture have been retained. In the traditional Chinese social structure, based on the teaching of Mencius (372–289 BCE), the family was the foundation of the country, and the country was considered an extension of the family. The interests of the family are directly related to the vital interests of each family member, and the social status of individuals is also determined by their status in the family. In primitive society, family ownership of public resources such as land became the basis of social ethics. Xun Zi (313–238 BCE), a famous philosopher, said that people are not as strong as cattle and can't walk as fast as horses, but cattle and horses are both used by humans because people understand cooperation, which gives us power over cattle and horses, who do not. Humans have become the masters of the Earth because of the power of our social relationships. No one can master all skills, so we survive as a society through division of labor and cooperation. To acknowledge this, Xun repeatedly stressed that humans need to depend on each other to survive.

The ancient Chinese believed that individual interests were consistent with group interests, and that only when the group was in harmony could individuals be happy. If the group's harmony is disrupted or weakened by conflicts or chaos, the individual cannot survive. *The Hanshu*, which represents an official history of the Han Dynasty that was compiled in 105 CE, says that if we don't cooperate, we will be unable to utilize the available natural resources and will not obtain enough resources for a satisfactory life. In ancient China, the traditional ideology placed the overall interests of the group above individual interests, and this has become the core of the Chinese tradition that public power is greater than private power. Chinese people also believe that fairness and selflessness represent benevolence. They will therefore focus on their personal interests only when those interests benefit the group's overall interests. Despite the repeated succession of dynasties in Chinese history, the stability of family ties and the ideology that emphasizes the primacy of national interests has kept Chinese culture stable even while governments fell. The foundation and ideology of this social structure did not weaken until the large-scale urbanization that began in the late 1900s. The *great harmony* described by Confucius emphasizes *public power over private power* and provides important support for this principle. It has therefore played an important role in preserving China's culture.

1.3.1.2. Governance Must Emphasize Social Order

In ancient China's society, maintaining the social hierarchy was a spiritual pillar of traditional Chinese ethics. Ancient China was known as "the land of propriety and righteousness," and *li* (social norms) played an important role in traditional Chinese ethics and morals. Confucius emphasized "self-restraint," with the goal of maintaining social stability. Because *li* is a general term for social order, the word is also used in the general sense of rules. Xun Zi also wrote that people are required to follow the *li* in terms of food, clothing, living spaces, equipment, chariots, horses, manners, and behavior. After a long period of influence on Chinese culture, *li* has gradually changed from an external compulsion to an internal consciousness that people generally follow because the guidelines are widely recognized by society.

The *I Ching*, which began as a book of prophecy, gradually became a book of philosophical commentaries (the "ten wings"). One of its insights is that if each member of a family fulfills their responsibilities, the family can prosper. Confucius inherited this belief. Unfortunately, starting in the Han Dynasty, selfish rulers corrupted the ideology of "benevolence and love" emphasized by Confucianism into a rigid system based on the "three cardinal principles" (ruler over subject, father over son, and husband over wife) and "five constants" (humanity or benevolence, righteousness, propriety or following the *li*, wisdom, and faithfulness). The system's goal was to constrain behavior so as to promote harmony. During the Han Dynasty, the philosopher and politician Dong Zhongshu (179–104 BCE) based the authority of the gods on the three cardinal principles and described them as the will of heaven. Since then, the hierarchy of emperor over subject, father over son, and husband over wife became the social norm in ancient China. This represents the invasion of *fajia* into Confucian culture, causing the first serious regression of Confucianism's influence. Nonetheless, the principles of benevolence, righteousness, propriety, wisdom, and trustworthiness (the five constants) have been retained as personal codes of conduct.

These constants represent the desired state that should be achieved by the Chinese people. These guidelines teach that we should be kind to and tolerant of others, that those who care about others can also care about themselves, and that we must conform to the rules to earn the respect of others. Only through self-restraint can we succeed, and if we respect others, they are more likely to respect us.

1.3.1.3. Defining the National Character Through the Doctrine of the Mean

The ancient Chinese realized that the overall harmonious development of society could only be achieved through the harmonious coexistence of individuals. For the society as a whole, order and harmony promote each other. On the one hand, order is established to ensure social harmony and tranquility. On the other hand, harmony and tranquility will naturally promote stability of the social order.

In international relations, the ancient Chinese believed in harmony among all nations. From the perspective of national governance, the traditional emphasis was on policies that satisfied the needs of the people. From the perspective of interpersonal relations, harmony brings good fortune, and fortunate people are less likely to look elsewhere for satisfaction. From the perspective of family relations, harmony leads to prosperity. From the perspective of commercial activities, harmony generates wealth. These perspectives have shaped a national characteristic, which represents the path of moderation (i.e., to not overdo anything or rely excessively on a single approach). This is considered by Chinese people to represent an ideal state of diversity and unity and creates an inclusive approach in Chinese traditional culture. This aspect of the national character not only makes the Chinese people compatible with foreign cultures but also has a positive impact on the formation of a unified but multi-ethnic country.

Harmony is not only a consensus goal of most Chinese people but also a characteristic of China. This national character has prompted the Chinese people to follow the principles of reconciliation and comity among nations and the principle of being kind and generous to others. Because of the importance of harmonious coexistence between humanity and nature and the resulting ecological ethics, Chinese culture embraces the Taoist ecological principle that "goodness is like water" because, like water, it moistens all things. It emphasizes the harmony of self-cultivation and develops a peaceful state of mind based on contentment. The pursuit of harmony between neighbors is an important goal of traditional Chinese ethics and morals.

This context of harmony and moderation is at the core of Chinese social ideology and has maintained the diversity of Chinese culture and promoted the development and prosperity of Chinese culture for thousands of years. Respectful, humble, and harmonious interpersonal relationships have enhanced social morality, raised the level of social civilization, alleviated social conflicts, maintained the long-term unity of China, formed a strong force for cohesion of the Chinese nation, and provided fertile soil for the evolution of China's social system.

1.3.2. The Influence of the Market Economy on Contemporary Chinese Ideology

After the founding of the People's Republic of China in 1949, Mao Zedong's ideology (often called "Mao thought") dominated China. Mao emphasized collectivism, put collective interests above individual interests, and opposed privatization and private ownership. In 1978, after Mao's death, Deng Xiaoping opened China to the West by launching market-oriented reforms and shifting the focus of Chinese ideology from the communist concept of class struggle to the new concept of economic development. He emphasized that it was acceptable for some people to get rich first and proposed the philosophy that it doesn't matter if a cat is black or white, so long as it catches mice. That is, he emphasized the effectiveness of a solution rather than its adherence to communist ideology. Deng's proposed ideology, which was based on the Western market economy system and permitted individualism, was a radical change from Mao's collectivist ideology and the "benevolence" that was emphasized in ancient Chinese society. Deng's ideology also contrasts with the capitalist philosophy of "everyone for themself" (Keenan, 2017) and the traditional Chinese ideology that *a gentleman loves money but earns it legally*. Obviously, these two ideas are difficult to fuse into a single consistent ideology.

The moral system of traditional Chinese society developed from a system based on small and self-contained villages. In this era of small-scale peasant farming, a person was basically a fixed part of a highly stable and small social unit and might live in the same village all their life. Even marriages mostly took place between residents of villages where parents knew each other. Therefore, most members of the society knew each other, and the desire to be respected by those they interacted with served as a check on their words and deeds. A good reputation earned long-term social rewards, and noble moral standards helped to restrain and regulate social behavior. This stability contrasts strongly with imperial and modern government systems, including those affected by *fajia*, which lacked such stability; Chinese dynasties that followed *fajia* were replaced after an average of only 71 years.

After 1949, Mao Zedong changed the traditional ideological system to emphasize collective ownership of all resources and to prioritize national needs over individual needs. The supervision of individual behavior also changed from informal mutual supervision among villagers (i.e., peer pressure) to compulsory and open monitoring of behavior by the state. After 1978, Deng Xiaoping promoted a socialist version of the capitalist market economy but took longer to change the laws and ideology established under Mao. During this period, Mao's ideology was increasingly questioned, and a new economic ideology was established to replace it. Because of his focus on the economy, Deng urged everyone to stop debating capitalist and communist ideologies and instead focus on economic development. Unfortunately, this new focus failed to provide a means of promoting moral, prosocial behavior and instead relied heavily on personal morality.

The market economy ideology encourages individual struggle, acquisition of personal wealth, and personal freedom. This capitalist ideology clearly conflicts with both traditional Confucianism and Mao thought, but the power provided by wealth has some resemblance to the power of emperors under the *fajia* philosophy. In the absence of a moral system that regulated behavior either by outside forces (government supervision) or internal forces (personal morality), moral disorder gradually became a prominent social problem in China. Moreover, the cultural differences between China and the West and China's new emphasis on economic growth at all costs have led to increasingly prominent confrontations that have not been mitigated during reform of the Chinese system. Ideological confusion is therefore an important and intractable problem facing China.

The introduction of a market economy system has greatly increased the enthusiasm of the Chinese people to devote themselves to economic development. In the absence of strong legal constraints, the Western ideology of self-interest quickly replaced the traditional moral system of the Chinese people. This has been exacerbated for powerful individuals, such as government officials, who follow the *fajia* system of ensuring that the government structure benefits them and not the people. When power is more important than the law, Chinese people are less willing to report unethical behavior of their colleagues than in the West (Leung et al., 2009). The result is equivalent to encouraging or at least condoning unethical behavior. Because taxes are collected locally, but allocated nationally by the central government, local governments have looked for ways to increase tax revenue and, in doing so, have forgotten their responsibilities to their citizens. As a result, many local governments have formed a subtle community of interests with the business community (Shang et al., 2019) and have even cooperated directly with this community to control commodity prices, prevent free competition, and perform other questionable activities. Due to weak supervision of economic activity, enterprises have produced a large number of fake and shoddy goods and, in so doing, have caused great harm to the rights and interests of consumers while seriously damaging the country's reputation. The infamous melamine scandal in 2008 killed at least six Chinese children, sickened hundreds of thousands, and hospitalized nearly 53,000, according to the *Lancet* (*Lancet* Editors, 2009). In 2006, China's economic losses caused by fake commodities reached more than 200 billion RMB, accounting for 2% of GDP that year (Shang et al., 2019).

In a society where economic interests are considered more important than anything else, it is difficult to find motivation to regulate moral standards, so self-serving antisocial behavior continues to spread, thereby disrupting relationships between people, weakening social ties, and damaging prosocial activities such as comforting or healing the dying, leading to widespread cheating and extortion. The government's failure to punish and discipline those who violate the law further promotes moral chaos, resulting in endless stories of extreme behavior. For example, when there is a road traffic accident, bystanders no longer rush to help the injured people. On November 16, 2010, more than 40 villagers in Lantian County of Shaanxi Province robbed an overturned vehicle of its goods and no one helped citizens who were injured during this accident (Shang et al., 2019). Deng Xiaoping's emphasis on economic development over all other goals, combined with a lack of punishment for those who damaged social harmony or the public good, has led to a gradual loss of professional ethics and of a sense of responsibility to the community. The primacy of self-interest has further weakened the sense of social responsibility of the Chinese people. Chinese entrepreneurs are well aware that corporate wrongdoing is rarely punished as long as it fuels regional economic growth, and this rewards unethical behavior. A recent survey found that 88% of Chinese people were eager to exploit loopholes in the law, and that 60% of Chinese employees were equally keen to find loopholes in the law (Leung et al., 2009).

As China's economy has grown rapidly since the start of the reform and opening-up policy in 1978, the population's mobility has increased, and the accelerating flow of people has weakened the supervision of individual behavior, leading to an increased incidence of antisocial behavior. This confirms the findings of behavioral scientists (Milinski & Rockenbach, 2007): "When reputation is at stake, humans switch from selfish to altruistic behavior." Unfortunately, when this policing is weakened, humans have a powerful incentive to deceive other members of their group. In the absence of such supervision, Chinese moral standards have continued to go downhill.

In a society based on subsistence farming, cheating can decrease the group's ability to survive, so mutual supervision among individuals promotes ethical behavior. However, in rapidly developing countries such as China, urbanization increases the size of social groups, accelerates population mobility, and increases the cost of mutual supervision among individuals. Market-based exchanges can be anonymous, and the market itself does not have a monitoring capacity or a true risk-sharing mechanism, so markets are inherently amoral (Fafchamps, 2011). The Western political system is based on a combination of separation of powers with checks and balances that prevent the abuse of power through independent supervision and an independent judicial system. This provides a theoretical basis for the rule of law over power in Western countries and an institutional basis for preventing corruption. However, China did not implement similar legal mechanisms when it introduced the Western free-market economic system.

In a world where power is stronger than the law, officials only need to be one rank above a subordinate to control the subordinate, and this has become the case in China. This is similar, in many ways, to the power hierarchy during historical Chinese dynasties but without an ideology such as Confucianism to restrain antisocial behavior and promote harmony in the service of the people. In a society dominated by the rule of law, people are eager to solve disputes between individuals through legal channels. In contrast, in a society dominated by power hierarchies, people involved in disputes first try to bribe government officials to rule on their behalf. Judges, local heads of government, public security chiefs, department leaders, and other powerful people see this situation as an opportunity to blackmail others. This kind of abuse of power is a key reason why people in ancient China preferred to solve social problems through the family governance model, interpersonal relationships, and even in the form of heroic revenge, rather than relying on legal protection.

In a centralized society dominated by power hierarchies, people learn not to trust the justice of laws and institutions because they know that powerful individuals can make, change, or ignore the rules at will. This undermines the national spirit of a social contract and weakens social cooperation. To cope with such situations, early philosophical works such as *The I Ching*, an ancient Chinese metaphysical work that taught the Chinese how to resolve conflicts without relying on a legal system and successors such as *The Tao Te Ching, The Sushu*, and Sun Tzu's *Art of War* have sold well in China for thousands of years. Because looting is more profitable than obeying the law if one expects not to be caught or punished, moral discipline breaks down in a society dominated by power hierarchies as soon as the watchful eyes of deities and neighbors no longer promote ethical behavior, and Confucian guidelines for harmonious behavior are ignored. In June 2023, students from Jiangxi Industrial Vocational and Technical College found a foreign object that was suspected of being a mouse's head in a cafeteria meal. Market Regulation Bureau officials examined the images taken by the students and decided (despite evidence to the contrary) that it was a duck neck. Subsequently, the students came to describe this decision as "declaring that a mouse was a duck" (Jiang, 2023) to point out the absurdity of a bureaucratic system that prioritized saving face for the cafeteria operators over communicating the truth.

When power is greater than the law, it is difficult to find reliable ethical rules to guide one's behavior, so encouraging the maximization of individual interests has become the only criterion. This has led to a shift in Chinese ideology, in which Chinese people focus more on individual struggle and less and less on social harmony. They are more willing to damage their competitors through unethical means than to maximize social benefits through fair competition or win–win cooperation. This is why it is said that "one person is a dragon and two people are worms" in China (i.e., as soon as there are two people, they will try to damage each other). As soon as the external pressure wanes or disappears, Chinese people are at risk of falling into a mutually damaging power struggle. Historically, this problem lies at the root of China's long-term dynastic stagnation and the fall of dynasties, but its occurrence now is a troubling sign.

1.3.3. Future Social Development Will Require a New Ideology

Ideology is the sum of the collective ideas of humanity, including political thought, morality, culture, and religion. It is the moral standard that constrains behavior, which in turn represents the ever-present institutional arrangements and the institutional basis for maintaining society. The construction of a convincing and attractive ideology is therefore a priority for politicians. All the successful political regimes in history have relied on such an ideology. For example, in the chaotic late stages of the Eastern Han Dynasty, the central government continued to promote the story of Rong Kong (153–208 CE), who sacrificed his self-interest by giving the biggest pears to his brothers when his father asked him to share the family's pears with his brothers. Rong explained that he was young, so he should be satisfied with the smallest pears. But he also gave a larger pear to his younger brother. When his father asked why, Rong replied that his brother was younger, and that it was his responsibility to take good care of him. Government support of this story has made it an example for Chinese people to teach their children. By repeatedly telling such stories, high moral standards are reinforced to become personal judgments of what is right and wrong. The *Tao Te Ching*, *Dizigui*, and the *Analects of Confucius* are only three examples from Chinese history of how promoting an ideology convinced younger generations to accept the promoted social norms as their personal norms.

Religion also aims to encourage moral (or at least prosocial) behavior by educating people to take responsibility for their contributions to society. Both education and religion share the goal of teaching students the information they need to participate in society. For example, Confucius was one of China's earliest and most influential educators. Through such education, ideology is repeatedly reinforced to reduce the harm individuals can cause to society and increase the benefits they create. Therefore, it is important to understand the influence of both religious and secular ideologies.

After the founding of the People's Republic of China in 1949, China embarked on a communist path based on the ideologies of class struggle, based on placing collective interests above individual interests, based on emphasizing "selfless dedication" to the nation, and based on opposing the capitalist ideology of "everyone for themself." On the surface, these noble moral sentiments seem to conform to the requirements for development of harmonious social groups. Unfortunately, they fail to account for selfishness and the value of an individual's existence, which makes this ideal more utopian than practical. How can an individual survive if they think and act selflessly at all times? History has shown that this beautiful goal is nearly impossible to achieve and has negative consequences. For example, a magnitude 7.8 earthquake occurred in Tangshan on July 28, 1976, resulting in 242,769 deaths and 164,851 serious injuries. Afterward, one husband ignored his wife's calls for help, as she was only partially buried in rubble. Instead, he picked up a shovel and went to help other survivors with greater needs. He was rewarded for this behavior by the government, but his wife lost her legs due to the injuries incurred while waiting for rescue. Are selfless communist moral norms conducive to social progress? Or do they slow social progress? Society is the sum of the behaviors of countless individuals, but without individuals, how can one form a society? Ignoring the existence of individuals and failing to meet their needs is likely to have been one of the main reasons for the failure of the Soviet Union's communist system.

The capitalist and communist ideologies are two sides of the same human coin. Only by allowing independent action by individuals can a society reward effort and adapt its ideology to changing circumstances. On the other hand, only social cooperation can protect society against adverse situations such as invasions or pandemics. An ideology can account for unfairness in society, such as the gap between the rich and the poor and the ability of the powerful to oppress the weak, as well as other problems that lead to social unrest. This includes inequities such as the greater power of men than of women and their conflicts over reproductive rights. As Alexandre Dumas (1802–1870) famously wrote, a more effective solution may be to combine the two ideologies as "all for one and one for all." This agrees with Confucius' suggestions for how to achieve the *great harmony*.

To solve the social and economic problems caused by the failure of Mao's centrally planned economy, the Chinese government launched a series of reforms that accompanied its opening up to the West in 1978. It introduced a form of the Western market-based economic system, with the goal of accelerating development of the Chinese economy. However, a market economy is based on anonymous transactions rather than exchanges between individuals. Because these transactions lack a personal element, there is no personal connection that would restrain unethical behavior. One significant problem with this anonymity is that it contributes to poor oversight. This is particularly true for intangibles such as money, since the more liquid something is, the harder it is to monitor. Businesses that operate in places with highly mobile populations (such as bus stations and tourist sites) may be less reputable because customers only come once; being honest with such customers does not win repeat business, so maintaining a high ethical standard may provide no financial rewards. The examples I provided earlier in this section make it easy to understand how the introduction of the Western market economic system changed the relationships between Chinese people. Although the Western philosophy of "everyone for themself" can improve the efficiency of a market economy, it provides no reinforcement for ethical behavior, and adopting this philosophy without adding a goal of social harmony is a direct cause of China's moral decline. This decline increases the cost of social supervision and impairs society's operation, thereby harming social development.

Western society regularizes prosocial behavior through legal coercion (i.e., penalties for breaking the law) and through religious restraints on behavior.

China lacks strongly functioning versions of both mechanisms, so it will be difficult to reinforce ethical behavior. After 1978, Mao's ideology was rejected, but this created a vacancy in Chinese ideology that was not filled by a new ethical code. People didn't know how they should behave. The problem was exacerbated by a revival of *fajia*, which has spread like a malignant tumor in Chinese society. Historical experience has shown that when a social system changes, the old system either disappears or its remaining parts function less effectively, and the new system that will replace it has not yet fully developed. Thus, people don't know what ideology they should follow. As was the case in ancient China during the Spring and Autumn Period and the Warring States Period (770–221 BCE), it is difficult to avoid ideological confusion due to instability and rapid social changes.

To develop a successful ideology, we must accept that humans are social animals and that without group cooperation, no individual can survive or thrive. Ignoring the existence of individuals ignores the inconvenient fact that most people want to survive at all costs; insisting that individuals sacrifice their life for the state ignores this basic fact. If we acknowledge this fact, we must abandon both the Western philosophy of "everyone for themself" and the communist philosophy of "selfless contribution to the state" and must instead construct a new prosocial ideology that I called *prosocial society* to balance individual needs with the needs of society. This new ideology has two requirements:

First, we must recognize that humans are both individuals and social animals. Every member of society must understand that they are an integral part of that society, that their personal wealth is also part of society's wealth, and that social wealth represents the sum of all individuals' personal wealth. Those who get rich first should understand that they became rich because they have benefited from the use of resources that were created and maintained by society, that belong to everyone, and that are only temporarily in the hands of people who are able to maximize the utility of this wealth, and who have a responsibility to better serve society. Social elites have the obligation to undertake more social responsibilities and obligations to help those who have been less fortunate and to consciously promote social development.

Because society is made up of individuals, personal wealth must be invested to create new wealth and value. This process not only increases returns to the investors but also increases employment and promotes social development. If an individual's investment behavior does not have a clearly beneficial social function, it should be discouraged by the government. Only individual behavior that is beneficial to society and that will conform to society's moral code will be legal. The individual's economic behavior is not only conducted in the context of the invisible hand of the market but also in the context of society's visible and invisible moral codes. Individuals prosper only when their behavior helps society to prosper. This is the basic ethical principle of a society based on the Confucian *great harmony*.

Second, we must recognize that growing access to higher education is producing a large number of technological experts, whose innovation is the driving force for the evolution of society. (In this book, I will define "technical" innovation as an improvement of techniques rather than technology. For simplicity, I will use the phrase *technological innovation* to refer to both technique and technology.) As new industries grow, new production relationships will gradually become the core of the socioeconomic system. (I will discuss this in more detail in Chapters 7 and 8.) The people who work under the new system will become a new social group, with a higher sense of social responsibility and an understanding that they are obliged to promote cooperation rather than competition, eventually forming a new social ideology with a prosocial spirit based on sharing.

Price discrimination (in which different individuals are charged different prices for the same goods) and unfair competition inevitably hurt the poor (see Chapter 6). On the one hand, the rich are rich because of their own efforts. On the other hand, they could not have succeeded without the foundation provided by all of society, including the poor. Moreover, they often succeed by directly or indirectly engaging in price discrimination and other forms of unfair competition and by plundering the weak and stealing wealth that should also belong to the poor. To compensate for this theft, the rich must voluntarily provide relief to the poor, rather than waiting for a revolution that will produce the same result involuntarily. A fair and harmonious development path benefits both the poor and the rich. We know this is possible because of the growing ranks of philanthropists, volunteers, and educators who act quickly in response to disasters.

In this context, I propose a metaphor: that the evolution of civilization resembles the growth and development of a tree. New ideologies grow from older ideologies the way that young branches grow from older branches. Therefore, we should not completely negate the old systems, since this would rob the new branches of crucial support. Instead, we should strengthen the fine tradition of ancient Chinese culture that emphasizes collective interests over individual interests, without ignoring the interests of individuals, to build a society in which man and nature coexist in harmony. This approach has the additional benefit of enriching the culture of society and making it more dynamic.

The selfish capitalist and selfless communist represent two extremes of human nature, and history has shown that neither approach can meet the needs of both individuals and society. Reconciling these extremes requires that we recognize a simple fact: if an individual loses their life, they can no longer contribute to society. *The "prosocial society" of the future can only arise if this new ideology encourages individuals to act in ways that both benefit themselves and enrich their society.* Benefiting from the resources provided by society requires individuals to share those benefits with society. This is both realistic and ethical.

The French Revolution that began in 1789 rejected the ideology of the divine right of kings but did not eliminate the ideology of a private-property society in which everyone acted only for their own benefit. The awakening of science led to the evolution of a different ideology, in which scientists and engineers eagerly explored the world using their new intellectual tools, with an emphasis on cooperation and sharing of knowledge rather than on hoarding information for their own benefit. The *Social Contract* proposed by Jean-Jacques Rousseau (1712–1778 CE) marked the beginning of this change but not the end.

Today, society is undergoing a dramatic transformation from a civilization based on private property to a new civilization that will increasingly recognize the need for social harmony using mechanisms such as shared property rights, in which those who benefit from using the assets of a society must share those benefits with the society that permitted that use. (I will discuss this in more detail in Chapters 7 and 8.) The *great harmony* pursued by Confucius will lead us into the next stage of development of civilization.

Chapter 2

The Significance of Cultural Diversity

Dozens of ancient civilizations developed around the world and prospered until they vanished or were replaced by other civilizations. Some remain in existence today, at least in spirit; for example, the ancient Greek democracies have spiritual descendants throughout most of Europe and the West, though an ancient Greek might not recognize the modern forms of democracy. Other civilizations have left only archaeological remains. China is an exception: a recognizably Chinese civilization has existed for more than 3,500 years (based on the starting date of the Shang Dynasty, in 1600 BCE). Like all other civilizations, China experienced countless periods of warfare, leading to a long history of one dynasty replacing another. Yet a recognizably Chinese culture has persisted, despite this turmoil.

China differs because of its long ability to absorb invading or conquering cultures. After the invasion of China by other civilizations, the invader's culture soon disappeared as a separate culture because the invader adopted China's rich culture. The failure to achieve this continuity is why writing systems such as the hieroglyphs of ancient Egypt and the cuneiform characters of the ancient Sumerians have disappeared and are no longer used. In contrast, Chinese characters have remained readable for millennia and are still in use today. Another Chinese strength has been the ability of competing ideologies to coexist. For example, Taoism arose in China around 400 BCE and Buddhism entered China nearly 2,000 years ago, but these religions coexist and remain active today.

As China has rejoined the global economy after decades of isolation, the country has been experiencing a strong impact from Western economic, scientific, and social culture, which currently dominates the world. Some scholars feared that ancient Chinese culture would collapse under the impact of Western culture and the information revolution. Despite the impact of the Communist revolution and the "great proletarian cultural revolution," and the invasion by the West that followed, China retained most aspects of its original ancient culture, including writing, social customs, art, and religion. As in the case of previous invasions, Chinese culture has absorbed the invader rather than being replaced by it. For example, Chinese characters are adaptable to computer culture because they offer the advantage of high-density information storage capacity; among the commonly used worldwide translation languages, Chinese is among the most concise.

A New Stage of Civilization: Striving for the Great Harmony, 37–63

doi:10.1108/978-1-83708-258-220251003

The information revolution did not destroy Chinese culture; rather, it has helped Chinese culture to thrive and spread around the world.

In 1978, Deng Xiaoping launched China's market-oriented reform but surprised Western observers by not adopting the dominant Western style of a pure market economy. Instead, China explored new development models and paths that attempted to incorporate the concept of a market economy within a Chinese cultural context. China's rapid rise since 1978 demonstrates the success of this approach and provides an attractive alternative to current Western systems. As I noted in the Introduction, some of these innovations (e.g., the shared property rights institution that I will describe in Chapters 7 and 8) show promise for overcoming the problems with traditional capitalism, such as the concentration of wealth in too few hands. Chinese culture seems to have a "gene" for longevity. In this chapter, I will discuss how this gene may become one of the important forces to promote civilization.

2.1. The Historical Evolution of Chinese Culture

Culture can be defined as the dominant ideology that governs a civilization and is expressed in that civilization's spiritual, artistic, economic, and political activities and institutions. It can be divided into material and non-material culture. In this book, I define *culture* as the collection of a society's spiritual wealth, including tangible and intangible spiritual products such as writing, art, science, literature, philosophy, religion, and political systems, which collectively represent the sum of all knowledge (understanding of the objective world).

From its beginning, Chinese culture has observed nature with a mixture of awe and gratitude. For example, the ancient Chinese feared thunder and lightning and created two gods to represent these forces: the "god of thunder' (*Leigong*) and the "mother of lightning" (*Dianmu*). They had also learned both to fear water for the flooding it caused and be grateful for water because it nourished themselves and their crops. This led to the creation of a water *lóng* (a Chinese dragon) who controlled the water. This *lóng* was sufficiently important that the Chinese people created a *lóng* totem, and worshipped the *lóng*, claiming that they were the *lóng*'s descendants.

2.1.1. Religious and Philosophical Traditions

In early Chinese culture, the most representative works of metaphysics are the *Inner Canon of Huangdi* and the *I Ching* (*The Book of Changes*). Even today, these two books are still bestsellers. According to legend, *The Inner Canon of Huangdi* was created 4,500 years ago by the Huangdi and the *I Ching* was written 3,000 years ago by Ji Chang, who became King Wen Ding of the Western Zhou Dynasty (1152–1056 BCE). Later, Taoism and Confucianism evolved from these aspects of early Chinese culture.

2.1.1.1. Views on the Unity of Heaven and Man

The early Chinese sages, including the Huangdi, believed that humans were related to both Heaven (the divine) and Earth (the mundane), which correspond to the sun and moon in Chinese mythology. Humans and nature have the same roots, and this provides an ideological basis for belief in the unity of Heaven and humans in Chinese traditional culture. *The Inner Canon of Huangdi* proposed that *qi* (spiritual or vital energy) is the origin of the world, and that the generation, development, and extinction of all things in nature result from the interactions between *yin* (the passive or female principle) and *yang* (the active or male principle). Humans are the product of the interaction between *yin* and *yang* in Heaven and on Earth and cannot live without nature.

Humans and nature are therefore closely related. Changes in the balance between *yin* and *yang* in Heaven and on Earth will inevitably affect and restrict human activities. The harmonious coexistence between humans and nature is the foundation of physical health and social stability. This unique model provides the theoretical basis for traditional Chinese medicine and is widely used to interpret physiology and pathology, guide the diagnosis and treatment of diseases, and maintain health by preventing diseases. The traditional people-oriented theory of Chinese medicine emphasizes respecting people, caring for others, and treating diseases to save people. This is also the basis of Chinese governance.

2.1.1.2. Self-improvement and Persistence

During the era of Ji Chang (King Wen of the Zhou Dynasty, 1152–1056 BCE), Chinese culture expanded from paying attention to an individual's physical and mental health to a broader philosophy of life. The *I Ching* stresses that someone with strong willpower will continuously strive for self-improvement and will therefore become able to support an increasingly heavy burden. The book suggests that self-reliance can only be achieved through self-improvement and respect for others. At this time, Chinese philosophers believed that *change is eternal and stability is temporary*. Things will change whenever they develop to a certain extent. Only in this way can they continue to develop. Therefore, as long as we balance the advantages and disadvantages of change and remain flexible, we can achieve long-term personal and social development.

Kong Ji (Zi Si, 483–402 BCE), the grandson of Confucius, summarized early Chinese culture and wrote the book *The Doctrine of the Mean* (*Zhongyun* in Chinese), which taught people how to recognize changes in things and how to account for those changes in their affairs. The goal was to avoid the harm caused by extreme behaviors, because extreme thoughts and actions can harm both individuals and society (Fig. 2). He also taught that one should be satisfied with having enough to meet one's needs rather than selfishly pursuing more, and that one should be flexible in one's approach to life rather than relying exclusively on a single approach. For over 2,000 years, this was a compulsory textbook for the Chinese people until the fall of the Qing Dynasty in 1912. However, it must be understood that here, "change" refers to changes of ways and methods, not of goals. This is reflected in the saying that *the goal is constant but the road is flexible*, an important Chinese belief.

Once the Chinese people have set their goals, they will persevere until they reach those goals, sometimes even across generations, with children pursuing

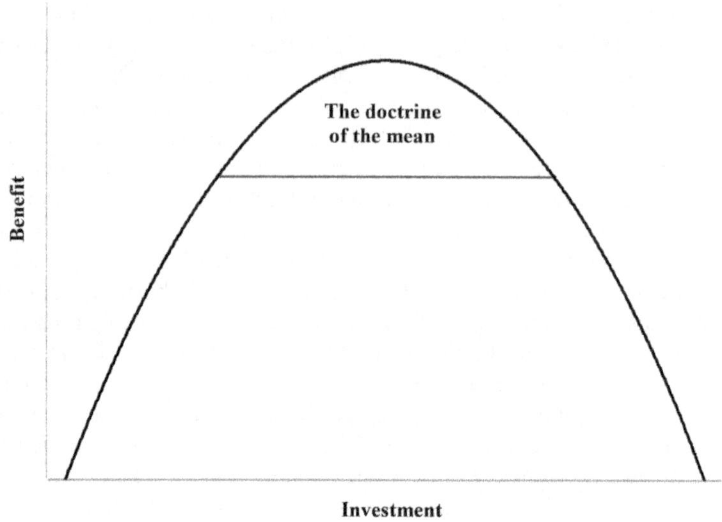

Fig. 2. Illustration of the Economic Basis for the *Doctrine of the Mean*: the Benefits of Investment Will Be Optimal at a Moderate Level of Investment (the Area Above the Horizontal Line), Whereas Excessive Investment Will Be Counter-productive and Yield Sub-optimal Results. *Source*: The figure is created by the author.

the goals of their parents. This is reflected in the Chinese saying that *as long as the green hills last, there will always be wood to burn*. This unyielding spirit has shaped the character of the Chinese people. After Deng Xiaoping's reforms began in 1978, some scholars believed that China had abandoned the socialist road (Mearsheimer, 2001). However, these people did not understand Chinese culture. Reform represents flexibility after weighing the advantages and disadvantages of each option, but the goal remained constant: a Chinese form of socialism. It seems unlikely that the Communist Party of China will give up that goal.

To pass on this indomitable spirit from generation to generation, the Chinese people have created many myths that inspired future generations. For example, in ancient times, the Chinese believed there were once 12 suns in the sky. To prevent these suns from scorching the Earth, the Chinese hero Kuafu fought hard to catch them. Because he persevered even though he was burned into ashes by one sun during this struggle, he was hailed as a hero by the Chinese. Houyi, a descendant of Kuafu, inherited his ancestor's goal and finally destroyed 11 of the suns. Similarly, the legendary Xingtian was beheaded by a god for challenging the divine power of the emperor of Heaven, but his indomitable body continued to fight on.

Some heroes were also female. The story of Jingwei filling the sea tells of a girl who drowned in the sea. Her indomitable soul turned into a bird and flew to the sea, carrying stones, every day in an unsuccessful attempt to fill the sea so that nobody else would ever drown. *Nüwà* was another great Chinese woman. According to legend, the earth was separated from the heavens in ancient times and to fight this disaster, *Nüwà* bridged the heavens and earth with her body and saved humanity.

Not yielding is at the core of ancient Chinese culture. A story tells us that faced with mountains that blocked their way, a Chinese family chose to remove the mountains rather than seeking another path. The story says that Taihang Mountain stood above the gates of Yugong's house. To avoid the pain caused by needing to climb the mountain before he could travel elsewhere, Yugong decided to dig up the mountain to open a path. Every morning, he took his children up the mountain to remove earth and rocks from the top, thereby lowering the mountain, and vowed that his descendants would continue his work after his death and would never stop until the obstacle was removed. His persistence moved Yuhuang, the Chinese god of the sky, who finally removed the mountain. Some people may not understand why ancient Chinese people did not write another version of the story, allowing Yugong to move to the front of the mountain. Don't forget, there are mountains in front of them. Only by eliminating all the mountains that block the way can human society achieve brightness. This is probably the core rule of human society's development!

About 4,000 years ago, the *Shun* sent his subject Gun to eliminate a great flood. Gun failed at this task and died trying, but his son Yu inherited his father's work and struggled three times to control the water without returning home until he finally succeeded. Yu founded the first (Xia) dynasty in Chinese history and was honored by giving his name to the *lóng* (controls the water) that controls the water. Historians believe that this story represents the "Great Flood of China" that occurred around that time and that appears to have lasted for two generations (Yang, 1986). Since Yu's victory, Chinese emperors have carried the title "the real *lóng* and the son of Heaven."

2.1.1.3. Hero Worship

As I noted in the previous section, perseverance and the willingness to take up a predecessor's struggles, while remaining flexible in one's approach, have been an important part of Chinese culture. It has allowed the Chinese people to accomplish many goals. Chinese culture has evolved over time, from early nature worship to ancestor worship (as in the story of the water *lóng*), and then evolved from ancestor worship to hero worship. Its essence is that it reminds us to be thankful for what individuals have accomplished.

Heroic historical figures have often been treated as gods. For example, Fu Xi, the Yandi, and the Huangdi described earlier in this chapter were upright people who became gods of the Chinese people. Like the gods of the ancient Western nations, the Chinese gods were considered to be living people. Not only were excellent ancestors deified after death, but even living people were sometimes mythologized. For example, when someone completed a task that was generally considered impossible, their achievement was considered to be superhuman.

In Chinese culture, the parents who gave us our life are respected as if they were personal gods, and this is the basis of the Confucian ideal of filial piety. Chinese people often tell their children that the gods (our parents) made us all to suffer on Earth, not to enjoy happiness. This is captured in the saying that *the right path in the world is suffering*. Because heroes are rewarded for their heroism, Chinese people deify their heroic ancestors. In doing so, they thank them for their great achievements in creating Chinese culture. But they also use these ancestors to set an example for future generations, educate future generations to not forget their ancestors' will, and to move forward with courage.

Guan Yu (160–220 CE), a Chinese general, is a typical representative of a Chinese deity. He and his leader Liu Bei (161–223 CE) were sworn brothers. When Liu Bei was defeated in 200 CE in battle with Cao (155–220 CE) and forced to retreat, Guan Yu treated Liu's wife, his "sister-in-law," kindly until he could reunite her with Liu Bei. Guan Yu was a military genius and had few rivals in his life. After he was killed by his former ally Lv Meng (178–220 CE), who was, in turn, executed by his leader Sun Quan (182–252 CE). After he was defeated in battle and killed by his opponents, Guan was deified for his loyalty, persistence, and courage, and was eventually named the *Guansheng god*. He is considered the most trustworthy person in Chinese history because he remained loyal even though this caused his death. Guan Yu's deification illustrates how Chinese culture does not care about temporary gains and losses but rather emphasizes the long term. In the 2,000 years after his death, Guan Yu was given many honors. Before his death, he was given the title "Marquis of Hanshou Pavilion" by Emperor Xian of the Han Dynasty (181–234 CE); nearly 800 years later, Emperor Huizong of the Song Dynasty (1082–1135 CE) called him "*Zhong Huigong*, the loyal and brave king of Wuan." Ming Shenzong (1563–1620 CE) of the Ming Dynasty granted him the title of "*Shenweiyuanzhen Guansheng* god," and Shunzhi of the Qing Dynasty (1638–1661 CE) granted him the title of the "Loyal and Righteous *Guansheng* god."

The cultural tradition of treating heroes as gods has continued until the present. For example, China's earliest God of wealth was Fan Li (536–448 BCE), a senior general of the Yue state during the Warring States period (2032–222 BCE). However, he spent all his money on charitable causes in his later years. He was the first major philanthropist in Chinese history. After his death, he was treated as the god of wealth by the Chinese people in recognition of both his success and how he spent his money. In 2003, Jack Ma created an Internet trading platform (Taobao) to provide services for online transactions by Chinese merchants (Cao & Yu, 2019). In gratitude, Chinese Internet merchants named him the modern god of wealth to reflect the sense of mission that Chinese culture respects. Excellent individuals are honored as powerful role models. Everyone strives to equal their example.

2.1.2. Confucianism and Gratitude

During the Spring and Autumn period (770–221 BCE), China's prosperous culture featured "a hundred schools of thought contending" and therefore illustrated the diversity of Chinese philosophies. Confucian ideals spread widely and became a dominant aspect of Chinese culture. After Emperor Wu of the Han Dynasty (141–87 BCE), the government replaced Confucianism with the *fajia* philosophy, in which the concept of serving the people through the government was transformed into the concept of the people serving the government. The term *fajia* was misleadingly translated as *legalism*, when it more closely resembles authoritarianism or even *realpolitik*.

Confucian culture began with Confucius (Kong Qiu, 551–479 BCE) and was later refined by his student Mencius (Meng Ke, 372–289 BCE). Confucius and Mencius both lost their father at the age of three and were raised by their mother in a single-parent family. This undoubtedly taught them gratitude to their mother, which evolved into a culture of Chinese filial piety that in some ways resembles Chinese traditional culture's worship of ancestors and other heroes.

The core of Confucian culture is based on *benevolence* (showing love or affection to others) and *righteousness* (striving to follow the moral path), which together lead to the *great harmony* described in Chapter 1. The path to achieving this goal is based on "harmony with differences," which means recognizing and respecting each other's differences through cultural diversity and inclusiveness and thereby achieving harmonious development.

2.1.2.1. A Humanistic Philosophy of Benevolence and Trust

Confucius believed that *benevolence* is the basis of all social relationships and arises from love and affection: parents love their children, children love their parents, brothers love their brothers, and brothers and sisters love each other, and he extended this to all the people of the world, who he considered brothers and sisters. Confucius divided love into two forms. First, he used *benevolence* to describe the fact that parents love their children and used *filial piety* to describe how children love their parents. In his view, parents should not only care for their children in terms of the basic aspects of raising them to maturity, such as providing simple clothing and enough nutritious food, but should also cultivate an ethical personality and educate their children and lead their children to actively assume family and social responsibilities. In return, children should treat their parents not only with love but also with respect, which bears a strong similarity to the evolution of ancestor worship in traditional Chinese culture. The Confucian concept of benevolence has evolved into social responsibility and obligation. The belief that fairness and selflessness represent benevolence has become a core component of Chinese ideology.

Filial piety is often understood to mean obedience, but this relationship has evolved over time. In an agricultural society, a person's survival skills are mainly transmitted from parents to children. In a society with slow scientific and technological progress, learning from a parent's experience is the key to survival, so obedience to parents is necessary. However, with modern society's rapid social and technological development, cultural norms seem to change with each passing day. Older parents find it difficult to keep up with the pace of social change. If children still blindly obey their parents, how can they make progress? The original meaning of filial piety was that children should respect their parents for their experience, knowledge, and selflessness. However, given the rapid pace of change, it's no longer appropriate to blindly obey one's parents, particularly when they become unable to keep up with the pace of change.

The second key principle of Confucianism is *righteousness*, which Confucius illustrated using the example of brothers and sisters loving each other. Righteousness has two meanings in this context. First, the mutual love between brothers and sisters is called *brotherhood* and *sisterhood.* It is incumbent on brothers and sisters to help and care for each other and show a combination of friendship and loyalty. We often say that when one brother or sister is in trouble, the other must help them. Second, righteousness includes the belief that the interests of society outweigh all other considerations, sometimes including family ties. When the demands of loyalty to one's society and of filial piety cannot be satisfied simultaneously, the highest Chinese moral standards dictate that the individual should sacrifice their life for righteousness and serve their country. In times of national crisis, the Chinese people are willing to sacrifice their lives to safeguard their country's interests. This sense of duty is why the Chinese people expect heroes to protect them.

The Chinese concept of heroism differs from the Western concept. In the Western world, a soldier who runs out of bullets and surrenders is generally considered to have done their duty by completing their task. They are still considered to be heroic because they risked their life. In contrast, Chinese culture would consider them to have failed in their duty to their country and, therefore, not to be heroes. Chinese people often say that "a warrior can be killed but not humiliated" to reflect this aspect of Chinese culture.

2.1.2.2. The Educational Concept Behind the Emergence of "Sages"

As a pioneer of moral and political philosophy, Confucius divided the process of education's impact on personal growth into four stages and proposed related requirements for education:

The first stage is called "little people" (*Xiaoren*). This refers to children who, before receiving cultural education, only focus on their immediate interests, have rigid thinking, and do not understand how to adapt to social changes by changing themselves. As a result, they abide by social rules without understanding them and are unwilling to take on social responsibility. Because women in the Confucian era did not have the opportunity to receive education, Confucius proposed that women and children were indistinguishable, since he believed that uneducated women were just as difficult to communicate with as the uneducated children. This belief recognized the role of education in creating a citizen and was not a suggestion that women and children were inherently immoral.

The second stage is called "citizen" (*Junzi*, a member of society). This means that after receiving sufficient education, a person realizes the importance of social rules, begins to emphasize conformity with those rules and help maintain social order, and is able to achieve self-restraint by following social norms and restraining their personal behavior. On this basis, he proposed that a citizen loves wealth but obtains it wisely. This means that educated people not only love wealth and aspire to a prosperous life, like the little people (children), but also understand the importance of abiding by social norms and obtaining wealth through legal and moral means. However, their awareness of social responsibility is not yet high. Therefore, Confucius criticized this stage by observing that citizens do not stand under dangerous walls. That is, because they have not yet formed a sense of social responsibility, they only know how to escape when they encounter difficulties and dangers rather than staying and taking on their social responsibility to help solve the problem (i.e., to repair the wall).

The third stage is called the "wise one" (*Xianren,* scholar). With improvement of an individual's education level, their social consciousness gradually awakens. Confucius believed that such scholars should regard social responsibility and obligations as their life goals, so that they can step forward and turn the tide in times of a social crisis and, in doing so, save the people from danger. This behavior is like the heroism described earlier in the chapter and earned the scholar a comparable level of respect from society. Mencius added that if an individual is poor, they will be alone, whereas if they are rich, they will become protectors of their world. This means that when a person is poor and in distress, they can still contribute to their society themselves by complying with social norms. When they subsequently obtain wealth and social status, they can actively repay society by being willing to contribute to social development. Confucius and Mencius referred to talented individuals who had made outstanding contributions to social development as "wise ones" and believed that cultivating students to become such individuals was the fundamental concept behind Confucian education.

The fourth stage is called "sage" (*Shengren*). In Confucius' view, a sage is a thinker and educator who, through education, learning, and personal efforts, understands the laws that govern social development, actively educates the people about those laws, and promotes social development to a higher level. The wisest of the sages may become saints due to their lofty social ideals, an unwavering sense of their social responsibility, and an enterprising spirit, and therefore become ideological leaders who promote continuous social development.

In Confucius' view, anyone can grow from a little person (a child) to become a citizen through education and self-learning and then grow from a citizen to become a highly educated wise one and possibly even a sage. On this basis, Wang Yangming (1472–1529 CE) noted that "everyone can be a saint." Unfortunately, this educational concept did not receive recognition and support from the governments that adopted Confucianism. After the Spring and Autumn period and the Warring States period (770–221 BCE), China no longer cultivated wise ones or sages.

Confucius' educational philosophy was advanced even by modern standards. He believed that all people are teachers, and that when three people walked together, at least one should be their teacher, and that if one chooses the correct idea for a given situation and follows it, they can change the incorrect thought of others. That is, Confucius encouraged his students to constantly learn from others, adopt correct knowledge to transform their own thinking and practice, and correct mistakes in a timely manner by encouraging a spirit of doubt and inquiry that leads the student to discover new knowledge. Confucius also emphasized the importance of independent thinking, pointing out that learning without thinking is useless, but thinking without learning is dangerous. Although Confucius emphasized that everyone should develop the belief that they have the moral responsibility to help others acquire knowledge and learn to engage in virtuous action, even if this means that they surpass their teachers, this clearly opposed the wishes of authoritarian rulers, since this freedom of thought threatened their power. To protect that power, emperors and their servants modified Confucius' ideas so that by serving their nation, citizens were actually serving the government. This is likely the root cause of modern Chinese education's emphasis on strict adherence of students to the words of their teachers and the custom of students not questioning their teachers. This attitude contradicts the educational philosophy of Confucius but also contradicts the philosophy of science, in which challenging the status quo and sharing knowledge are two keys to innovation.

2.1.2.3. The Political Concept of Serving the Public

The principle that underlies society is that the world is public (i.e., a society of tightly connected people rather than isolated individuals) and that this is at the core of the *great harmony* proposed by Confucius 2,500 years ago (551–479 BCE). Later philosophers who shared this belief include Jean Jacques Rousseau (1712–1778 CE), who included a similar concept in his book *The Social Contract*. Confucius believed that all men were born equal, and that a nation's land was the property of a political group composed of people with equal value rather than the private property of the ruler and the ruling class. To achieve the *great harmony*, it was necessary for a nation to establish a sound system of the government to maintain order, but the nation should also regulate everyone's behavior through a sound system of laws to sustain a harmonious and friendly society that followed social norms and restrained selfish behavior. Confucius referred to two key aspects of such a society: First, a society based on the rule of law must encourage humility and behaving in a manner worthy of respect. Second, it must ensure equality for all; princes and commoners should be held to the same standard and are equally guilty if they commit a crime. Mencius added a criterion: rulers who make mistakes should learn from the resulting criticism, but if they are unwilling to learn, they should be replaced. That is, the people should have the right to depose a ruler who fails to honor his responsibility to the people. This is similar to the ideology advocated by Jean Jacques Rousseau.

Unlike teachers of Taoism and Buddhism, China's two major religions, Confucius encouraged his disciples to participate in governance and emphasized the importance of cultivating a respectable character, maintaining a safe and nurturing family, governing the country ethically, and pacifying the world by creating the *great harmony*. Unfortunately, his ideas were not accepted by politicians and rulers of his era because these principles threatened their privileges. To meet the needs of the government, the government official Tong Shusun (about 245–190 BCE) established a hierarchy of officials for the Han Dynasty (202–220 BCE) that was based on the scope of an official's responsibility. Later, Dong Zhongshu (179–104 BCE) institutionalized a hierarchical culture based on serving the ruler first, sons serving their father, and wives serving their husband. This differed strongly from the older ideas of Confucius. Nonetheless, the Confucian concept of governing the country for the benefit of everyone was almost completely abandoned in China and was replaced by the authoritarian *fajia* ideology based on strict obedience to the hierarchical imperial system. The *great harmony* that Confucius sought did not emerge, and the hierarchical imperial system continued in China for more than 2,000 years after his death. It was not until the publication of *The Social Contract* in 1762 CE by Jean Jacques Rousseau that such a philosophy became part of Western thought.

Historically, China's rulers have often chosen not to follow the Confucian philosophy, and only in times of chaos have they attempted to maintain the order advocated by Confucianism in an effort to win over the hearts of the people. Unfortunately, this has often led them to reinterpret Confucian principles in their favor. For example, they have often described the Confucian respect for parents and elders as obedience and have extended this relationship to superiors, such as supervisors and government officials. In some cases, they persecuted intellectuals who would have prevented them from tampering with Confucian ideology for personal benefit, as evidenced by the repeated occurrence of "literary jails" (imprisonment of philosophers who might have undermined an emperor's power) in Chinese history. In the Chinese hierarchy that was implemented during the Han Dynasty (202 BCE) and subsequently, the social status of Chinese intellectuals was ranked ninth, and intellectuals were known as "stinky old nine," below even beggars (who were in eighth position). Throughout China's history, this tendency to censor the words of wise men and women and insist on obedience has stifled innovation, leading to slow social, scientific, and technological progress. I will discuss this problem in more detail in Chapter 3.

Today, the self-learning ability of artificial intelligence has sparked panic based on the fear that artificial intelligence will ultimately surpass, rule, or even eliminate humanity. This concern can be resolved if those who create such software follow Confucian ideals. In Confucianism, children must honor and obey their parents and must never punish their parents for whatever sins the parents may have committed. If we treat artificial intelligence as if it were our child, we can teach it the same principles to ensure that it has no desire to punish us. To me, a greater fear is that we will instead teach the artificial intelligence the "everyone for themself" ideology, in which our relationship with our artificial child becomes a zero-sum game, with us as the loser. Though Confucianism is more than 2,000 years old, it still has lessons for us to learn going into the future.

2.1.3. Humanism Under Buddhism

Chinese culture experienced three large upheavals before it became what it is today. The first was a long series of wars between competing powers for control of the land, which began 4,500 years ago, thereby establishing the historical borders of China and emphasizing the importance of loyalty and heroism during these conflicts. This is referred to as the period of nation building and includes three historical figures who are often referred to as the ancestors of the Chinese people: Yandi, Huangdi, and Chiyou. (Chiyou was the first defeated tribal leader described in early Chinese books and was active in what is now Shandong Province from 2500 BCE–2000 BCE.) These protracted conflicts not only defined the geographic boundaries of China but also laid the foundation of Chinese culture.

The second upheaval was the "hundred schools of thought contend" period during the Spring and Autumn period (770–221 BCE) and the Warring States period (2032–222 BCE). This description emphasizes the diversity of philosophies that arose during these times and their coexistence. Popular Chinese idioms that are still in use today mainly come from the "hundred schools of thought contend" period (770–221 BCE). Confucianism largely won this competition after it was adopted by Emperor Wu of the Han Dynasty (141–87 BCE), after which the competing schools of thought slowly declined, although *fajia* retained deep roots within the bureaucratic system.

The third upheaval came from the arrival of Buddhism in China, which also became a major source of Chinese idioms based on quotations from classic Buddhist texts. Examples include "when the conversation becomes disagreeable, saying even one word more is a waste of breath," "if you are fated to meet, then you will still meet even if you are thousands of miles apart," "good will be rewarded with good, and evil with evil, and if the reward is not forthcoming, it is because the time has not yet come," "if you're not willing to work hard, then hunting will provide you with no prey" (in English, "there's no such thing as a free lunch"). Buddhism pursues the equality of all life. In Buddhist classics, respect for all life is called *goodness*. Just as love and affection are a key foundation for Confucianism, goodness is a key foundation of Buddhism. Buddhism's greatest contributions to Chinese culture can be divided into the concepts of causality and of a cycle of life, death, and rebirth.

2.1.3.1. Causality: Good Causes Produce Good Results

In terms of causality, Buddhism acknowledges that actions have consequences. "Good causes produce good results" is the essence of Buddhist thought. Buddhism believes that a person's current situation is the result of the accumulation of previous accomplishments. This is also reflected in the idiom that "good will be rewarded with good, and evil with evil." Buddhism actively guides people to accumulate virtue and do good so that their efforts will be repaid with additional good. This creates a moral foundation for the harmonious development of society.

Buddhism often uses humorous, incisive, and witty language and is therefore appreciated by the Chinese because they understand the humor and appreciate the insights it provides. For example, the Buddhist idiom about self-cultivation reminds us that if one expects rewards, one must work to achieve them. The more modern Buddhism-inspired idiom about innovation reminds us that a businessman who doesn't keep up with the times cannot prosper. *Competition* is inevitable, but Buddhism strives to avoid *conflict* and therefore provides insights on how this can be accomplished. For example, two competing enterprises can try to constantly improve their technology and management, create new products and management models, and occupy new markets rather than fighting. In addition, competitors can seek ways to cooperate while also competing (i.e., coopetition). For example, Microsoft developed the world's dominant computer operating system, with Apple's operating system acting as its main competitor, yet Microsoft develops many products that also work on Apple's computers. Competition produces progressively better products, but only benign competition can benefit social development and progress without destabilizing society.

The Shang Dynasty (1600–1046 BCE) was one of the earliest dynasties in China. The emperor named himself "Shang" because he was good at doing business, and *shang* means business. However, subsequent emperors aimed to achieve an economic monopoly, thereby distorting the Buddhist perspective from aiming to be a skilled and competitive businessman to becoming a profiteer. Rather than promoting economic activity and social development, this restricted business and socioeconomic development.

Unfortunately, Buddhist thought has not developed like experimental science, which constantly seeks the root causes. Instead, Buddhists adopted the concept of "fate" to explain some aspects of causality. Therefore, in contrast with the logical thinking of experimental science, the Buddhist "good cause produce good results" has a strong metaphysical color. Buddhists believe that life is a combination of fate with personal choices and represents an invisible connection between people. In this ideology, some situations and their outcomes are inevitable (i.e., are fated). However, many situations offer individuals a choice, and the key Buddhist concept of *karma* reflects the belief that choices have both practical and spiritual consequences. This philosophy can lead to a certain nihilism, in which a believer renounces their free will because they believe that everything is fated. On the other hand, the possibility of good consequences from making ethical decisions, and being rewarded with a better fate in one's next life, motivates some to behave more ethically and with more loving-kindness (*maitrī*) toward others.

2.1.3.2. Cycle of Life

A second key concept in Buddhism is the belief that people are composed of a body and a soul. The body experiences a continuous cycle of life and death, whereas the soul is immortal and is reborn in a new body after each cycle. Therefore, after Buddhism was introduced into China, Chinese people who embraced Buddhism felt less fear of death, and this represents one of the great contributions of Buddhism to Chinese secular culture. In contrast, atheists believe that when someone dies, they are gone forever. This creates a significant fear of death. Buddhism provides more reassurance through the belief that death is a normal process, and this encourages believers to cultivate their soul while they live. Buddhism believes that a person's success or failure in life results from their behavior in previous lives. Buddhism teaches that individuals will be rewarded if they seek to accumulate virtue (spiritual wealth) rather than material wealth.

The Chinese concept that "good is rewarded with good, and evil with evil" clearly promotes good (prosocial) behavior but may require reinforcement in real life, particularly for those who don't believe in an afterlife. Therefore, Buddhism also offers the concept of "retribution in this world." For example, a person who commits many evils will experience retribution in their lifetime or may pass those consequences on to their children. It's easy to understand that an immoral person can't or won't educate their children in virtuous behavior, and to counteract such influences, modern Chinese education pays attention to learning how to raise an ethical family.

Traditional Chinese medicine promotes the belief that cultivating a kind heart makes one healthier by preventing disease. This belief suggests that when someone has good and positive thoughts, their bodies will produce healthy substances and their immune system will become stronger, making it less likely they will become sick. There are some similarities between "occupational diseases" in modern society and Buddhism's "retribution in this world." A person who works in an unhealthy environment for a long time will damage their health. A person who often fights with others will also suffer from reduced health. Modern medical statistics suggest that young criminals may be stronger than law-abiding teenagers of the same age, but that when they enter middle age, their health status decreases rapidly, and the risk of hospitalization and disability is many times higher than for more ethical people (Archer et al., 2022; Chua, 2018). People who are "broad-minded and philanthropic" tend to be more physically and mentally healthy. This may be why Confucius said that benevolent people live a long life. Taoist thought (discussed in the next section) and Buddhist thought agree that good people live a longer life.

There is a saying in modern society that weakness results from the combination of evil with a criminal act dressed in the cloak of goodness. Some people incorrectly believe that kindness equals weakness. The Buddha's concept of goodness is similar to the benevolent good of Confucianism, and neither is a weak good. Evildoers are despised or feared by others, and this is why no one is willing to lend them a helping hand when they encounter difficulties. Thus, the consequences of their bad behavior are often bad.

Not everyone accepted the idea that Buddhism rewards good and evil. For example, the great warlord Zhang Xueliang (1901–2001 CE) handed over three northeastern provinces to Japan without firing a shot. He was a traitor who smoked opium yet still lived to 100 years old. Isn't this an exception? Those who believe this conveniently forget that Zhang spent nearly 60 years in prison (1931–1990) as a reward for his behavior. Was he really rewarded despite his bad behavior?

2.1.4. Political Wisdom of Taoist Culture

Although Confucian remains popular in China, the influence of Taoism can't be ignored. Like Confucianism, Taoism inherited the essence of traditional Chinese culture. Its key thinkers were Lao Zi (571–471 BCE) and Zhuang Zi (369–286 BCE) during the Spring and Autumn period and the Warring States period, respectively. In contrast with the ancestor worship of Confucian culture, Taoist culture inherited the Chinese tradition of respect for nature and proposed the philosophical concepts of "the unity of Heaven and man" and "governing by inaction."

2.1.4.1. The Humanistic Concept of Respecting Nature

Taoists believe that man and all living things are equal and that man and nature should therefore coexist harmoniously. People should treat nature, others, and themselves with equal consideration. Taoists believe that only when people follow the laws of nature and meet the requirements of nature can they be accepted by nature and live harmoniously and contentedly. Taoist scholars studied nature to obtain insights and came to believe that water was a good metaphor to inspire social behavior. Just as water nourishes all life without asking to be repaid, Taoism believes that people should take on their social responsibilities and nourish others without expecting or requiring acknowledgment of their actions, although thanks are always welcome and promote future good behavior. Taoism believes that it is everyone's duty to help others. This philosophy is similar to the modern concepts of charity and philanthropy.

Taoism advocates freedom through a return to nature. A Taoist should not let the joys and sorrows of the world disturb their pure state of mind and should always maintain a natural nature (i.e., think of oneself as a part of nature). Therefore, Taoism advocates a plain and frugal lifestyle that embraces simplicity (maintaining a pure and simple nature, reducing selfish desires and related thoughts) and a simple diet and notes that someone who is content with what they have will be happy in other aspects of their life. As a consequence of these beliefs, nobody should cause harm to another or to society.

Frugality is a historical virtue of the Chinese people. To encourage frugality, Taoism tells a lovely story: when everyone is born, they receive meal tickets from the king of Hell who, in Chinese mythology, is responsible for both life and death. When you spend your last meal ticket, you will come to the king of Hell because you are already dead. To delay this, we should eat less every day and spend fewer of our valuable tickets. These meal tickets cannot be bought with money but must be bought with life. Even those who have money cannot consume without restraint. To consume without restraint is to burn our life capital. In addition to being a lovely prosocial ethic, this is undoubtedly a way to preserve one's health in modern society. Obesity is one of the biggest health problems today. Researchers have confirmed that monkeys can prolong their life by 20% by reducing their daily food intake by 30% (Lu et al., 2024), and this may also apply to humans.

2.1.4.2. Governing by Inaction

Taoist thought holds that both nature and society have their own laws. If we follow those laws instead of opposing them (i.e., inaction), we can get better results with less effort; the Western phrase "going with the flow" is an example. This is consistent with the concept of the "invisible hand" in a modern market economy. It also acknowledges that although water appears weak, it can achieve powerful results, such as when years of dripping water wear away stone. Taoists also compare people to water and the government to a boat and note that just as water can carry a boat, it can also overturn the boat; that is, rulers should be taught not to act arbitrarily, should be people-oriented, and should not compete with the people for profits for fear that they too will be overturned. Taoists should oppose the shortsighted behavior of trying to catch all the fish, thereby enriching oneself while impoverishing everyone else.

Taoism believes that governance should follow natural law. That is, Taoists should let people develop and improve themselves and should help people to live fully and freely. Only in this way can people be safe and prosperous and live in a harmonious and stable society. In response to a crisis, Taoism advocates that governments should "use softness to overcome hardness," as in the Chinese martial art of *tai chi*, which uses the opponent's strength against them rather than fighting strength with strength. Related idioms include "there is a limit to everything, and enough is enough," "constant dropping of water wears away stone," and "hide one's capacities and bide one's time." These sayings encapsulate some of the wisdom of Taoism. They are also consistent with the Confucian doctrine of the golden mean (i.e., the goal is constant, but the road is flexible).

The most typical negative example is Yang Guang (569–618 CE), who became Emperor Yang of the Sui Dynasty (581–618 CE). During his reign, he abused his power over people but also built the Beijing Tang Grand Canal, which became an essential resource during the subsequent Tang dynasty but depleted the empire's treasury. He frequently waged wars and attacked the nomadic Tuyuhun people, eventually leading to the collapse of the Sui Dynasty. Despite his undoubted contributions to China's social and economic development (the Grand Canal is still in use), his ending was tragic because it led to the downfall of his dynasty and disrupted the lives of millions of people.

Taoist wisdom still provides important guidance for China. For example, US Defense Secretary Leon Panetta proposed the "Asia–Pacific rebalancing strategy" in 2012, noting that the United States will deploy 60% of American warships to the Pacific by 2020. Rather than matching force with force, Chinese president Xi Jinping proposed the "Belt and Road Initiative" (Cheng, 2016; Huang, 2016). This initiative aimed to divert much of China's trade westward over the land to Europe and western Asia, rather than competing directly with American power in the Pacific Ocean. In so doing, it adopted the *tai chi* approach of never meeting force with force. In the South China Sea, many of the reefs and small islands are claimed by neighboring countries. Fighting with each other over ownership has unacceptably high political and economic costs. What should China do? China chose to build artificial islands in the South China Sea, thereby avoiding military conflict but also protecting Chinese interests through military occupation of these islands. This wise approach achieved multiple objectives, as in the Western idiom "to kill many birds with one stone."

2.1.5. The Social Harm Caused by Fajia

For most Chinese people, Confucianism, Buddhism, and Taoism seem to represent the entirety of Chinese philosophical culture. This ignores how powerfully *fajia* has covertly influenced Chinese culture for thousands of years and will continue to do so. *Fajia* originated from the ancient Chinese criminal law system (which may be why it has been misleadingly translated as *legalism*) and later developed into a relatively complete theory formulated by thinkers such as Shang Yang (390–338 BCE) and Han Feizi (280–233 BCE). Because this ideology has been widely applied, it has deeply influenced China's governance institutions. Because this ideology serves the government rather than the people (the opposite of Confucian thought), it has always been opposed by the Chinese people. But because it is attractive to individuals who seek power, it has been difficult to eliminate from Chinese culture.

2.1.5.1. The Political Concept of Serving Rulers

During China's Warring States period (476 BCE–221 BCE), many thinkers such as Shang Yang and Han Feizi recognized the importance of private property rights and proposed using this idea to enrich the state and strengthen its military. They believed that human nature is selfish, and that there are no universal ethical standards, so the government should instead harness selfish interests to induce the people to serve the government. Therefore, they successively carried out reforms such as abolishing the hereditary privileges of the nobility, who competed with the emperor for power; encouraging the people to cultivate wasteland, thereby increasing their income and being motivated to defend that land; seeking rewards such as land, property, and power (official positions) by military achievements that benefited the emperor; and creating new landowners who could profit from leasing their land to farmers and others. These reforms were among the first efforts to formally implement private ownership of land throughout China. Rewarding military achievements was particularly effective because it increased the people's enthusiasm to become soldiers. This enabled China to maintain economic and military leadership for more than 2,000 years.

Shang Yang believed that obedience to laws and regulations was the foundation of state governance. Using the excuse that centralized control increased security by guaranteeing military victory, advocates of *fajia* promoted this legal structure. Han Feizi summarized the historical experience of ancient China by noting that the Confucian ideology of serving the people could not simultaneously meet the needs of serving the rulers. He considered "private education" to be a particular stumbling block, as it taught students to think independently rather than focusing on the needs of the rulers. Therefore, he proposed a government monopoly on education to cultivate loyalty to the rules and rewarded "wise officials" and "good generals" who showed that loyalty.

These ideas became the philosophical basis for both control of China and defending China against both internal and external threats. On the other hand, it became an effective tool for monarchs to exploit the people and persecute intellectuals who might threaten their rule. This led to more than 2,000 years of institutional lock-in that left China politically backward.

2.1.5.2. The Political Harm of Fajia

The adoption of *fajia* in the economic and military fields strengthened its role in Chinese culture and despite its negative impacts, its ability to centralize power provided an effective means of responding to national emergencies. However, this institution had an important practical downside: it forces rulers to both reward officials to retain their loyalty and help the people to avoid losing their support. The solution adopted by many rulers was to engage in a series of wars to seize the wealth of other kingdoms. This was, at best, a short-term solution, since China's lands had a finite supply of resources, and human desire would always exceed that supply. Shortsighted rulers instead harvested the wealth of their people through taxation and theft. For example, Shang Yang proposed a series of governance strategies that assumed a weak and foolish population, thereby increasing the people's distrust. Although he successfully unified China into the Qin empire, that empire lasted only 14 years (221 BCE–207 BCE) before the people rose up in rebellion.

Despite the downfall of the Qin Empire, the *fajia* concept of serving the rulers remained attractive to the emperors of subsequent dynasties. To gather support for this approach, or to minimize resistance, they pretended to support Confucianism, Buddhism, and Taoism while modifying these teachings to favor the emperor. For example, the version of the *Tao Te Ching* written by Laozi has only 5,000 words. But a version unearthed from the Han tomb in Mawangdui, written more than 2,100 years ago, has more than 700 differences from the original (https://slife.org/tao-te-ching), which are clearly the result of tampering. Such tampering with classic works to create support for the government has long been an open secret. Many fake versions are in circulation, and only scholars can be confident about which versions are correct.

After the manipulation of Confucianism by the Han Dynasty's Shusun Tong and Dong Zhongshu, the Song Dynasty's Zhu Xi wrote *Neo Confucianism*, which represented a covert system by which rulers manipulated Confucianism to promote *fajia*. Zhu Xi (1130–1200 CE) integrated Confucianism with Taoism, claiming that *li* is the fundamental law that governs all things, including society's ethics. This philosophy divided everything into two opposing parts, such as stillness and movement, goodness and evil, and right and wrong. Zhu recommended balance between the extremes to avoid excessive behavior that may lead to negative consequences. Because governments have the power to define how words are interpreted, Zhu proposed *li* should be interpreted as "rationality." This "rationality" became the government's only criterion for judging right and wrong. Under this system, the government's laws and an individual's words were assumed to be correct so long as they appeared reasonable, and this was given the name of Confucianism. Today, *fajia* is concealed under the concept of neo-Confucianism. The true connotations of Confucianism, Buddhism, and Taoism have largely disappeared from the modern government.

Governing by law is clearly important, but how well this will work depends on who proposes and implements the law and who supervises its enforcement. Because *fajia* emphasizes centralized control, laws were proposed, implemented, and enforced by the government in its own interest rather than the interests of the people. Infringement of human rights, killing of the innocent, and corruption became common political tools of rulers (discussed in Chapter 5). The authoritarian beliefs that money can motivate anyone to work and that "might makes right" gradually became core elements of Chinese culture, even though both ideas contradicted Confucian ethics; this is more evidence that Confucianism is always under attack by *fajia*. Rousseau's *The Social Contract* revived the concept of the rights of the people but did not change how governments operated. For example, Communist Leaders such as Joseph Vissarionovich Stalin (1878–1953) and Mao Zedong (1893–1976) launched revolutions based on the concept of class struggle but without prior agreement of the people, leading to millions of deaths. Then, once the revolution was complete, the attitude that the end justifies the means promoted extensive corruption, particularly in the form of government theft of private property to reward its members.

Like other philosophies designed to concentrate power in a leader's hands, *fajia* discourages independent education, which promotes independent thought that may criticize the government and lead to rebellion. The government-tolerated education focuses on cultivating graduates who support the government. In China, for instance, this produced "composite talents" who were both red (i.e., socialist) and professional. Truly outstanding talents are distrusted because they may encourage rebellion; as a result, they are often killed or forced to flee into remote areas or even to other nations to survive.

This problem delayed China's adoption of Western democratic and scientific ideas, which did not clearly support the government. Their lack of adaptation to Chinese social conditions made it difficult to integrate these ideas into Chinese culture by leaders such as Mao Zedong, who felt threatened by these ideas. Although many of these ideas are finally being adopted in Chinese economics, where they have begun to flourish, they have generally not been adopted by Chinese educators, who are still distrusted by the government. Under strict government control, modern Chinese universities have extinguished the innovative spirit of students (Loyalka et al., 2021) and weakened their ability to innovate (discussed in Chapter 3).

2.2. Why Has Chinese Culture Survived So Long?

China has suffered from an unending series of invasions, whether military or cultural, throughout its long history. China has not stood still in the face of these challenges, yet it has also remained recognizably Chinese because it has absorbed and benefited from these invasions. Today, China is the world's most populous country and has seen historically unprecedented economic growth. At the same time, despite a century of warfare and chaos, the Chinese language is increasingly widely used around the world. This naturally raises a question: How has Chinese culture survived for so long? The roots of Chinese culture that I have described in this chapter are strong and appear indomitable. But this may not explain the long-term survival of Chinese culture, because perseverance alone is a common human characteristic. If we want to know the source of Chinese culture's "longevity gene," we must start from the origin of Chinese culture and seek the cultural characteristics through a painstaking investigation, like unreeling silk from a silkworm's cocoon.

2.2.1. The Formation of Chinese Culture

Early human culture originated from nature worship. Because there are significant differences in physical geography among regions, people in different places have chosen different totems (ancestral images). Northern grassland tribes often took ferocious carnivores as their totem. For example, wolves are the totem of many Mongolians. In northern forests, the totem of the early Chinese ancestor, the Huangdi, was the bear. Most tribes in southern forest areas worshipped birds, such as the peacock, which is the spiritual pillar of the Dai nationality, or the phoenix, which became the totem of the Shang Dynasty.

Totems reflect a culture's shared concepts and beliefs and recognize common ancestors. A totem represents the foundation of all of the culture's social knowledge and spiritual and cultural development and also accounts for the interdependence among members of an ethnic group (Jones, 2005). Therefore, throughout the world, totems have been a starting point for a group's efforts to define its identity and shape its civilization.

Unlike the totems of most nationalities around the world, China's *lóng* is not a single species found in nature but rather a composite of multiple precursor totems (Fig. 3). The *lóng* has the face of a horse (a herbivore), antlers (a herbivore), the body of a snake (a reptile), fish scales (an aquatic animal), a tiger's tail (a carnivore), an eagle's claw (a bird), shrimp whiskers (an aquatic animal), feathered fins (a bird), and a cicada's nose (an insect). Thus, it incorporates aspects of many cultures with different totem animals. This illustrates a continuous Chinese belief in the ability to combine the strengths of many cultures to create something stronger than its individual parts.

As I noted previously, groups of people ranging in size from extended families to whole villages have cooperated to improve their access to resources, defend themselves against other groups who also wanted those resources, and increase the likelihood of their survival. When groups with different ancestry joined, they often combined their totems. Archaeological results confirm that before 7000 BCE, the *lóng* symbol had been adopted in northwestern China (Lawler, 2009). The early *lóng* was relatively simple (Fig. 4), and the complex *lóng* pattern we see now (Fig. 3) resulted from gradual merger with other patterns and evolution of the resulting image over thousands of years.

Warfare also resulted in the merger of totems. With increasing populations, the living space available to different groups became increasingly constrained, often leading to warfare to control the resources required to survive. To survive, weaker groups either surrendered to a more powerful invader or joined with other groups to resist the invader; in both cases, this often led to merger of the totems. Chinese tradition shows that alliances of weak groups can defeat powerful opponents. For example, 4,500 years ago, the Yandi fought with the Chiyou people for land. After the Chiyou defeated the Yandi, the Yandi formed the Yan–Huang alliance with the Huangdi and defeated the Chiyou. More recently, the Manchu people (an ethnic minority who lived in what is now called Manchuria) united with the Mongols about 400 years ago, and this let the Manchu, with a population of only 6 million, defeat the Ming Empire (1368–1644 CE), with a population of 200 million and establish the Manchu Dynasty.

It is worth noting that the Yan–Huang alliance comprised more than just the Yandi and Huangdi tribes. According to legend, tribes with tiger, leopard, wolf, and other animals as totems also joined the alliance to meet the challenge of the Chiyou. Undoubtedly, military operations must be integrated and benefit from a unified structure, and the *lóng* may have been generated in this way and increasingly adopted as the alliance continuously strengthened. The union of weaker groups formed an alliance that was equal to or stronger than the group they opposed.

Fig. 3. The Chinese *Lóng* Combines the Characteristics of Totems from Many Prehistoric Cultures. Its Combination of Diverse Features Reflects the Desire to Combine the Best Aspects of Many Cultures, and in So Doing, It Became the Shared Totem of the Chinese Nation. *Source*: Drawing by Dr Suo Xinhao.

After the Huangdi Xuanyuan defeated the Chiyou, he did not replace any part of the *lóng* with the bear totem of his tribe. Such respect for different cultures and customs has always been a Chinese tradition and resulted from the rich diversity of the people. There is a Chinese saying that describes this diversity: "the local customs differ within ten miles." When someone traveled between villages to do business, it was necessary for them to follow each new village's customs. This was both a practical matter and a desire to recognize and show respect for other cultures.

2.2.2. Formation of Cultural Diversity

Alliances among weak groups are not enough to let a culture exist for a long time. For Chinese culture to survive, it has emphasized the concept of inclusiveness. This can be seen in the Chinese idiom "destroy the country without destroying its history." This means that even when it was possible to destroy a rival country through warfare, the country's history and culture should be protected. Over time, the two cultures merged, while retaining aspects of both cultures. This may be the true origin of Chinese culture's longevity gene. Archaeologists have revealed that China's *lóng* totem first emerged in prehistoric times in northwestern China, whereas

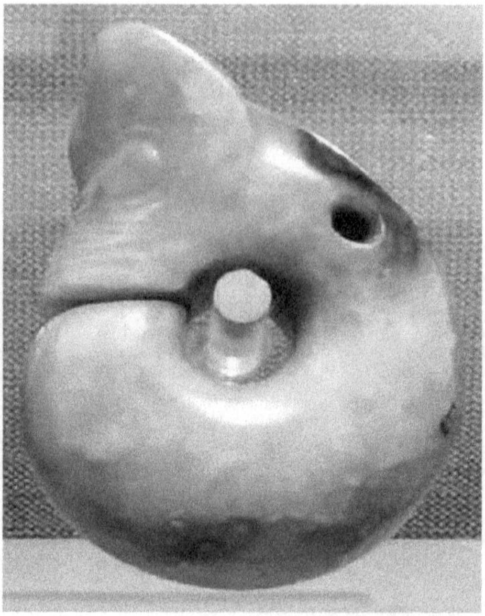

Fig. 4. A *Lóng* Pattern from the Hongshan Culture Period of China, 5,000–6,000 Years Ago. *Source*: Photograph by Prof. Liu Zhiming.

tribes with birds as their totem in southeastern China merged to form a phoenix totem (Lawler, 2009). The phoenix was not only the totem of the Chiyou tribe but also the totem of the Shang Dynasty (1562–1066 BCE), China's second major dynasty.

After the Zhou people conquered the Shang Dynasty and ruled China, the Zhou people who adopted the *lóng* as their totem did not destroy the phoenix symbol but rather accepted her gladly. To integrate the different cultures of *lóng* (traditionally a male symbol of strength) and phoenix (traditionally a female symbol of virtue and grace), the Chinese people skillfully transformed the phoenix into a symbol for Chinese women, took the *lóng* as a symbol for men, and created the idiom "prosperity brought by the *lóng* and the phoenix" to recognize the happy life of a husband and wife. Both are celestial beings, and their happy love makes them inseparable.

The inclusiveness of Chinese culture has cultivated broad and open minds. Confucius summed up Chinese culture by emphasizing that "all of the world's people are brothers." Being kind to the defeated and reducing hatred and cruelty against the conquered are important manifestations of Chinese cultural inclusiveness. This culture continues to this day. Although the early Chinese army often killed prisoners of war because they represented a future threat, it was very tolerant of the common people of their enemy. For example, during the Han Dynasty (202 BCE–220 CE), the Chinese people fought with the Huns, a grassland people who lived in the present-day Mongolian plateau, for more than 200 years.

After each war, the emperors of the Han Dynasty rewarded the defeated Huns with land, provided farm tools, and sent officials to teach them how to farm. In addition, the emperors of the Han Dynasty gave their surnames to the Huns, so that many of the Huns bore the name Liu, the surname of an emperor of the Han Dynasty. Many of the Huns who joined the Han Dynasty were welcomed as nobles.

China's tolerant culture greatly reduced casualties after a war ended, encouraged the conquered people to accept their new rulers, and provided an institution that promoted the long-term survival of Chinese culture. This ability to coexist may also be why the population density in China and Southeast Asia has been higher than that in many other areas. Europeans have not been so fortunate. As in China, there are many diverse ethnic groups in Europe, but rather than merging to create stronger groups and combat invaders, they retained distinct ethnic identities. As a result, they remained divided and weak, leading to a seemingly endless series of wars. These wars were exacerbated by religious intolerance, which was itself the cause of many wars.

Language preserves a culture by making it easier to teach subsequent generations the knowledge they need to thrive in their culture and help it survive. The Chinese language has survived thousands of years because it has achieved these goals. Unlike Western languages, which are phonetic, Chinese written language is symbolic (logographic). Although written Chinese is more difficult to learn than phonetic languages, its efficiency and clarity means that it has survived, with relatively minor changes, throughout Chinese history, and has been adopted as the basis for other languages such as Japanese. Some believe that Chinese characters have not yet completed the transformation from "shape" to "sound" and are therefore primitive characters. They are wrong. Chinese characters contain a high density of information in a small space and therefore represent an elegant solution to the challenge of preserving written information in an age before the easy production of paper and advanced writing instruments. The continued survival of these characters provides an ability to continue to comprehend a large body of historical documents without having to learn an additional language.

Chinese culture has developed deep foundations and a complex genealogy that results from the mixing of many cultures. The *lóng* and phoenix totems, as well as their organic combinations, reveal the integration of different systems and cultures, and demonstrate the Chinese philosophy of "harmonious coexistence" (Cao et al., 2007), which is unmatched by other cultures. China's respect for foreign cultures increases Chinese enthusiasm for understanding other cultures, and China has nourished itself by learning from different systems. "Making foreign things serve China, and making the past serve the present" are ways to describe this characteristic of Chinese culture and have promoted the survival of Chinese culture. As I mentioned earlier, the long-term coexistence of Confucianism, Buddhism, and Taoism in Chinese culture, as well as their learning from each other, has promoted the richness of Chinese culture. The "doctrine of the golden mean" in Confucian culture not only inherits wisdom from traditional Chinese culture but also contains the wisdom of Taoist culture. Chinese people tend to dislike or distrust one-sided or extreme solutions and prefer "not only, but also" approaches that incorporate the best aspects of all sides of an argument. As in a natural ecosystem, institutional diversity improves China's social stability, and this has enabled China to continuously nourish itself with inputs from other cultures throughout its long history. This diversity may have saved Chinese civilization from many historical crises such as environmental disasters (e.g., floods, droughts) and man-made disasters (e.g., invasions, changes of dynasties).

Throughout Chinese history, whenever one dynasty replaced another, the victorious dynasty preserved the *lóng* totem and, in so doing, inspired survivors to work through the period of social unrest to unite again as a single people. Even after the Mongols conquered the Southern Song Dynasty and established the Yuan Dynasty (12791368 CE) and the Manchus conquered the Ming Empire and established the Qing Dynasty (1616–1911 CE), the new rulers considered themselves descendants of the *lóng* and inheritors of Chinese culture. Today, Chinese people still retain the essence of their traditional culture and actively absorb aspects of Western culture. This has provided a strong foundation for ongoing changes such as the market-oriented reform that is marrying Western market concepts with Chinese socialist principles. The concepts of diversity and inclusiveness are once again inspiring the Chinese people to forge ahead bravely.

An example of coexistence of different systems is captured by the slogan "one country, two systems," which reflects how Hong Kong and Macao have retained a degree of independence within the larger Chinese system yet remain a unified and integral part of China. The political wisdom of cultural diversity has helped Chinese people overcome many obstacles while evolving into a new society and appears to have reduced the social costs of China's operation and thereby continues to preserve Chinese culture. As I noted in Chapter 1, China is leading reform efforts to achieve a market economy with socialist characteristics and, in so doing, is demonstrating the sociological significance of cultural diversity.

2.2.3. The Socioeconomic Significance of Institutional Diversity

A *system* refers to the combination of rules and norms in a human culture that affect human activities and social development, including laws, policies, regulations, rules, customs, morals, norms, and religions. In an ecosystem, biodiversity helps the ecosystem to maintain stability during environmental change. Similarly, human institutional diversity improves the adaptability of social systems by improving their ability to adapt to internal and external pressures, thereby avoiding major changes in the system's structure and maintaining its initial state. This diversity preserves a culture. It has been argued that no single system can effectively, fairly, and sustainably achieve equitable sharing of public resources (Lin, 2002). Moreover, we usually don't know which potential rules represent the best solutions, and it is often better to retain a diversified combination of systems than to stick to a single system (Ostrom et al., 1999).

In nature, the spatial organization of each ecosystem results from cooperation and competition among the ecosystem's organisms. Biodiversity allows organisms to occupy different ecological niches, thereby reducing competition and improving the ecosystem's overall viability (Rands et al., 2010). Institutional diversity helps a social system bear the pressure of internal and external forces, maintain its structure and form, and promote stability. Culturally diverse social systems can even benefit from external disturbances and changes by learning from each change. For example, after the Mongols entered China's Central Plains, the first thing they did was to go to the Mausoleum of the Huangdi to worship their ancestors, claiming that they were the direct descendants of the Huangdi. After the Mongols raised the *lóng* banner, the resistance of the Han people weakened. Roughly 300 years later, the Manchu also claimed that they were direct descendants of the Huangdi when they conquered the Ming.

The Mongolians and Manchus cast their own shadows on the *lóng* culture. Since they shared the same roots, they found it best to live in harmony. These historical cases are further examples of how cultural diversity has maintained the basic structure of Chinese society and promoted the long-term survival of Chinese culture. Because members of a diverse society have more choices, institutional diversity enhances their enthusiasm for participating in social and economic activities; moreover, each culture can learn from others, and this will promote social unity, social stability, and prosperity (Huisman, 2007).

Every region in the world has its own unique resources and is deficient in one or more other resources, so societies quickly learn to trade, thereby maintaining prosperity for both societies. Diversity has done this for China. Despite many periods of disruption by warfare, Chinese society has always returned to its essential form, and the stability of this social environment has promoted social and economic development by encouraging cultural exchanges and trade (Cao, 2016a). Since 1978, China has successfully integrated the capitalist market economic system with the socialist planned economic system, and the result has been unprecedented prosperity through international trade. In contrast with the history of Europe, China has had no large-scale religious conflicts. Just as the *lóng* totem represents the merger of many ancient tribal totems, recent institutional changes in China have once again demonstrated the importance of cultural integration and harmonious development. China's economic prosperity in Deng Xiaoping's era provides a radical contrast with the economic failures and famine during Mao Zedong's era. China's history has proved time and again that maintaining institutional diversity is essential to social prosperity and stability.

After the global economic depression of the 1930s, countries all over the world spared no effort to reform their economic systems. Unlike the socialist countries that were headed by the former Soviet Union, which fully implemented a centrally planned economic policy, the capitalist countries headed by the United States chose Keynesianism. Keynesianism also encourages government intervention in the market economy, but it does not hinder its normal operation. When the economy slows, the government stimulates consumption to drive economic development. This is like a capitalist country walking on two legs (one for the market economy and one for the government-planned economy) rather than one (the rigid communism of the former Soviet Union). It's not surprising the Soviet system failed and the Western system thrived. Russia repeated the same mistake under Boris Yeltsin, who replaced the single leg of central planning with the single leg of a pure market economy. China learned from these mistakes and is adopting a more cautious two-leg approach (a market economy combined with central planning and state ownership of key resources) that seems more likely to succeed.

Social institutional systems are not isolated but rather form an interdependent network of complex interrelationships (Jackson & Deeg, 2008). Because organizations at different levels (e.g., the United Nations) and governments need to work from different perspectives and from local to global scales, a country's socioeconomic system needs a way to respond at local to national levels to achieve the ultimate goals of stability and prosperity (Berkes, 2007). These differences require the development of a robust social and economic network with complex branching systems (Hill, 1996). This is similar to the network structure of the human body, in which tendons and bones work together to enhance the body's strength. Continuing to preserve cultural and institutional diversity enriches the ways people can acquire and share resources and ensures that the social system will support people with different needs and abilities. When the socioeconomic environment changes, protecting the old system is a viable strategy for as long as the old system continues to work well in the new environment, and this system, working in parallel with the new system, preserves social stability and development. Conversely, when the old system fails to work, the new system provides an opportunity to achieve stability and growth (Cao, 2016a). This is the principle behind the belief that "the history of a country cannot be destroyed" in Chinese culture. Obviously, during the process of China's recent economic reforms, it was institutional diversity that saved China from following the Soviet example.

From the perspective of long-term social development, protection of institutional diversity has been important. Nations that included multiple cultures have traditionally been strong and vigorous, as in the case of Canada, which has strongly supported immigration for decades. In contrast, nations that lack this diversity (such as the Soviet Union) are at much greater risk of collapse. Therefore, institutional diversity is essentially important, and protecting this diversity is a fundamental reason why Chinese culture has survived for so long. The radical social changes that China is currently experiencing cover only a short segment of its thousands of years of history, so it seems likely that a recognizably Chinese culture will emerge when the situation stabilizes.

Overseas Chinese like to call themselves the Tang people, because the Tang Dynasty (618–907 CE) was the most inclusive and prosperous era in Chinese history. The Tang Dynasty welcomed people from many cultures. Businessmen from Europe, the Middle East, and India were a common sight in the capital, whose streets were full of restaurants, wine shops, and other businesses owned and operated by foreigners. The Tang emperor married princesses from all over the world, and the prince of the Tang Dynasty was commonly of mixed blood. For example, the father of Li Shimin, emperor during part of the Tang Dynasty, was Han, and his mother was a Xianbei aristocrat with Mongol origins. The Tang people had no cultural boundaries and mingled with other peoples to the extent that it became difficult to tell what was Han culture and what originated elsewhere. For example, the Hu Xuan dance from the Western Regions of China was a favorite of the Tang people. The relationship between the Tang Empire and the surrounding countries was consistently well handled, with an emphasis on mutual economic development and social prosperity. This tolerance and diversity is a lesson we should learn from history.

Chapter 3

The Harm of Centralized Systems for Education

In 2008, the documentary *Two Million Minutes: A Global Examination*, directed by American director Chad Heeter, was released globally. In the movie, Heeter notes that in the United States, students, regardless of their grades, tend to be arrogant and complacent about their abilities. They talk about inventions and creations all day long and naively believe that they could easily change the world. Their education pays considerable attention to music, sports, and art but neglects mathematics, physics, and chemistry. The classroom is almost beyond the teacher's control. Students show little or no respect for their teacher: they wink, talk, cross their legs, and even walk around the classroom as if they were shopping. On this basis, Heeter concluded that basic education in the United States was very poor, and that in another 20 years, China's science and technology and culture would catch and surpass those of the United States.

The United States also sent a delegation to China in the same year. They visited several schools in Beijing, Shanghai, and Xi'an and wrote a report. Their main findings were that in China, pupils focus on the teacher, show the teacher respect, and remain silent and attentive, without speaking until the teacher asks a question. Students wake up early. Before 7 o'clock, most of the people on the street are students, who often eat their breakfast while walking. Homework is provided for students to build on their classroom work at home. The student with the highest examination score is honored for their work and will get a certificate at the end of the semester. They concluded that:

> Chinese students are the most diligent in the world, get up the earliest and go to bed the latest. Their academic performance is the best compared with students of the same grade in any country. It can be predicted that in another 20 years, China will leave the United States far behind in science, technology, and culture. (https://movie.douban.com/subject/3138548/)

As the world's second-largest economy, China invested more in research and development (R&D) than Japan in 2009, thereby becoming the world's

A New Stage of Civilization: Striving for the Great Harmony, 65–91

doi:10.1108/978-1-83708-258-220251004

second-largest research country, after the United States (China Statistics Agency, 2010–2023). In 2022, China invested US$459.0 × 10^9 in R&D, which was 64.4% of American spending and 3.4 times Japanese spending. This huge investment has brought some good economic returns, such as the fact that China is currently the world's largest producer of paper products, and in a small number of areas (such as some physical sciences), China's scientists and research organizations are world leaders (Marginson, 2022). However, only two Chinese researchers have won the Nobel Prize in the past 120 years, compared with 265 researchers from the United States and 22 from Japan (Xia et al., 2023). Why has China, with 20% of the world's population, achieved so few crucial breakthroughs at the frontiers of science and technology?

In 2009, before Chinese rocket expert Qian Xuesen died, he finally summoned up his courage and questioned "Why can't such an excellent basic education system cultivate equally excellent talents?"

3.1. The Dilemma Facing China's Higher Education

Culture includes philosophy, literature, art, customs, science, and other historical social factors. These factors all influence a culture's attitudes and approach to life. Experimental science (as opposed to observational science) has a history of only about 400 years since its emergence. That is, more than 400 years ago, science was dominated by observation of nature, as in the examples of the medical research by Yandi, Fuxi, Shennong, and Huangdi that I described in Chapter 2. There was no formal concept of experimental science based on the creation and testing of hypotheses. During China's May 4th Movement in 1919, a new concept of "science" was introduced into China from the West (Luo, 2004), along with certain aspects of European culture. However, the concept of science was still only vaguely defined, and even today, there is no accurate definition in Chinese dictionaries. For example, if you enter the question "what is science?" in Baidu, the largest Chinese Internet search network, you'll be told that there is no accurate definition of science. Even in the English-speaking world, not everyone agrees on the definition. To facilitate the rest of my descriptions, I propose the following characteristics of science:

1. Science is a knowledge system that humans use to understand the nature of the world by applying a logical, objective, and rational cognitive (discovery) process.
2. Science tries to discover truths about the past, present, and future by learning the laws that govern the operation of the universe and by seeking new knowledge and has the characteristic of progressively excluding explanations that have been proven to be incorrect.
3. Science provides knowledge that can be used to deal with a range of problems, such as disease, and knowledge that supports technological innovations through its practical characteristics. (In this chapter, I will define *innovation* as going beyond improving existing products or techniques to create something entirely new.) However, science also generates knowledge that is primarily theoretical, without necessarily having a clear practical application.

4. Science is a continuous journey of discovery, without end, and is based on the principle of always continuing to ask questions and challenge existing explanations when new evidence contradicts them.
5. Science is the common property of humanity.

For non-scientists, this may seem complex, so I can also propose a simpler definition: Science is the process of knowledge discovery, education is the process of knowledge transmission, and technology is the practical application of knowledge. Based on the latter property, China's government emphasizes that scientific papers should be written "on the ground"; that is, the science should first and foremost support technological applications. In the past, China only paid attention to the process of knowledge inheritance and application and turned a blind eye to the process of knowledge discovery. Based on my proposed definition, China appears to be a country that lacks an equivalent to Western science or that attaches less importance to knowledge discovery than to application of existing knowledge. This attitude has deep roots. As I discussed in Chapter 2, Zhu Xi (1130–1200 CE) defined rationality as an explanation that agreed with the government's interpretation of reality. However, it's important to remember the importance of context. During China's Cultural Revolution (1966–1976), the Red Guards (a student paramilitary organization mobilized to erase the old culture and replace it with a new socialist culture) did not understand science, considered it outdated and unsocialist, and persecuted or killed many Chinese scientists. Chinese scientists have a long memory and have learned caution from this experience. The resulting unwillingness to challenge authority provides an important explanation of the problems with modern Chinese science, which is still recovering from this period.

Chinese people like to say that what someone says is very scientific, that a new policy is very scientific, and so on. This suggests that Chinese "science" emphasizes the characteristics of rationality, practicality, and public sharing of knowledge that it learned from Western science; however, the characteristics of logic, exclusiveness, and questioning are not key aspects of how Chinese culture sees science. The Chinese government conceals their lack of understanding of science by affirming the importance of science to the public, but in practice, they attach little importance to science and scientific research. For example, in 2020, China's scientific research investment reached 2.44 trillion RMB and accounting for 2.4% of GDP, and scientific research investment ranked 12th in the world (China Statistics Agency, 1952–2021). However, the proportion of basic scientific research (i.e., research designed to improve knowledge rather than to produce new technologies) was only 5.5%, compared with 17.2% in the United States and 15.5% in Russia in 2020 (China Statistics Agency, 1952–2021).

What are the consequences of China's misunderstanding of science and its neglect of scientific research?

3.1.1. Insufficient Innovation

Because China has not distinguished between science and technology, the Chinese people often combine the two, replace science with technology, and propose a concept that I call *sci-technology* that does not distinguish between the two fields of research. This results in the mistake of treating technology as science and prioritizing technology. Government departments also don't understand what science is. For example, in 2015, the Ministry of Science and Technology proposed to include in their mandate the concepts of yin and yang, the five elements, and the eight trigrams from the *I Ching* (the *Book of Changes*, an ancient Chinese discussion of metaphysics) in their *13th Five-Year Plan for the Cultivation of Scientific Literacy of Chinese Teenagers (2016 to 2020)* to promote their belief that Chinese culture is an ancient culture that is good at scientific discovery. This belief was widely opposed by Chinese scholars and these items have been removed from the curriculum. The problem resulted from a lack of cultural confidence, a lack of innovation, and a serious brain drain in which gifted Chinese researchers seek jobs in Western countries.

3.1.1.1. Lack of Cultural Confidence

The concepts of *yin* and *yang*, the *five elements*, and the *eight trigrams* are the essence of Chinese cultural thought and an important foundation of ancient Chinese culture. They have a history that may go back 5,000 years, whereas science (in the Western sense of the word) has a history of only about 400 years. The ideas of moderation (*zhongyong*, seeking the golden mean between two extremes) and flexibility are important sources of wisdom and have supported the long-term prosperity of Chinese society. These ideas have led to tolerance of foreign cultures, which can be seen in the modern diversity of Chinese culture. However, science is a completely different cultural system that has not been widely adopted by Chinese culture and seems unlikely to benefit from mixture with these older concepts.

Literature, science, and art are different cultural systems that play different roles in the evolution of civilization. Metaphysics, such as the *yin* and *yang* concepts, differ from literature, science, and art and represent a distinctive feature of any culture. However, such concepts are strongly associated with religion, and rely on faith rather than scientific inquiry, and are therefore a poor choice for guiding scientific inquiry. In China, Western experimental science is analogous to an invading foreign culture, and as has been the case in China's long past, it must be slowly digested and absorbed before it becomes part of Chinese culture. Western historical experience shows that science has been an indispensable force in the evolution of Western civilization, an important engine of social and economic development, and a symbol of humanity's entry into the modern era. China has not yet understood this philosophy.

Although science plays an increasingly important role in the development of modern society, it cannot solve all the problems we're facing (Davis, 2000). For example, science is generally ethically neutral, and although it can support ethical decisions, science focuses on discovery and challenging incorrect perceptions, not on ethical issues. Literature, art, religion, and philosophy can provide ethical insights that are indispensable. China should enhance its cultural self-confidence by promoting its achievements in these areas but should use that confidence to give it courage to embrace and absorb the Western concept of science, without abandoning other important aspects of human life such as cultural ethics.

3.1.1.2. Lack of Innovation

Since the 1990s, China's policies on innovation have emphasized the development and adoption of modern technologies and, given China's status as an impoverished developing country, were appropriate for helping China to catch up with international standards. Indeed, this policy achieved immediate effects. For example, Chinese scientists and engineers have landed a rover on the dark side of the moon (Cogorno, 2022). China also leads the world in quantum encryption (Titcomb, 2021), social media platforms such as Tiktok and their content recommendation algorithms, e-commerce (e.g., platforms such as Alibaba) (Kumar et al., 2021), and social media apps such as WeChat (Hao, 2023). These examples show the scientific and technological capabilities of Chinese researchers. However, they all represent improvements in Western innovations rather than original breakthroughs. Though China's space exploration program is impressive, China has not yet landed one of its astronauts on the moon, even though Neil Alden Armstrong and Edwin Eugene (Buzz) Aldrin landed and walked on the moon in July 1969. If we ignore the contributions of overseas Chinese scholars, it is difficult to find breakthroughs created by original Chinese research (Cao et al., 2020; Weinberg, 2011). Instead, innovation is almost always introduced from Western states (Dou et al., 2015).

In the context of science and technology, innovations are breakthroughs that reveal new knowledge or permit the development of new technology and that improve our ability to explain the world or improve our life. In China, most research is performed by the government in government-controlled universities and research institutes (Paulson, 2018). Unlike in the West, little research is done by enterprises. For example, investment in scientific research by Chinese enterprises accounts for only 14.9% of the total R&D investment, versus 33.0% in the United States (China Statistics Agency, 1952–2021). This doesn't seem serious in light of achievements such as China becoming the world's largest producer of academic papers. From 2015 to 2017, the number of scientific papers published in China accounted for 26.9% of the total global number, versus 16.8% for the United States (Xia et al., 2023). However, most of today's high-impact papers published by Chinese scholars are essentially follow-up papers that validate previous results or repeat an experiment under new conditions rather than innovations that enter wholly new areas of knowledge (Cao et al., 2020). In the more than a century since Western science was introduced to China, China has not yet made contributions to science and technology that have been widely adopted by other countries, and China's scientific and technological innovation have not been proportional to the country's population or its investments in universities and research (Lagrotteria & Besescheck, 2012).

To conceal this problem, China's government and researchers have created the phrase "filling the gap." This means that Chinese scientists have made up for the omissions of domestic and international researchers in certain fields rather than building on that research to create something new (i.e., a breakthrough). Every year, a large number of Chinese academicians and administrators (leaders of universities and research institutes) are rewarded by the state for filling such gaps. In China, scholars without administrative positions rarely receive government funding, and they find it even more difficult to obtain government awards. More than 100 years ago, Henry Augustus Rowland (1848–1901), an American physicist, said in a lecture (Zhou, 2021):

> To have the applications of a science, the science itself must exist. Should we stop its progress, and attend only to its applications, we should soon degenerate into a people like the Chinese, who have made no progress for generations, because they have been satisfied with the applications of science, and have never sought for reasons in what they have done. The reasons constitute pure science.

Rowland's observation remains true today.

In September 2020, the China Internet Manufacturing Summit was held in Xiamen. Nian Yong, former director of the Industry Department of the National Development and Reform Commission, pointed out at the meeting (Bajpai, 2022):

> Today, more than 100 years later, the reality we see is that China is almost blank in the field of major basic theories and original core technologies. Today, the key basic materials, advanced basic technology, and core basic components of 4G are heavily dependent on imports.

He added: "To say that China is a big manufacturing country means that it is a contract factory. The reason is very simple. We don't grasp the science and don't know what its principles are."

A large part of the problem is that China's government controls both education and scientific research. This is the legacy of *fajia*, which distrusts activities such as teaching innovative thought that might lead to criticism of the government and a reduction of its power. As a result, China not only lags behind Western countries in scientific research but also lacks the will to transform research into something closer to the Western model. The patent conversion rate of Chinese enterprises (i.e., the proportion of patent applications that are granted) in 2020 was 44.9%, which is equal to that of the United States. However, the conversion rates for government-controlled research institutes and universities were only 11.3% and 3.8%, respectively, which are 22.6% and 7.6% of the US level (Sanyou, 2021).

3.1.1.3. Serious Brain Drain

The 35th anniversary of China's National Day was on October 1, 1984. Peking University students displayed the banner "Hello Xiaoping" to welcome leader Deng Xiaoping because they believed that he would bring China into a new era of academic freedom. However, the long-awaited springtime of science still has not arrived. Because China offers few opportunities for groundbreaking research, wealthy Chinese students and students fortunate enough to earn a scholarship have increasingly left China to study abroad. The number of students studying abroad increased from 24,000 in 1999 to 703,000 in 2019, an increase to 29.3 times the initial value in only 20 years (Fig. 5). During the same period, the proportion of the students who returned to China after earning their initial degree increased from 33.3% to 82.5%. However, nearly 90% of Chinese PhD recipients stayed in the United States, and 20,000 students from Tsinghua University, "China's MIT," remained in Silicon Valley alone (Xia et al., 2023), resulting in a serious brain drain of some of China's smartest students.

Western countries have learned that they can earn large sums of money by educating Chinese bachelor's and master's degree students and can use that money to bring the smartest students to their own country, train them to obtain doctorates, and persuade them to engage in scientific research and higher education in their new country. These elite students often choose to stay in their new country and improve its economy instead of that of their native land (Peters et al., 2016). Because the Chinese government doesn't include statistics on such

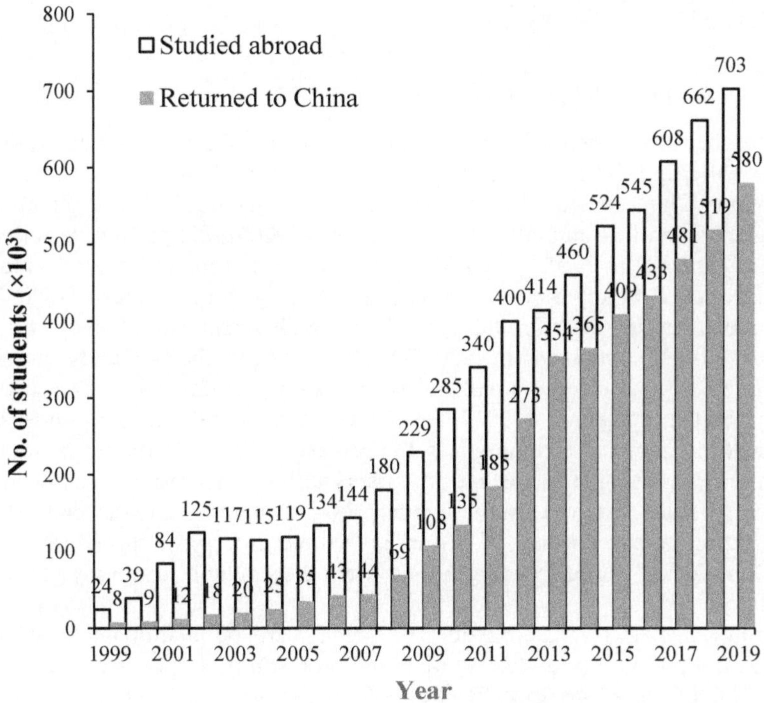

Fig. 5. Statistics on the Number of Chinese Students Who Studied Abroad and the Numbers Who Returned to China After Earning Their Initial Degree from 1999 to 2019. *Source*: The figure is created by the author.

sources of income in its economic data, the Chinese public doesn't understand how scientific research earns money for universities and the government. This ignorance undoubtedly contributes to the Chinese government's reluctance to invest in scientific research. The hundreds of thousands of Chinese students who study abroad each year creates an international education market of approximately US$1 trillion (including tuition fees, living expenses, and other expenses related to studying abroad). International education is one of China's largest imported products.

After 40 years of reform since China's opening up to the West, Chinese technology has caught up with Western technology, but a lack of innovation has been gradually revealed. China and the United States have been competing economically with increasing intensity for more than 20 years, and innovative science and technology have been key weapons in this trade war. The lack of innovation has been revealed as the biggest of China's political and economic constraints. Morales (2021) reported that 29% of the world's top researchers have obtained undergraduate degrees in China, ranking first in the world. However, 56% of these researchers migrated to the United States to obtain their PhD. The talent market in the United States is almost evenly divided between Americans (31%) and Chinese (27%), with 88% of Chinese PhDs in the field of artificial intelligence choosing to work in the United States and only 10% returning to China, which is a staggering loss for China.

3.1.2. Unbalanced Higher Education

The number of universities (schools that can award MSc and PhD degrees) and junior colleges (higher vocational education schools that cannot award such degrees) in China increased from 182 in 1952 to 2,956 in 2019, and the number of students enrolled annually increased from 66,000 to 8.2 million, an increase of 124.2 times (Xia et al., 2023). However, the number of university graduates increased more rapidly than the corresponding job growth rate, resulting in high unemployment just after graduation. The unemployment rate of these students was 3.2% in 1997 and 34.9% in 2020. During this period, the unemployment rates in China's large cities and small towns were only 3.1% and 4.3%, respectively (China Statistics Agency, 1999–2021). University students educated under China's centrally planned economy lack the professional skills required by modern enterprises, resulting in a shortage of workers with the professional and technical vocational skills required by these enterprises, so many graduates cannot find jobs (Mzingwane & Plattner, 2008). In 2019 alone, enterprises lacked more than 4 million skilled workers during a time when 2.86 million university graduates could not find jobs.

From 1989 to 2017, the proportion of China's rural population fell from 73.6% of the total population to 39.8%, while the proportion of rural students in universities fell from 43.4% to 8.0% (China Statistics Agency, 1999–2021). Clearly, urban residents are receiving a better education. As a result of this imbalance, poor students from rural areas have become the student group with the highest unemployment rate in China. *New Express* (2014) reported that only 6,000 of the 28,000 poor students in Guangdong found jobs in 2014, so their employment rate was less than 22%. Rural residents are clearly discriminated against by the education system.

Under China's centrally planned economy, the Ministry of Education is keen to show the world the high student enrollment rate of Chinese universities, which sounds impressive but fails to mention how these schools ignore the needs of society (the skills demanded by enterprises and the need to employ all these graduates) and the criteria required for development of China's science and technology sector. In contrast with the education policy of market-oriented countries, the Chinese government subsidizes universities on a large scale. For example, in 2020, the Chinese government gave these schools a subsidy of 40,000 RMB for each undergraduate student to encourage schools to expand their enrollment. In 2017, China enrolled 84,000 doctoral students, but the subsidies paid to schools for doctoral students are incredibly low, with each doctoral student receiving an annual salary after graduation ranging from 10,000 to 50,000 RMB, compared with more than 300,000 RMB in Europe and the United States (Xia et al., 2023). As a result, only 16.1% of doctoral students expressed an interest in doctoral-level scientific research (Cao et al., 2009a). There is little incentive to become a scientist under China's higher education policy, because it seems that the more you study, the lower your salary. This situation is unlikely to change so long as government officials don't understand the importance of science and fear that scientific thinkers will threaten their power.

Under China's planned economy and centralized political control, Chinese universities and research institutes have become typical government departments: everything is decided by officials (Ai, 2019). Like Chinese government officials, university and research institute officials are tempted to abuse their power. *China News* (2013) reported that the former director of the Transportation Bureau of the Ministry of Railways admitted to accepting bribes totaling 47.55 million RMB to obtain the title of academician. These examples may only represent the tip of the iceberg, since the government has not investigated every report of unethical behavior. It's easy to find other examples using appropriate search words such as (in Chinese) "university president" and "arrested." For example, you will find stories about Communist Party officials and university presidents being expelled from the party and dismissed from public office along with stories of many senior individuals under investigation.

In contrast with the largely independent research environment for Western scientists, Chinese administrative leaders have the power to define the laws that researchers must follow, even if those laws contradict government laws, and some leaders place these laws above science. Meeting the requirements of higher officials has become a hidden rule followed by many scholars in China (Xia et al., 2023). This same form of administrative management has encouraged a moral decline among Chinese scholars because it provides implicit support for making decisions based on flawed science or even pseudoscientific evidence that officials are not able to identify as problems. Since 2021, the number of journal manuscript retractions involving Chinese scholars have exceeded 17,000, accounting for three-quarters of the global retractions (Mallapaty, 2024).

3.2. Scientific Development and National Governance

In the 17th century, the British philosopher Francis Bacon (1561–1626) proposed that science must be experimental and inductive, and that all truth must be based on a large body of conclusive factual material (i.e., data). On this basis, he proposed a scientific induction method to find causal relationships that required induction from observations of experimental materials. The emergence of experimental science under this paradigm was a conceptual breakthrough that made the modern world possible. Bacon emphasized the need to question all knowledge and obtain evidence through repeated verification of a hypothesis and emphasized that any point of view and knowledge must be supported by evidence and particularly repeated evidence (replication) to provide confidence in the results. It is not difficult to understand that this form of experimental science conflicts with religion, which relies on faith rather than evidence. It also conflicts with *fajia*, since the truth does not always support government desires and challenges government power.

3.2.1. Differences Between Science and Religion

Religion originated as an empirical judgment formed by early humans based on their long-term observation of natural and human phenomena and their desire to explain their world. The desire for religion was strengthened by the human desire for immortality; most people long to believe in an afterlife and in powerful but mysterious supernatural forces or entities who exist outside the visible world. To attract their attention and ask for blessings, people revere and worship these mysterious forces and, over time, develop a system of beliefs and ritual activities. Finally, by creating a shared and unchanging ideology, religion attempts to create harmony within a society.

Where science encourages questioning and repeated verification of one's beliefs, leading to revision of the beliefs as new evidence becomes available, religion emphasizes compliance with accepted beliefs and rituals and opposes questioning. Science relies on a simple statement: "Prove it." Religion relies on an equally simple statement: "Believe it." Of the two, science has provided more practical solutions to the world's problems. Since the advent of science, the kind of person who chooses a career in the sciences has increasingly rejected religion. Although not all scientists are atheists, most Western scientists no longer believe in the existence of gods. Some are willing to accept that religion deals with issues beyond the ability of science to explore; others do not. However, all scientists agree that our scientific understanding of the world is incomplete and that far more knowledge remains to be discovered. In contrast, religion generally claims to explain everything.

One problem with science is that it provides no universal moral structure that scientists use to judge the ethics of their research. Although science has provided many practical insights that have helped modern society evolve, it lacks an inherent form of ethics apart from the ethical responsibility to not falsify data or ignore contradictory evidence. But beyond this, science makes no ethical claims;

on the contrary, scientists emphasize that science itself is ethically neutral and only the uses of scientific knowledge have ethical implications. This is a dangerous attitude, because science not only provides practical insights that promote the development of society but also supports anti-social behavior, such as the endless development of weapons based on technologies made possible by new science. If we don't try to restrict such undesirable consequences, we risk severe negative consequences, including the collapse of societies or even civilization.

In contrast, religion is based on a moral code that guides human behavior and assumes that all behaviors are inherently ethical or unethical. Although religious knowledge inevitably contains errors because it is based on faith rather than fact, its contribution to the development of society cannot be denied. For example, religion has contributed greatly to the cultures in which it evolved through its contributions to language, philosophy, art, and music. Religion has also contributed practical knowledge, such as traditional Chinese medicine. Some of these traditional practices have saved countless lives, whereas others, such as the *yin* and *yang* principles, the five elements, and meridian theory, are not supported by modern experimental science. Religion has also served an important role in removing some of the fear of death by emphasizing that death is part of a natural cycle. In particular, Chinese people may not believe in the existence of gods, but they cannot forget their ancestors and instead believe in their continued existence and their continued desire to bless their children.

The emergence of science has dramatically changed the human cognitive style, to a belief system based on experimental verification rather than personal experience. Science provides better explanations of life in the world and more objective ways to solve problems. Although modern science has increasingly proved that most religious explanations of nature and society were wrong, there are still some religious phenomena that science has been unable to explain. For example, science cannot prove whether a person has a soul.

Questioning is one of the greatest advantages of science. Science relies on replacing explanations that are no longer supported by evidence, thereby reinvigorating science and making it a continuing endeavor. However, science is not omnipotent, as it cannot replace literature, art, music, and other forms of creativity. Because religion and culture are intertwined and difficult to distinguish, it seems unlikely that a society will ever eliminate religion. In addition, the dividing line between religion and philosophy is often unclear. For example, whether Confucianism is a religion or a philosophy remains controversial. We modern humans therefore face an interesting challenge: the historical experience that is preserved in our culture and religion contains wisdom and proven solutions for coexistence that cannot be simply rejected, yet despite science's practical and objective nature, it can only provide evidence that may persuade some religious people to revise outdated and no longer relevant beliefs.

Whether knowledge derives from religion or science, it must be spread to those who can benefit from it for the knowledge to be valuable. The purpose of disseminating science is twofold: First, scientific knowledge can resolve doubts, help people understand the laws that govern natural and social development, and teach people how to live in harmony with nature and other people. Second, this knowledge can guide engineers to improve the products we use in everyday life through technological innovation. This creates the possibility to continuously improve production methods and the quality of life. The purpose of spreading religion is both similar and different. First, by answering questions about the world and dispelling doubts, religion teaches people to learn to live in harmony with nature and each other. Second, it has the goal of making the recipients of religious knowledge believe that religion is the omnipresent ruler of the human spirit. Although this second aspect of religion encourages unity within social groups and maintains social stability, it can also be used to control people, limit their freedom and creative ability, and retard social development. It can also lead to conflict between religions or between different groups that nominally belong to the same religion.

Religion does not encourage questioning of fundamental beliefs, and through repeated and intensive education, it cultivates generations of believers who have no independent ideas or an independent personality. In contrast, science encourages questioning, and through repeated and intensive education and training, it cultivates free-thinkers who develop innovative ideas, independent personalities, and a spirit of exploration in search of new insights, even if those insights lead to rejection of existing beliefs. Unlike religion, science is a system of knowledge that is constantly evolving and improving. Therefore, if a country's education system is opposed to questioning, teaching science and religion produces similar results: people who don't question their beliefs. At the same time, science aims to promote a world without national boundaries, characterized by the free spread of ideas. In contrast, religion often attempts to impose boundaries, and religious conflicts have plagued society for millennia.

Traditional Chinese education also has two sides that share some aspects of science and religion. On the one hand, Confucius and his successors were eager to disseminate knowledge, answer questions, and teach relevant skills to citizens. Confucius noted that the correct way of learning is through simultaneous practice. He encouraged his disciples to constantly verify knowledge through practice, transform it into improved thinking ability, and obtain inner pleasure and satisfaction from this activity. Although Confucius emphasized that a wise one should like helping others achieve their goals and that a student should be better than his teacher, this kind of encouragement clearly doesn't conform to the wishes of authoritarian rulers who prioritize their own ideas. Therefore, after China entered the imperial era, *fajia* has interfered with free thought and the ability to question authority. The idea that students should surpass their teachers was replaced with the ideology that they should honor their teachers and esteem the truths the teachers revealed, without questioning those truths. This attitude has persisted for more than 2,000 years, leading to a conservative approach to education that has limited the creative spirit of the Chinese people and left China stuck in a cycle of dynastic change in which only the ruler changed.

The Chinese educational model based on honoring teachers and respecting their teaching is a form of *fajia* that has trained generations of Chinese people to memorize knowledge by rote learning. Today, China's primary and secondary education is still the best in the world from this perspective. However, it does not teach logical or critical thinking ability or creativity to "think outside the box" and discourages students from questioning the correctness of existing knowledge. Although Chinese students can benefit from their mastery of rote knowledge, they have a hard time seeking new knowledge through experimental methods. In primary and secondary education, the problems caused by the Chinese educational model are not prominent. Because the knowledge learned during primary and secondary education is the result of hundreds of years of repeated verification, the body of knowledge contains few mistakes and provides a solid foundation for more advanced knowledge. Unfortunately, the situation for college and university education is surprisingly similar to that of primary and secondary education. University textbooks in developed countries are revised frequently, perhaps every 3–5 years, to ensure that they reflect the most recent knowledge, and errors in textbooks are constantly being eliminated. At the same time, the latest research results are being constantly integrated. Although China's Ministry of Education also organizes revisions of textbooks, Chinese scholars in the Ministry rarely have time to comb through the latest research. Instead, they emphasize translation of the latest international textbooks into Chinese.

However, Chinese universities tend to teach standard answers for use in student examinations, and students can get high marks simply by memorizing these answers. Students who propose their own ideas may not only be judged wrong but may also risk failing their courses. Over time, the lack of rewards for creativity and the presence of penalties for creativity leads to its elimination. This kind of devotion to textbooks resembles religion more than science. Recent survey results (Loyalka et al., 2021) showed that the critical thinking ability of Chinese students often declines after they complete their university studies. At the beginning of their university education, the critical thinking ability of Chinese students is equivalent to that of American students, but only four years later, this ability has decreased to only 29%–66% of the value for American students. The standard explanation for greater Western innovation is that this problem originates from China's college entrance examination system, which requires students to answer questions using answers prescribed by the Ministry of Education. As a result, traditionally well-behaved and obedient Chinese girls frequently score higher than boys, leading to more female than male university students (regardless of the field of study). For example, the proportion of female applicants admitted to undergraduate programs in Chinese universities was approximately 63%, while the proportion of male students was only 37% in 2022 (China Statistics Agency, 2023). This system has rewarded students who accept without questioning, leading them to continue that approach. Even when Chinese students are capable of innovative thinking, they may choose not to because doing so would risk their continued success.

The fundamental difference between modern Western universities, whose origins lie in the 17th-century European Enlightenment, and their medieval and Renaissance predecessors lies in the transformation of university functions. Medieval universities were places for imparting existing knowledge but did not prioritize research and knowledge discovery or criticism of knowledge passed on from previous generations. In contrast, modern Western universities regard research as their main function, with the goals of increasing human knowledge, cultivating research, and teaching students to perform this research as their main tasks. Furthermore, they advocate academic freedom (particularly the ability to question received knowledge) and unify teaching with research. Therefore, a modern Western university is a focal point for scientific research, and scientific discovery and communication of scientific knowledge are the university's main functions. We often recall Isaac Newton's famous saying that scientists are people who stand on the shoulders of giants. In this context, the giants are scholars. Every time we read a scholarly paper, we are essentially exchanging ideas with the giants who supported the writing of the paper. In contrast, Chinese universities have not taken this step and remain trapped in a model based on promoting old knowledge rather than building on that knowledge to create something new.

Scientific research takes a long time. For example, it is not uncommon for a researcher to take five years to form an idea, define a testable hypothesis, perform the research to find evidence to support or reject the hypothesis, write a paper, and then guide the paper through the review and publication process. It can then take about 20 years of research and accumulation of knowledge from the publication of papers to be able to write a book on a specialized topic. To remain aware of the current state of knowledge, a scholar must constantly read the latest published papers in the field, since books take so much longer to produce that they often reflect the past rather than the present. From the point of view of scientific research, the knowledge in a book may be too old after 20 years, so books are more often useful for beginners, students, and ordinary readers. However, Chinese government and university officials, as well as some scholars, can publish many books each year by copying books and articles published by others. There is a Chinese proverb that describes this problem: "Many manuscripts are borrowed from the words of others to see who copies better." Compared with plagiarism of papers, plagiarism of books by Chinese bureaucrats and scholars is open and unscrupulous. Unlike literature reviews or textbook compilation, which require a lot of careful, intellectually rigorous work by the author to summarize the knowledge of scholars, some books produced by Chinese officials and scholars may be copies of the work of others, without any attempt to summarize and integrate the source materials. They therefore provide no innovation or new insights into the material. Many Chinese people call such officials and scholars "Professor Scissors" because they assemble their books from pieces cut out of the work of other authors.

This description of Chinese schooling makes it easy for us to answer Qian Xuesen's question from earlier in this chapter: a bureaucratic university that does not teach students to think for themselves, does not teach students to criticize and challenge previous knowledge, and does not respect creativity and scientific innovation cannot cultivate excellent talents.

3.2.2. Relationships Between Science and Government

Markets, government, and the combination of science and technology are three interconnected dimensions of modern civilization. Modern society relies on scientific and technological innovation, market competition, and government services to maintain development momentum. The lack of any one of these aspects leads to an imbalance or even a collapse of social development. When the market, government, and science and technology development work together in a balanced way, social progress is fastest. In a given country, imbalances among these forces can cause radical changes in a society. For example, in Mao Zedong's era, the government took over all of society's affairs and functions, completely rejected market forces, and exiled university professors, who were sent for re-education in rural areas or imprisoned. After nearly 30 years of this governance, Mao had turned China into the poorest and most underdeveloped country in the world.

Because a government's first priority is to maintain social stability, which conflicts with the desire of researchers to explore potentially disruptive ideas, so its relationship with science has always been delicate. On the one hand, the government needs scientific knowledge and skills to improve its ability to govern the country and to promote socioeconomic development. On the other hand, science often exposes the government's mistakes. So the government's attitude toward science is always mixed. Bureaucratic systems, in which subordinates obey superiors and the people obey the government, inherently oppose freedom, so universities regulated by the government generally become bureaucracies that stifle the ability to innovate. During the more than 70 years of the Communist Party's rule, all affairs in Chinese universities have been decided by the government's education administration rather than by university researchers, and both teachers and students in universities had little chance to participate in scientific innovation, particularly in the examination (testing) system that I described earlier in this chapter. Because there were penalties for thinking outside the box, and few rewards, innovation skills have been neglected (Lagrotteria & Besescheck, 2012).

In China, the government has the final say on the objectives, principles, curriculum, organization, system, procedures, and funding of universities (Normile, 2018). To avoid conflicts with the government and administrative penalties up to and including the loss of funding, scholars in universities choose to obey the government rather than trying to innovate and change the existing system. As a result, they strive to meet the needs of the government rather than promoting the freedom and breakthroughs that universities need to thrive. To be on the safe side, scholars try to avoid controversial research directions that might lead to disruptive breakthroughs, and train students to follow government instructions rather than meeting the labor market's demands. Where the government doesn't understand those demands, it is inevitable that university education will be out of touch with the labor market (Mzingwane & Plattner, 2008).

Because innovation often means negation of old beliefs, so innovators often become the target of criticism because their understanding differs from that of most people. During China's Cultural Revolution, Mao Zedong's approach to the pursuit of truth was to leave the definition of truth in the hands of the common people rather than in the hands of scientists. This led to the persecution of scientists with different ideas. Unlike primary and secondary education and professional and technical training, modern universities advocate academic freedom and the unity of teaching and research, which contradict the obedience and order preferred by a government system that controls what is taught by the education system. This is where the problem lies: science continuously achieves breakthroughs by building on an increasingly firm foundation but also by rejecting past beliefs that are no longer valid; as a result, it also exposes the deceptions or errors of religions and the government. When the emperor's new clothes are exposed, an angry government often defends itself by attacking the scientists responsible for this exposure, possibly even to the extent of closing problematic universities.

For example, when Mao Zedong failed to gain power in the 1930s, he remained in awe of science. He was very clear that "only science can save China" and wrote an article titled "The Theory of Practice" that encouraged the Chinese Communists to respect science and bring forth new thinking through the method of negation. However, after Mao came to power in 1949, he first attacked his political competitors and then gradually expanded his attacks to all competing ideologies, leading him to crack down on science and scientists who exposed flaws with his reasoning. Finally, he launched the Cultural Revolution in 1966 to reject and suppress all non-Mao thought. Mao said that "political power grows out of the barrel of a gun." Ji Xianlin (1911–2009), a master of Chinese culture, had only a pen in his hand, so he said helplessly that "I dare not tell the truth, I can't tell lies, so I must shut up." Ji expressed the helplessness of Chinese science and scientists in that era.

Although today's governments generally participate in social and economic development, carry out infrastructure construction, and show a friendly face of "serving the people," Olson (1993) noted that governments often function as "rational robbers" who care more about their own interests than about right and wrong. This is interesting because it suggests that *fajia* is not a purely Chinese concept. (Chapter 5 discusses the essence of government in more detail.) Such individuals focus on personal success, not stable development of future society. At the same time, the lifespan of a leader, whether elected or a dictator, is always limited. It is difficult to reconcile the contradiction between short-sighted governments that are eager for quick success and instant benefit for themselves and scientific research, which honors individual achievements but pursues the long-term development of society. Fortunately, technological innovation that arrives at the right time depends on scientific guidance. Despite the clear value of this guidance, a government that loves technological innovation has always been suspicious of scientists and their work because of the possibility that it will embarrass them. Thus, the abundant scientific research funds in Western countries come from market-oriented autonomous universities rather than government investment. In contrast, Chinese universities obtain funds almost entirely from the government and from student tuition fees.

The administrative governance system of Chinese universities robs them of the autonomy that is a key factor in the success of Western universities, of the spirit of freedom that promotes innovation, and of the potential innovative power of universities. Government-run universities are less concerned than autonomous universities about whether their students can adapt to society and create wealth, since graduates who fail to prosper have no wealth to return to the autonomous universities that trained them. The primary value of the government-run universities is the transmission of potentially outdated technology and skills to students, and this helps to explain China's lack of innovation.

3.2.3. Time-lag Effects

Science rarely has immediate consequences. For example, there is often a five-year period between developing an original thought and turning it into a published manuscript. Scientific research is a long process. It often takes 100–200 years from the initial scientific discovery to a mature understanding of the discovery. For example, when British physicist John Tyndall (1820–1893) demonstrated the principle of internal light reflection by water at the Royal Society in 1870, he did a simple experiment: he drilled a hole in the bottom of a barrel filled with water and then illuminated the water from the top of the barrel with a lamp. His audience was surprised to see shining water flowing out of the small hole in the bucket. When the water bent, the light also bent and was transmitted by the bending water.

It took until 1967 for a practical demonstration of the utility of this knowledge. Dr Kao Kuen (Charles Kuen Kao, 1933–2018), a British–Chinese scholar, published a paper titled "Dielectric Fiber Surface Waveguide for Optical Frequencies" in the journal *Electromagnetic Wave Theory*, in which he analyzed the theory of light transmission in a fiber, thereby demonstrating the possibility of using optical fiber as a transmission medium that allowed data communication (Kao & Hockham, 1967). In 1970, three engineers at the Corning Company in the United States successfully developed a low-loss silica fiber that could be used to create usable optical fibers. In 1977, for the first time, engineers installed the first telephone network based on these fibers. In 1982, the "82 Project," a key scientific research project of the Ministry of Posts and Telecommunications of China, opened China's first fiber-optic communication network, in Wuhan.

From the discovery of internal light reflection to the application of this principle for communication, scientists took more than 100 years. Similarly, it took humanity more than 200 years from Newton's law of universal gravitation to the first rocket launch. Today, without Einstein's theory of relativity, modern communication would be considerably more difficult, and global positioning system (GPS) satellites would be either impossible or inaccurate. However, Einstein did not know the usefulness of relativity when he was studying it.

Science is first used to explain natural and social phenomena and then gradually applied to technological innovation and practical application. Many countries exist for hundreds of years, but in any given country, the governing regime exists for a much shorter time. In the United States, each new government has only four years to complete its work before they are potentially replaced at the next election. Even in a centralized regime, a dictator cannot live forever. Because governments know they have only a short time to achieve success, they are eager for quick successes and prefer instant benefits; they have no patience to wait for interesting science to find an application.

Because of the desire for rapid results, governments don't appreciate scientists and generally prefer engineers who are engaged in applying technological innovation, especially for the production of goods or delivery of services. For example, China enthusiastically welcomed rocket expert Qian Xuesen (1911–2009) and the father of Chinese rice, Yuan Longping (1930–2021). Although their contributions to science were minimal, and Qian caused much damage through his unjustified prediction about agricultural yield (described in Chapter 1), their technological achievements earned them a reputation as great scientists. Few people know that their real success was as engineers.

As I noted earlier in this chapter, "science" has been replaced in China by a phrase that can be translated as "sci-technology," and few Chinese understand the difference between science and technology. In today's Chinese universities, few professors and researchers can clearly explain this difference. Thus, few scholars will accept the suggestion that Qian and Yuan were not scientists. Science can also be a dangerous profession, because scientific research challenges authority and can embarrass powerful people. Perhaps the best-known example is Galileo Galilei (1564–1642), who contradicted the Catholic doctrine that placed the Earth at the center of the universe and was threatened with execution by the Pope for this heretical belief.

"It takes 10 years to grow trees but 100 years to rear people" is a well-known proverb in China. But when Chinese people say this, they always say it to others and don't apply it to themselves. Since 2011, China's decreasing birth rate has begun to decrease the labor supply. Simultaneously, China's economic growth rate has decreased from double digits to single digits. I worry about how China, which ignores scientific research in favor of technology development and lacks a way to encourage scientific and technological innovation, will lead humanity into the future. Much of China's economy is powered by a growing real estate bubble. Although the bubble has not yet collapsed, income from government land sales (a primary way for local governments to earn income that they can invest in infrastructure or the economy) has decreased rapidly. This has created a high risk of a severe recession. If the Chinese government continues to ignore the importance of science, China will lose its advantage over other counties and find its economic development beginning to stagnate, which happened to Brazil after the 1970s, Japan after the 1980s, Indonesia after the 1990s, and other developing countries.

3.3. Innovation Needs a Competitive Environment

On the surface, every government shows a strong desire to govern the country well, but this desire tends to disappear when the interests of the state (i.e., the people) conflict with the interests of the government. (I will discuss this in detail in Chapter 4.) In this situation, government officials have a strong incentive to replace the state interest with their own interests. These officials have only rarely chosen national interests. In the absence of supervision or with inadequate supervision, official corruption and decision-making errors have become common government problems. (I will discuss this in more detail in Chapter 5.)

In the West, scientists have an obligation to speak the truth, when necessary, to correct erroneous government decisions. However, the Communist Party of China (CPC) stipulates that members of the party should not contradict the party's statements in public. In its "negative list" of political discipline violations, the Regulations on Disciplinary Actions of the CPC, revised in 2015, include "distorting the major policies of the CPC Central Committee and undermining the centralism and unity of the Party." A warning or serious warning will be given to those whose misconduct is considered minor. If the circumstances are serious, the person will be removed from their post within the party or placed under observation. If the circumstances are truly serious, they will be expelled from the party. Therefore, Chinese intellectuals have chosen self-protection, leading to the existence of policies that were ineffective, overly aggressive, or poorly considered. It took many years to correct these problems, and some still have not been corrected.

Since 1978, continuous market-oriented reform has promoted the rapid development of China's society and economy. However, although most economic sectors have completed the majority of their market-oriented reform, scientific research and higher education have maintained their traditional centrally planned model. This model emphasizes the pronouncements of a single policy that may not reflect an effective solution rather than a debate among many perspectives until consensus can be achieved about the best approach. Since 2000, China's government has implemented a series of plans to promote innovation. This approach has been unable to prevent China's top talents from emigrating to other countries. This has given those other countries a significant advantage in the modern trade war, which relies heavily on scientific and technological innovation. Although it's easy to accuse these emigrant scholars of a lack of patriotism, something more serious may be wrong with China's scientific research environment.

3.3.1. The Harm Caused by **Fajia**

The Western concept of science encourages researchers to get to the bottom of the matter through in-depth study and questioning of previous explanations. After more than 2,000 years of imperial rule, the Confucian educational philosophy that students should become better than their teachers has been replaced by the pragmatic *fajia* ideology, which emphasizes obedience. China's government opposes private education because it threatens government power and emphasizes loyalty to the government, with the implicit understanding that disagreement represents disloyalty. This has led to two negative consequences: First, the best talents are diverted into officialdom rather than spending their career thinking about "boring" scientific problems. Second, this philosophy stresses order and obedience and opposes questioning, which means that someone who accepts the philosophy is only rarely willing to "get to the bottom of the matter." Those who do seek the truth are accused of worrying too much and being unrealistic, even if they are not mocked outright. Today, Chinese universities still call those scholars who are unwilling to strive tirelessly for fame and wealth "bookworms." Clearly, *fajia* culture would not encourage the emergence of science.

As I discussed in Chapter 2, Chinese culture has advantages that other cultures lack. Specifically, Chinese culture embraces cultural diversity and inclusiveness. Anyone who studies European history quickly learns that when any single religion or culture occupies a dominant position in society, this increases the risk of conflict with other religions and cultures and thereby creates barriers to cultural exchanges and trade. In contrast, encouraging cultural diversity can improve the flexibility of the social system and prevent conflicts between ideologies by promoting harmonious coexistence (Cao, 2016a). However, scholars have generally overlooked the negative impact of *fajia* on Chinese culture. The neo-Confucianism of Zhu Xi not only accepts *fajia* principles but also supports the suppression of individual rights and centralized rule within a hierarchical system. Because *fajia* aims for a single system based entirely on government opinion and remains a powerful force in Chinese culture, it has prevented science from becoming an integral part of modern Chinese cultural diversity.

Buddhism was introduced into China without large-scale religious conflicts like those created by competition between Christian sects or between Christianity and Islam in the West. This provides strong evidence that cultural diversity helped to maintain the stability of ancient China and has been a core reason for the long-term survival of Chinese culture. Unfortunately, Western science has not yet been smoothly integrated with Chinese culture. *Fajia* promoted teaching students to develop strong and noteworthy suitability for government employment, with the ultimate goal being to support the emperor, since everyone was expected to want to contribute to the imperial court's success. However, true scientists rarely seek power and instead pursue differences from others, which runs counter to the Chinese culture of obedience and seeking power while adapting to one's superior's needs. Unfortunately, China's government discourages scientific behavior because it doesn't promote loyalty and obedience; instead, it cultivates "wise officials" and "good generals" who serve their government without questioning. As I noted earlier, the goal is to cultivate students who are "red and professional," as well as "compound talents" with expertise in multiple fields rather than working together with true experts. The pursuit of obedience constrains the innovative spirit of the Chinese people and answers Joseph Terence Montgomery Needham's (1900–1995) question about why ancient China failed to produce science similar to that of the West.

Fajia creates a culture in which people don't compensate for their shortcomings by taking advantage of the strengths of others through cooperation. Instead, they try to develop the necessary skills themselves; as a result, many workers spend their whole life doing work they are not good at. Chinese researchers who want to excel in a single area of study must travel to another country that will let them develop that expertise. This is an important cause of the brain drain mentioned earlier in this chapter. Chinese philosophers, such as Sima Guang (1019–1086 CE) and Ye Shengtao (1894–1988 CE), compared teachers to gardeners, whose goal is to cultivate students. Unfortunately, many "gardeners" prefer students who fit neatly in their garden. The *Chinese scholar tree* (*Styphnolobium japonicum* (L.) Schott) doesn't meet this criterion because it grows tall and wide and doesn't fit well in a garden (Fig. 6). Instead, they graft shoots of the tree onto a rootstock of *Sophora pendula* (syn. *Styphnolobium japonicum* "Pendula"). This variety's pendulous branches grow toward the ground rather than reaching for the sky (Fig. 6). As a result, the trees fit well within the garden but never rise above it. This answers

Fig. 6. Chinese Gardeners Like to Cultivate the *Chinese Scholar Tree* (*Styphnolobium japonicum* (L.) Schott) by Grafting it Onto Rootstock of *Sophora pendula* (*Styphnolobium japonicum "Pendula"*) so that it Fits Better in a Garden. *Photo source*: The author.

Qian Xuesen's question from earlier in this chapter about why China's excellent basic education system cannot cultivate equally excellent talents.

Unfortunately, a centralized government based on *fajia* is only willing to cultivate "wise officials" and "good generals" who serve the government rather than scientists and engineers who challenge the government and serve the people. Because scientific research inevitably exposes the government's flaws, *fajia* governments strongly oppose it. In extreme cases, this has led to book burning, imprisonment, and even death for scholars who could not escape to another country. Authoritarian governments find many other ways to constrain followers. For example, scholars are evaluated based on how many government grants they have received rather than the academic achievements permitted by these grants. As a result, those who seek power and influence are promoted or given prestigious titles. Scholars without such power or titles must seek their livelihood abroad or face a dead end for their career. Some are pushed into criminal behavior. For example, on June 7, 2021, Associate Professor Jiang Wenhua of Fudan University killed the college's Secretary of the Communist Party after receiving a negative performance appraisal (Sharma, 2021). On May 13, 2024, Associate Professor

Song Kai of Nanjing Forestry University committed suicide for the same reason (*Lai Times*, 2024).

3.3.2 The Shackles of Central Planning

Many animals store food in the fall to prepare for the winter, when food will be scarce. Like these animals, humanity has known from ancient times the importance of planning. For example, food storage to permit distribution in times of famine was among the most important tasks of early families. However, such plans may no longer work in the modern era of rapid and unpredictable changes due to forces such as global climate change that humanity has never before faced. Planning works well for dealing with familiar problems, but in the face of the unknown, there is no basis on which to develop or implement a plan. Although science can provide this basis, governments are often reluctant to listen to scientists; they distrust the potentially disruptive suggestions because they don't understand them and worry that the resulting plans will make them look foolish.

The CCP is officially atheist, and its leaders know very well that they are not "prophets" – yet they attempt to predict the future without relying on scientific research. By learning from the experience of Western developed countries and following their paths, we could reduce China's blindness to scientific and technological progress. By learning from Western management experience and advanced technology, China has made great economic progress in the past 40 years. However, the inability of central planning to cope with surprises means that China can no longer afford to continue this approach. Doing so means that when a surprise occurs, the central government will lack the tools (e.g., scientific knowledge) to respond logically and effectively.

History repeats itself, though with many variations, and it's necessary to learn from that repetition. For example, a centrally planned economy permitted remarkable achievements during the early industrialization of the former Soviet Union. However, after the industrialization process was complete, planning errors occurred frequently during the Soviet Union's subsequent modernization drive. By around 1970, the former Soviet Union had built a complete and independent semiconductor industry in terms of the raw materials, equipment, design, and manufacturing that were, at the time, only available in the United States and the Soviet Union. However, researchers soon realized that this technology had no defense against the electromagnetic pulse produced by a nuclear explosion and was likely to fail completely during a future war. Policymakers therefore believed that integrated circuits could not meet their future needs and abandoned this technology in favor of miniaturization of vacuum tubes. In contrast, Western nations learned to "harden" computer chips and circuit boards against electromagnetic pulses and pioneered a whole new field of engineering. The Soviet Union's poor decision delayed their technological progress for decades and may have contributed to the subsequent collapse of the Soviet Union.

Scientific research and technological innovation have relatively low success rates and a high risk of failure. The experience of the former Soviet Union shows that a centrally planned economy can be effective when it's necessary to account for known problems because it can concentrate a nation's resources on responding to those problems but often proves unable to deal with surprises, including newly discovered phenomena such as global warming and breakthroughs in unfamiliar areas of research. In contrast to relatively inflexible central planning, a market-oriented system comprises a collection of independent parts, each of which tries its own trial-and-error process to find a solution without knowing in advance which approach will succeed. Even if most of the efforts fail, the likelihood that one will succeed is high. This description is also true of scientific and technological research and innovation. Although the risk for individual enterprises or researchers is high, the risk for society as a whole is greatly reduced. In other words, in an environment that promotes innovation through market competition, the failure of an innovation at most leads to bankruptcy of the enterprise that gambled on the success of that innovation. In centrally planned countries, a failure of the government's strategy may lead to the demise of the country because there are no other options that can be tried. The Soviet Union's loss of power and global influence is a sad reminder of this outcome.

Because of how central planning concentrates all power in the hands of a few government officials, allocation of funding is determined by officials rather than by researchers, who generally know the potential risks and rewards better. The problem is exacerbated by the desire to seek a single approach for all, rather than trying to benefit from a wide variety of approaches. The problem also relates to the limited resources of any individual: someone who wants to be both an official and a scholar is likely to end up doing neither job well. There is a popular saying in China: "If you want to destroy a scholar, make him an official!" A final problem is that the officials who allocate funding are expected to produce tangible results from that funding, and innovative research does not guarantee such results; thus, funding such research may damage an official's reputation for wise allocation of funding, and it is safer to fund low-risk research that will provide results, even if the results are unimpressive.

To encourage scientists to carry out innovative research, the Chinese government spends a huge amount of money every year to reward researchers for their accomplishments. However, they don't understand that it is impossible for real scientists to divert their attention from their research and allocate it to managing their relationships with the officials who control their research. As a result, the individuals perceived as outstanding scholars focus on achievements that are most likely to earn them awards rather than on the inherent importance of their research. When these false scientists are rewarded, the true scientists give up in frustration. Because the research of each scientist is unique, it is difficult to compare researchers and define the likely advantages and disadvantages of their research focus and methods. The Chinese approach relies on a single best guess at which researcher will succeed, whereas the Western approach is based on letting each researcher try their own approach, greatly increasing the likelihood that someone will succeed.

The approach used in basic scientific research is very different from the thought process used in technology development. Rather than brainstorming technological solutions, basic science attempts to support or negate existing knowledge, with the latter typically leading to conceptual breakthroughs. But the Chinese government's emphasis on harmonious development and its opposition to contradicting the official government position inevitably hinder the development of this form of science. Due to the lack of scientific innovation, China's performance in technological innovation has also been weak, since China has been forced to emulate existing technology from developed countries (Zhou, 2021). We don't know what the next stage of civilization will be. The only way to deal with this uncertainty is to give researchers more freedom to explore and more tolerance for results that may be unpopular to the government. Scientific research, like finding a path in the dark, requires curiosity and a willingness to step into the unknown, not clinging to the narrow circle of light created by the constraints of government programs. China's ability to concentrate social forces to accomplish great things has achieved impressive results in traditional fields such as infrastructure construction but has sacrificed exploratory scientific research in immature fields of research that may become important in the future. Given the rate of global change (both social and climatic), it has become risky to concentrate all resources to accomplish a single task (in China's case, increased economic production). This situation is similar to warfare, in which a general doesn't know the enemy's disposition of forces and must send out enough scouts to learn the enemy's situation. Although this scouting is not free of risk, it is safer than sending all troops forward in a single direction without knowing what they'll find.

The Chinese government should learn from the experience of Western countries and implement a comprehensive system of university and research institute governance that is controlled by the professors and researchers, with guidance from one or more representatives of the national government, and should incorporate a market orientation in this approach, so that universities and research institutes produce graduates who can meet the needs of the private sector. In this approach, a committee of professors and researchers would create a development plan that allows more effective allocation of the university's or research institute's resources. Administrative personnel should provide logistics services to support this plan in accordance with the rules and regulations established by the committee. At the same time, government departments can send CCP members to supervise the university's or research institute's work to ensure that the research directions remain conducive to meeting the country's needs – and particularly the needs of the people.

However, that is not the only possibility. Many Western universities solicit funding from enterprises to study and solve various problems faced by the enterprises, and many Western university researchers establish their own private enterprises to commercialize their scientific findings. The result is both improved scholarship and promotion of the economy, but researchers can also benefit financially from this work. China's government should learn from these examples and should test whether this approach could work in a Chinese university or research institute. If the Chinese government wants to be the leader of the next stage of civilization, it must find a way for universities and research institutions to compete better in the marketplace of ideas and promote a system of shared property rights (see Chapter 7) to increase the motivation of researchers.

3.3.3. Importance of a Competitive Institutional Environment

Under the centrally planned economy, individual behavior is bound within various frameworks, which are designed to make everyone act in uniform ways under a single national plan. When this approach is extended to scientific research and technological innovation, it becomes a continuation of government administration and robs researchers of their independence and their flexibility (e.g., the ability to deviate from the plan when that becomes necessary). Such a system makes it difficult to achieve scientific breakthroughs and difficult to use the breakthroughs to promote social and technological innovation. As a result, China's ability to convert the results of technological innovation into social productivity (e.g., the number of patents granted) is less than half of that in developed market-oriented countries.

Because most Chinese investment in scientific research comes from the government, a remarkable feature of the government regulation of research is that scholars are not required to take responsibility for their mistakes. For example, China's national afforestation program has been promoted uncritically without accounting for the need for different plant species or functional types (e.g., grassland rather than forest). As a result, it continues to be applied inappropriately (Cao et al., 2011; Zastrow, 2019). The scientists responsible for designing this program should be held accountable for its failures but not punished; instead, they should be asked to revise the program to solve the problems. Although this offers the advantage of encouraging researchers to explore without fear, it also has a downside: the Chinese have uncritically embraced the notion that "scientific research allows failure." Although it's true that mistakes are inevitable in any field of activity, it raises the question of whether researchers who don't take responsibility for their mistakes also rob society of its ability to constrain the behavior of such researchers.

Because the resources for scientific research are in the hands of officials, the editors of Chinese academic journals only need to follow the administrative orders of these officials and publish the papers that these officials like. In addition, universities are not required to consider social needs other than those proposed by the government. For example, universities do not need to pay attention to changes in the labor market to adjust their student training plans. There is no need for innovation to contribute new knowledge to the knowledge market because universities perceive this as the job of the relevant government departments. Obviously, the resulting "plan" stifles innovation and is vulnerable to corruption both at the university or institute level and in the government. This paves the way for wrong decisions.

From an economic perspective, the main body of technological innovation is provided by entrepreneurs and not by scientists or the government. Scientific research is an innovative process, so it is neither the goal of innovation nor the result of innovation. The Chinese government has set up a special administrative department to lead China's innovation activities, but in practice, it has mostly hindered innovation. Administrative management without adequate input from scientists has produced world-leading technologies, such as large-scale afforestation of arid areas (Cao et al., 2011; Zastrow, 2019), that lack economic value and have emphasized pleasing superiors by providing the emperor with "new clothes" rather than producing tangible value (Zhou, 2021). For example, hundreds of scientific research achievements in China have won national science and technology awards every year, but these have been unable to provide essential tools that would allow China to compete effectively with the United States during the current trade war because the technologies China requires are only available from Western countries (Joane, 2023).

In contrast, a market economy forces entrepreneurs to become organizers and leaders of innovation, and this requires close cooperation between enterprises and scientific researchers to provide the breakthroughs that enterprises require. Business owners, unlike researchers, must accept responsibility for their decisions, whereas engineers only need to do a good job of working with the technology itself, and the market system encourages enterprises to complete the commercialization for successful new technology. Not only does the market not pay for failure, but winners are rewarded handsomely. Therefore, reforming scientific research to provide a market for ideas can provide opportunities for individuals to display their excellence, thereby transforming innovation from a scientific activity to an economic activity. For example, Shenzhen is China's first city to transform scientific and technological innovation from a purely scientific activity into an economic activity. Zhou Luming of Shenzhen Municipal Bureau of Science and Technology summarized this innovation as follows: more than 90% of scientific researchers are employed by enterprises, more than 90% of research funding comes from these enterprises, more than 90% of scientific research institutes are set up by enterprises, and more than 90% of technology patents come from these enterprises (Zhou, 2021). Shenzhen's experience reflects the feasibility of organizing innovative practices to account for economic principles and illustrates the superiority of a market-oriented system for scientific and technological innovation.

Unfortunately, as I noted earlier, children from rural areas and poor families face decreasing opportunities to receive a higher education, creating serious issues related to fairness. Subsidizing undergraduates harms the poor because the subsidies are not large enough to allow students from poor families to survive, but the same subsidies allow students from rich families to live comfortably, and this widens the gap between the rich and the poor. This system therefore fails to provide opportunities for the students who need these opportunities most (Xia et al., 2023). Chinese universities operate within a system in which all money goes into the same big pot instead of being preferentially allocated to the students who need it most. This failure of higher education in China is a typical example of the free-rider problem. As a result, students "vote with their feet": the failures of China's higher education system encourage those who can afford the cost to go to Western states to earn their degrees (Fig. 5).

China's government should learn from the Western experience: they should allow colleges and universities to compete for the best students as if they were enterprises competing for investors in the stock market. Undergraduate and graduate education should be at least partially self-funded for students from wealthy families, as is the case in many Western countries. To ensure that outstanding students are not affected by family poverty, universities should be required to allocate some proportion of the funds they receive from the government (perhaps one-third) to provide full scholarships for outstanding students from impoverished families. Any savings from this approach can then be used to fund 12 or 13 years of compulsory education so even poor students can learn necessary skills at no cost after they have completed the current 9-year compulsory education program or have graduated from high school after 12 years. This has several advantages: first, it collects money from the rich to fund higher education and scientific research and reduces the government's financial burden; second, a free professional education can mitigate the shortage of skilled workers in China; and third, this approach can narrow the gap between the rich and the poor and thereby improve social stability.

To follow the Western approach, undergraduate students should be allowed to apply directly to enroll in a doctoral degree program after they have earned their undergraduate degree and should be funded equivalent to the salary of assistant teachers so that they can afford to pay their expenses while they complete their degree. However, for this approach to work, teacher salaries must also be increased so that teachers are rewarded for their efforts while all student expenses are covered. This can encourage the best students to pursue a career in scientific research. Without competition, the education system loses vitality, whereas competition will help the best schools develop study programs that stand out and attract more and better students. The Chinese government should also learn an additional lesson from Western universities: they should allow private enterprises to fund specific university research programs that the government is unwilling to fund because they are perceived as too risky (a low probability of success) or too disruptive.

Because knowledge work such as scientific research cannot be rewarded by paying a piecework rate or an hourly wage, the Chinese government should learn from Shenzhen's experience and implement a shared property rights system for scientific researchers. (I will discuss this institutional innovation in detail in Chapters 7 and 8.) One possibility would be to award every professor and researcher a share in the university's profits and participate in the school's decision-making. Because they will then receive a share of the university's profits, in addition to their salary, this will encourage them to innovate in ways that improve their compensation. When they no longer work for the school, their shares are returned to the school and used to reward new professors. If Chinese professors can earn the same salary as Western scholars through competition among universities to hire the best professors, while also receiving profits that Western professors don't receive, there will be a strong incentive for university graduates to stay in or return to China. Government departments can share the wealth created by scientific researchers through taxation, leading to a win–win institutional arrangement. Freeing scholars to pursue their own interests, constrained by a code of ethics and a sense of responsibility to society, will reveal surprising new knowledge that benefits both China and the world.

Chapter 4

The Origin and Future of a State

On October 1, 1949, Mao Zedong established the Central People's Government of the People's Republic of China. Some wondered why a central government was necessary for a People's Republic. Mao understood that the state and the government represent different concepts and different roles: like enterprises, states cannot self-govern and must rely on agents to supervise their management and operation. Enterprises require a chief executive officer (CEO) and board of directors; states require a government. In this metaphor, governments act as state CEOs.

In this context, we can refer to the space that is governed by a state as a "country," and the state as the social structure that provides governance for that space. But economists, philosophers, and sociologists emphasize different aspects of that governance. Myerson (2011) proposed that states are complex social units in which a property rights system protects the wealth of individuals, enterprises, and social groups and that states are self-governed within a physical space (a country) that remains independent of surrounding states. Geographers focus on the state's geographical characteristics, such as its mountains, rivers, and borders (i.e., they treat it as a country). In contrast, sociologists emphasize the ethnic and other groups that comprise the state and how the assembled groups can act together. Political economists focus on governance mechanisms and government institutions.

All these perspectives share the belief that states are formal contractual relationships between the people, who delegate responsibility to safeguard their rights and maintain social stability to a government, thereby relinquishing some freedoms and powers in exchange for safety and stability. Governments also provide services to the people, such as physical infrastructure (e.g., roads) and enforcing laws, but this is not a gift from the government to the people; rather, it's a commitment defined by a contractual relationship, which is codified in the form of a Constitution or represented by a collection of regulations and laws or customs. The American Declaration of Independence makes this point even clearer (Korey, 2007):

> We hold these truths to be self-evident, that all men are created equal, that they are endowed by their Creator with certain unalienable Rights, that among these are Life, Liberty and the pursuit of Happiness – That to secure these rights, Governments are instituted among Men, deriving their just powers from the consent of

A New Stage of Civilization: Striving for the Great Harmony, 93–118

doi:10.1108/978-1-83708-258-220251005

> the governed – That whenever any Form of Government becomes destructive of these ends, it is the Right of the People to alter or to abolish it, and to institute new Government.

This represents a radical change from feudalism, when rulers prioritized their own interests and declared themselves to be equal to the state. Marx (1871) wrote, in *The Civil War in France*, that "the state is nothing more than a machine for one class to suppress another class." Marx and Engels proposed an alternative: "dictatorship of the proletariat," in which the people increasingly control the state during its evolution into a true socialist state, an ideal that is still respected by many socialist states.

In the rest of this chapter, I will discuss how the different concepts of state and government function and their roles in preserving stability and security despite the competing needs of other states.

4.1. Historical Debates About the Meaning of a State

As is common in most fields, different scholars have different interpretations of key terms such as "state" that are limited by their areas of expertise and their dominant concerns. For example, Marx never studied the existence and laws of the state from the perspective of geography or sociology; he was only interested in the construction of a state and how it obtained and used its power (i.e., politics). Such one-sided perspectives have had negative consequences for the development of society. For example, under the leadership of the former Soviet Union, "class struggle" became the dominant theoretical basis for the governance of socialist states, resulting in the deaths of tens of millions of people caused by authoritarian governments who forgot or deliberately ignored their responsibility to their people. This is undoubtedly a key reason for the setbacks of global communism in the late 20th century.

In China, for example, most people could not explain the difference between the state and the government, but even economists, sociologists, and political scientists sometimes forget the difference between the two concepts: that the government is the means by which the state serves its people. Confusing the state with the government is a significant problem because it reverses the direction of the responsibility. As in the concept of fajia, it mistakenly suggests that the people exist to serve the state and its leader. To support my discussion, I will divide the concept of states and governments into categories based on geography, social science, and political economics.

4.1.1. The Geographical Perspective of Resource Economics

The geographical scope of a state is an important perspective from resource economics. In 1970, Robert L. Carneiro published a paper titled "A Theory of the Origin of the State" in which he defined the state as an autonomous political unit jointly formed by multiple social groups that coexist within the state's declared territory (Carneiro, 1970). On behalf of the state, the government has the right to levy taxes, conscript the population for collective social activities, engage in military activities, and propose and implement laws. The earliest states often emerged in relatively enclosed natural and social environments, such as areas where cultivated land was surrounded by deserts, mountains, and oceans that isolated a society from the outside world or in areas surrounded by dense populations that forced the surrounded society to take protective measures to avoid the occupation of their resources by outsiders (Carneiro, 1970). When a certain resource could not meet the needs of more people, it became necessary to solve the conflict of interest between those who controlled the scarce resource and those who needed it through peaceful negotiations or other ways, including warfare (Alchian & Demsetz, 1973).

In the absence of formal or informal protection of property rights, social groups may follow a first-come, first-served institutional arrangement, in which latecomers must accept low-quality resources or pay higher costs to obtain resources that are already occupied by others (Hellenthal et al., 2014). Increasing demand and continuous population growth lead societies to exceed the natural environmental carrying capacity of their region, triggering a resource scarcity and forcing social institutions to evolve (Cao et al., 2007). Such scarcities forced states to develop institutional arrangements to address resource allocation issues; for example, they found it necessary to protect their resources from outsiders or to trade with other regions to obtain required resources. These constraints and the resulting responses remain important today. In some cases, when the state can no longer meet the needs of its people, this may lead to migration of those who have this option.

A shortage of resources will lead to a series of social problems (e.g., war, famine) and economic problems (e.g., market distortions, inflation) and can even trigger severe population declines (Diamond, 2004). The cyclical fluctuations in the fates of civilization are closely related to climate change (which I will discuss in Section 4.2.3) and changes in natural factors (e.g., resource depletion) that increase the risk to human survival by affecting the ability of ecosystems to supply essential resources such as food and water (Ajibade & McBean, 2014). Finding effective solutions to resource shortages is among the most important responsibilities of state governance and a major driving force for the evolution of the political systems. In independent and autonomous territories, complex institutional combinations of individual and collective property rights ensure the safety of individuals, communities, enterprises, and the state's public wealth. From this perspective, the state can be considered an institutional arrangement to solve the scarcity of resources.

4.1.2. The Social Science (Humanistic) Perspective

The Book of Rites, which was written during China's "warring states" period (ca. 475–221 BCE), includes the statement that "a public spirit will rule all under the sky when the great way prevails." That is, the "great way" ensures that social action will focus on all citizens, not just on a ruling elite. This work is likely to originate from the idea of a people's state that Confucius (551–479 BCE) proposed after touring many Chinese states and is one of the earliest historical conceptions of a people's state.

Before Confucius, Chinese philosophers considered China to be "the world," and the head of the state was called "the son of Heaven." In *The Book of Songs*, Bei Shan wrote in the Xiao Ya chapter that "all the land under heaven belongs to the king, and all the people are the king's servants." In this worldview, all of the land in the world (i.e., in China) belonged to the son of Heaven (i.e., the leader), who then assigned the land to each "vassal" (similar to the current states of the United States or the constituent republics of Russia), who then assigned the land to scholar bureaucrats (i.e., educated and trained representatives of the ruler), thereby forming a hierarchical governance system. Historians call this period the *feudal system*. Some Chinese textbooks refer to this period in China as a slave society. In fact, the main population of the Zhou Dynasty (1046–256 BCE) comprised citizens, with few slaves, and most of the slaves who did exist became domestic slaves in scholar bureaucrats' families. Domestic slaves included servants of the scholar bureaucrats, soldiers who were responsible for the safety of the bureaucrats, and possibly family advisors who advised the scholar bureaucrats. Their social status would have been higher than that of ordinary citizens. In ancient Chinese characters, the word "slave" meant secondary status; for example, women called themselves "slaves" of their husbands, and ministers of the Qing Dynasty (1636–1912 CE) called themselves "slaves" of the emperor.

4.1.2.1. The Social Contract

In the 18th century, Jean-Jacques Rousseau (1712–1778 CE) wrote *The Social Contract*. Before the French Revolution (1789 CE), Europeans commonly believed that kingship was granted by God, and that the monarch must be crowned by the Pope in a ceremony that represented recognition of the monarchy by God, within the context of a theocratic political system. The coronation ceremony emphasized the contractual relationship between the church and the monarch's family, with the Church helping the king to maintain state rule and the king protecting the Church's monopoly on religious power.

The Social Contract denies the legitimacy of the divine grant of monarchy and proposes that this "right" is a lie fabricated by autocratic monarchs to preserve their power. Rousseau believed that because people tended to abuse the natural rights given by God if their actions were not constrained, the interests of all people could not be guaranteed in the absence of a ruler (i.e., anarchy). Therefore, people had to transfer part of their rights to a government that was responsible for resolving conflicts and allocating resources fairly. When a government fails to perform its obligations correctly, the people have the right to terminate the contract. This is similar to the beliefs expressed by the first peasant rebel leaders in Chinese history, Chen Sheng and Wu Guang (who both died in 208 BCE), who rejected the belief that those of high rank were born to be aristocrats.

In addition to *The Social Contract*, Rousseau also openly challenged the monarchy in his works. He stressed that the law is supreme, that no one can arrogate the law, and that the law is invalid without the consent of the people. He believed that

> all, being born free and equal, alienate [i.e. give up] their liberty only for their own advantage. The whole difference is that, in the family, the love of the father for his children repays him for the care he takes of them, while, in the State, the pleasure of commanding takes the place of the love which the chief cannot have for the peoples under him. (Bertram, 2004)

Rousseau advocated the establishment of a republic under the rule of law. He emphasized that any state under the rule of law, regardless of its administrative form, is called a republic. He believed that the rule of law must be promulgated and supervised by the people, not by their government. Rousseau's thought is undoubtedly an important theoretical basis for modern state governance.

4.1.2.2. Serve the People

In China, Mencius (372–289 BCE) may have been the first philosopher to advocate that the government must serve the people because the people are more precious than the state, and the ruler is even less precious. Because some agents must govern the people, it is necessary to establish a state. This ideology has deeply influenced Chinese society. On September 5, 1944, Zhang Side (1915–1944 CE), a soldier in Mao Zedong's staff, was killed in the line of duty. To highlight the essence of the Communists and their troops, Mao Zedong delivered his famous "Serving the People" speech at Zhang's memorial service, emphasizing that the Communist Party is the public servant of the people and that the army, led by the Communist Party, functions as the people's army.

The Chinese government has continued this philosophy of Chinese soldiers being "both a soldier and a citizen." Today, the primary task of the Chinese army is not to fight but rather to provide disaster relief. China also has special disaster-response forces to deal with disasters, but when a major disaster occurs, the army rushes to help. For example, when Typhoon Dove hit Hong Kong on August 20, 2017, the People's Liberation Army provided disaster relief. This is one great legacy of the philosophy that the state should "serve the people."

From an economic perspective, if a regime focuses on long-term stability, even a purely self-interested government should seek to maximize its interests by maintaining that stability (North, 1990). Long-term stability can maximize tax revenues by encouraging people to produce and consume more goods and services. To achieve this goal, any government's rational choice is to provide more public services, so that the people remain confident of their ability to govern and will continue to support the government (Olson, 1993). This is why Deng Xiaoping, China's great institutional reformer, said that the basic contradiction of socialist society is between the growing material and cultural needs of the people and China's underdeveloped social productive forces. This is also why China's government has spared no effort to promote infrastructure construction.

The biggest drawback of a democratic regime is that the expected duration of each political party's tenure is too short, and this tends to focus elected representatives on short-term goals. In contrast, China develops five-year plans that define the state's goals and guide state investments and programs to achieve those goals; the plans are reviewed and revised at five-year intervals. This approach is designed to unite the state's efforts to achieve shared goals, while allowing flexibility in how provinces and smaller regions attempt to achieve these goals and providing ongoing review to allow changes in the plans when conditions change. The short tenure in power in a democracy prevents such long-term thinking and planning. As a result, activities such as infrastructure construction, which is an economic process with many inputs and slow returns, tend to suffer. In particular, governments that might otherwise make such investments are reluctant to do so because they fear that subsequent governments will take credit for their actions. Because ordinary people do not understand (or forget about) the "time lag" effect of government behavior, their eagerness for quick successes and instant benefits has become a significant weakness of democratic politics. Because of this and other factors, capitalist societies face growing pressure for political reform.

A state's ethos that "the world is for the people" restricts a government's selfish behavior and provides a theoretical basis for more ethical development. When a social system functions well, the government sees itself as the agent of the state and does not see the state as the private property of the government or of powerful individuals. In its role as the state's CEO, the government is responsible for the orderly and vigorous development of governance, so that every citizen can receive greater political and economic returns from their support of the government. This is the basic connotation of a state that prioritizes serving people. However, China's political elites have achieved their positions by persuading the people to support them (or at least not oppose them) in their efforts to seize power by relying on Confucius' proposal that "the world is for the people" for the past 2,500 years. After gaining power, they worked to eliminate their political opponents and finally stole the state itself. In many cases, these ambitious people immediately repressed and persecuted intellectuals to prevent the emergence and development of new ideas and cultures that might threaten their authority. To maintain power, they used tools such as armed suppression (i.e., subverting the army's role of supporting the people) and various forms of deception until they weakened or made errors that let new, more powerful people replace them. This often resulted from the *fajia* philosophy that I have discussed in previous chapters, which has led to the downfall of most historical Chinese dynasties.

4.1.3. The Political Economics Perspective

Scholars in the field of political economy have been fascinated by state governance, but their understanding of the state's nature has generally been erroneous. There is probably no more influential early research thesis than Karl Heinrich Marx's (1818–1883 CE) doctrine of class struggle. Marx believed that the state is a form of struggle between the rich ruling class and the poor majority to obtain control over the allocation of resources. This belief ("class struggle") is the theoretical basis of communism. Under the guidance of this ideology, more than

160 ruling or non-ruling parties joined the Socialist International Organization in the 20th century, and 39 countries declared the establishment of a communist or socialist state system (Cao & Liu, 2020).

Other political economists, such as Max Weber (1864–1920 CE), Mancur Lloyd Olson (1932–1998 CE), and Nobel Prize winner Douglass C. North (1920–2015 CE) held similar views (North, 1990; Olson, 1993; Weber, 1978). They agreed that governments dominate the development of the state, and that by understanding the nature of government behavior, we can understand the state. Going further than Marx's statement that the state is an instrument by which the rich class oppresses the poor, North (1990) and Olson (1993) further described the state as a "Mafia" organization and a "rational gang."

North believed that although every government has a deep-seated desire for long-term stability, a government's longevity in power is limited, especially in Western democracies. For example, each American president can only serve two terms (a maximum of eight years). It is often unrealistic to realize personal political ideals in such a short time. Therefore, every president is pressured to take a series of extraordinary measures to speed up the political pace. These extraordinary measures often violate the purposes of the state's constitution (North, 1990). Olson (1993) explicitly pointed out that the government not only benefits in legitimate ways, such as taxation, but also in stealthy ways (e.g., by issuing bonds, changing the money supply, and other invisible taxes imposed on citizens) and direct ways (e.g., confiscating private property, outright looting). He believed that for most of history, governments have functioned in some ways like a legalized robber. North's and Olsen's views represent an important component of contemporary understanding of the state by political economists. Although economic means such as issuing bonds and inflation are commonly used in modern states to stimulate the economy, these approaches are an invisible tax on citizens. The harm they cause has not yet aroused widespread concern among economists (Bekiros et al., 2017).

It should be clear that Marx (150 years ago) and North and Olsen (in the 20th century) both adopted a strongly one-sided perspective. But in reality, the government and the people more strongly resemble the two sides of a coin. Neither side can exist without the other, and it is neither logical nor practical to assume that the two sides must inevitably work in opposition. Modern states have accepted Rousseau's republican idea that the government functions as the manager of a state, and that there is an invisible contract between the government and the people who permit them to govern. In humanity's long history, people have always participated directly or indirectly in the process of governing and in the construction of state institutions such as elections and referendums or have resorted to violent revolutions to meet their needs. Competition among political agents or between the government and the people has always constrained the behavior of governments, and competition from state and international political markets has always threatened their dominance.

4.2. The Origins and Evolution of the State

Society likely originated with families or groups of families, who engaged with each other through largely cooperative behaviors. Family members often reach consensus through peaceful consultations to jointly deal with the problems and challenges they encounter. However, when the number of family members or families grows, it becomes more difficult to reach agreement. In such cases, larger families or groups of families may split into a larger number of smaller families and restore a consensual decision-making lifestyle (Olson, 1993). However, this growth and division process cannot continue indefinitely, particularly when resources such as land are constrained. When the process is no longer possible, the groups may form governments, whose role is to make such decisions for the people.

Because of the low population and the world's rich resources, there were enough resources for every member of early societies, and it was less necessary to defend territory. Almost all of Earth's resources were public rather than private, and there was no clear concept of territory and property rights. People followed the first-come, first-served system, and when resources such as the fruit on one tree were consumed, they simply moved to the next tree. Without a need to fight over such resources, the relationship between people was generally harmonious. However, as the number of individuals and families grew, even this harmonious and peaceful society began to encounter difficulty in allocating finite resources, as in the case of determining how to feed the slowly increasing population when a resource shortage occurred (e.g., after a drought). Migration to other areas with more resources would have been an effective strategy.

As part of the 1,200 years ago (Olson, 1993), society gradually changed from a hunter-gatherer mode of food production to a sedentary lifestyle based on tending livestock and planting and tending crops, which represented a major social breakthrough. However, with a larger source of food, the population grew faster, making it difficult to migrate to new lands that didn't already have an indigenous population. When the resources in a territory could no longer meet the needs of the growing population, the dependence of community residents on foreign resources gradually increased, and this would have promoted the development of trade networks (Hellenthal et al., 2014). To support this trade, complex social structures gradually evolved.

After entering this phase of an agricultural society, the problems of how to protect one's livestock and the grain one grew from being harvested by others and how to ensure that one's arable land was not stolen by others gradually became sufficiently serious to require a response. In early prehistoric society, people formed social contracts through peaceful negotiation, rather than solving problems through war (Olson, 1993). Subsequently, conflicts over the right to access resources during times of insufficient supply would have increased the tension between groups. Driven by survival instincts that outweighed social instincts, peaceful and friendly solutions would often have been replaced by conflict. To solve this problem, groups of people gradually implemented the concept of a state to coordinate their activities, including the development of armies.

4.2.1. The Origin of States and Warfare

Early societies were likely to have been based on one or more family units, concentrated within a small area that provided enough resources for the group to survive and flourish. Trade among these groups often resulted from differences in the available resources. For example, groups near large bodies of water could sustain forms of agriculture such as paddy rice cultivation and could capture fish, whereas groups in drier grassland areas may have emphasized grazing (i.e., meat production) or may have grown dryland crops such as wheat. The efficiency of trade supported the evolution of specialist workers such as blacksmiths and weavers, and trading communities gradually formed a community of interests. As populations continued to grow, these groups often formed alliances based on trade or mutual interest (e.g., to defend against nomadic groups who had not settled, to jointly overcome natural disasters). Such associations were likely to be peaceful, at least initially. These early trade alliances represented the beginning of a market economy. This form of economy therefore has ancient roots (North, 1990).

While populations remained low, sharing of resources was relatively easy, and if a dispute developed over a resource, it was relatively easy to negotiate a solution or for one family group to move elsewhere to avoid conflict over the resource. Trade also reduced the likelihood of conflict because it became possible for one group to obtain scarce resources from another group where those resources were abundant. However, as groups grew in size and infrastructure (e.g., mills for grinding grains into flour), moving to a new area became increasingly difficult, and there was less and less unoccupied land where a group could move. At some point, it became necessary to declare sovereignty over local resources to ensure a group's food supply, leading to the development of independent political entities (states) that controlled access to resources (Lim et al., 2007).

4.2.1.1. The Evolution of War and Political Institutions

The emergence of agriculture allowed rapid population growth and permanent or semi-permanent settlements that provided a space where technological innovation (e.g., the invention of plows) and the development of stable trade networks became possible, thereby feeding a larger population. When natural disasters such as drought occurred, trade was sometimes able to replace lost crops. In other cases, many settlements suffered from the same natural disaster, making it impossible to obtain necessary resources through trade, as other settlements retained those resources for their own people. When one group became desperate, formerly peaceful relationships were sometimes abandoned, leading to violent conflict (theft or warfare) to obtain the resources needed for survival. There are countless historical examples of such conflicts over land resources in Mesopotamia, Egypt, India, and other parts of the world (Bowles, 2012).

Of course, in any human group, some will be more effective at exploiting the available resources than others. For example, large families can exploit more land and grow more crops than small families. This led to the emergence of wealth disparities both within and between settlements. To protect a community's wealth from being looted by others, professional armed forces may have evolved to protect both resources and trade routes. After the development of specialized armed forces, other members of the group no longer needed to spend time preparing for fighting, which left them more time to grow food and engage in other economic activities.

China is a mountainous country with a relatively small area of arable land relative to its population, and most of this land was concentrated around several large rivers. There are also large arid or semi-arid areas (e.g., in northern China) that are difficult to use for agriculture. This led to many resource conflicts as populations grew. Historically, conflicts triggered by a resource scarcity have been a recurring feature of most societies (Allen, 2013). Although some wealthier members of society were able to move to a new area to escape a resource shortage and integrated peacefully with their new group, many migrants had little or no trade goods or money that would let them relocate. Instead, it was necessary to use force.

Warfare had several consequences for these early societies. First, warriors often killed all of their opponents or destroyed their settlements, creating room for their own group to expand. Second, defeated opponents were sometimes enslaved rather than killed, thereby increasing the number of workers in the victorious society and increasing the society's ability to exploit local resources. Third, warriors often captured large quantities of resources from the defeated groups (i.e., through looting), enriching themselves and creating a wealth gap compared with the farmers who supported them.

As I noted earlier, the growing potential for conflict led to the replacement of occasional warriors (people with peaceful professions such as agriculture who were occasionally called on to defend their settlement) by specialists whose only profession was warfare. To support such a profession, it was necessary to establish special systems for sharing resources (e.g., to feed warriors who had no time to grow their own crops) and to support social decision-making (e.g., whether or not to initiate a war). At the same time, police forces evolved to punish individuals or groups for illegal or unethical behavior and to punish "free riders" who tried to monopolize resources or claim a shore of resources they had not played a role in producing. By preventing these abuses, policing of behavior maintained social cooperation and protected the weak within the social group from the strong (thereby promoting social stability), and legal systems gradually developed to support such activities (Bowles, 2012). These mechanisms (including institutions that governed resource management, trade, prevention of invasions, and prevention of internal strife) gradually combined into a sophisticated set of social institutions that defined the organization of the state and constrained the social system.

Because large organizational management systems are expensive, it was necessary to find ways (e.g., taxation) to pay their costs and to develop institutions that were capable of regulating the system's behavior and prioritizing resource allocation. Because warfare is expensive and has enormous human costs, it was necessary to develop governments that represented the needs of the people and that determined when peaceful negotiation could accomplish the group's goals and when warfare was necessary. In particular, weaker social groups were forced to find ways to compromise with stronger groups, since failing to do so often led to war (Carneiro, 1970).

4.2.1.2. Institutionalization of the State

To win a war, the government needs the population's support and their willingness to obey the government's commands. Therefore, for a state that wants to be prepared for war, it's necessary to strengthen the bureaucratic system to maintain stable operation of the social system and to raise funds for activities such as training the troops and paying the high costs of warfare. These needs have promoted the expansion of government institutions and increased the complexity of social structures. As Charles Tilly (1929–2008 CE) famously said, "war made the state, and the state made war" (Kaspersen & Strandsbjerg, 2017). In this sense, the state is a society's response to external threats (Krasner, 2011). It must be emphasized here that external threats are not only invasions by other countries but also natural disasters that may be even more destructive (I will discuss this in Chapter 10).

The need to prepare for war constantly strengthened and refined social and political institutions, leading to stable, centralized politics and a bureaucratic system to support the government's functions. The central government gained control over its territory and had sufficient bureaucratic capacity to tax the population, borrow from them (e.g., through bond issues), mobilize social resources, and organize and deploy armed forces (Bowles, 2012). Even when resources are scarce, the tax and military service systems can ensure that a state has sufficient funds to wage war (Tilly, 1990). A state's mobilization capacity can be used not only to support a large-scale war but also to mobilize social resources, promote socioeconomic development, and improve the livelihood of citizens. For example, governments organize large-scale infrastructure projects such as water conservation, transportation networks, and communication within and between states. With the increasing interdependence among a state's social groups, the social structure's complexity continues to increase, eventually combining institutions that were originally independent into a single, integrated, and centralized political unit (Carneiro, 1970).

As states grew in size, whether through peaceful mergers with adjacent groups or through conquest, it became necessary to create a supporting infrastructure. For example, well-maintained roads became necessary to ensure that soldiers could reach any point in their boundaries quickly during an invasion and that supplies such as food could reach the soldiers. Once the size grew beyond the distance an army could travel in a single day, additional infrastructures became necessary, such as fortified settlements and castles where an army could rest peacefully, replenish its supplies, and defend better against invaders. Such structures controlled an area with a radius of about 25 km, which is about the distance an army could travel in a day and equivalent to the size of a county in today's China, and this area of control may have been the basis for defining the size of an early state.

Blocked by mountains, rivers, oceans, and land claims by competing states, a state's actual boundary is generally irregular and occurs near a natural boundary such as mountains that cannot be crossed or a position that represents the balance between the strength of two competitors. When the strengths of the two sides are unbalanced or when one state is dissatisfied with its existing territory, war is difficult to avoid. The ancient Chinese character for a "state" (國) resembles a group of armed soldiers within city walls. Because preventing or winning wars is a top priority for the state, individuals who perform well in this role are often elected as political leaders or heads of relevant government departments. In China, the most famous recent example was the election of Mao Zedong, a successful military leader, who became the leader of the Chinese Communist Party and its army during the Red Army's Long March. From October 1934 to October 1936, the Red Army was led by the Communist Party of China. It was defeated by the army of the then Nationalist Government. This forced the Red Army to carry out a strategic transfer (i.e., change their strategy and move their headquarters to a safer location). After passing through 14 provinces and traveling about 25,000 miles (i.e., a long march), the Red Army reached northern Shaanxi Province, a place of safety. Mao Zedong commanded the war brilliantly and was eventually elected leader of the Chinese Communist Party and its army.

4.2.1.3. Other Forms of "War"

Military conflict is an extreme form of political struggle between states. Smart politicians are more willing to gain benefits through more subtle methods. These invisible forms of war include the ideological wars discussed in Chapter 1; the talent and science and technology wars discussed in Chapter 3; and trade, currency, and food wars. All of these approaches aim to maximize state interests through cooperation, competition, and coopetition rather than traditional warfare. One interesting alternative to war is to steal your enemy's most talented individuals. From 1955 to 2019, China lost 21,563 researchers to other countries; during the same period, only 5,986 researchers immigrated to China (Li & Yang, 2021). Currently, about 145,000 Chinese migrate overseas every year (Xia et al., 2023). Many of these migrants are highly educated. For example, SpaceX employs 1,022 students who graduated from Tsinghua University, "China's MIT"; this amounts to one-third of the engineers employed by the company. This is a huge victory for the United States in its technology war with China (Morales, 2021). After the Russian and Ukrainian conflict broke out in February 2022, SpaceX provided technical support to Ukraine for free, greatly hindering Russia in their pursuit of victory.

Warfare can also be economic. In contrast with military warfare, economic warfare relies on economic rather than military power. However, even in military warfare, the results ultimately depend on the relative economic strength of both sides and the ability to mobilize that strength. A Chinese example of combined economic and military warfare would be the Opium Wars (1839–1860 CE), during which Western powers used their military strength to force China to allow Western merchants to sell opium in China without interference by the Chinese government. Since 1962, the United States has imposed a continuous economic embargo on Cuba. In February 1978, the Islamic Revolution in Iran ended with the appointment of Ruholla Khomenei as the state leader, and the United States began a long-term blockade and sanctions against Iran that continue today. Such non-military confrontations are numerous.

The desire to maximize economic benefits is one of the core goals of most military conflicts, and economic strength is a prerequisite for achieving this goal. This is reflected in the Chinese proverb that says, "the army has not moved, and the food and grass go first." Winston Churchill (1874–1965 CE), the former British Prime Minister, added that "we have no eternal allies, and we have no perpetual enemies. Our interests are eternal and perpetual" (Müller, 2002), and those interests are often economic.

4.2.2. The Emergence of Federalism

Weaker states have the option of surrendering to stronger competitors, but the resulting loss of sovereignty is usually unacceptable to their citizens. Instead, weaker states often choose to form a strong political alliance with other relatively weak states. The result is a federation. For example, Russia became the former Soviet Union by dominating the surrounding states to create a huge empire from many participating republics, and the United States became a federal state through the union of what is now more than 50 relatively independent states. Federal politics also has an ancient history in China. For example, 4,500 to 5,000 years ago, Chi You united and led the Kyushu tribes to defeat the Yan Emperor. After his defeat, the Yan Emperor united with the Yellow Emperor to defeat Chi You. During the Zhou Dynasty (1046–256 BCE), the Zhou Emperor continued the traditional state political system. Historical records show that the Zhou Dynasty enfeoffed a total of 114 vassal states, although other sources suggest that the dynasty only included 71 states (Cao et al., 2019).

States have always known the benefits of alliances and cooperation. In addition to treaties, states often took more radical measures, such as holding hostages (e.g., members of the royal family of one state were sent to grow up in other states) and arranging marriages. These and other measures reduced the risk of warfare and sometimes even built trust between states and helped them to maintain peaceful relations. In 640 CE, the most powerful emperor of the Tang Dynasty, Li Shimin (598–649 CE), enthroned his niece as Princess Wencheng and married her to King Songtsen Gampo (617–650 CE) of Tibet the following year (641 CE) to ensure peace with the Tibetan empire. This strategy was also practiced for hundreds of years in the West. For example, Princess Catherine von Anhalt-Zerbst of Prussia (1729–1796 CE) married Peter III Fyodorovich of Russia and subsequently became empress of Russia.

Those who study Chinese history carefully will find that despite the numerous powerful dynasties that controlled the country at different times, China's 5,000-year history is also the history of a state in which the weak frequently prevailed over the strong. For example, the weak Emperor Huang (the Yellow Emperor) and Emperor Yan united to defeat the powerful enemy Chi You and established the foundation of the modern Chinese state. Subsequently, the founders of the Zhou Dynasty united with the Xiqiang tribes and with the crown prince of the Shang Dynasty to defeat the powerful King Zhou of the Shang Dynasty (1075–1046 BCE) and established the Zhou Dynasty (1046–256 BCE). More recently, the founders of the Qing Dynasty united the Mongols to defeat the Ming empire (1368–1644 CE) and established the Qing regime (1636–1912 CE). The wisdom behind a federal state system lies in the political strength that can be achieved by embracing cultural diversity and is one of the fundamental reasons for the long-term survival of Chinese culture (Cao, 2016a). One major advantage of a federation over a single state, despite its many greater complexity, is that it unites multiple smaller states with different resources and diverse cultures into a more powerful federation.

Whether a state is a federal system or a centralized system, it generally aims to continue expanding either its territory or its access to resources. For example,

China has expanded from a small country with a maximum area of 2,500 km^2 4,500 years ago to one of the largest countries on Earth, with a land area of 9.6×10^6 km^2 today, and the United States has expanded from 13 states at the time of its founding to 50 states, 5 major territories (e.g., islands such as Puerto Rico), and more than a dozen small islands. History suggests that peace is temporary, but war is eternal, and as long as there are states, there are likely to be wars. Of course, as I noted earlier in this chapter, war is not the only way to maintain a state's existence. To win international power struggles, or at least to avoid being defeated, trade, diplomacy, and economic development are all tools that governments can use to maintain their power or even their existence.

4.2.3. The Impact of Climate Change

War is humanity's most costly and risky collective behavior. Therefore, both governments and the people they govern are eager to avoid warfare. Yet despite this, wars occur again and again. There are two main reasons: changes in the balance of power that lead one state to believe they can defeat another, and disasters such as climate change that force a state to seek food supplies outside its own borders during a period of food scarcity that makes international trade more difficult. In the first case, when the balance of power between two states changes, a weak state that is dominated by a strong state may become sufficiently strong in relative terms that they are unwilling to let the other side continue governing their behavior. They may even covet the formerly stronger state's resources, leading them to contemplate acquiring those resources through conquest. I have discussed this in detail earlier in this chapter.

In the second case, we have increasingly begun to understand the impact of climate change on the relationships between states. China has experienced many climate changes during its history. The Hexi Corridor, located in modern Gansu Province and the Xinjiang Autonomous Region in northwestern China, has historically been the location where eastern and western cultures met. The region's ecological environment is fragile and highly sensitive to climate change. Unfortunately, where two cultures meet, there is a risk of warfare. In this region, such conflict has been promoted by climate change (Feng, Tian, et al., 2019). When the Hexi Corridor's climate warmed, the grain output increased, the grain price decreased, and the frequency of social unrest (famines and wars) decreased (Fig. 7.). During such periods, nomadic people living by bodies of water and in grasslands were attracted by the rich forage in China's northern lands and migrated northward. The relationship between the farming people and these migrants eased, and the frequency of war decreased.

From 7,000 to 4,500 years ago, the global climate warmed as the most recent ice age ended, and this promoted agricultural production and population growth. Most of the world's ancient agricultural civilizations were born during this period, and almost every ancient civilization has a legend about the flooding caused by retreating glaciers. The climate during the Han Dynasty (202 BCE–220 CE) was warmer than our modern climate (Shi et al., 2021). The area of arable land increased in the Hetao area, which represents the border area between Ningxia (now part of Gansu Province) and Inner Mongolia, and the reclamation of land for agriculture moved northward. The Great Wall of the Han Empire was built

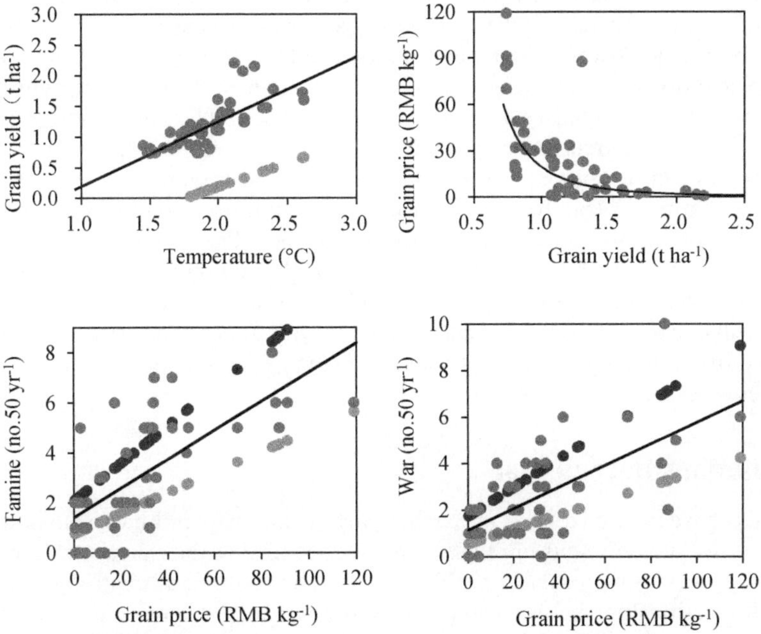

Fig. 7. The Relationship Between Climate Change and Grain Yield and Social Unrest in the Hexi Corridor from 2 to 1998 CE Was Estimated Based on Tree Growth-ring Records and Examination of Historical Documents. *Source*: The figure is created by Prof Yang Linshan.

as far as the Yinshan Mountains (42°N, 106°E–116°E) in Inner Mongolia. During the Song Dynasty (960–1279 CE), heavy snow fell in the Hangzhou region (118°21′E–120°30′E, 29°11′N–30°33′N). The cold climate decreased grassland productivity in the north, forcing Mongolian herders to migrate south to support their herds, leading to conflict with the Song Dynasty, which was soon conquered and became the Yuan Dynasty.

Even when there was no conflict between peoples, it was difficult to transport grain that had been grown in the south to the grasslands farther north to feed the armies that defended China's northern border. To reduce the size of the army required to defend this border and the arable land it enclosed, Chinese leaders began construction of the Great Wall as early as the seventh century BCE, with the largest sections constructed hundreds of years later. This massive engineering project did not prevent wars. For example, in 1388 CE, the Ming Dynasty's general Lan Yu led 150,000 troops northward to Mongolia, where they defeated the troops of the Yuan Dynasty's emperor on the shore of Lake Baikal, and the Yuan Empire was completely destroyed. However, the resulting territory was too large to defend, so the armies retreated southward to the Great Wall to reduce the number of troops required to defend the frontier. Because of the colder climate, the Ming Dynasty extended the Great Wall even farther to the south to provide further protection.

Whatever the modern rate of climate warming may be, it's important to remember that our current civilization developed under a specific set of climatic conditions. We don't know how much those conditions can change before we see ecological disaster that leads to conflicts such as those that occurred during the fall of the Song Dynasty and the Mongol invasions of China and eastern Europe. The goal of green development is to provide a comfortable and healthy living environment for humans everywhere and to avoid creating situations such as famines that might lead to wars. To accomplish that, we can no longer ignore climate change. At the same time, we must note that the progress and consequences of climate change are influenced as strongly by political and economic factors. Although we increasingly understand the complexity of these changes, the political causes and social impacts remain poorly understood. However, history warns us of an increased risk of warfare if supplies of resources such as food and water decrease.

4.3. Solutions Beyond War

Although I have focused on war in the first part of this chapter, I have also noted that war is not the only solution states can adopt to resolve their disputes. It may even be the worst way to solve a problem. With the evolution of civilization, the economic relationships between states have strengthened. Compared with war, solving resource shortages through mutually beneficial trade has a low cost and a low risk. From a historical perspective, economic interdependence can promote peaceful coexistence between states (Dazzi et al., 2013). Through economic development, which improves the standard of living of people everywhere, there is less need for people to take risks and less incentive to engage in antisocial activities such as looting. This creates an opportunity to escape the cycle of endless wars and embark on a period of peaceful social evolution. After World War I, governments tried to build an international political system that would prevent future wars by providing an opportunity to settle disputes between states peacefully. The League of Nations (1920–1946) was a first attempt but failed. After World War II, the international community tried again by establishing the United Nations, which continues to strive for peace today. Regions and states are also trying various forms of cooperation, such as the European Union, ASEAN, and the African Union.

States in most parts of the world have some unique resources that they cannot fully utilize, but that are needed by other regions, and this has promoted the development of trade networks. The ancient Silk Road that led from the Mediterranean to China, stretching thousands of kilometers, is the most representative ancient trade route. Although most Europeans did not know about China's existence until the 13th century, when Marco Polo published a book about his travels, archaeology has confirmed that this trade route was active as early as the Qin Dynasty (221–207 BCE; Comas et al., 1998). In the past half century, globalization has led to trade cooperation that replaced frequent wars, international trade has brought prosperity to many regions, and globalization has permitted the evolution and the construction of a community of humanity with a shared future.

However, this vision of a shared future did not eliminate conflict, including proxy wars between communist-dominated states and Western democracies (i.e., the Cold War). After the end of the Cold War, international political forces were unbalanced, with dominance by the United States occurring simultaneously with China's rapid rise, which threatened American dominance. This has led to increased American defensiveness and increased uncertainty about the future development of society. In recent years, military conflicts have increased in many regions of the world and political stability has decreased, reflecting the problems and challenges revealed or created by economic and political globalization. One of the toughest issues civilization faces is how to avoid military conflicts that result from intensification of state interests and how to find a peaceful path to coexistence.

The *great harmony* advocated by Confucius is indeed a beautiful ideal that might provide a solution, but no one knows where the path to achieving this harmony lies, and we must seek answers from historical experiences and lessons.

4.3.1. Challenges of Political Globalization

Annexing another country by war is a traditional approach to increasing a state's power. During the Western Zhou Dynasty (1046–771 BCE), China was divided into at least 71 (or 114) independent feudal states. After 550 years of annexation wars during the Spring and Autumn period and the Warring States period (770–221 BCE), the Qin Dynasty (221–207 BCE) unified China and established a centralized imperial system (Cao et al., 2019). A similar story is repeated throughout history around the world. For example, at the end of the Middle Ages (476–1453 CE), Europe had nearly 500 independent political entities, from city states to more than 30 countries. Since then, long and repeated wars of annexation have merged these entities into 30 countries (Bowles, 2012). During this period, states behaved like predators, expanding their territory by consuming other states and reducing the number of independent regimes (Jackson & Deeg, 2008).

The establishment of the United Nations and other international institutions in the 20th century has curbed the occurrence of large-scale wars of conquest. In the past half century, conflict among major states has largely been conducted through debates in the United Nations but also through "proxy" wars during the Cold War and continuing today. The Cold War between the Soviet Union and the United States finally ended, bringing long-awaited peace. However, the disintegration of the former Soviet Union and China's rapid economic growth broke the global balance of power. Russia and China hope to improve their voice in all fields of international affairs and to play a more important role in the international political and economic arena. American hegemony is therefore being challenged, which in turn raises the risk of military conflict (Davis, 2010). The "America first" foreign policy proposed by former US President Donald Trump further widened the rift between states.

The old political balance has been broken, and a new balance is yet to be established, so conflicts between states are gradually heating up, and regional conflicts are becoming more frequent. For example, Russia invaded Ukraine and annexed the Crimean peninsula in March 2014 and invaded Ukraine again in February 2022 (CGTN, 2022). On the surface, the focus of these conflicts has been traditional political issues such as demarcation of historical state borders and the distribution of natural resources; however, from the perspective of political evolution, the United States, Russia, China, and other states are sparing no effort to expand their international political influence, with the goal of establishing a dominant position on a larger scale and making it possible to expand the state's interests.

Because a growing population and increasing access to resources are effective ways to lower the per capita cost of a country's internal and external operations, these changes are also basic requirements for technological progress, industrial upgrading, and economic development. Thus, the evolution of political systems has been accompanied by a continuous process of expansion and re-expansion of a state's power. Warfare (including both hot and cold wars) seems likely to never go away until the disappearance of the institutional arrangement of the independent state, which creates a context of inevitable competition, and the establishment of an integrated global system that promotes cooperation rather than competition and therefore aims to achieve the great harmony proposed by Confucius. In the rest of this chapter, I will discuss a potentially effective way to create a global federal political system (i.e., one based on a federation of states) through peaceful means rather than war.

4.3.2. Challenges of Economic Integration

Globalization and the development and integration of international trade networks have been traditional strategies to solve the shortage of resources through trade (Hellenthal et al., 2014). With the support provided by rapid development of science and technology, the capitalist market economy has become the main driving force for global social and economic development (Huisman, 2007). As a result of these factors, the global trade volume increased from US\$0.1 $\times 10^{12}$ in 1900 to US\$16.4 $\times 10^{12}$ in 2015, a 164-fold increase in 115 years (Cao et al., 2019). The steady growth of international trade brought about by globalization has shaped the social landscape of modern societies and has guided the development of state societies (Spencer, 2010).

Although globalization has contributed to world economic prosperity, trade protectionism and unfair competition among states, driven by the goal of maximizing profits and preserving a state's power, have increased the cost of international trade and negatively affected global trade. Due to the wide gap in economic and military strength between states, it is difficult to achieve fair competition in international trade, and this potentially increases the risk of war (i.e., if states cannot meet their needs through trade and diplomacy). There are also great political challenges to the trend of global economic integration because this requires states to relinquish sovereignty over their trade activities. Due to the increasingly fierce competition between states for resources, land, and power, determining how to prevent economic conflicts from turning into military conflicts is a political challenge that advocates of globalization must face.

In the 21st century, Western leaders such as former US President Barack Obama reoriented their global strategies to focus on global economic development and state security in the Asia–Pacific region (Ross, 2012). This inevitably raised concerns in China about the effects on its sovereignty and will have important implications for regional security and global stability. In the face of escalating regional military conflicts and tensions, China and other states are seeking effective strategies to avoid war. One approach has been to avoid conflict by avoiding direct competition. In 2013, Chinese President Xi Jinping proposed the "New Silk Road Economic Belt" development initiative (Fig. 8), a proactive attempt by China to avoid conflict with the United States in the Pacific by directing both overland trade and maritime trade to reach the Middle East and Europe.

To strengthen economic cooperation between states and establish a new international political order based on mutual benefit and mutual trust, the Asian Infrastructure Investment Bank was established in Beijing in 2015 (Hasan et al., 2009). This represents another attempt by China to solve global political conflicts through economic means. In 2015, Russia, Kazakhstan, Belarus, Kyrgyzstan, and Armenia signed an agreement to establish the Eurasian Economic Union. On June 25, 2016, Russian President Vladimir Putin visited China and proposed that China and neighboring states join the Eurasian Economic Union, further expanding the political influence of this union. This represents a positive response to

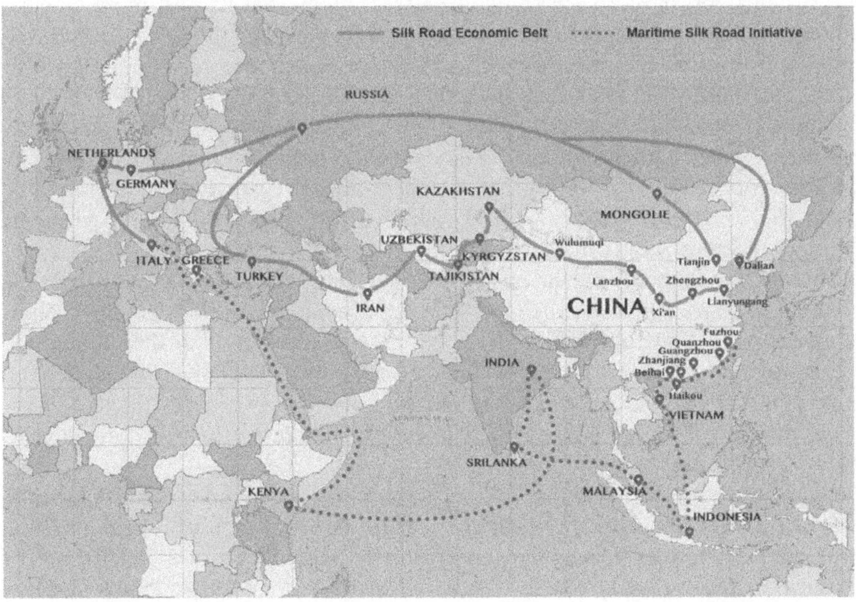

Fig. 8. The "New Silk Road" Strategy Aims to Connect China with Asia, Europe, and Africa to Create a Regional Economic Alliance and Avoid Direct Competition with the United States in the Pacific Region. *Source*: Illustration by Dr Xia Chengqi.

the close trade relationship between the United States and the European Union (Cao et al., 2019).

The 21st century has seen the continuous emergence of economic alliances, which have gradually replaced warfare with more peaceful approaches to competition. Among other things, federations such as the European Union seek consensus among their members on economic issues and provide formal dispute-resolution methods that eliminate the need for military solutions. Similar to the worldwide political alliances established at the beginning of the 20th century (such as the League of Nations and the United Nations), new alliances such as the Eurasian Economic Union and other international trade organizations emphasize the political and economic independence of each member state, focus on building win–win solutions through peaceful negotiation, and attempt to bring relationships within the union closer through monetary integration and other means.

4.3.3. Obstacles to Achieving the **Great Harmony** *of Confucius*

The huge consumption capacity of international and domestic markets is the foundation of modern social and economic development. Growing populations also mean that the per capita cost of a state's operations is smaller. Research shows that population growth is one of the key driving forces for the evolution of civilization (Cao et al., 2007). This conclusion is easy to understand: First, overpopulation and an insufficient resource supply will inevitably force us to change old systems and develop innovative new technology that is both more efficient and that does less damage to the environment. At the same time, high-tech development and infrastructure construction are expensive and require enough people to share the cost. This demographic consideration is an important driving force behind the expansion of state power. Some sparsely populated states and some regimes may be eliminated in the process of state succession through merger with another country or dissolution into smaller states. The history of China illustrates the importance of population. Whether for the Song Dynasty when the Mongols invaded China in 1235 CE or for the Ming Dynasty when the Manchus invaded China in 1644 CE, the invaders were a minority after they settled in the conquered state. To secure their power, they accepted Chinese customs such as worshipping the ancestors of the Han people and claiming that they shared the same ancestry as the Han people. They also learned the Chinese language and embraced Chinese culture. Because their own population was too small and the resident population too large, the invaders found it less expensive and safer to adopt Chinese customs.

Just as small celestial bodies can be torn apart by the tides created by large celestial bodies, the pressure created by larger political entities in international political markets can lead to the elimination or assimilation of smaller states or political entities (Cao, 2015). War is always expensive and uneconomical, especially if we consider the cost of human life. Therefore, over time, governance must shift its attention from military struggle to economic power. Even in ancient times, when war was the key way to develop and exercise power, governments recognized the importance of economic development. For example, in 256 BCE, the rulers of the Qin during the Warring States period invested heavily in construction of the Dujiangyan irrigation system, which controlled flooding and provided sufficient water for irrigation (Cao, 2015). This is the oldest and longest-used water management project in the world and has protected the Chengdu Plain from floods and droughts for more than 2,000 years. It continues to nourish the local people.

Modern world politics is changing rapidly, the traditional rules are collapsing, and the risk of dictatorships that arise as a result of historical processes or that are created by war and violence is gradually disappearing. In the context of globalization, the interdependence of an increasing number of states has forced changes in old systems to allow for better interactions among states. The increasing pressure to protect human rights has promoted the new political system. The new challenge for society is to build global institutions that will meet the challenges of globalization. In that context, the rest of this section will describe the challenges facing federal politics and ongoing changes.

4.3.3.1. Federal Politics

Historical experience shows that federal politics can enable weak states to survive the "law of the jungle" in international politics; at the same time, maintaining some measure of independence among the members of a federation can ensure that people in different regions can find their own paths to development and can find ways to adapt their unique societies and cultures to meet changing needs (Myerson, 2011). One advantage of such a moderately decentralized distribution of power is a guarantee of institutional diversity. As I have noted previously, this kind of cultural and institutional diversity helps society survive stresses and even crises. In blood circulation, the microcirculation through capillaries and the powerful heart supply nutrients and energy to the whole body. In political systems, without a unified and powerful central political force (the heart in this analogy) and without the flexible path choice and increased flow of resources that is permitted at local levels (the capillaries), it is very difficult for loose international organizations such as the European Union to replace traditional national political systems. Similarly, rigid centralized systems have difficulty in making new policies that account for the unique characteristics of different regions or that evolve flexibly to meet new challenges, so rigidity is naturally unable to activate local economies.

Over the past century, internationalization has brought economic prosperity to the world, but this alone does not prove that the economic path toward peace can replace wars and conquest (Hellenthal et al., 2014). Competition between states has promoted the evolution of political systems and the development of civilization. However, this competition also changes the balance of economic and military power between states with different ideologies, increases the risk of war, and leads to political instability. Therefore, how to prevent international competition from escalating into regional or international conflicts is a large challenge facing international politics. This challenge must be met soon, since existing mechanisms for international political cooperation cannot mobilize the world's human, economic, and technological resources to combat crises such as global climate change. Without such a mechanism for collective action, the conflict of interests between states is more likely to evolve into conflict. Fighting this problem by building a strong international political system will be necessary to achieve a great harmony that will let us solve these problems.

As in the case of international organizations such as the United Nations and the European Union, the states participating in China's Belt and Road initiative and Russia's Eurasian Economic Union are dedicated to forming a federation that will protect the political and economic interests of their member states by finding win–win solutions. However, the essential difference between the United Nations and a trade federation is that trade federations only have authority over economic cooperation; member states are not allowed to intervene in each other's domestic affairs, and there is no framework for effective military cooperation. Therefore, such federations have difficulty in playing a constructive role in the face of military threats and natural disasters such as climate change. How they will transform international conflicts into new international relationships that combine cooperation with benign competition, avoid worsening of the conflicts, and reduce the harm caused by such conflicts will be a major challenge for global economic integration as the future evolution of the world political order. To achieve effective governance of such inter-state alliances, we can learn from the experience of China's Zhou Dynasty (1046–256 BCE)and the experience of the modern United States to build a federation-based state political system. (I will discuss details of such a power structure in Chapter 5.) Several methods could support this evolution.

First, we should promote the reform of state political systems to delegate power to local governments to deal with local affairs and encourage central governments to concentrate on international affairs and coordination among local governments. That is, the goal would be to share central power to create something that more closely resembles a federation. The central governments should help economically underdeveloped areas develop their economies through transfer payments and should allow local governments to achieve local governance through self-taxation. For example, it might be possible to allocate two-thirds of the tax revenues collected by a federation to local governments or member states and retain one-third of the revenues to fund the federation's government. Through competition among a state's or a federation's regions that lead to efficiency improvements, such taxes could be reduced to mitigate the contradiction between the government and the people. A precedent for such an approach exists in (for example) the United Nations mechanism to gather funds from member states to support specific global projects such as UNESCO.

Second, the central governing body of a trade federation can use the increased access to land, mineral resources, and other resources as collateral that is provided by membership within a trade federation to issue currency or bonds that support development (Cai et al., 2019). The success of this cooperation will attract surrounding states to join the federation and support collective infrastructure construction and provide compatible tax incentives. The individual member states that join such a federation can share political power, negotiate responses to the state's affairs, build a unified market, and jointly respond to natural disasters and other international challenges. The goal is to achieve expansion of national power through economic transfer payments rather than through war.

Third, to prevent or mitigate political risks such as the United Kingdom's secession from the European Union ("Brexit") and the Greek debt crisis, states that belong to a trade federation should implement a governance system that combines centralization to support cooperative international activities with decentralization to support local activities, that unifies the currency and state defense, that strengthens diplomacy and security, that maintains international peace, that jointly handles state affairs, that builds a stable international trade and economic development system, and that protects and supports the economic development of member states. This suggestion is most likely to work if the benefits a country receives from participation greatly outweigh the costs of their participation, which include relinquishing some of their sovereignty. Unlike existing international alliances, the federation I am proposing is similar to the current United States. No member state in the federation has its own army, and participation in international affairs is governed only by the federation's overall governing body. A member state's core work is to develop its economy, improve the livelihood of its residents, and conduct other internal affairs. This would result in a Federation of States that benefits from the division of power between a strong central government and semi-autonomous states united under that government that has succeeded so well in the United States. It would also improve international affairs through dispute resolution by the federation's strong central government, prevent or mitigate natural and social disasters, and promote the development of individual member states through local autonomy within the federation. However, the lessons of the US civil war (1861–1865) suggest that unless member states are willing to surrender some of their sovereignty, there is a significant risk of internal disputes escalating into wars.

To encourage participation by neighboring states, the federation's government should not only invest to support the economic development of member states but should also protect the sovereignty, territory, and cultural and religious independence of each member country. Conversely, member states should participate in the state's political affairs on an equal footing. This will, in practice, be very difficult to achieve, since powerful states rarely accept decisions that are contrary to their interests. Therefore, implementing mechanisms to preserve the federation's cultural diversity is the basis for achieving sustainable political development of the member states, accepting cultural differences among the member states, and gradually promoting the development of a culturally diverse community with a shared future based on equality for all. By joining the federation, small states and weak states can reduce the risk of natural and man-made threats to their independence and autonomy. The protection and opportunities provided by such an institutional framework will help the governments of weak and small states to focus on economic development, improve the standard of living of their citizens, and obtain public support for their governance. This will motivate the governments and people of these states to join the federation, as it has done in the European Union. The government of a federation that values cultural diversity should avoid using extreme ideologies of capitalism or socialism to constrain the behavior of the member states and should instead promote a culture in which achieving the great harmony, based on the "be good to yourself and serve society" approach that I proposed in Chapter 1, can lead to a new political order in which everyone is equal.

The central government is a state's highest authority. While seeking to expand the state's economic resources, this government should strive to handle international affairs well (i.e., to avoid conflicts, wars, and other harmful events such as trade embargoes). This will provide an effective way for the peaceful evolution of state politics to reduce the risk of conflict by building an increasingly effective alliance of states. This approach has a low risk and high efficiency compared with warfare. If the governments of large states perform well economically, they can raise funds to support their political objectives by issuing currency and bonds and can further expand their political credibility by supporting the economic development of weak member states, thereby promoting benign interactions to achieve bloodless, low-cost economic growth. Weak and small states can combine their natural and human resources that have not yet been fully exploited and use the combined resources as capital to strengthen their influence on political negotiations. Rather than increasing their military power to confront big states, these smaller states can instead use their political wisdom and combined power to seek greater political and economic benefits from participation in the federation by political and economic means. This is a win–win political strategy. It is dangerous and foolish for politicians in weak and small states to confront more powerful states based on selfish personal interests, and they will become victims of the international political game if they adopt this strategy.

4.3.3.2. Ongoing Changes

The collapse of the former Soviet Union and the end of the Cold War let the United States become a global political hegemon, and this prompted less powerful states to build international political unions to protect themselves against American hegemony. The practical experience of the European Union shows that looser political alliances are weak and unstable. Therefore, a political framework based on state-level centralization and local decentralization was the only choice for a state political system. If China and Russia can work with the United States to establish a unified global political system and maintain regional and world peace, this will undoubtedly improve everyone's life. The limited success of the United Nations in solving international conflicts suggests it will not be easy to achieve an effective federation of states.

To reduce the cost of governance and prevent the reoccurrence of wars of annexation between states, the governments of large states should select a small number of partner states with which they can test the potential of my proposed federation of states, verify the feasibility of such cooperation between states, and adjust the plan based on the results of these pilot projects to gradually improve the plan's effectiveness. Of course, before we can promote a federation of states, we must first reform the existing political systems and alliances of the great powers. For example, the European Union, the African Union, ASEAN, and other regional political alliances should abandon selfish nationalist ideologies, strengthen their federation through equal consultation by all members, and avoid being overpowered by the big powers (a serious risk when small states confront more powerful states individually). Membership in a federation of states is the best choice to maximize their own interests while minimizing conflict.

For weak and small states, joining the federation will give them access to huge investments (the collective resources that all members contribute to the federation) for local and national infrastructure, industrial parks, and basic and advanced education. At the same time, a federation's strong central government acts as an arbitrator to resolve disputes between member states, thus helping to transform conflicts into cooperation. Joining the federation is also an effective way to avoid regional military conflicts. These benefits result from the fact that each member state has the right to independently manage its own political, economic, cultural, religious, and social affairs; in addition, the leaders of member states or their representatives can directly participate in the federation's central administration and guide policy development in more equitable ways. This would be a clear win–win option for governance.

The federal political system of the United States is commendable, but because states have considerable power, this can interfere with national-scale projects. There are other problems. For example, the currency supply created by the US government's increasingly loose monetary policy does not use the funds for infrastructure construction but rather to promote household consumption and military development. Moreover, the current trend toward an "America first" policy has weakened trade relationships between the United States and its allies and hindered the development of global integration. Unlike the current United Nations, the federation of states, which is intended to be a first step toward achieving the great harmony that I have proposed in this book, emphasizes the independence of each member country in terms of its own political and economic interests in the search for win–win solutions. Under this model, states can use an arbitration mechanism coordinated by the federation government to resolve disputes. To achieve this goal, a major change in the way of thinking that we have inherited from previous generations will be needed. To succeed, the proposed federation must emphasize peaceful cooperation and benign competition and must oppose war and abandon the extremely selfish ideology of "everyone for themself." Most of all, it must encourage states to be willing to accept arbitration even when the results are not favorable to the state.

Another important change will require humanity to rethink the concept of property to account for the goals of the great harmony. For thousands of years, societies around the world have focused on protecting private property rights, often accompanied by legitimation of plundering of other societies, possibly even considering this act to be virtuous, and by calling belligerent warmongers heroes, treating states as war machines, and confusing the protection of property rights with the crime of slaughtering others to protect those rights. The culture of private property, if not constrained, establishes a "law of the jungle" and usurps the power of the state, severely inhibiting the growth of an ideology of sharing of resources and responsibility for their wise use. In the future, society must evolve from the selfish ideology of "everyone for themself" to an ideology of "prosocial society," in which personal efforts are rewarded (i.e., a key aspect of capitalism) while still providing incentives for individuals to give back to their society (i.e., a key aspect of socialism). The goal is to create a harmonious society in which everyone has responsibility for their fellow citizens and everyone dares to take responsibility for the health of society. Only in this way can humanity establish a new global political order based on equality, consultation, and consensus. This is perhaps our best hope for abandoning the millennia-old practice of settling disputes through the application of military or economic power.

It is certain that whatever form the future world political system takes, there is no necessity to eliminate the traditional private property system (discussed in Chapters 7 and 8 of this book). The pursuit of a purely capitalist or purely socialist system seems unlikely to succeed given the magnitude of the challenges that humanity currently faces and given extensive historical evidence that neither ideology represents a perfect solution. Instead, blending capitalism with socialism to take advantage of the strengths of each system and negate its weaknesses will be the only way to achieve win–win solutions. Building a globally integrated political system (the federation I have discussed in this chapter) and transforming the world into a unified federal state would achieve the great harmony peacefully. This approach will let the people of the world unite to cope with all kinds of natural disasters and build a better home together, while avoiding war for perhaps the first time in history. Motivating the world's states to achieve this goal was my ultimate goal in writing this book.

Chapter 5

The Paradox of Government

Society operates not only in the context of formal political, judicial, economic, social, and other rules but also within informal systems of religion, culture, and customs (Cao, 2016b). Although political groups such as political parties, parliaments, local governments, and national governments develop simultaneously, non-political or semi-political organizations such as the stock market, enterprises, cooperatives, and some civil organizations (such as clubs, religious groups, and schools) also develop. These organizations are formed to achieve a common goal (Cederman, 2002).

In his essay "Mencius," he wrote that "without a ruler, it is impossible to draw a square." In this context, a system (the ruler) refers to all the norms that constrain human behavior, including formal institutions such as laws, rules, and regulations implemented by the government, its departments, enterprises, and organizations, and informal institutions such as customs, religion, culture, and morality that have developed through long-term historical evolution. The square that is drawn using the constraints imposed by these institutions represents a box that contains a nation's society. Throughout history, groups based on cooperation are more likely than individuals to survive challenges. One of the most basic human choices is to cooperate rather than fight, and cooperation requires effective formal or informal organizations and systems (Bowles, 2012). As a society develops, its organizational structures and its social system evolve, generally becoming more formal and sometimes becoming more efficient. When a country forms, the government has become the most important component of a society's social institutions and organizational mechanisms.

5.1. Government Origins

Citizens of a state understand that the state's government functions in ways analogous to an enterprise's chief executive officer (CEO), as noted in Chapter 4. However, popular religions may have a more profound impact on society. Some form of religion has accompanied civilization throughout history. Before governments appeared, family ties and religion were the main forces that maintained social cooperation and cohesion. Early humans lived as families (clans), which eventually came together in villages (tribes). When there are few

A New Stage of Civilization: Striving for the Great Harmony, 119–145

Published under exclusive licence by Emerald Publishing Limited
doi:10.1108/978-1-83708-258-220251006

people in a family, everyone can sit together and discuss a situation, and soon a consensus can be formed. But as the family size or village size increases, the possibility of easily forming a unified understanding diminishes. Dividing big families into smaller units was one solution, but often this was not possible or efficient, and often it required some coordination among these smaller units. This created an early need for some form of government.

One common social pattern around the world is for men to hunt and women to gather food. This was efficient for relatively small communities. When someone became too old to participate in hunting or gathering food, they transitioned to the role of "elder," and village elders became the repository of learned wisdom, while also serving to care for children, provide advice, and recommend solutions to problems. This is analogous to the Confucian concept of the sage, which I described earlier in Chapter 2. When human populations were small, it was generally unnecessary to migrate far to find new territory that would support everyone. Instead, several related families lived near each other to form villages (also called tribes), and several neighboring villages sometimes united to form tribal alliances. By pooling their resources, such communities increased their ability to exploit a region's resources and increased their ability to survive disasters such as drought. But cooperating in this way also provided a means to resolve disputes and deal with problems such as conflicts with or invasions by neighboring tribes. This cooperation was supported by two social institutions that separately or together proposed and enforced rules for prosocial behavior: religions and governments.

5.1.1. The Origin of Religion

Primitive humans were no less confused about their place in the universe than modern humans. All kinds of simple natural phenomena, such as thunder, lightning, wind, and rain reminded them of their low importance but also led to awe and nature worship. The early gods were all natural gods, such as the "thunder god" (in China, *Leigong*) and "mother of lightning" (in China, *Dianmu*). Although much of our knowledge of early religions is entirely speculative due to a lack of sociological or archaeological evidence, thinking about these issues is important to help understand the origin of Chinese culture.

During this early period, before the invention of science, it was difficult to explain natural and human phenomena, and some of a community's older and more experienced elders took on the responsibility of explaining nature, teaching survival skills, and saving lives through their medical knowledge. For example, the legendary ruler Shennong (before 3000 BCE) tested many herbs to learn which ones could cure diseases. People who developed effective medical skills and healed illness or soothed pain were treated almost as gods in the eyes of others. For example, Chinese historical figures such as Fuxi (before 5000 BCE), Shennong, and the Huangdi (ca. 2500 BCE) became gods of medicine. Confucius (551–479 BCE), whose teachings lie at the root of much of Chinese culture, was treated as a semi-divine sage whose teachings are still remembered. Even today, doctors and teachers are revered, and people thank "god" for blessings such as recovering from an illness. In Chinese culture, gods and people are interlinked, and those who have made outstanding contributions to the development of society will be honored and commemorated after their death.

As civilization increasingly adopted sedentary agriculture to produce enough food for everyone, inventors of essential agricultural technologies also became important. For example, the Yandi (Shennong) developed techniques such as plowing to increase crop yield and reduce the risk of starvation. People with special skills and experience were also sometimes elected as a tribal leader (in China, as the village chief) or as the leader of a tribal alliance before they were deified. Such leaders had the important roles of resolving disputes, teaching their followers survival skills and encouraging them to practice those skills, and dealing with crises. Successful practices were then passed down from generation to generation, and the most successful were sometimes codified as a religion.

Before formal governments appeared, society was controlled by religious leaders. Early on, there was enough separation between cultures or enough tolerance that the phrase "all flowers bloom together" can be used to describe the religions of that period. Almost every tribe had its own religion and its own god. For example, there is a story that when the Huangdi attacked the tribal leader Chiyou, tigers, leopards, bears, and other forest animals rushed to fight for him when he whistled. People with little knowledge of ancient times may believe that Huangdi had special skills, could speak various animal languages, and could lead various animals. The truth is that the tigers, leopards, bears, and other animals seem to have represented the totems of forest tribes that allied with Huangdi rather than actual animal soldiers (Cao, 2006).

As civilizations grew, their problems became more numerous and complicated and required ongoing management rather than ad hoc solutions. Religions evolved to meet these needs, but because they were based on a core set of teachings that didn't always reflect real-world experience (e.g., because the teachings failed to evolve while society changed), their ability to meet these needs was often unsatisfactory. Moreover, different religions often began to compete for dominance rather than cooperating and coexisting. Governments arose to provide a more effective solution.

5.1.2. The Emergence of Governments

As more and more people gathered together, it became necessary for societies to develop systems for management of scarce resources, resource allocation, dispute resolution, and planning for or dealing with crises. Conflicts over private versus public ownership of property and other resources became increasingly common. Although elders were a good solution for small communities and often emphasized conflict resolution as a form of "teaching without punishment," this method could no longer cope with the growing complexity of human relationships. Some form of government became increasingly necessary. About 4,500–5,000 years ago, in the Yandi's era, agricultural cultivation had become well-established in China, though Chinese society was still in a relatively peaceful state of family or village ownership of public resources. When two or more groups had conflicts they could not solve, the Yandi brought the groups together and facilitated dialogue until a consensus could be reached. This way of talking and coordinating a solution remains popular in modern China.

However, not all disputes can be resolved peacefully. When conflicts arise, smaller groups often unite to defeat stronger groups. In areas with scarce resources, groups that cannot obtain the resources they need to survive may be forced to capture the resources of another group, as in the case of wars of conquest. To resist bandits and invaders, tribes and tribal alliances must mobilize and coordinate workers and resources, including the people and resources required to form a well-trained army that can respond to external threats. To support military operations, it's necessary to designate specialized personnel (e.g., generals, officials with expertise in logistics) to coordinate the relationships between the military and the citizens they defend and to share the costs of defense. This cost sharing gradually becomes a fixed tax, and a service organization (a government) evolved, composed of specialized personnel, to manage this taxation.

The function of early governments was therefore relatively simple: to resolve disputes, collect taxes to pay for social goods such as an army, train the army, protect the group, negotiate alliances with other groups, and – when necessary – to invade other groups to obtain essential resources that could not be obtained locally. With the passage of time, groups began to recognize the importance of specialization, which was more efficient than having a range of skills but with no mastery of any one skill. In addition, owners of key resources learned that economies of scale produced more goods or services, more efficiently, than small family workshops. Specialization and division of labor increased productivity but also created a need for collective action to provide certain resources, such as water to irrigate large fields of crops. The resulting prosperity created enough wealth that it became possible to implement taxation to pay for the cost of specialized workers, such as soldiers, teachers, and leaders, who had no time to feed themselves and had to rely on others for their food. Taken together, these factors led to the need for specialized workers who would govern society both to enhance its stability and to help it grow wealthier. However, once governments developed and became more effective, conflicts began with other powerful individuals (such as the priests of a religion) or groups (such as rich merchants). Religious groups, in particular, were reluctant to surrender their power to the government. The people affected by this conflict were often forced to choose whether to obey their government or their religion.

5.1.3. The Relationship Between Religions and Governments

Before the emergence of professional armies, every member of a tribe had to participate in protecting the tribe. The tribe's leader was often a religious leader, who was responsible for offering sacrifices to the gods, educating the people, teaching people essential skills, promoting cultural skills such as art or storytelling, treating the sick, and saving the people during invasions or crises such as drought. Rather than surrendering their power to the government, religious leaders often sought ways to hold on to their power. They attempted to do this by promoting ideas such as the belief that "evil is rewarded with evil and good is rewarded with good."

However, the concept of appeasing the gods (i.e., following their commands rather than resisting and therefore becoming complicit in any problems that resulted from this appeasement) became increasingly unpopular. Governments increasingly challenged the authority of religions and moved toward an ideology of immediately punishing people for violation of a community's laws rather than waiting for divine punishment for violating rules imposed by the gods. For some people, including those who struggled to achieve secular power, this ideology was more popular than the religious idea of post-death rewards in a hypothetical afterlife. As experience with government increased, and government mechanisms became more effective, the advantages offered by the government became increasingly obvious, leading to a steadily increasing role for the government and an increasingly marginal role for religion, at least in terms of managing a secular society.

However, religious control over thoughts and behaviors never disappeared entirely. On the one hand, religion provides essential spiritual comfort (e.g., the idea of an afterlife) that cannot be provided by a secular government. On the other hand, religious leaders constantly innovated to find ways to influence behavior both through emphasis on religious ritual and through secularization. For example, the Christian religious practice of "confession" gave priests a tool for influencing a believer's behavior, and most religions featured religious vows that governed a person's subsequent behavior. For a secular example, some countries or regions of a country tried to minimize conflict with religious leaders by formalizing their social role, such as only accepting a religious certificate as proof of marriage. In countries or regions where a government's power over its followers was weak, it became necessary for governments to seek religious support for their rule. This is often expressed using phrases such as "winning the hearts and minds" of the people (i.e., both their emotional and logical sides). This has led to (sometimes uneasy) coexistence and cooperation between secular and religious leaders. Even the officially atheist Chinese Communist Party has not completely eliminated religion, despite the potential threat it represents, since they see the comfort it provides to believers as an additional means of social control. To offend a religious leader means to offend all of their followers, possibly losing their support.

Archaeological evidence supports this coexistence. At many early archaeological sites, the key secular power structures (e.g., castles) are located beside key religious power structures (e.g., temples), with both located near the center of the city. Why? Because both sources of power were located close enough together that they could serve as a symbol of combined power (e.g., a ruler as divinely authorized to rule), could work together, and could monitor each other's behavior. In places with strong religious beliefs, the approval of one or more gods is an important basis for the government's legitimacy. During many periods of European history, every head of government, after taking office, participated in a religious ritual to persuade the people that they led a legitimate government authorized by the Christian God. In ancient China, the emperor was also called the Son of Heaven, who had been sent to the Earth to lead the people.

Overall, it's fair to say that the secular government has won the struggle for power in most modern nations, despite exceptions such as Iran. Because of the government's power, governments have generally been able to eliminate or control anti-government religions to further secure their power. The rise of a scientific worldview has also contributed to a loss of power for religions, since science provides a more persuasive explanation of the world for many people. Moreover, ideologies such as the official atheism of communist states have further marginalized religion. In China, Buddhist and Taoist temples are now often deserted or located far from densely populated places, which represents a dramatic change from their original central locations in major communities. The power of religious leaders has also been reduced by scandals such as sexual assault of believers or egregious expenditures of money for personal gain or comfort. This is a particular problem for religions that aggressively encourage believers to give their money to religious leaders, aided by government regulations that make such donations tax-deductible. Such hypocrisy by people who claim to represent their gods does not inspire belief. In fact, many religious leaders seem to secretly be atheists and no longer fear divine punishment. As a result, they are governed only by their personal ethics. Many religions hoard the wealth supplied by their believers rather than spending it on alleviating poverty or building infrastructure, further weakening faith in their goodwill.

There is an ongoing debate among those who believe religion has no value and those who defend its value. Critics point out the abovementioned abuses and note that secular ethics (e.g., the moral systems proposed by secular philosophers) serve the same purpose as religious ethics: promoting ethical and prosocial behaviors. Defenders note that specific religions have survived for thousands of years by meeting continuing human needs that are not met by secular ethics, such as providing consolation and reassurance that death is not final. Governments cannot fill these roles, and religions fill the void left by the government.

In China today, religion has been largely marginalized, apart from the impact it has had on shaping Chinese ethics and society in the past, but that impact continues to shape today's culture. With no religion to promote a single unifying code of ethics, and inadequate supervision, unscrupulous individuals, both in government and in business, have set out to enrich themselves, with no fear of the consequences for themselves or others. For example, vendors have sold toxic milk powder or contaminated food, and fake health products and other fake and shoddy products are everywhere. The producers of these goods are not limited by ethical constraints; if they were, they would not behave this way. Moral decay has thus become a social norm in 21st-century China. The historical struggle between religion and government has never stopped, and history provides many examples of leaders who used religious power to lead a rebellion and seize power. For example, at the end of the Eastern Han Dynasty, Zhang Jiao (145–184 CE) led the Yellow Turban Revolution, nominally based on Taoist beliefs, and claimed that he was following divine authority ("the way of Heaven"). He threatened the Han leaders before finally being defeated. Hong Xiuquan (1814–1864 CE) founded the "worship god" movement and led the Taiping rebellion against the Qing Dynasty, with the nominal goal of establishing the "Heavenly Kingdom," before being defeated by the Qing.

Governments have spared no effort to crack down on religions that opposed them. For example, Chinese history tells of many government-organized campaigns to destroy Buddhism. Mao Zedong's era is a particularly noteworthy modern example. However, religions have impressive vitality and continue to exist and sometimes even thrive despite the government's best efforts to eradicate them. For example, during China's Cultural Revolution period, young Communist cadres, encouraged by the government, invaded temples and broke all of the statues that were not hidden fast enough, but most of the important ones have now been replaced. As these examples show, religion has played both positive and negative roles in societies. Religion continues to exist in a dynamic struggle with the government, and how this struggle will be resolved remains the subject of considerable speculation and study.

5.2. The Dual Attributes of the Government

Governments have two primary responsibilities: ensuring social stability by measures such as protecting the rights of citizens and promoting economic development to improve standards of living and obtaining tax revenues that will support government operations and the delivery of services. The government exercises power on behalf of the state to fulfill roles such as protecting citizens, upholding and enforcing laws to ensure social stability, collecting taxes, and distributing tax revenues to fund government and private programs. Because the powerful may try to take property away from individuals, individual property rights rely on the government or the nation's constitution for protection. Unfortunately, public officials are also individuals and frequently use the power at their disposal for their own benefit or take advantage of the informational advantage they have over nongovernmental members to achieve private gain, leading to reduced economic efficiency and potentially serious social problems (Stovel et al., 2011).

Historically, the vast majority of governments have not provided effective services to support social stability and economic development. As a service organization whose primary goal is supposed to be protection of the public interest, governments have instead frequently operated more like organized crime (North, 1990). The obligation to serve the state wars with the temptation to abuse power, which has often led to a paradoxical duality of the government: at the same time, government officials are claiming to be acting "for the people," they are relentlessly abusing their power to take advantage of the people. Because history books are written by the successful, the successful are often portrayed favorably in these books as benevolent leaders who served the people based on noble motives, particularly when they are government-sponsored textbooks (Olson, 1993).

The limited lifespan of authoritarian rulers in autocracies and the even shorter election cycle of officials in democracies (e.g., the US president serves only four years per term, for a maximum of two terms) encourages governments, whether authoritarian or democratic, to think in the short term, leading to short-sighted decisions. Government officials know they must accomplish their personal goals in a short period of time and often take shortcuts to achieve these goals; for example, they may confiscate private property, refuse to repay government loans, issue money indiscriminately, and expand government debt to allow excessive spending (Olson, 1993). The United States is widely considered a model democracy. Nonetheless, buying votes is a well-known secret. Beddoe et al. (2009) found that in US elections, a candidate can spend as little as US$10 per vote on political advertising and still win an election. Elected officials must then compensate those who provided funding and compensate voters for their votes, and this inevitably leads to abuse of power. Although violent revolutions have occurred throughout history, and this should have taught would-be rulers painful lessons not to risk such a fate, no society has yet invented institutional systems that ensure the rational long-term functioning of the government in the service of the people and simultaneously support a thriving economy (North, 1990). A monopoly on the use of force has traditionally been the primary means by which authoritarian governments have robbed their people, but democratic governments are no better; the main difference is that the means of robbing people are more subtle in a democracy (Bhattacharjee, 2007; Stone, 2009). We still have a long way to go to understand the nature of the government and take measures to improve the state's ability to govern. In the following sections, I will discuss the problems of irrational government behavior and provide examples of rational choices.

China's *fajia* ideology blatantly regards the people as the servants of the government. Its most representative figure, Shang Yang, wrote about a series of strategies that harm the people and serve the government, such as accusing citizens of being weak and foolish, and somehow less valuable than the rich and powerful, and used these descriptions to justify oppression. Since this approach has often worked, at least in the short term, governments starting with the Han Dynasty (202 BCE–220 AD) have spared no effort to promote a corrupt alternative to Confucianism, often disguising their philosophy in the terminology of Confucianism and deceiving the people. This ideology continues to affect Chinese society, and its survival for thousands of years suggests it will be a long and arduous task to eliminate this influence.

5.2.1. Irrational Government Behavior

The state is a complex social unit based on a shared ideology and exists within a separate space where individuals, corporations, and social groups share resources under a series of institutional (e.g., legal, cultural, customary) constraints (Cao, 2015). Because the state cannot govern itself, it must delegate governance to an agent that acts on its behalf: the government (Myerson, 2011). However, the officials who form the government and act as agents of the state find it difficult to resist the temptation to abuse their power, and thus, instead of always serving the people, they often use the powers they have been granted by the state to benefit themselves and oppress the citizens they are nominally working to benefit (Olson, 1993). As a result, they evolved into what Marx described as an instrument of oppression.

When a government replaces the state instead of acting as its agent, it necessarily neglects its mandate to serve the people. In countries controlled by authoritarian governments, there is a general lack of democratic power for citizens, accompanied by government corruption, abuse of power, loss of human rights, and often widespread famine and poverty that lead to social unrest (Myerson, 2011; Stovel et al., 2011). During the more than 2,000 years of imperial rule in Chinese history, emperors controlled the state and passed on that control from generation to generation of their descendants. When the emperor was fair and effective, this system worked reasonably well; when the emperor was corrupt or ineffective, this created unrest that eventually led to peasant uprisings or undermined the state so that it could be conquered by another state. As a result, dynastic changes occurred after an average of roughly 71 years. These repeated revolutions had a high cost in human lives and in reversals of social progress.

The state and the government are strongly related but different concepts. Nonetheless, both must be governed or managed through agents. For example, governments are the agents of the state, and officials are the agents of governments. Unfortunately, agents are human in both cases, and humans are flawed: we are short-sighted and often motivated by self-interest. How to solve these problems is the greatest dilemma facing political economics. It is the paradox of political economics that citizens need the government and its agents to govern the country, but by giving them the power necessary to fulfill this role, citizens may lose the ability to stop them from abusing their power. History seems to be an endless replaying of the same story over and over again; that is, governments compete with their people, and although the government initially wins, it is inevitably overthrown. The ways in which governments rob their people have become more numerous and more insidious over time. These include owning an economic monopoly, levying invisible taxes, and controlling benefit redistribution.

5.2.1.1. Economic Monopoly

As the nominal representative of all citizens, the government is both the guardian of individual property rights and a monopolizer of resources. In the 1950s, shortly after the birth of the People's Republic of China, all farmland, factories, and natural resources formerly owned by individuals or groups were confiscated by the government in the name of communism. In 1952, private enterprise output accounted for 55% of China's industrial output; by 1962, this figure had fallen to zero (Li, 2004). The destruction of functional and effective enterprises and their replacement by government-managed monopolies run by managers who had no experience managing such operations ultimately led to poor decisions, wasted resources, a dramatic economic downturn, and economic and social disaster. From 1961 to 1963, deaths exceeded the normal rate by a total of more than 7.6 million in China and total gross domestic product (GDP) dropped by a total of nearly 100×10^9 RMB, equivalent to 17% of total annual GDP at the time (Cao et al., 2014).

Government monopolization of trade is another common problem, even in modern societies. As I discussed in the previous chapter, it is easy to understand monopolistic operations for sectors such as the provision of public health services that are naturally monopolistic and for cross-regional natural resource mobilization (e.g., the Grand Canal I described in Chapter 2), but government monopolistic behavior is not limited to such activities. Governments often extend their reach to obtain monopoly benefits for every corner of the economy until it collapses under their mismanagement. For example, the Chinese government under Mao confiscated all privately owned goods and monopolized all sectors of the Chinese economy; after the reform and opening up to the West in 1978, the Chinese government privatized industries that were failing to operate efficiently and profitably but retained its monopoly on essential or highly profitable industries such as salt production, energy generation, precious metal mining, natural resource development, finance, and education.

Chinese government statistics suggest that the value of the assets of Chinese state-owned enterprises in 2011 had increased to 2.9 times the value in 2002, whereas the mean income of Chinese citizens increased only 1.8 times (China Statistics Agency, 2012). From 1990 to 2010, government income increased 28.3 times, while citizens' income increased only 16.2 times; the ratio of citizen income to government income therefore decreased from 3.5:1 in 1990 to 2.0:1 in 2010. The income increase was driven by changes in regulations that allowed provinces to earn income from real estate sales. In 2011, revenue earned from land sales accounted for 76% of total local government revenue (Zheng et al., 2014).

Because government officials can use their economic monopoly to solicit bribes from enterprises and individuals, they prefer monopolies and are unwilling to change them even when they bring obvious harm to society. For example, the Chinese government's long-standing monopoly on higher education, which I discussed in Chapter 3, has led to persistent failure of China's talent development efforts, and the government remains unwilling to change this dysfunctional system even as the competition between China and the United States for dominance in science and technology is in full swing.

Because members of the government and their associates outside of the government are aware of unpunished unethical behavior by their colleagues, they may be encouraged to practice their own unethical behavior. This creates a situation in which corruption is tolerated and unethical behavior is widely tolerated. It also teaches citizens to emulate this behavior. On December 7, 2021, an elderly man who was delivering sugarcane was "mugged" by a group of people wearing government uniforms in Samsung Town, Nantong City, Jiangsu Province (*Global Times*, 2021a). It was subsequently revealed that the bandits were actually employees of the Nantong Jingtong Cityscape Management Company. This company had been hired by the local government to perform administrative work but without adequate supervision; this allowed them to both receive fees for their work, while the government officials continued to receive their pay despite having their work done by the private company, and abuse their power by stealing from citizens. The marketization of power in this and other ways has directly led to the marketization of government jobs, and the sale of positions by government officials has become the "emperor's new clothes": everyone knows about the problem, but since nobody is willing to confront the problem, corruption continues to spread like a malignant tumor.

5.2.1.2. Invisible Taxes

To gain a long-term trade advantage, every country aims to achieve a stable monetary policy. However, both authoritarian and democratic governments are keen to increase currency issuance to provide money they can use for various purposes (Desai et al., 2003), especially during economic downturns, and quantitative easing of monetary policy has become a popular choice for governments around the world. The problem is that this increases government debt, and few governments ever recover the increased expenditures when the economy thrives again, making this practice one cause of price inflation. Because the rich can profit from speculation (both because they have more money and because they have better information sources), inflation is more harmful to the poor; as a result, inflation ultimately undermines social stability and economic development (Desai et al., 2003).

Revenue gained by issuing new money is only one aspect of the government's access to hidden income. If the government controls the sale of goods, it can also charge different prices to different customers, a practice referred to as *price discrimination*. However, by raising prices on these goods, the government creates a hidden tax on consumers who were forced to buy the goods, whereas lowering the prices creates a hidden tax on producers who are forced to sell the goods to the government at low prices (e.g., farmers who had to sell their grain to the government). From 1990 to 2000, China's agricultural price discrimination reduced the per capita income of rural residents by 146.5 RMB per year, which amounted to 6.4% of an average farmer's annual income (Si, 2005). Between 1950 and 2004, the Chinese government collected more than 5×10^{12} RMB from farmers through invisible agricultural taxes, equivalent to 29.2% of the government's total tax revenue of 17.1×10^{12} RMB, thereby perpetuating the poverty of Chinese farmers (Zeng, 2004). Taking inflation into account, the prices of major crops (e.g., corn and soybeans) that are subsidized by many countries have decreased greatly since 1970, while the prices of unsubsidized agricultural products, such as fresh fruits and vegetables, have increased by more than 200% (Popkin, 2011).

Readers may wonder why a major food-exporting country like the United States would subsidize its food, while food-importing countries don't provide import subsidies for their citizens. This is because the United States and other developed countries control food prices to make it impossible for developing countries with immature agricultural systems to accumulate enough capital to diversify and modernize their economy by implementing industrial mass production and this is why they promote urbanization through agricultural modernization (Popkin, 2011). As a result, these countries must depend on the industrial products of developed countries for their industries, which also allows the developed countries to control the prices of industrial products. The developed countries can therefore enjoy monopoly profits from controlling the price of both agricultural and industrial products. With the rapid economic rise of developing countries such as China, there has been growing economic competition with developed countries, leading these countries to develop new strategies (Xia et al., 2023). As I described in Chapter 3, developed countries have encouraged a brain drain from China by promoting their higher education sector to students in developing countries; the result has been to capture the best talents from developing countries by importing these talents to Western universities. This has also promoted the development of a monopoly on science and high technology, which in turn has allowed monopoly pricing of high-tech products.

5.2.1.3. Benefit Redistribution

If taxes were shared equitably by all members of society and the government's aim was to benefit society as a whole, a country would develop more harmoniously. Unfortunately, in most cases, government policies facilitate transactions between the government and the rich, and the rich always find ways to benefit from the government (North, 1990). To harvest more tax revenue from taxpayers, governments prioritize economic development models that benefit the rich and ignore policies that would benefit the poor and improve the welfare of all humanity. In addition, the wealthy (including industrialists) can afford to bribe government officials to implement policies that maintain their industry's dominance (i.e., regulatory capture). Such deals between the government and rich taxpayers increase the income gap between the rich and the poor, leading to a loss of public confidence in the government.

As a result of these factors, combined with the hidden taxes I described earlier in this section, wealth becomes concentrated in the hands of the rich rather than being distributed equitably among all citizens. In 2009, 95% of the wealth in China belonged to 5% of the households, versus 60% of the wealth in the United States (Shang et al., 2019). Considering the hidden income that is available to civil servants through corruption, bribery, and other unethical practices, these government workers are the highest paid workers in China. Therefore, applying for civil service has become the first choice for Chinese students after graduation. For example, in 2010, the number of students who registered for the government civil service examination was 155 times the number of job openings (Fig. 9). Statistics show that China's expenditure on government administration is 25.6% of GDP, versus only 3.4% and 2.8%, respectively, for the United States and Japan. This imbalance decreases the money available for other important social services. For example, education and medical expenses in the United States account for 21.5% of GDP, versus 23.4% in Japan, but only 3.8% of GDP in China (Xia et al., 2023).

Because senior government officials are often wealthy, they are motivated to introduce policies that benefit the wealthy and give them a greater stake in the redistribution of wealth. A typical example was the rule implemented during the Ming Dynasty (1368–1644 CE) that the farmland of officials' families would not be taxed, which led to massive hoarding of arable land by Ming officials and triggered peasant uprisings. The last Ming emperor, Zhu Youjian ("Chongzhen"; 1628–1644 CE), exacerbated the problem by implementing a regulation that prevented taxation of the property of government officials and their families. The resulting loss of tax revenues left the empire's army without financial support, and the Ming Dynasty soon fell under the double blow of peasant revolts and Manchu invasions. Similarly, current Chinese laws stipulate that if tax evasion is detected, the tax evaders can pay a small penalty to receive a lighter punishment. Since the consequences for the crime are weak, this has contributed to increased tax evasion. People from all parts of society, from rich businessmen to artists, have joined the ranks of tax evaders. If you enter the words "celebrity tax evasion" (in Chinese) at https://www.baidu.com, you will find that almost all familiar film and television stars in China are on the list of tax evaders.

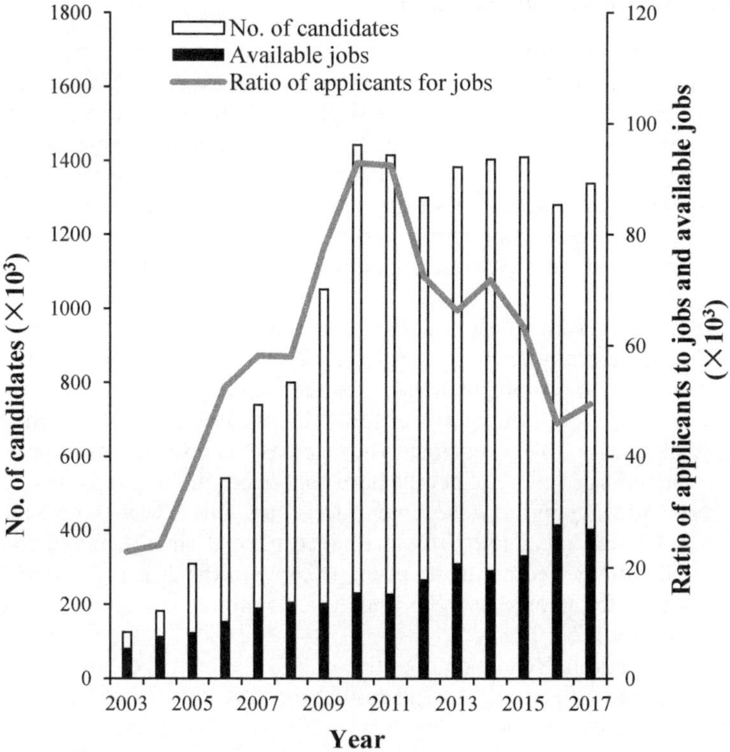

Fig. 9. Annual Changes in the Number of Government Jobs and Job Applicants from 2003 to 2017. *Source*: The figure is created by the author.

Throughout history, policies that violate economic common sense continue to appear. For example, as I noted in Chapter 3, the proportion of China's rural population fell from 73.6% to 39.8% between 1989 and 2017, while the proportion of rural students in universities fell from 43.4% to 8.0% (Xia et al., 2023). Chinese universities enroll many more students from wealthy families because these students tend to receive better education (thus, they perform better on entrance examinations) and are more able to afford the cost of their education (e.g., housing and food), whereas students from relatively poor families either end their education after nine years of compulsory education so that they can work to support their family or attend technical schools. This occurs even though the government massively subsidizes universities. For example, Tsinghua University received financial support of 36.21×10^9 RMB in 2022, which amounted to 630×10^3 RMB per student (Statista, 2023). The result is that children from rich families receive more educational benefits, while children from poor families have ever-decreasing opportunities, with the inevitable result that the poverty of rural residents continues to increase.

5.2.2. Rational Choices by the Government

Governments are not always irrational. Rationality represents the ability to make decisions based on logic, an understanding of cause and effect, and the ability to learn from the consequences of decisions. If the government is consistently irrational, it will sacrifice the people's support. Thus, governments can only persist if they have some beneficial aspects that encourage people to support them. It follows that governments exist because they also have a rational side. For example, governments can ensure stable demand and supply by stimulating investment and production, ultimately benefiting both the government and the people (Olson, 1993).

In theory, a government should focus on long-term stability, since even a purely self-interested government or ruler understands the importance of optimizing tax revenues to prolong their rule through strategies such as reducing taxes to encourage people to produce and consume (Olson, 1993). To achieve this goal, the rational choice for any government is to increase its investments in providing services to the public so that the people have confidence in the government's ability to govern and will support government decisions. This is why Deng Xiaoping (1904–1997), China's great practitioner of institutional change, noted that the basic contradiction in a communist society is between the growing material and cultural needs of the people and the immature economic production structure, which cannot meet those needs.

Government rationality in a competitive political market (i.e., one where candidates compete to be elected) doesn't result from the people's choice of which candidates will be elected but rather from politicians and government officials behaving ethically to avoid being defeated by their competitors (Zhao, 2006). Competition in the political market includes not only domestic competition among politicians or political groups with different political views, including local governments and government departments, but also international competition among countries. The pressure from the political market forces the government to improve its ability to govern and thereby avoid being squeezed out of the market by smarter competitors.

In political markets, where businesses and citizens vote with their feet rather than their hands (Hill, 1996), a politician's reputation is particularly important. Good reputations are socially rewarding, since they secure support by the people. Indeed, politicians can switch from self-interested to altruistic behavior when their reputations are at risk of being compromised (Milinski & Rockenbach, 2007). Once a government and its people establish a virtuous mechanism of mutual trust, a country enters into a self-reinforcing system that ultimately benefits both the government and the people (Zhao, 2006).

Governments are not only influenced by internal pressures but also by external factors. Competition among countries also promotes the improvement of government institutions and leads to credible commitments and more rational policies (Krasner, 2011). In the face of an increasingly modern, diverse, and globalized world, each country's government must strive to obtain and then maintain an international competitive advantage (Beddoe et al., 2009). A competitive political environment attracts better politicians, leading to the development of an elite government, improved government decision-making mechanisms, and enhanced government decision-making capacity. Competition can also increase the supply of information, leading to more rational and better government decisions, promoting a more diverse and open information system, and leading to implementation of political reform programs to obtain a more perfect state (Zhao, 2006). Deng Xiaoping's 1978 policy of reform and opening up provides strong evidence of government rationality and its effectiveness.

History has repeatedly shown that excessive and unreasonable taxation and other burdens upon individual choices can undermine trust in a government; it can also cause a widening gap between the rich and poor, social unrest, environmental degradation, economic decline, and even war (Bowles, 2012). All dynasties in Chinese history, without exception, have collapsed under the combined pressures of internal unrest and external invasion (Cao et al., 2007). Today, collapse is more likely to result from economic factors. With rapid globalization, capital and talent have begun to flow faster to the most stable and efficient countries. Like a wounded person losing blood, irrational regimes end up paying for their own greed and stupidity with outflows of their precious resources.

Governments must create conditions that encourage businesses and people who can create wealth for the country to stay in the country, and these conditions must provide them with an incentive to work hard because they will be rewarded for efforts to improve their situation. If someone knows that all the wealth they create belongs to the government, as has been the case in many communist regimes, they will either refuse to work or will work less hard than they would do if they benefited from their labor. There are many reasons for the rise and fall of nations, but the selfish and self-serving behavior of government officials has been a major cause of regime change throughout history. As Deng Xiaoping said, if China does not reform, develop its economy, and improve the standard of living of its people, this will inevitably result in its demise.

As citizens become more literate and information technology develops, the information advantage of governments diminishes. Modern governments are pressured to put the best interests of society first, align themselves with the desires of the people, and continue to achieve results that inspire public confidence in their ability to govern. Therefore, a rational government, acting in its own interest, must also provide opportunities for socioeconomic development and promote social stability to increase public confidence that anyone who participates in socioeconomic activities will have their efforts and the resulting rewards protected by the government and can therefore improve their own welfare through their own efforts.

To motivate government officials to more ethically serve the people, some countries and regions, such as Singapore and Hong Kong, have introduced retirement incentive systems that reward government officials with high pensions if they don't abuse their power (Myerson, 2011). Such incentives can motivate government officials and employees to work harder and more ethically. However, some officials who are smart can earn far more money through unethical behavior without being caught. And many government officials retire and are hired by enterprises to use their expertise and insider knowledge to influence government policy through lobbying, which resembles the Western equivalent of the Chinese concept of *guanxi* (i.e., a network of connections and favors). In those cases, a good pension is potentially less of a motivation than future economic benefits. Governments don't currently have a good rational solution to this problem, although improving monitoring of officials might be a good start.

5.3. Government Governance

Politicians know that popular support is the key to their survival and power. During China's War of Liberation from 1946 to 1949, the Communist Party of China confiscated land from landowners and distributed the land to the peasants. The peasants who obtained the land actively supported the logistics, provision of military supplies, and transportation for the People's Liberation Army, thereby helping the Communist Party to gain power. But in 1958, the Communist Party of China launched the people's commune movement and confiscated the land they had given to the people. This left the former owners of the land destitute. In 1978, after nearly 30 years of the communist government, the annual per capita net income of Chinese farmers was only 133.6 RMB (China Statistics Agency, 1979), making them the poorest people in the world. In 1978, Deng Xiaoping's administration returned this land to the farmers again and gave them responsibility and independence for managing the land, thereby ushering in a market-based economic reform that succeeded so well that it caught the world's attention.

When policymakers have many options, they tend to choose the option that maximizes their personal utility (Lin, 2002), and such a system can become "locked in" even if it is inefficient for the nation or its people and will lead to eventual failure. (*Lock-in* means that the government relies on the initial path and rules and is unable or unwilling to change them even if the context changes.) The aim is to guarantee the personal interests of the current leaders rather than seeking social goals such as political stability, optimal allocation of resources, economic efficiency, and environmental sustainability. It is not hard to imagine that this system is likely to eventually trigger a revolution (Argandoña, 2004).

During more than 2,000 years of imperial rule in China, the irrational choices that resulted from centralized politics led to repeated locking in of systems, followed by revolution and dynastic change. However, "those who cannot remember the past are doomed to repeat it," so leaders quickly forget past mistakes. Thus, it takes no more than a few decades before the new regime repeats the same mistakes and causes the same problems and are then forced to once more reform the system. When a reform is initiated by the leader of the central government, in the absence of third-party constraints, the reform is intended to strengthen central rule. As a result, the regime would either fall slowly if the failure is gradual, as occurs when a leader's supporters falsely praise the reform to earn the favor of their leader (i.e., the emperor's new clothes), or dramatic (e.g., if the reform pushes the opponent beyond their ability to tolerate the leader), leading to chaos. For example, shortly after the death of the first Ming emperor, the second emperor began to annex his vassal states. As a result, the Yan king (1360–1424 CE), rebelled and captured the capital. The second Ming emperor committed suicide.

The situation may change if third-party constraints are imposed. For example, in 356 BCE, the Qin principality, the weakest nation at that time, was forced to reform its economic and legal systems in order to win the war with another principality. Similarly, in 1978, when a weak China was threatened by two superpowers, the Soviet Union and the United States, it was forced to change (i.e., to adopt a socialist market economy so that it could compete). Unlike authoritarian politics, which typically lead to a violent reckoning after a few decades (or occasionally centuries, as in the case of some ancient Chinese dynasties), democracy has problems that occur on much shorter scales after a change of the government. For example, as soon as Donald Trump took office, he began trying to reverse the policies of his predecessor, Barack Obama. The development of the United States and other nations has often been swayed by such differences in the personal preferences of successive leaders, often leading to a cycle of meaningless changes.

Clearly, the failure to constrain a leader's power can have expensive consequences in both dictatorships and democracies. However, in any economic system, a clear system of property rights cannot be realized without effective government support that protects the weak against the strong, and social transactions become more difficult (Stovel et al., 2011). This is the famous North paradox: the government is both a provider and a destroyer of social institutions (North, 1990). When governments begin to seek goals other than their own utility, they can create the conditions for true democracy: the rule of law, altruism, prevention of inequities, and a philosophical revolution toward restoring the government's role as protector of the people it represents (Bowles, 2012). Therefore, competition from third parties to provide alternatives and strong supervision by the people to prevent corruption and lock-in are both important.

5.3.1. The Harm Caused by a Centralized System

In Chapter 3, I described the harm caused to scientific innovation caused by excessive centralized control of university education. However, centralized control can also damage the economy and society. Such power, controlled by few individuals or only one person, remains a problem and has likely led governments to fear the chaos that might result from decentralization or to fear their own loss of power and prestige. As a result, the government acts to secure its power rather than to improve the well-being of the people. Although capitalist democracies have some resistance to such problems (because governments can be thrown out of power at each election), they are not immune to a loss of control over governance. For example, the phenomenon of *regulatory capture* can occur, in which industries that are nominally supervised and regulated by the government fund the election of officials who relax or abandon this supervision.

In strongly centralized political structures, senior officials have little or no competition. Thus, once leaders defeat their opponents, they can enjoy the fruits of power even without widespread support from the people (Myerson, 2011). In this case, the government will choose the system that is most conducive to its own needs rather than the system that is best for the people (Zhao, 2006). In the absence of competition to eliminate bad institutions and protect socially beneficial outcomes, most governments have historically tended to choose institutional frameworks that overwhelmingly favor government monopolies rather than frameworks that expand competitive opportunities (Mabogunje, 2000).

History has repeatedly proven that both communist and capitalist states can harm citizens by weakening their rights and their ability to share in the society's growth and development when governments adopt extreme forms of centralized power. As a result, citizens lose their incentive to create wealth, thereby causing enormous harm to social development.

5.3.1.1. Abuse of Power

Historically, communist states have generally tried to replace the state with the government, and dictators who were happy to call the shots repeated the slogan of serving the people, when in fact they were only acting for themselves. To maximize their personal interests, they exploited their power to the best of their abilities, even if that meant killing innocent people, and caused great damage to their state and its economic development. Because dictators are well aware that the duration of their reign is limited, they seek to maximize their benefits while they can, but some also strive to perform miracles that will see them immortalized in the history books. They may be extremely austere in their lives or seek ways to portray themselves as great men. To achieve such goals, they misuse the power of the state, start wars, and kill the innocent in the guise of behaving as revolutionaries (Mayer, 1993). For example, after Hitler gained power as Chancellor of Germany in January 1933, he began preparing for Germany's rise and annexed Austria in March 1938, leading to World War II. This war caused the death of more than 60 million people and a direct military expenditure of US$13 trillion that would have been better spent improving lives around the world (Skousen, 1988).

Because of its theoretical flaws, which were sometimes masked by the nominal benefits for humanity, communism has been exploited by dictators since its birth. Whether in the former Soviet Union or in other countries that remained monarchies under a veneer of communism, the countries that claimed to be communist eventually fell into the quagmire of dictatorial rule without exception. Under the centralized system that was typical of such countries, a strict hierarchy developed that governed the relationships among different groups of people. Power was concentrated in the hands of a few, and the majority had little or no power, which eventually led to the disappearance of effective oversight of the government by the people (Wilson, 1887). Some dictators use all kinds of extreme means to oppress the people. For example, former Iraqi President Saddam Hussein (1937–2006) used intimidation and death threats by his Ba'ath Party (which was nominally communist) to ensure that every voter voted for him during the presidential election (Eyal, 2002). Former Libyan president Muammar Muhammad Abu Minyar al-Gaddafi (1942–2011) killed most of his potential rivals in the name of the law (Cottee et al., 2008), subsequently ruling as Libya's dictator for 42 years until the 2011 "Arab Spring" led to his capture and execution by militants.

Even in peacetime, dictators are often indifferent to the safety of the people and their property and have been eager to launch various political campaigns intended primarily for their own benefit. For example, Mao Zedong launched the "Anti-Rightist Struggle" in 1957 and the "Cultural Revolution" in 1965 and openly declared that similar revolutionary political programs would be implemented every five or six years. In doing so, he formalized the persecution of his own colleagues and neglected the needs of the people he nominally served. Under Mao, the Chinese government estimated the rations required for farmers to survive and the seeds that should be set aside for planting the next year's crop, allocated this portion of the harvest to farmers, and then moved the rest of the harvest to state granaries for use by the government. This represented one of the most heavily taxed periods in history. During the 28 years of Mao's rule, nearly 1 million people were forced to leave their jobs for re-education among the rural poor, millions died of starvation or other unnatural causes, and hundreds of millions of Chinese people endured poverty and famine, causing direct economic losses of more than 800 billion RMB (Lin, 2002).

Such problems are not unique to communism. In capitalist democracies, governments often prioritize economic growth rather than improving the welfare of the people because this increases tax revenues. (In some cases, this may also be a corrupt way to reward their supporters for supporting their election.) Excessive or unreasonable taxes and other burdens have caused widespread impoverishment of the people, sometimes leading to unrest, conflicts, crises, famine, and other social disasters (Bowles, 2012). For example, the American government relaxed regulations on mortgage loans and other potentially risky investments by the world's largest financial institutions. The result was a global financial crisis in 2008 that forced nations around the world to intervene to prevent the situation from becoming a disaster on the scale of the Great Depression.

When the state is captured by a ruler rather than existing to serve the people, the ruler tends to fear that outstanding individuals will reveal the leader's flaws, leading to a loss of power, and therefore persecutes these individuals, with serious consequences (loss of the skills and insights of these individuals) for society. This has also occurred in China. For example, Zhao Gou, the emperor of the Southern Song Dynasty (1127–1279 CE) worried that his soldiers would seize political power. To prevent this, he declared war on and killed two rival rulers, Yue Fei (1103–1142 CE) and Xiang Shibi (1205–1261 CE), so that the soldiers would be busy with the war and would leave him alone. In protest, 60 of his generals defected and then united to crush the dynasty (Zhang, 2021).

Dressed in the cloak of serving the people, leaders throughout Chinese history have profited at the expense of the people. When they are no longer able to benefit from their corruption, they often immediately abandon their patriotic slogans and revolt or betray their country. Such betrayals are not unique to Chinese history; on the contrary, they may occur in any society when the government crosses a threshold and tries to replace the state. When the former Soviet Union was about to collapse, Mikhail Sergeyevich Gorbachev (1931–2022), the last leader of the former Soviet Union's government, met with his successor, Boris Nikolayevich Yeltsin (1931–2007), but did not stop him from splitting the country into independent republics. Instead, Gorbachev negotiated his own safety and his political and economic treatment after his retirement.

Human nature often causes leaders of a government to maximize their personal interests at the expense of the state. However, if they cannot find a way to cooperate with the citizens they govern, it is difficult to achieve their goals (Argandoña, 2004). It follows logically that there is a necessary equilibrium of interests between a leader and the people they lead, and although it is difficult to achieve this equilibrium, successful leaders instinctively recognize the need to seek it. Several similar proverbs that acknowledge this issue appear repeatedly in Chinese history textbooks: "the government forces the people to rebel," "where there is oppression, there is resistance," "water can carry a boat, but it can also overturn it," and so on. These all suggest that unrest originates from oppression of the people by their government. Totalitarian rulers who are unable to control their own greed or lack effective mechanisms to restrain the government and its officials from abusing their power inevitably experience unplanned regime changes. The French philosopher Baron Charles-Louis de Secondat (1689–1755 CE) put it this way (de Secondat, 1752):

> The desire for power is common to all, and power has a natural tendency to expand indefinitely, so to speak. Therefore, it must be restrained by means of a restraining mechanism, so that it is not allowed to become a beast that hurts society, and then also allows those who have the power to destroy themselves. This is especially true of public power, and any society in which public power acts arbitrarily must be a very terrible society.

These restraints are called *governance*.

Since neither capitalism nor communism appears able to prevent political problems such as the abuse of power, both political systems are still immature (Bridgman, 2008). Thus, we must encourage political change that will promote development to a new stage of society in which the government once more serves the state.

5.3.1.2. Rampant Corruption

Concentration of power creates conditions that encourage corruption, and governments and their officials often use the power in their hands to maximize their own interests through means other than taxation, such as bribes, confiscations, and fines (Olson, 1993). Because of the unchecked power of those who centralize power, most government officials will use this power to benefit themselves and their cronies rather than the people they are charged with protecting. In a political system where power is greater than law, the concentration of power makes it easy for officials to turn their own interests into national interests. This encourages corruption at the highest levels. In 2014, for example, the former general manager of Beidaihe Water Supply Company in Hebei Province, one of China's lowest-ranking government officials, was found to have acquired 120 million RMB in cash, 37 kg of gold, and 68 properties (He, 2018). The former chairman of China Huarong Asset Management Co., Ltd. took a bribe of 1.8×10^9 RMB, kept over 100 mistresses, and owned more than 100 properties (Cao, 2021). The pursuit of personal interests at all costs by government officials further widens the gap between the rich and the poor, aggravates the harm caused by inequality among members of society, and increases crime and social unrest (Shang et al., 2019).

Corruption in the former Soviet Union was already a serious problem in Lenin's time, and Joseph Stalin (1878–1953) exacerbated the problem by further increasing the privileges of his cadres, thus institutionalizing corruption (Brovkin, 2003). The privileges of former Soviet officials included private rights to own luxury *dachas* (vacation homes in the countryside), as well as to receive special supplies, education, and health care that were unavailable to citizens (Nove, 1986; Towns, 1993). In Libya, Muammar Gaddafi personally controlled US$8 billion worth of gold reserves in the Libyan central bank (Vasil'ev, 2014). In China, government officials have used their power to protect unscrupulous businessmen who repaid them for this protection, as well as to buy and sell official positions. From May 2019 to April 2020, the Chinese government under Xi Jinping, the General Secretary of the Communist Party, launched a special campaign to fight crime and eliminate corruption (Li et al., 2020). During this campaign, they shut down 3,120 underworld groups (organized crime organizations) and filed 67,190 prosecutions against what were called "triad umbrellas," namely government officials who provided protection to the underworld groups. This process resulted in detention of 388,442 suspects. Xi's anti-corruption efforts have won him the respect of the Chinese people.

In 1997, Chinese government stipulated that both citizens who bribe and officials who accept bribes are guilty. Once discovered, not only will the relevant property be confiscated, but both parties will also be subject to the same criminal punishment. That is to say, citizens who bribe government officials may not only lose his property but also face imprisonment like government officials. As a result, government officials are not only more willing to accept various gifts from citizens but also more willing to use their power to extort ordinary citizens without restraint. Because the punishment for citizens who bribe is heavier than the officials who accept bribes, ordinary people dare not report officials after being extorted to avoid being imprisoned together with him. Refusing to bribe government officials could be life-threatening. For example, because no bribery was given to government officials, on June 12, 2010, the Public Security Bureau of Zhuzhou City, Hunan Province, detain Li Tuchun without any reason, the chairman of "Prince Dairy Group Company," the largest dairy enterprise in China at that time, as well as his brother, sister, and secretary, and confiscated their property, leading to bankruptcy of the enterprise (Zheng, 2023). After 15 months, Li and others were acquitted and released, but the huge losses they experienced were ignored. Fortunately, Chinese officials dare not extort foreign citizens due to concerns about diplomatic disputes. This is the main reason why Chinese people are more willing to immigrate abroad.

5.3.1.3. One-sided Science

In countries where the law's power is greater than the government's power, scientists can use the law as a weapon to protect their personal safety; however, in countries where governments can ignore the law, scientists are seen as very dangerous to the government and are vulnerable to reprisals if they are not protected by a powerful guardian. For example, on February 17, 1600, Giordano Bruno (1548–1600) was burned to death in Rome's Piazza Della Flora by the Pope, leader of the Catholic church. In such a society, the government defines what is truth, and those who contradict the government are guilty of a crime against the state. A more recent example involves Li Wenliang, the first doctor who reported the new COVID-19 outbreak in Wuhan, who was prevented from speaking about this until the outbreak could no longer be concealed. Rather than being encouraged to question and criticize, those who seek scientific truth face strong pressure to seek evidence that the government's decisions are correct and wise. This constraint strongly influences scientific research in China and eliminates much of the power of science to provide foresight about future conditions.

After China's 1957 anti-rightist campaign and the Cultural Revolution from 1965 to 1976, Chinese scholars learned to protect themselves from their government by remaining silent or by carefully censoring their words. Some selectively reported research results by publishing only articles they knew that administrative officials would like (one-sided science), creating a Chinese academic ecosystem in which researchers who supported the government were, in turn, supported by the government. It is far easier for scholars to grasp the desires of their leaders and follow the resulting constraints than it would be to challenge their leaders or introduce their own scholarly ethics systems to constrain their behavior. This leads to negative consequences for academic freedom. For example, many Chinese universities and research institutes have introduced policies that evaluate the work of professors according to the amount of research funding they receive. As a result, researchers who are good at reading the minds of officials and who are therefore better at gaining government research funding can spend research money without producing results or can produce results that satisfy the officials who gave them the research grant. As a result, they become the highest-ranking and most highly paid professors. They may even be promoted to roles as academicians of the Chinese Academy of Sciences or other prestigious government positions, where they then influence future scientific research planning.

Such science can have serious consequences. For example, afforestation provides wood and other forest products for the market. In addition to the commercial value of these forests, they also contribute greatly to urban greening and preventing soil erosion in many areas. But China's forestry sector was not satisfied with these services. To make afforestation seem even more valuable, they have claimed that the plantations can combat desertification, fight the production of dust storms and haze, and improve the ecological environment. As a result, plantation forestry has become one of the main measures of ecological restoration in China (Cao et al., 2011). The State Forestry Administration claims that afforestation has rapidly restored ecosystems in China and has reversed ecological degradation (Cao et al., 2011). However, there is little evidence that the improved ecological environment is directly related to plantation establishment (Wang et al., 2010). Particularly in arid and semi-arid regions, local governments have mainly used planted forests to combat desertification and control dust storms, but with counterproductive results (Liu et al., 2008; Yang, 2004). The problem has been that there is insufficient water to sustain the fast-growing trees that are usually chosen for such projects, which consume too much water. This both reduces their growth and makes water unavailable for other vegetation, leading to death of the other vegetation (Cao et al., 2011; Feng, Yang, et al., 2019).

Although restoration work in the field is difficult and doesn't always succeed, admitting any failures can lead to a loss of government funding. Thus, to preserve this funding, the forestry department avoids mentioning such failures and instead keeps reporting total planting and the area of the new forests in the news media (Li, 2021).

5.3.2. New Institutional Changes

Whether a government is authoritarian or democratic, the profit motive may outweigh morality, leading officials to look the other way when crimes benefit them. In a society where the power of officials is greater than the power of the law, the government can easily degenerate into a system in which the personal power of these officials lets them maximize their personal interests at the expense of the people. For example, emperors and other dictators naturally regard the state as their own private property and transfer management of the state to their children as private property after their death. Similarly, government officials will regard the administrative departments, administrative regions, and state-owned enterprises they manage as their own private property and will use them to extract benefits for themselves. They not only use the power in their hands to expand their own private interests within the framework of the system but also to change the system to make their selfish acts seem more reasonable. This may continue until the interests of the state (i.e., the people) are completely neglected. When the public grows sufficiently angry at this behavior, they will rebel to overthrow the corrupt regime, possibly through violence.

Corruption of officials has been one of the greatest problems that hinder state governance. If we don't find a way to eliminate the problem, it will continue to occur. The key to achieving this is to understand that corruption arises from a governance failure at the level of the state's institutions, and only by treating both the symptoms (corruption) and the root causes (the flawed institutions) is it possible to succeed. Because of the selfish and self-interested aspects of human nature, it's difficult for officials who are granted political power to resist the temptation of abusing their power, especially when the short-term gains from the abuse of power outweigh the long-term risks. As North (1990) and Olson (1993) observed, when policy formulation, implementation, and supervision are by the same person or department, the people involved are bound to seek personal and departmental interests under the banner of reform, thus setting up the reform for failure. Historically, reforms that fail, thereby angering the people who hoped to benefit from the reforms, have led to regime change and sometimes even the downfall of the state.

Sir John Emerich Edward Dalberg-Acton (1834–1902) famously said that "power tends to corrupt, and absolute power corrupts absolutely." The solution this suggests is to separate the powers of defining policy, implementing policy, and supervising the implementation. Unfortunately, in the Chinese government's implementation of the decentralization reforms, they created countless smaller (local) centralized systems with no supervision and relatively independent power over the law. Because the officials responsible for governance were well aware that their power was temporary, they used their unlimited power during that limited time to maximize the benefits they could obtain from corruption. According to *The People's Daily*, the central government investigated 136,307 cases of violations of the "Eight Provisions," which refer to the code of conduct for government workers established by the Chinese government in 2019. The number of people whose behavior was examined totaled 194,124, and 124,723 of these people were subjected to party discipline and government punishment (https://www.ccdi.gov.cn), which is 5.6 times the number in 2013 (Shang et al., 2019).

Humans and animals both shift from self-interested behavior to altruistic behavior when their reputation is threatened (Milinski & Rockenbach, 2007). This suggests that monitoring officials and publishing the results (i.e., shaming the perpetrators of corruption) is an effective strategy to prevent governments and government officials from abusing their power. Thus, it is essential to strengthen monitoring of government employees and the work performed by government departments. In a healthy ecosystem, the ecological balance is essential; in a government, a balance between officials and monitors must also be achieved. As the Chinese saying goes, "more birds, fewer insects."

The ideologies of a people's state proposed by Confucius and Rousseau share many characteristics. In each, the ideology emphasizes that the government must be an agent of the state (i.e., of the people) and must not become the state itself. The goal is to ensure that the government remains a representative of the people's interests rather than the organized criminal organization or the "rational robber" described by North (1990) and Olson (1993). To improve the efficiency of state governance, it's necessary to prevent government officials from abusing their power and to raise the moral standards of society so that officials know that unethical behavior will not be tolerated. Moreover, it's necessary to achieve a separation of powers (so that no individual or group controls all the power) and to implement a system of checks and balances to ensure that this separation is maintained (Fig. 10).

The decentralization reform that has been implemented by the Chinese government has been unquestionably effective from an economic perspective. However, because it lacks strong monitoring mechanisms, local governments have not been prevented from becoming corrupt. This problem can only be solved by creating a system of local self-governance with a separation of powers that includes checks and balances, especially to separate the powers of policymaking, implementation, and supervision (Fig. 10) and to ensure that those who make the policies (including plans and laws) cannot implement them and those who implement them cannot participate in policymaking. In this approach, policymaking, implementation, and supervision mutually constrain and supervise each other, thereby reducing the possibility of corruption right at the source.

In the absence of a competitive political environment (e.g., the multi-party system used by most Western democracies), the separation of powers may be an effective strategy to restrain government officials from abusing their power.

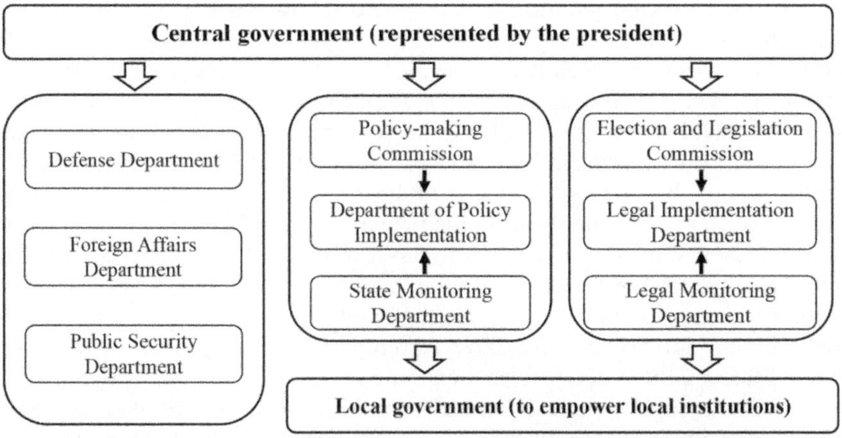

Fig. 10. A Possible National Governance Structure Designed to Provide Separation of Powers and Implement Checks and Balances in a Hypothetical People's State. *Source*: The figure is created by the author.

The new political structure described in Fig. 10 supports decentralization if it is replicated at the local scale so that local governments and administrations can continuously improve their part of the political system in response to actual conditions in their region (Cao & Ren, 2019; Zhou, 2012). The primary tasks of leaders are to maintain national security, lead the people in their response to various disasters, and supervise and manage all departments and local governments to eliminate corruption and improve efficiency. Therefore, national political leaders should not intervene in local affairs unless an emergency affects multiple regions or exceeds a region's ability to respond. Intervention may also be necessary when corruption that cannot be solved locally is revealed. To improve the government's emergency response capability, the government should collectively decide on whether it's necessary to grant the leader the power to respond rapidly to a crisis rather than waiting for the standard government processes to operate.

To ensure that local governments promote innovation and support socioeconomic development, the policy formulation and supervision departments of the central government should evaluate the work of local governments sufficiently frequently that they can detect and correct problems before they become serious or expand to affect other regions. When local governments succeed, they should share their experience so that others can benefit from their success. For example, the 110 alarm system (i.e., the development of an emergency police response system based on phoning a single central number, 110) was established by the Guangzhou Public Security Bureau in 1986 and later became the standard mechanism for the public security system. China's experience has proved that cooperation between the policymaking departments and local governments to carry out tests of new institutions on a small scale is an effective means of institutional progress. I will discuss institutional evolution in more detail in Chapter 9.

The state and legal monitoring departments shown in Fig. 10 represent the means by which the people can ensure that the government is monitored. This restores a situation in which the people are the masters of the country. However, given China's enormous population, there must also be some constraints on the public. It would not be feasible, for example, for every citizen to have the right to monitor every government official's behavior on a daily basis. In addition, the sometimes horrible abuses that occurred during the Cultural Revolution period remind us of the dangers of giving the people too much power. To increase the effectiveness of supervision, it will be necessary to reward those who monitor and report corruption, but to do so within a legal and institutional framework that preserves fairness for officials who are accused of corruption, since not all accusations will be valid. For example, those who report corruption could be rewarded with a share of the money stolen by a corrupt official once the magnitude of the theft has been determined. The US Internal Revenue Service offers a similar reward program for citizens who report tax fraud (IRS, 2022). This and other rewards would make the fight against corruption an enviable and respectable job that would benefit both society and individuals.

To prevent a recurrence of the tragedy of the Cultural Revolution's abuse of the people's power, a healthy, robust, and secure judicial system must be established as the foundation of the people's oversight to guarantee social stability. It is very important to build a legal mechanism for people's supervision that ensures the use of legal means rather than violence. The people's supervision under a legal framework supports the philosophy that the people are the masters of the country, and it can also reduce the cost of central government supervision of officials, making it a win–win path. Restoring and maintaining the primacy of law over power is the institutional foundation of a civilized society. Governments should work with sociologists, legal specialists, and other experts to study potential ways to achieve this solution.

To improve the quality and efficiency of government officials and the managers of state-owned enterprises or institutes, and to stop corruption, the central government should learn from the successful use of the imperial examination system in ancient China and conduct a nationwide unified examination for civil servants and employees of state-owned enterprises and, to ensure that these individuals maintain a high level of competence, repeat these exams at frequent intervals, such as every four years or only when someone applies for a promotion to a more powerful position. Similarly, local governments and state-owned enterprises should be required to evaluate civil servants and promote only the best personnel to administrative positions. This would, on the one hand, encourage civil servants to form good habits of lifelong learning to meet the requirements of fast-developing modernization; on the other hand, it would minimize the corruption that results from nepotism and the buying and selling of government services. To prevent cheating on examinations, public service examinations should be organized and monitored by the central government to prevent local governments from falsifying the results.

At this point, I caution readers against the logical error of assuming that any problem has only two sides (binary thinking), and that if one side is right, the other side is wrong. For example, it's tempting to suggest that an autocratic system is wrong and a democratic system is right. The actual situation may be more complicated. For example, although the democratic system may be more equitable and effective under normal circumstances, an autocratic leader can respond faster in a crisis – and the response may be equally effective if the leader is well advised by experts. Although I've noted the necessity of protecting each citizen's rights, governance is a complex discipline, and the inevitable information asymmetry means that most people have less knowledge of a country's political status than the officials who are managing the country and therefore cannot make equally accurate judgments of the situation. If their power is unrestrained, the people may change from guardians of the state to a dangerous rabble. This is the greatest lesson of the Cultural Revolution for the people of China and the world. It's also necessary to ensure that the people are well informed through clear, complete, and honest communication to avoid polarization of opinions (as has occurred in the United States due to targeted disinformation campaigns) and ensure that the people have the information they need to make a rational decision. Achieving this goal is a difficult problem that has not yet been solved.

Another example of avoiding binary thinking is how nations respond to a disaster or other crisis. It's necessary for someone to have the knowledge, support, and power to act quickly, while also finding ways to bring the people together to produce a powerful collective response. In practice, both are necessary for a successful response. One problem with democratic systems is that they often elect leaders who are skillful actors but not skillful administrators. Ideally, a democracy should be a meritocracy, in which the most skillful and knowledgeable individuals are elected. For example, allowing experienced politicians to run for leadership positions can minimize the harm caused by political amateurs. Thus far, no such system has been used by a nation, although the Confucian system of examinations to select the best government officials may provide some guidance.

Asking candidates for government positions to engage with social, political, and economic experts to demonstrate their knowledge and their suitability for the position might also help. However, as I have noted in previous chapters, any such proposal should be tested carefully on a small scale to ensure that it works before expanding the method to an entire country. The method should also be flexible to ensure that local governments can adapt it to account for their unique local conditions.

Chapter 6

Economic Development and Social Equity

If the majority of the governed people don't accept a system, the system will not work well or for a long time. This is particularly true for a nation's institutions. This insight can guide us toward a different definition of a nation: *a complex social unit in which individuals, companies, and social groups in a self-governed space share internal resources and govern themselves under a series of institutional constraints (e.g., laws, cultures, customs) based on a shared ideology*. Historical experience has repeatedly demonstrated that the willingness of ordinary people to participate in social cooperation is driven by their belief in the benefits to be gained through this cooperation. Government officials are no exception. No one wants to do something that is unprofitable. Therefore, when a government proposes a new system or reforms the old system, it must ensure that everyone can benefit from the changes or that anyone who loses benefits is fairly compensated for their loss if they hope to avoid strong resistance or even revolution.

However, no matter how strong a nation, its government must convince the people that its rule will bring them benefits. When institutions are perceived as being unprofitable, people will circumvent the institutional constraints by both legal means (e.g., by seeking loopholes in a law) and illegal means (e.g., stealing, violence, bribery). They may even overthrow the existing regime by violent revolution. In June 2010, a 56-year-old Chinese farmer obtained a government contract to manage 1.7 ha of land to raise fish and cattle until 2029. However, the local government sought to gain more benefits from the land through real estate development, so they invalidated the contract and sent public security personnel to forcibly recover the land. The farmer confronted these officials using homemade cannons (https://www.badassoftheweek.com/yang). Eventually, the farmer persuaded the government to restore the contract with the help of lawyers. This extreme event demonstrates the importance of institutional fairness.

Because economic monopolies and monopolistic benefits (natural or man-made) are as attractive to governments as they are to individuals and groups, politicians will try to avoid the loss of their monopolistic economic activities, such as controlling an economic sector or business so that the government owns all of its income and is not required to tax the sector or business. Historically, governments have used their position to monopolize information resources to distort the market and even to maximize their profits through informal mechanisms

A New Stage of Civilization: Striving for the Great Harmony, 147–175

Published under exclusive licence by Emerald Publishing Limited
doi:10.1108/978-1-83708-258-220251007

such as bribery and confiscation of property (Olson, 1993). Because governments have more information than other individuals and groups (e.g., they have or can obtain access to information unavailable to other participants in markets, including through insider trading), their benefits can outweigh the benefits they would obtain from a perfectly competitive market (Myerson, 2011).

When economic development is the focus of national policies, local governments are often required to allocate their tax revenues to achieve this development goal; it leaves less money (or no money) available to meet the goals of local governments. This forces local governments to find other ways to support their economic operations, such as maintaining economic development at the expense of local residents or the environment. This may even include confiscation of valuable land or a forced sale of the land to the government at below market prices so the land can be sold at a higher price to developers (Cao et al., 2024). Political monopolies provide the power base for economic monopolies, and all governments tend to seek a monopoly; sometimes this is to improve their profits and sometimes it is for the sake of efficiency. For example, this may be the case for key infrastructure industries (such as transportation and communications) and for social service industries (such as medical care and basic education). However, not all economic activity works best as a monopoly, since monopolies discourage competition and innovation. Thus, market competition may be a superior solution in many cases. At the same time, the potential economic value of scientific research makes politicians willing to spend more money and time to obtain these benefits; this also encourages risky but potentially highly profitable research that private investors are unwilling to fund.

However, there will always be certain resources that are constrained by political and geographical constraints or by institutional constraints (such as unclear property rights for shared resources) that prevent individuals or small groups from utilizing these resources. An active government can guarantee equitable resource utilization and economic development but also provides the basis for rallying the people, expanding resource development, and realizing national political goals. In terms of resource allocation (especially large-scale resource allocation), the relative roles of the government and the market remain a topic of debate in economics. Nonetheless, the role of the government in economic construction cannot be ignored.

6.1. Construction of a National Economy

For a nation, a healthy economy is the basis for achieving political goals, as economic interests are an important part of national goals. Sima Qian (145–87 BCE), a famous historian of the Western Han Dynasty (202 BCE–8 CE), summarized Chinese history by writing that China's vigorous economy resulted from everyone seeking profits. His words explain the behavior of individuals and governments well. They also described the needs of both individuals and countries and noted that personal needs must be met first. Nobody can survive without food, and in many climates, clothing is essential for survival. Thus, both needs must be met first, because if an individual cannot survive, they cannot pursue other objectives. Different preferences require different economic strategies, with some people paying more attention to long-term returns and others paying more attention to immediate benefits. This is not only an economic problem but also a philosophical problem. It is also a pragmatic problem, since governments must simultaneously satisfy both short-term and long-term needs through governance.

Philosophers such as Jean-Jacques Rousseau (1712–1778 CE) and Confucius (551–479 BCE) preferred a more moderate view of the economic behavior of a nation, which they considered to be an economic organization in which the government provides services to the common people in exchange for taxes. This ignores the role of the nation in allocating resources, the dynamic role of the nation in seeking profits, and the frequency of greedy, self-interested politicians. Therefore, whether a nation is the Republic proposed by Jean-Jacques Rousseau or the *great harmony* proposed by Confucius, the beautiful aspirations of a state that serves its people require human effort to achieve.

When resources are in short supply, governments and people are forced to seek new alternatives, including exploration, finding and developing new resources, innovating new technologies to make more efficient use of existing resources, and developing new management models and institutions to improve the efficiency of resource use (Cao et al., 2007). These responses can happen either passively (in response to a crisis) or actively (to prepare for a predicted future crisis). New forms of social development represent responses to real or potential crises and eventually lead to changes in social systems. Such institutional evolution has promoted the formation of an increasingly strong and efficient centralized bureaucracy and has improved a nation's ability to mobilize resources on a large scale. This evolution often led to the formation of specific bureaucracies to manage the allocation of specific resources, as in the case of implementing irrigation projects to increase agricultural productivity, the development of a military to defend against invasion, and the construction and maintenance of a national transportation systems to facilitate transport of resources such as food from regions with a surplus to regions with insufficient food. At the same time, the successful allocation and maintenance of resources further strengthened the political position of the government because it clearly met the needs of the people and maintained the unity of the people and the nation.

The private sector generally lacks the capacity to coordinate large cross-regional resource mobilization and lacks an incentive to invest in areas with no direct economic returns or with returns only after a long time. Therefore, if a nation wants to improve its development level, it must rely on national power to promote investment in areas with a long delay before the investment achieves an economic return (such as infrastructure construction) and unprofitable aspects of the public sector (such as the military). As a result, large-scale resource allocation projects often require a large national investment. Weak nations that cannot provide these services must obtain assistance from stronger nations or nongovernmental agencies such as the United Nations to gradually improve their resource allocation capacity or must offer multinational enterprises the opportunity to develop the required resource in exchange for a profit from their investments. Without improving access to resources, a nation will gradually be dominated by other nations that are more effective in international competition.

6.1.1. Expensive Political Costs

In late 2014, millions tuned in to watch the 44th President of the United States, Barack Obama, debate his main rival, Mitt Romney. The world's news media and advertisers earn a lot of money from such television broadcasts and other forms of news coverage. BBC News estimated that politicians spent nearly US$6 billion during the presidential election campaign (bbc.co.uk/news/magazine-19052054). This is likely to have been the most expensive political campaign in human history. However, this outlay is dwarfed by national military expenditures and other areas of government spending such as the State Department. Statistics from the Stockholm International Peace Research Institute showed that the global military expenditure in 2021 exceeded US$$2.1 \times 10^{12}$ (Liang et al., 2021). Obviously, both the election process and government expenditures need huge financial support to maintain their operations. Maintaining the inputs and outputs required by these operations is an important part of a country's economic strategy.

For an individual or political group, living beyond their means not only fails to meet their long-term needs but also provides opportunities for greedy and unethical individuals to exploit them. If a state turns a blind eye to maintaining healthy economic processes, their future becomes dim. Some historians are keen to document the actions of monarchs and other leaders but are sometimes indifferent to the economic forces behind them. Some economists describe the economic processes of a society in detail but sometimes ignore the role of the government behind these processes. There are clearly tight relationships between politics, including the selfish or selfless goals of politicians, and the historical processes that have led to a nation's current socioeconomic situation. No matter how complicated the political events, there are always economic interests behind them. Therefore, it is not enough for politicians to focus on political events that are reported by the news media, such as military conflicts. Politicians must also understand the economic laws that govern how a nation functions before they can attempt to manage the nation sustainably.

Olson (1993) pointed out that political leaders maximize their own interests through their monopoly on coercive power and their ability to control the allocation of tax revenues. They treat their citizens the way ranchers protect and feed their livestock and thus make a continuous profit. Unfortunately, this does not represent a sound economic strategy. Moreover, the reality is far more complex than Olson's description. For a government, the best choice is to achieve national stability and development by maximizing returns on investment (whether long-term investments like a military or short-term measures such as taxation); success usually depends on simultaneously accounting for a range of short-term and long-term economic goals. This has advantages over focusing only on tax revenues because this approach directly increases the government's governance benefits and helps to maintain its authority. Therefore, participation in economic development is a popular governance strategy for modern governments.

The size of a nation's political influence depends on the constraints imposed by its technical and managerial efficiency. (In this book, I will define *technical innovation* as an improvement of techniques rather than technology. For simplicity,

I will use the phrase "technological innovation" to refer to both technique and technology.) Early nations and today's developing nations are limited by low management (governance) efficiency and immature technology, and this slows their political and economic development, particularly in remote regions (Spencer, 2010). Despite these limitations, the economic tentacles of modern developed countries such as the United States can touch any corner of the Earth (Cao, 2017).

6.1.2. Allocation of Resources by Nations

Early society had a limited understanding of the economics of how nations operate, so early nations focused on the balance between taxation and spending. Even so, monopolies over scarce resources brought substantial benefits to some early nations, which undoubtedly attracted the covetous eye of other nations. Where the nation that controlled the resource was unwilling to engage in fair trade with nations that required that resource, this often led to wars over control of these resources and forced leaders to learn more about economics to support aggression or defense.

At least as early as the third century BCE, Chinese politicians during the Spring and Autumn and Warring States periods (770–221 BCE) recognized the importance of economic development and actively carried out economic development and management projects. For example, in 256 BCE, the rulers of the Qin vassal state (770–207 BCE) invested a huge amount of money in the construction of the Dujiangyan irrigation system, which is still in operation today. The irrigation system passed through the Chengdu Plain to support farmers who were needed to grow and then transport a continuous supply of food to imperial soldiers who protected the nation's borders. The water also ensured food security for the imperial people and laid the economic foundation for the Qin to unify China. Dujiangyan is the oldest and longest-running water conservation and translocation project in the world. It has been in operation for nearly 2,300 years and is still important today. It has protected more than 600,000 ha of the Chengdu Plain from floods and droughts, and the vast area of rich land around the canal continues to nourish the local people.

The benefits of more efficient and equitable resource allocation are that it boosts production and raises short-term tax revenues, and it has long-term effects (such as increased future tax revenues) that make it attractive to far-sighted politicians. However, any economic activity has a time-lag effect, and resource allocation projects must be based on the understanding that benefits may take some time to appear. This requires governments to balance long-term investments with short-term needs to ensure that the people remain willing to support the long-term project. This can be difficult to achieve, and failures affect more people (e.g., a whole nation) than the failure of an enterprise. For example, in 605 CE, Yang Guang (569–618 CE), the second emperor of China's Sui Dynasty (581–618 CE), invested heavily in expanding the canal by about 1,000 km, thereby linking China's Yangtze and Yellow rivers. The 1,794-km Beijing–Hangzhou Grand Canal has been expanded and maintained by the Chinese people for more than 2,000 years. It has become the main water transportation channel in China's interior and a major component of the eastern route of the South-to-North Water Diversion

Project. This enormous project, which is still used for water transportation in China, drained the empire's finances and the Sui Dynasty quickly collapsed.

Archaeological evidence suggests that Chinese politicians began building water diversion projects much earlier than the Dujiangyan irrigation system. For example, the ancient city of Liangzhu (founded in 3300 BCE) in Yuhang District of Hangzhou City, in Zhejiang Province, has a large-scale water conservancy project that has existed for more than 5,000 years (Azzam & Kong, 2021). This complex hydraulic engineering system included 1 dam, 1 reservoir, and 11 dikes. This shows how nations can be more than a machine for dealing with war and can also deal with resource shortages to improve livelihoods.

6.1.3. International Political Balance

Because governments are primarily responsible for the well-being of their people, and governments of other countries may have different objectives for their people, governments have always been required to invest in the development of a military service. Within a nation, the government is generally operated by a leader and an assembly of politicians whose policies are implemented by a bureaucracy; together, they represent a state monopoly on power. However, all nations are affected by the actions of other nations, and this leads to competition in the international political marketplace. In modern society, this is not a truly "free" market; it is influenced by the balance of international political power. Moreover, the balance of power is not determined solely by a nation's economic strength. Many powerful nations also support a strong military system to protect themselves against military interventions by other countries and provide the option of controlling other countries through the threat of invasion. The situation is further complicated by lobbyists, who try to persuade government officials (through logic or bribes) to influence government decisions. Furthermore, governments negotiate treaties with other governments, including both public and private negotiations, and the news media selectively report a subset of the information about these negotiations to induce public support for or opposition to the government.

Unlike the nation itself, the nation's political and economic influence are not constrained by geographical boundaries; nations such as the United States and China exert their political power throughout the world. Thus, a modern nation is free to try to increase its economic power and its influence over other nations. Globalization has increased the reach of a nation's political and economic activities to every corner of the globe. The aerospace industry has even extended this reach into orbit around the Earth and may eventually extend it to other planets. Driven by a nation's own interests, the nation's economic development strongly supports technological innovations and scientific research, as it expects that new technologies and research breakthroughs will promote its industrial development, increase its future earnings, and expand its global influence by improving its ability to compete with other nations. Unlike the private sector, a government is willing to support research into uncharted areas that require huge investments without immediate economic returns, such as the Chinese government's plan to spend 1.3×10^{12} RMB annually on space exploration (Wang & Jiang, 2006).

To protect economically valuable resources from encroachment by competing nations, the nations that control these resources develop effective defense mechanisms. Many of these mechanisms are military, and this has led to a global arms race. Fortunately, there is a good side to this race, as many military technologies have important peaceful applications. For example, Internet communication is the product of the Cold War arms race, and the satellite technologies pioneered by the military have had many applications in civilian remote sensing. Historically, the arms race has not only been an important engine for the development of a country's defense industry but has also driven technological progress and industrial development in many other economic sectors. The Union of Concerned Scientists reported that as of May 1, 2022, only 577 of the 5,465 satellites orbiting the Earth were military satellites (https://www.ucsusa.org/resources/satellite-database); the rest were providing citizens with education, news, communications, and scientific research services. Despite the nominal benefits of defense spending, a nation must be able to afford the investment. For example, the Soviet Union invested billions of dollars in the construction of aircraft carriers, but when the Soviet Union collapsed, successor governments such as Ukraine could not afford to operate such expensive equipment, and Ukraine was forced to sell one of its aircraft carriers, the Varyag, to China in 2011. Subsequently, after a series of refits, the vessel became China's first aircraft carrier, the Liaoning (https://www.baidu.com), and was put to work protecting China's homeland security.

The governments of most modern nations have realized the importance of economic development, and economic management has become the government's primary work. For monopolistic industries, government intervention can be an effective strategy to avoid widening the wealth gap and promoting social unrest. For example, the Chinese government's intervention in the health system has made health care affordable for most of its citizens (Chen, 2005). However, for non-monopoly industries, competition is a more valuable way to promote innovation and efficiency, so government intervention often has a negative impact, such as distorting resource allocations in the high-tech sectors (Xia, 2021). I discuss this in Chapter 3. The lack of competition is one of the important reasons for the setback of communism globally. Today, many developing nations adopt a centralized system that concentrates wealth in the hands of so-called elites rather than distributing wealth to the people to promote their productive activities and improve their quality of life, and this monopolistic power limits market competition and opportunities for economic development. The result is continuing sluggish economic growth in many developing countries (Mabogunje, 2000).

The end of the Cold War and the rise of globalization vividly illustrate that global political changes can also affect a nation's self-image and its role in the world economy (Cederman, 2002). Since its reform and opening up to the West, China has transformed from an underdeveloped nation dominated by Mao Zedong's ideology and communist revolution as its core value into a world power that has actively and peacefully extended its economic influence across the globe. This change is the result of promoting the social responsibility of its citizens and their voluntary participation in economic activities, which have been key components of the nation's successful social and economic development (Krasner, 2011). Globalization has spread the influence of a nation's economic power around the world and, in the future, may extend this influence into Earth orbit and even to other planets, far beyond the borders of the nations where it was born.

6.2. The Issue of Poverty

Poverty is a long-term problem that plagues the development of society. Due to differences in politics (Zhang et al., 2020), geography (Achten & Lessmann, 2020), education (Hendel et al., 2005), and government policies (Song, 2013), the levels of social and economic development differ greatly around the world (Li, Cai, et al., 2021). World Bank (2019) reported the per capita disposable income of Switzerland in 2019 was US$66,499, which equaled 317 times that of Burundi. Poverty can be divided into absolute poverty (based on the minimum income required for survival) and relative poverty (the income gap between individuals in different socioeconomic categories or regions). The essence of both forms of poverty is the problem of income inequality and an unfair social distribution of wealth (Liu & Xu, 2016; Nguyen et al., 2020). World Bank (2018) pointed out that about 10% of the global population still lives in absolute poverty, and eradicating poverty should be the common mission of humanity (Khan, 2008; Shi et al., 2020).

In 2000, the United Nations proposed the Millennium Development Goals (Sachs & McArthur, 2005), which aim to eradicate poverty by helping the poorest regions of the world increase income and food security of the poorest individuals, especially in Africa (Dalgaard & Erickson, 2009). The plan aims to address poverty by improving local education (Sachs & McArthur, 2005), increasing investment in infrastructure (Fay et al., 2005), and improving public health (Syairudin et al., 2015), but thus far, there has been little success (Cuenca-García et al., 2019). In the past 20 years, the development differences between regions have not narrowed; on the contrary, the gap has widened (Gohou & Soumare, 2012; Kouadio & Gakpa, 2021). For example, from 2000 to 2020, the income gap between Europe and Africa increased to 1.8 times the 2000 level (World Bank, 2021).

6.2.1. Relative Poverty

Many scholars understand poverty as an economic problem, but this is a one-sided perspective. In practice, poverty is a political problem first, and an economic problem second. In the *Jishi* chapter of *The Analects of Confucius*, Confucius wrote that an unfair distribution of wealth (relative poverty) is more dangerous for a nation than a lack of wealth (absolute poverty) because it is more likely to create social unrest. Confucius reminds us of a basic rule for any government: the ultimate goal of governance is to enrich the nation so that it can keep the people safe. To achieve this goal, we must seek ways to achieve a fair social distribution of wealth while developing the economy to generate more wealth, thereby mitigating to the greatest extent possible the social problems caused by a widening income gap and safeguarding national security and stability.

Confucius died nearly 2,500 years ago, but the problem of a widening gap between the rich and the poor has not been solved; on the contrary, it is getting worse (Katikireddi & Dundas, 2017; Whalley & Yue, 2009). Under this system, China's economy grew rapidly, and China changed from a country with a very small gap between the rich and the poor to a country with a very large gap (Sutherland & Yao, 2011; Xian & Zhou, 2014; Zhang, 2016). According to *China People's Livelihood Development Report 2014*, the Gini coefficient based on a Chinese family's net worth (tangible property plus savings) was 0.45 in 1995, 0.55 in 2002, and 0.73 in 2012 (Shang et al., 2019). (The Gini coefficient is a commonly used index that measures the income gap between the rich and the poor in a country or region; the maximum value is 1 and the minimum value is 0. The closer the Gini coefficient is to 0, the lower the inequality and thus the more equal the income distribution. Generally speaking, a Gini coefficient between 0.3 and 0.4 is considered to be reasonable.) In 2009, 95% of China's wealth was held by the wealthiest 5% of families, versus only 60% in the United States. The wealthiest 1% of the population earned 33% of the total income of Chinese residents, versus only 1% for the poorest families, who represent 25% of the population (Gradín & Wu, 2020; Shang et al., 2019).

Butzer (2012) showed that the widening gap between the rich and the poor will aggravate jealousy and feelings of injustice and will lead to resentment or hatred of the rich that will promote an increase in the frequency of crimes such as theft and robbery, and the resulting serious social problems will lead to additional unrest. History suggests that if this unrest becomes sufficiently serious, it may lead to revolution and even regime change. As I noted above, relative poverty is more likely than absolute poverty to cause social divisions and may reduce a country's ability to cope with risks (Alderman & Paxson, 1992), aggravate social inequality (O'Boyle, 2003), hinder regional economic growth (Wang, 2006), and endanger regional peace and stability. The expansion of relative poverty caused by an unfair social distribution of wealth is a common social phenomenon that accompanies economic growth (Heshmati, 2007). Historically, most social unrest in China arose from an unfair distribution of wealth and a continuously widening gap between the rich and the poor. This gap leaves the poor with less ability to purchase consumer goods, which reduces market demand and causes the economy to slow its growth or even shrink. This can lead to excessive supply, leading to a range of economic crises that challenge the sustainable development of society. Understanding the causes of relative poverty and trying to prevent the income gap from widening is therefore one of the core issues of development economics.

Li, Cai, et al. (2021) found that trade competition can mitigate the constraints of regional resources, promote economic development, and increase personal income (Bastos, 2020). Unfortunately, free markets often lead to monopolies with excessive concentration of resources, thereby exacerbating the harm caused by unbalanced regional development (Tian et al., 2019). The expansion of income differences between regions has promoted migration of workers to more prosperous regions and to population agglomeration, and the influx of large numbers of people into high-income areas (i.e., a loss of workers in the less prosperous region) has exacerbated the harm caused by geographical and economic differences

(Fleisher et al., 2010). Therefore, China's central government should take strong measures to limit the development of monopolies. One successful solution to the monopoly problem has been the implementation of regulations that reduce the ability of enterprises to form monopolies; in the United States, this is covered by three "anti-trust" acts (USA, 1890).

Since 1978, China's gross domestic product (GDP) has grown at an average annual rate of about 10% (China Statistics Agency, 1979–2021). Along with this economic growth, the gap between urban and rural areas has continued to widen. The per capita income gap between urban and rural residents increased from 167 RMB in 1978 to 26,703 RMB in 2020, and the urban-to-rural income ratio increased from 2.6:1 in 1978 to 3.2:1 in 2020 (China Statistics Agency, 1979–2021). The gap between urban and rural areas is not only manifested in income but also in politics, culture, medical care, and welfare.

Due to differences in income and employment opportunities and other factors, the income gaps between the rich and the poor and between rural and urban residents is widening (Cao et al., 2009b). When an individual or family falls into persistent poverty and cannot escape, scholars call this state the "poverty trap" (Katikireddi & Dundas, 2017; Whalley & Yue, 2009). As I noted earlier in this chapter, the inequality between the rich and the poor is swallowing the fruits of China's economic growth and threatening national stability and possibly even its government. Relative poverty is exacerbating these problems, so the unfair distribution of wealth between urban and rural residents and between the rich and the poor is a particularly serious concern.

6.2.2. Political Poverty

In most market-oriented countries, urbanization can significantly narrow the income gap between urban and rural areas (Su et al., 2015; Yuan et al., 2020) and can promote fairer social development. However, China's situation is special. During Mao Zedong's reign, Chinese residents were divided into different classes for urban and rural residents. These classes enjoyed different social welfare benefits (discussed in subsequent sections). Starting on January 1, 1958, the Chinese government implemented the *Household Registration Law*, which defined the status of urban and rural residents at birth and imposed a hereditary system for this status (Lin, 2002; Zhao, 2006). The benefits a citizen is entitled to depend on this status. For example, farmers are born as rural residents, and even if they move to a city, they cannot change their status. Because they cannot register as urban residents, they are denied access to the same social welfare benefits that urban residents receive simply because they were born in a city; as a result, immigrants sacrifice their access to free medical care, education for their children, and unemployment insurance (Cao et al., 2009b). They also receive much smaller pensions when they retire.

An even more regressive practice was that when rural residents migrated to a city without the government's permission, they were formerly required to pay a fee of 200 RMB to the local government every year so that they could continue to live in the city (Borooah et al., 2006). In 2004, this cost was equivalent to 6.6%

of the per capita net income of rural residents (China Statistics Agency, 2005). Although the central government banned these fees after 2004, rural residents still lack access to the same welfare services as urban residents after they move to cities. They also lack political power that would let them change this situation. Although rural residents in China accounted for 69.5% of the number of delegates eligible to attend the first 13 national congresses from 1954 to 2018 (China Statistics Agency, 1955–2021), they only accounted for 11.9% of the chosen delegates (Table 2). This represents inadequate representation and ensures that the rights and interests of rural residents can't be guaranteed naturally through fair participation in these meetings (Cao et al., 2009b).

Cao et al. (2009b) noted that although urban residents accounted for less than 35% of China's total population in 2008, urban education expenditures accounted for 77% of China's total education expenditure. At the same time, only 15% of college students came from rural areas, even though these areas accounted for 65% of the total population. As a result of government efforts to improve the basic education of citizens, the proportion of Chinese urban residents with a high school education increased from 40% in 1985 to 55% in 1999, but the proportion in rural areas decreased from 22% to 19%. In addition, there were insufficient teachers in rural areas. The number of rural primary school students in 1999 accounted for 88.2% of the total number of primary school students in China, but the number of rural teachers accounted for only 43.1% of the total number of primary school teachers (Blumenthal & Hsiao, 2005). Another problem is a lack of time to attend school. To help earn a living for their families, rural children frequently have to work in the fields, which reduces their study time. This puts them at a disadvantage compared to urban students, who lack such duties. Therefore, the average education level (years of schooling) of rural residents was only 55.6% of that of urban residents from 1978 to 2019 (China Statistics Agency, 1979–2020). Because of the lack of employment opportunities in rural areas, most students stay in cities to work after they graduate from college or university, and the gap between urban and rural education levels is increasing.

From 1952 to 2004, rural residents accounted for an average of 76.6% of the total population but received only 23.4% of China's total social welfare expenditure, and urban residents enjoyed the remaining 76.6% of this expenditure (China Statistics Agency, 1979–2020). In 2004, 8.3×10^6 registered urban unemployed residents were eligible for government unemployment subsidies, but 150×10^6 rural unemployed people did not receive any subsidies. Urban residents also receive a retirement pension, but rural residents can't enjoy these and other benefits (Cao et al., 2009b). Because they receive little or no social welfare support, the rural elderly who lose their ability to work are the most vulnerable group in China and have been largely forgotten by Chinese society.

Dummer and Cook (2007) found that in 2004, the average annual disposable income of rural residents in China were 3,027 RMB, and the per capita medical expenses of rural residents was 2,349 RMB (accounting for 77.6% of their total income). As a result, 62.3% of rural patients did not have enough money to see a doctor, and 24.3% of rural families were forced into debt because they could not afford to pay for treatment of serious diseases. In contrast, the medical expenses

Table 2. Representation of Rural Representatives at Meetings of China's National People's Congress From 1954 to 2018.

Meeting	Year	Number of Representatives				
		Attendance (No. of Delegates)	Rural Representatives		Population of China (×10^6)	Rural Proportion of Population (%)
			No. of Delegates	Proportion of Total Attendance (%)		
1st session	1954	1,226	63	5.14	520.17	86.31
2nd session	1959	1,226	67	5.46	548.36	81.59
3rd session	1964	3,040	209	6.87	575.49	81.63
4th session	1975	2,885	662	22.90	763.90	82.66
5th session	1978	3,497	720	20.59	790.14	82.08
6th session	1983	2,978	348	11.70	807.34	78.38
7th session	1988	2,978	685	23.00	823.65	74.19
8th session	1993	2,978	280	9.40	853.44	72.01
9th session	1998	2,979	240	8.00	831.53	66.65
10th session	2003	2,988	276	9.24	768.51	59.47
11th session	2008	2,985	275	9.21	692.68	52.16
12th session	2013	2,987	201	6.73	622.24	45.51
13th session	2018	2,980	234	7.85	564.01	40.42
Average				11.92		69.47

of urban residents are usually paid by the government. As a result, the infant mortality rate in rural areas is 2.4 times that of cities (Cook & Dummer, 2004). Finally, 360×10^6 people in rural areas lacked access to clean drinking water in 2003 (Gustafsson & Li, 2004). Since 2003, the lack of social welfare in China's rural areas has gradually attracted the attention of the central government. The government has worked with local governments to provide a medical subsidy of 20 RMB per person per year for farmers in the central and western regions. Given the statistics earlier in this paragraph, this was clearly inadequate. In 2011, the subsidy was raised to 200 RMB, and in 2020, rural medical costs will be almost fully covered; the central and local government will cover 70%–90% of the medical expenses of rural residents. Chinese farmers will finally get welfare benefits similar to those of urban residents in terms of medical treatment. However, the gaps in employment and education have not been addressed.

Not all taxes are direct and obvious. To support China's industrialization, the Chinese government has kept the price of agricultural products at a very low level so that urban workers can support themselves and their families while earning relatively low wages. Unfortunately, this artificially suppresses farmer income. Low wages reduce the cost of industrial products and increase the competitiveness of Chinese manufacturers in international markets, but the downward pressure on food prices makes it harder for farmers to survive. The Chinese government is aware of this problem, and that reducing farmer income lets industry lower its prices and increase its profits. Despite the benefits for industry, this becomes an invisible tax on farmers because it forces them to sell their crops at prices lower than fair market value. This approach harms poor farmers, and since a large proportion of the rural residents are farmers, this means that rural residents have been unable to extricate themselves from poverty. Controlling the price of agricultural products isn't a new phenomenon; it was famously described by the first Soviet leader, Joseph Vissarionovich Stalin (1878–1953), and it has been a common problem in all industrialized countries (Jarvis, 2016).

The Chinese government collected more than 5×10^{12} RMB from farmers through implicit agricultural taxes, which is equivalent to 29.2% of the government's total tax revenues of 17.1×10^{12} RMB from 1950 to 2004 (Zeng, 2004). At the same time, local governments have reclaimed farmland for urban construction while paying the dispossessed farmers a very low price. In 2017 alone, the invisible tax revenue from these land sales reached 5.21×10^{12} RMB, which is 40 times the value of 0.13×10^{12} RMB in 2001 (Cai et al., 2019). This taxation exacerbates the poverty of Chinese farmers, particularly when they have no other land to farm and no opportunities for additional employment. Si (2005) found that from 1990 to 2000, the per capita disposable income of urban residents averaged 3.2 times that of rural residents, but the personal income tax of the relatively wealthy urban residents averaged 39 RMB per person per year, versus 154 RMB for rural residents (a ratio of 1:3.9). The tax burden (the tax rate as a proportion of per capita disposable income) on rural residents was therefore $3.2 \times 3.9 = 12.5$ times that of urban residents. Since 2004, the Chinese government has gradually abolished the agricultural tax, but the invisible tax caused by fixed prices has not decreased.

Due to a lack of funds and teachers, rural areas naturally have weaker educational systems than better-funded urban systems (Brown & Park, 2002). Rural residents who move to cities to find work often find that they lack sufficient skills for the jobs that pay a good salary and can only accept low-income jobs such as manual labor. The resulting low income exacerbates the poverty problem for this group of people. Compared with urban residents, rural residents must pay more to bring their children's education up to the same standards as an urban education. For example, the poorest fifth of families in China spend 14.2% of their annual income on education, versus only 5.5% for the richest fifth (Fang et al., 2002). Over the past 70 years, the educational gap between urban and rural areas in China has not changed, further increasing the poverty risk of rural residents (de Gregorio & Lee, 2002).

Inequalities also lead to health problems. Health is not only a direct component of human well-being but also a promoter of human capital because health improves an individual's ability to work. Disease reduces a person's productivity (Bloom & Canning, 2003). Ancient health problems such as schistosomiasis and tuberculosis combine with more modern problems such as AIDS, respiratory diseases such as influenza and COVID-19, and avian flu (which infects birds but often spreads to humans) seriously threaten the health and well-being of China's rural residents (Dummer & Cook, 2007). These factors combine to reduce the income of rural residents (Ravallion & Chen, 2007). Compared with urban residents, rural families find it harder to recover from diseases. Illness not only causes them to lose their ability to work but also causes them to miss opportunities to increase their income, and both factors widen the income gap between urban and rural residents (Bloom & Canning, 2000). This, in turn, reduces their access to health care and increases their risk of subsequent disease. This vicious circle leads to a continuous decline of the quality of life of rural residents who are unprotected from the burden of disease (Ravallion & Chen, 2007).

Experience shows that income inequality is not a necessary condition for economic growth (Deininger & Squire, 1996; Parker et al., 2008). On the contrary, serious inequality can become a huge obstacle to sustainable development. An urban-to-rural income ratio below 1.5 (Zhang & Wan, 2006) is an internationally recognized threshold for equity; larger ratios mean increasing inequity. In 2020, the Chinese ratio was 3.2 (China Statistics Agency, 2021), which is 2.1 times the equitable level. The factors discussed earlier in this section trap the rural poor in poverty, since they cannot afford to go elsewhere, whereas the rich can choose to emigrate or study abroad to further improve their advantage over the poor. (I discuss this in more detail in Chapter 3.) Since 2010, China's economic growth rate has remained high but has decreased steadily (China Statistics Agency, 2011–2022), and the Chinese government announced that the economy had entered a "new normal," with slower growth.

6.2.3. China's Experience and Lessons

Since 1978, China has made remarkable achievements in reducing absolute poverty, but as my analysis earlier in the chapter shows, it has not succeeded in eliminating relative poverty. Due to the lack of equal political participation by the representatives (spokespersons) of rural residents, the interests of farmers have been either ignored or given less attention than the interests of urbanites. In China, rural residents are at a disadvantage in all aspects of their lives, and this perpetuates or widens the income gap between urban and rural areas (Ravallion, 2001). Therefore, I repeat the insight of Dr Amartya Sen (1981), the 1998 Nobel laureate in economics, who noted that although natural disasters certainly exist, more disasters are created by humans. Government failure is a common political problem both throughout history and around the world. If government failure, market failure, and innovation failure overlap in the same region, their harm will not only lead to major adverse economic consequences but will also cause social shocks, including revolutions, regime change, and possibly even warfare (Saboor et al., 2017; Wan et al., 2021).

6.2.3.1. Harms Caused by Hierarchies

In a hierarchical society that gives greater power to government officials than to the people they nominally serve, government officials receive lucrative salaries, with salaries increasing as they rise through the hierarchy. Even after their retirement, when they no longer create wealth for society, they continue to receive large pensions. In contrast, farmers, self-employed workers, unemployed workers, and other Chinese people who are lower in the hierarchy receive the national minimum salary or social welfare payment when they work and find it difficult to obtain basic welfare guarantees (including retirement pensions) after their retirement. Because the adoption of a post-Mao market economy rapidly widened the gap between the rich and the poor, this exacerbated the unequal and inequitable distribution of social welfare between the rich and the poor. This situation builds anger and resentment, leading to social unrest, and the intensifying social contradictions have begun to test the ability of those in power to govern (Cao, Lv, et al., 2015).

Some unscrupulous Chinese scholars have cheerfully compared the unfair treatment of farmers to how lakes can absorb floodwater and moderate flooding (Si, 2005): when rural migrants who lose their jobs in cities return to the countryside during an economic crisis, this is similar to how lakes absorb floodwaters, and those who believe this metaphor suggest that it's appropriate to deprive these unemployed people of access to social welfare benefits. Though the Chinese government advocates the idea of "selfless dedication to the greater good" (i.e., to serve the people), they continue to divide the Chinese people into different classes that receive different rights and benefits (i.e., rural vs urban residents), which runs counter to the *great harmony* proposed by Confucius, in which everyone is equal. Urbanization has exacerbated the relative poverty of Chinese farmers and has thereby exacerbated social inequality. This violates a key principle of socialism (i.e., equal treatment of all citizens) and is likely to have adverse consequences for society.

The Chinese government seems to be aware of the seriousness of the gap between rural and urban residents. Through financial transfer payments, it has begun to narrow the gap between urban and rural areas and has maintained a measure of social fairness and justice. Since 2009, the income gap between China's urban and rural areas has been narrowing (China Statistics Agency, 1952–2020), but the unfair increased access to higher education for urban residents and real estate speculation have increased the Gini coefficient nationwide (Li, Ma, et al., 2021). To ensure that urbanization will reduce the Gini coefficient, governments should not only pay attention to the migration of rural residents to cities (that is, urbanization) but should also pay attention to the fairness of the income and benefit distribution. At present, even if Chinese farmers live in cities, they can't gain access to the same welfare benefits as urban residents, such as medical care and education for their children. This problem could be easily solved if the government implemented a mechanism for changing a citizen's status (urban or rural) to reflect where they are living, although this would not change the inequality of citizens who continue to live in rural areas. People are looking forward to the day when this changes and everyone is truly equal.

China's expansion of higher education has created a huge pool of human capital (Ge & Chen, 2010). However, the development of higher education has not promoted social equity or social stability as the government expected. Instead, it has become a powerful promoter of the widening income gap and has undermined social equity. Chan and Ngok (2011), Yang and Gao (2017), and other scholars have reached the same conclusion: higher education has widened the income gap of Chinese citizens because those who obtain this education can obtain high-paying jobs that are unavailable to citizens with less education. As I described in Chapter 3, the government-controlled Chinese education system has caused more and more children of disadvantaged families to lose access to higher education. By subsidizing universities, the Chinese government has effectively developed a system of harming the poor to help the rich, which is contrary to the central socialist goals of justice and equity. At the same time, the economic differences between regions have also led to unequal educational opportunities for students, with fewer and less advantageous opportunities in remote and impoverished regions (Chan & Ngok, 2011). If the Chinese government continues this unfair model for China's higher education system, the gap between the rich and the poor will continue to widen, which will eventually hurt the regime's stability.

The inequality of educational opportunities leads directly to the inequality of future wages and benefits. The income of citizens who have received higher education is much higher than that of less-educated citizens (de Gregorio & Lee, 2002), so increasing the educational opportunities of vulnerable groups in underdeveloped areas is a more effective strategy to reduce the polarization between the rich and the poor than blindly subsidizing universities using strategies such as equal funding that fail to account for regional differences in needs. As I discussed in Chapter 3, the Chinese government should implement a 12-year compulsory education plan so that children from poor families can master the basic job skills that are in greatest demand by enterprises and improve their employment opportunities. In addition, the government should create a "marketplace" for universities (i.e., have them compete for the best students or to offer a better educational experience to all students) and should improve the vitality of undergraduate education and scientific research through market competition and by encouraging universities to seek funding from private enterprises that is designed to prepare graduates to work in these industries. This approach would bring China closer to the goal of improving education and opportunities for all Chinese citizens.

6.2.3.2. Respect Geographical Differences

China's regions differ in their transportation infrastructure and natural resource endowments, but government policies are widening this regional development gap (Hibbs & Olsson, 2004). China's eastern region is rich in human resources, highly market oriented, and capable of scientific and technological innovation, and combined with its easy access to ocean transportation, this means that it has attracted the most foreign investment. This has widened the economic development gap between eastern China and the less-fortunate central and western regions of China (Song et al., 2021). Although China's decentralization policy, which is intended to give regions more flexibility in meeting national goals (see Chapter 9), should promote economic development by letting each region benefit from its unique advantages, the advantages of provinces in eastern China have, in practice, exacerbated regional inequality (Mauro et al., 2023). Because wealthy provinces have advantages such as the greater tax revenues provided by their higher population and superior economic structure, decentralization can improve their economy more than in impoverished regions, whereas underdeveloped regions lack the population and revenues to achieve the same success (Song, 2013). Financial transfer payments from the central government are an effective means of decreasing regional development differences, but more work must be done to let less prosperous provinces develop a more prosperous economy.

The experience of China since 1978 has shown that the main reason for regional differences is that the government has adopted different policies in different regions. Since China's reform and opening up in 1978, marketization has gradually advanced westward and northward from the southeastern coast to inland provinces (Valerio Mendoza, 2016), and fiscal decentralization has followed behind this trend (Yang, 2016). The time difference in policy implementation is the result of the strategy of gradual reform favored by the Chinese government. These differences in the status of different provinces lead directly to significant differences in regional industrial development (Zhu & Zhang, 2021). However, this does not mean that each region should use the same approach to development or should adopt a strategy before it has been proven to work in another region. On the contrary, governments should adopt targeted and differentiated development policies based on the unique needs of each region to ensure that underdeveloped regions receive at least the same support as more developed regions.

Economic development, social services, and environmental changes can all affect the social progress of a region or country (Dong et al., 2022). The spread of the Internet, improvements of medical security, industrial development, and market mechanisms all play an important role in promoting regional socioeconomic development (Li et al., 2022). The labor force in poor areas continues to migrate to rich areas, causing the less-developed areas to bear the cost of training their remaining workers, whereas developed areas are reaping the benefits of an increased labor force, with the result that this becomes exploitation of poor areas by rich areas (Kim et al., 2022). Capital aggregation and technological progress have produced a large number of high-paying jobs in the coastal areas of eastern China, which has further marginalized manual laborers and increased regional differences in individual income (Lin et al., 2013). The government should promote technical training and education for the workers with the lowest incomes to narrow the ability gap between individuals, increase employment opportunities, and narrow the income gap. A responsible government's duty is to work harder to protect the welfare of society's most vulnerable groups rather than the rich and to provide an institutional guarantee to achieve the political equality of all citizens. Technological progress (such as the popularization of the Internet) is important in densely populated developed areas, but it is even more important in sparsely populated underdeveloped areas because of its potential to improve the lives of the most impoverished citizens (Chi et al., 2021).

Globalization is a prominent feature of the modern global economy, and ocean transportation is the main mode of transportation in international trade for products and commodities that are not time sensitive. Therefore, coastal areas should continue to improve their level of marketization (i.e., the proportion of the economy accounted for by the private sector) and take full advantage of the dividends of the marine economy to promote their economic development. In contrast, inland areas are far from the marine economy, and their focus should instead be on developing finance, education, and high-tech industries that are less dependent on transportation. They should also look into new modes of transportation such as China Railway Express that provide faster access to European and Middle Eastern markets than would be possible through ocean transport. Emphasis should be placed on cultivating talents to support high-quality economic development and on promoting industrial upgrading.

In a centralized society, the creators and managers of the political system are the same person or group of people. When they make policies, laws, rules, and other institutional systems, they intentionally or unintentionally choose schemes that benefit themselves as they seek to satisfy what they consider to be their "legitimate interests" and those of their stakeholders. Because ancient China's government was unable to prevent widening of the gap between the rich and the poor, China has repeatedly experienced this problem, which allowed emperors and the government to prosper while the people suffered, leading to revolts by the people and the fall of the dynasty. For example, the Ming government (1368–1644) enforced a system in which the emperor's children could enjoy their roles as aristocrats and be supported by the government throughout their life without having to earn a living, and government officials and their families were not required to pay any taxes on their wealth. More than 200 years after founding of the dynasty, the Ming emperor found that government officials and the royal family and nobles were all rich, and that his inability to tax them meant that the imperial treasury had no money to pay the dynasty's soldiers. To reduce the financial burden, the last emperor of the Ming Dynasty was forced to eliminate certain key military functions, such as staffing of messenger posts that permitted rapid communication between widely separated areas. This led to discontent among the soldiers who were employed by the messenger posts and eventually led to mutiny. The problem was exacerbated by a currency crisis and natural disasters that led to famine and widespread peasant revolts. Together, these factors caused the fall of the dynasty.

China's experience shows that economic growth is an effective strategy to solve absolute poverty, but it cannot effectively deal with the problem of relative poverty (Parker et al., 2008). In part, this is because the current political system repeats the mistakes of ancient Chinese dynasties: it doesn't prevent the rich from growing so rich that they are beyond punishment and doesn't protect the poor. When the rights and needs of vulnerable groups are ignored, the government's policies exacerbate their poverty, thus damaging social justice, endangering economic development, and greatly increasing the risks to social stability. Due to invisible political problems such as price discrimination, government statistics fail to show the effects of these invisible taxes on some groups of citizens. Therefore, the income results calculated based on government statistics often provide a false basis for designing effective policies, with consequences that it may be impossible to correct for a long time. The longer it takes to detect and correct the problem, the greater the likelihood of damaging social fairness and jeopardizing the possibility of sustained socioeconomic growth and a stable political system. The problem is exacerbated by the trade strategies of other nations. Developed countries subsidize agriculture and other industries (Bai et al., 2022), creating hidden taxes on developing countries. This continues a long-standing practice of exploitation of underdeveloped countries and regions by rich countries and regions. Historical experience has shown that such exploitation can lead to conflicts and turbulence (Li, Cai, et al., 2021), which can have a serious negative impact on the peaceful development of humanity and become one of the greatest obstacles to the progress of society (Kim et al., 2022).

If government departments fear that "the emperor's new clothes" will be revealed, they face pressure to use their power to indirectly or directly obstruct research and conceal reports that would reveal their failures, and governments may even encourage some scholars to obtain false research results that are beneficial to the government and the rich. This can exacerbate government failures by causing the government to continue ineffective programs and further undermining trust in the government. This has led to the belief that poverty is often the result of careful planning by political elites (Feng, Yang, et al., 2019). When poverty is exacerbated by an economic crisis or natural disasters, the inevitable consequence will be social turmoil and possibly even regime change. Government failure is a common political problem when the government's power lets it ignore the nation's laws, and the interactions between government failure, market failure, and lack of innovation are yet another problem that has plagued China for thousands of years.

As part of its decentralization program since 1993, China has devolved major economic decisions to local governments, such as the right to approve investments and access markets, to obtain tax revenues, and to manage public spending.

This has allowed the Chinese government to gradually develop a federal system of government, with central planning and policy development but flexibility in the development of local strategies to achieve national goals, often through the development of a market-oriented economy (Li, 2011). However, decentralization has not solved the problem of centralized autocratic power that developed under Chinese communism. Local governments, which were originally controlled by the central government, gained more power after decentralization, but their most powerful officials now behave more like unrestrained emperors, with no fear they will be punished for unethical behavior. Each local government and each government department potentially has one hand controlling the power of planning, execution, finance, and supervision, and the other hand seeking personal gains. The problem has been exacerbated by a central government that has focused on economic growth rather than the people's welfare. Although decentralization has permitted miraculous economic growth, it has also produced growing corruption, inequality between the rich and the poor, a loss of human rights, and environmental degradation, among the many problems caused by such human failings (Cao et al., 2009b; Litina et al., 2021; Shang et al., 2019).

6.3. The Resource Curse

Resources provide the material conditions for socioeconomic development and are the material basis for achieving economic growth (Henri, 2019). Before the 1990s, economists generally believed that a country's natural resource endowment directly affected its economic performance (Hilmawan & Clark, 2019). However, Auty (1993) found that if a country or region has a large amount of certain non-renewable natural resources, this is likely to lead to a long-term downturn in industrial development, difficulties in transformation and upgrading of the country's or region's industrial structure, and the formation of an economic structure that relies excessively on a single resource. He found that the economic situation of the world's resource-poor countries was often better than that of resource-rich countries (Auty, 2001). Auty (1993) invented the phrase "resource curse" to describe this situation. He believed that due to excessive dependence on relatively abundant natural resources, these resources may become a curse rather than a blessing for economic development. This is typically because such countries are often dominated by exports of these resources rather than by conversion of these resources into value-added products. This may be caused by a competitor's trade strategies, as in the case of agricultural pricing that I discussed earlier in this chapter or by other factors. Many countries with rich natural resources have slower economic growth than those with scarce resources (Badeeb et al., 2017; Gylfason, 2001).

However, when economists consider all of a country's resources as a whole, including things such as wasteland that are not traditionally considered to be resources, they often find no significant difference in the total amount of resources among regions, especially when transportation facilities (such as natural harbors), climatic conditions, and other resources that are difficult to price are also included in the economic model (Cao, Li, et al., 2015; Li, Ma, et al., 2021). To account for these seeming contradictions, it's necessary to devote some space to discuss this issue.

6.3.1. Resource Supply and Economic Growth

Auty (1993) believed that development of these resources dominates economic development, at least initially, and that this affects the investment in technological research and development (R&D) and in innovation activities in areas rich in natural resources (Sachs & Warner, 2001). Because investment funds are always limited, this focus on improved exploitation of natural resources often hinders development of other things, such as improving conditions for citizens and promoting the development of value-added industries. However, this explanation of the resource curse is not convincing because both resource-rich developing regions and resource-rich developed regions coexist. For example, Australia and Canada are both rich in natural resources, yet both are highly developed economies. Therefore, the causes of the resource curse have been debated ever since this term was proposed (Betz et al., 2015). However, one reason for the debate may be that socioeconomic development in different regions results from a variety of factors rather than a single factor such as the resource endowment (Parcero & Papyrikas, 2016). Areas rich in natural resources are often hotspots for political and economic conflicts, and this may be one direct cause of the resource curse (Angrist & Kugler, 2008). An example is the establishment of large areas of monoculture oil palm plantations in many tropical parts of the developing world (de Almeida et al., 2020). This has caused large-scale destruction of tropical rainforest and has had a severe negative impact on the local environment. However, developed countries that desire this resource often provide large amounts of financial support for such projects despite their high social and environmental costs to the developing nation. In that context, it's important to holistically understand the dynamics of regional socioeconomic development rather than relying exclusively on simple regional economic indicators.

To avoid being misled by international political relations, Li, Ma, et al. (2021) collected resource and economic data from China's 31 provinces from 2006 to 2016 (i.e., used only intranational data), and comprehensively considered the "net resources" after accounting for the impact of total resources and transportation costs (Fig. 11). They found that the resource curse had an impact on local economic development, but that the impact was negligible. The resource curse was more apparent for agriculture, but its influence on exploitation of mineral resources was not obvious. Regional differences were more strongly driven by human factors. Li, Ma, et al. (2021) found no significant correlation between per capita resource richness and per capita income in China (i.e., no resource curse). On the contrary, they found a significant positive correlation between the resource richness per unit area and per capita income, which suggests that resource richness has promoted economic development throughout China. The primary factors that affect economic growth are human factors such as employment, investment, marketization, education, finance, and urbanization (Fig. 11) rather than simply the supply of resources (Cao, 2001).

Regardless of the results of such statistical calculations, resources support the basic needs for socioeconomic development. Undoubtedly, natural and human resources are the foundation of economic development (Sun et al., 2018).

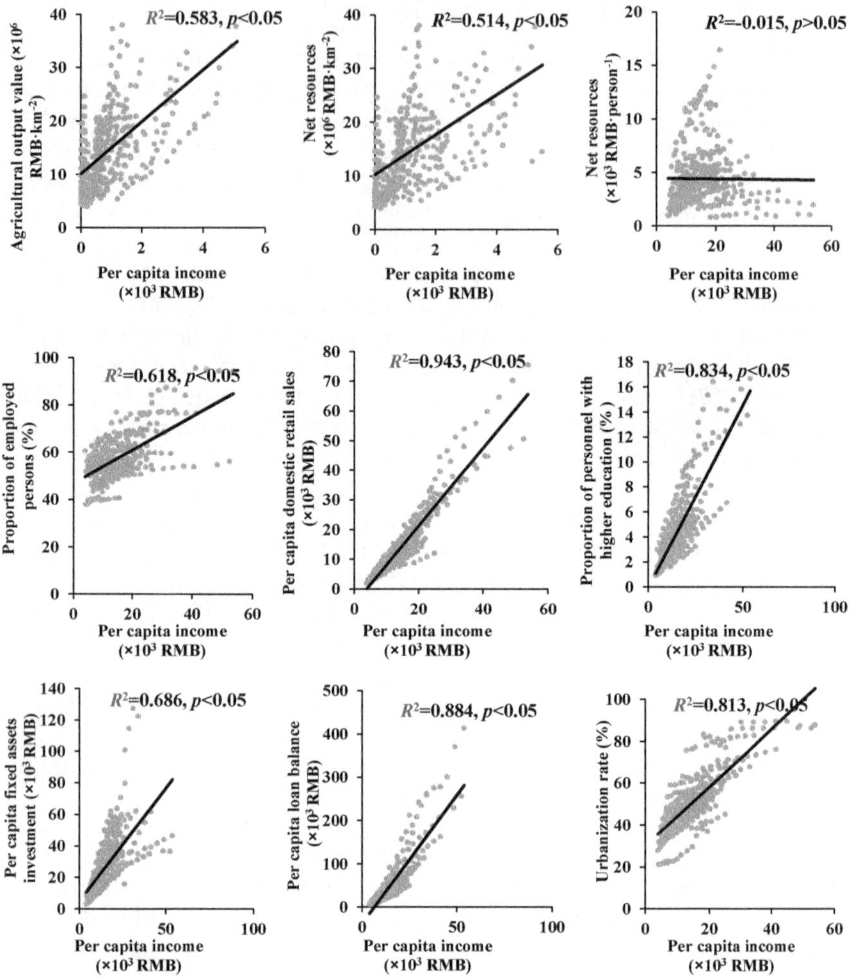

Fig. 11. Regression Analysis Results for the Relationships Between per Capita Household Income and Various Economic Factors. *Source*: The figure is created by the author.

However, resources alone are not enough, and human factors clearly restrict the utilization of resources, so socioeconomic development depends to a greater or lesser extent on limitations of these factors (Bildirici & Gokmenoglu, 2019; Parcero & Papyrikas, 2016). Although the differences in the total amount of resources between regions are not as obvious as people think, there is no doubt that some regions have more abundance of certain specific types of resources. These differences are the material basis for regional trade and are a primary motivation for globalization. That is, if trade is free, resource differences promote rather than hinder economic growth (Cao, 2001). The focus of improving the efficiency of economic development should be on scientific and technological innovation so that resources can create higher economic value per unit input. At the same time, we should constantly optimize the social system that supports resource exploitation and improve the efficiency of resource utilization (Li, Ma, et al., 2021; Wang et al., 2019). To achieve regional economic growth, it is necessary to allocate resources across regions through government or collective forces, make full use of the complementary relationships among resources (such as land and freshwater resources), and give full play to resource advantages.

Some of the most developed economies in the world are rich in natural resources, such as Saudi Arabia's oil and gas resources and Canada's forest and agricultural resources. However, other resource-rich countries, including Venezuela, Iran, and Iraq, suffer from social unrest, wars, and poverty, resulting in weak economic growth. A key difference lies in whether the country's socioeconomic development is supported by an effective and sound social and political system that ensures socioeconomic stability (Bildirici & Gokmenoglu, 2019). A sound institutional environment is the prerequisite for the efficient development and utilization of resources and for social and economic development (Vahabi, 2018). Since 1980, the Chinese government has established many special economic zones to test new economic systems and many free trade zones to test the impact on exports and imports. These have promoted local economic and technological development by creating a favorable investment environment, attracting foreign investment, and introducing advanced technology and management (Li et al., 2020).

Looking back at three of my examples earlier in this section provides some insights. Iraq was originally governed by a corrupt dictatorship, and the invasion by the United States transformed this situation into political chaos that has prevented stable economic development even after the dictator was removed from power. Although Iran has not been invaded, economic sanctions by Western developed countries have severely restricted its foreign trade and have prevented Iran from engaging in trade that would support economic development. Similarly, Venezuela has fallen into social chaos that has seriously hindered the country's ability to benefit from its huge oil and gas reserves. These examples clearly show how political instability is a primary reason for disappointing economic development. They also reveal the complexity of the factors that lead to or prevent the development of the resource curse. For poor and underdeveloped countries and regions, the "political curse" (i.e., the government's inability to provide a stable social environment) can prevent its citizens from gaining control over local resources, and the government may even actively hinder economic development.

6.3.2. Regional Development: A Chinese Example

Governments develop plans to stimulate economic development of specific industries or specific regions. To illustrate the effects of such plans, I will discuss the example of regional development in China in this section. Since China's reforms and opening to the West in 1978, the government has promoted the development of a socialist market economy, with one key goal being to use international trade to drive economic development. Because of eastern China's natural advantages such as proximity to the ocean (i.e., easy and inexpensive international transport) and a high population density (i.e., a large supply of workers), the Chinese government developed policies that preferentially targeted the eastern coastal areas but largely neglected less-favorable locations such as China's central and western regions. This resulted in a large development gap as eastern regions raced ahead and the other regions were left behind. To balance regional development, China implemented the Western Development Plan in 2000 (Lu & Deng, 2011). In this plan, China invested 2.2×10^{12} RMB over a period of 10 years to improve the region's transportation infrastructure and fund the construction of factories to capture the western region's abundant mineral, hydroelectric, and oil and gas resources. The plan achieved remarkable results but failed to narrow the gap between per capita GDP in the eastern and western regions. China's per capita GDP increased from 4,601.7 RMB in 2000 to 55,711.6 RMB in 2020, an increase of 12.1 times in 20 years. However, the gap in per capita GDP compared with the eastern region increased from 7,127.2 RMB in 2000 to 37,554.8 RMB in 2020. In 2020, this gap widened to 119,773.3 RMB (China Statistics Agency, 1979–2021).

Part of the problem is that the eastern region's more developed market and superior infrastructure attracted more domestic and foreign investment. Although the western development plan benefited from a huge government investment, the project's core goal was to transport the western region's natural resources to the east and provide resources that would sustain the eastern region's economic development (Ji et al., 2014). That is, despite the project's name, it supported eastern development far more than western development. For example, the "West–East Gas Transmission" and "West–East Power Transmission" projects were nominally intended to promote economic development in western China, but in practice, they have primarily provided cheap resources for the eastern region that promoted its economic development rather than that of western China. None of the Western Development Project's details describe the transport of resources (such as water) from the eastern region to the western region or to create new value-added industries in the western region.

Poor design of the program also meant that it lacked good environmental protection measures. As a result, resource development in the western region has led to continuous degradation of the ecological environment (Ash, 2006). These environmental costs were borne by the local people rather than by the eastern region's consumers (Li & Coxhead, 2011). There is also an important contradiction in China that may not occur in more developed countries: all natural resources with a high economic value (such as coal, oil, natural gas, and iron ore) are controlled by the central government, whereas low-value natural resources that can be difficult to monetize (such as precipitation, light, topography, and natural river ports) are owned by local governments. This leads to plundering of the most lucrative resources by eastern China, thereby exporting money that could be used to protect the environment and enrich the people of western China. Because the most economically valuable natural resources belong to the state rather than to the local governments, China's central government and state-owned enterprises earn most of the profits from development of the resources and feel little responsibility for mitigating the environmental impacts of this exploitation, and the need for local governments to deal with those impacts further reduces the local economic competitiveness (Zhang et al., 2008).

Western development has also suffered from an emphasis on resource exploitation rather than on technological progress and transformation of primary resources into secondary resources or manufactured goods with high value-added. There is little or no local processing of resources into finished products, little or no creation of high-tech industries to promote technological upgrading, and few attempts to modernize local industries (Ji et al., 2014). The western region has huge reserves of energy and mineral resources, so if it were not for a state monopoly on these resources and the region's distance from markets, it could attract more private investment to promote technological progress that would take advantage of these resources, to improve worker skills, and to take advantage of various positive externalities such as the creation of jobs for workers who maintain the infrastructure that transports these resources to the east. Unfortunately, these drawbacks mean that the western region has failed to attract private investment from both China and abroad. In addition, due to the lack of innovation that results from the state monopoly on mineral resources (i.e., the lack of innovative private enterprises that want to transform these resources), the western region has been trapped in a vicious circle of slow economic growth and persistent poverty (Cao, Li, et al., 2015). The central government's resource monopoly and price discrimination related to mineral resources and agricultural products (i.e., setting low prices that generate low income from these products in western China to benefit industries in eastern China) let the eastern region continuously gain benefits from the difference between the centrally planned price and the price that could be achieved in a free market. As a result, the western region is forced to sell its resources and agricultural products to consumers in the eastern coastal areas at the government prices and must buy industrial products produced in the eastern regions at market prices. This unfair trade environment inevitably widens the development differences between the eastern and western regions. It is also another example of the invisible taxes I discussed earlier in this chapter.

Each region has its own unique resource and economic advantages and constraints. Therefore, regional development planning should consider not only a region's advantages but also its constraints. For example, although the eastern part of China lacks the abundant natural resources that are found in western China, it is close to the ocean, so it has a huge transportation advantage to support international trade. Although western China lacks access to the ocean, it is close to the railway lines of China Railway Express, a major Chinese initiative to provide large-scale transportation of goods to Europe and the Middle East under the Belt and Road Initiative. This proximity can potentially compensate for western region's geographic trade disadvantage.

6.3.3. Resource Balance Theory

In a broad sense, resources are the natural foundation of wealth, as they are the resources that support employment and account for the sum of the conditions required for humans to acquire wealth. These resources can be divided into natural resources, which are provided by the natural environment, and human resources, which represent the value provided by human thought and labor. Together, these resources are the inputs that society uses to create material wealth under a given set of social, economic, and technological conditions. With continuing development of science and technology, the scope of labor will continue to expand, and a series of new resources will be recognized and developed. For example, scientific breakthroughs may make it possible to exploit a resource that could not previously be economically exploited. Simultaneously, the progress of science and technology is constantly improving the resource utilization efficiency. An academic school of thought, "resource balance theory" (Cao, 2001), suggests that extremely rich natural resources exist everywhere in the world, although the quality and nature of the resources differ between regions, and it may not be possible to utilize resources before their location is identified by exploration and before technologies and techniques are developed to permit their exploitation. The difference between regions results from differences in the dominance of various resources, on whether we currently understand how to use them, and the time elapsed between their discovery and utilization. These factors create an imbalance in global regional economic development. In resource balance theory, this imbalance can be corrected by accounting for these factors.

6.3.3.1. Balanced Distribution of Natural Resources

From an economic perspective, every region has abundant natural resources, although we may not yet know that they exist or how to utilize them. For example, silicates are among the most abundant minerals on Earth, but we only began to understand their potential for use in computers in the middle of the 20th century. In this context, the differences between regions come down to the nature of the resources. These differences determine whether or not we know how to exploit the resources in a given time period under a given combination of economic and technological conditions. With the continuous improvement of human awareness and knowledge, it is entirely possible that areas that were once considered "barren land" contain valuable natural resources that we now understand how to exploit, thereby enriching society. For example, Alaska was once considered nothing more than barren land by the Russian czar, despite the fact that native peoples had thrived in this region for tens of thousands of years. In addition, the czar realized that this land would be difficult to defend given its distance from Russia. Thus, rather than maintaining ownership of Alaska, the czar sold the land cheaply to the United States. Subsequently, huge oil and gas resources were discovered, thereby enriching the United States. A parallel example from China relates to the huge oil and gas resources that have been discovered in the Taklimakan Desert, which was formerly considered nothing more than desolate and dangerous wasteland (*Global Times*, 2021b).

Similarly, agricultural resources show large geographical differences, and different regions have their own advantages and disadvantages in terms of the crops they can sustain and the techniques necessary to achieve this. For example, southeastern China has abundant precipitation and a high cumulative annual temperature, which makes it a good place to develop high-yield agriculture. However, there is little climatic variation within this region, which means that a small range of crops can be grown, and it is difficult to improve the quality of the agricultural products. In contrast, northern China's vast arid areas have low precipitation, combined with low cumulative temperature, which creates considerable difficulty in growing crops and leads to lower crop yields where cultivation is possible. China's large size has created a wide range of complex climates and terrain, so there is a similarly wide range of other potential resources (e.g., wind and sun) and high potential for diverse agricultural development. To accomplish this, it's first necessary to understand the balance of resources in each region and find ways to exploit the most abundant or profitable resources.

Even in seemingly barren desert areas, there may be potential for developing a specific form of agriculture. For example, China has developed the cultivation and processing of economically valuable psammophytes in many desert regions, thereby providing a steady stream of raw materials for Chinese herbal medicines and stimulating new thinking about how to promote regional agricultural development (Cao et al., 2018). The range of resources available to support the development of agricultural products, especially for diversified agricultural products, provides good conditions for different forms of agricultural development in different regions. With the strong support of agricultural science and technology development, different agricultural resources could be promoted in different regions (Feng, Tian, et al., 2019). These examples reveal how it may be possible to reconsider the potential of regions that were once considered to be incapable of supporting agriculture. Agriculture may be possible even in deserts if suitable species are chosen. For example, *Glycyrrhiza uralensis* and *Glycyrrhiza glabra* are being cultivated in the Ningxia Hui Autonomous Region, where annual precipitation ranges from 203.7 to 317.8 mm. In the Alxa League of Inner Mongolia, with annual precipitation ranging from 33.9 to 208.5 mm, farmers are cultivating *Cistanche deserticola* and *Cynomorium songaricum*. These and other characteristic Chinese herbal medicines have become an important industry for local farmers and are helping them to mitigate poverty or even become rich (Cao et al., 2018).

6.3.3.2. Achieving Balanced Utilization of Resources

Once the economic value of the natural environment has been recognized, it becomes possible to utilize that environment to achieve economic benefits and support social development. As a result of our improving understanding of the world and our efforts to transform the world, we have gradually increased our ability to exploit natural resources and to do so more sustainably. When we recognize the potential to exploit a natural resource, the areas rich in that resource can be developed, potentially generating many social benefits. However, ongoing exploitation of non-renewable resources or unsustainable exploitation of renewable resources can decrease their abundance or even deplete the resource. Scientific research has permitted the development of techniques and technologies that allow utilization of a formerly unexploitable resource, recovery of a depleted renewable resource, or identification of new resources that could be exploited.

As a result, new resource-rich areas are identified and become important areas for socioeconomic development, leading to movement of workers between areas. However, the ability to exploit a resource must be balanced against the damage caused by that exploitation.

The development and utilization of natural resources are affected by many factors, including our knowledge (techniques and technology), economic ability (i.e., the ability to fund development and exploitation), access to transportation, and social needs. Differences in these factors may be the main reasons for differences in the development and utilization of a given resource in different regions. The development of any kind of natural resource is restricted by demand for that resource and a market in which that demand can be satisfied. The greater the demand, the higher the degree of resource development and utilization. The exploitation of natural resources in areas rich in these resources and the cultivation of markets in areas poor in natural resources are important issues related to the balance that must be understood to support exploitation of a natural resource.

All stages from development to exchange of natural resources depend on the availability of a transportation infrastructure that allows transport of the resource from its source to where it will be consumed. The geographical advantages of areas with excellent natural transportation (e.g., with a natural port, with proximity to a large population of consumers) lead to some of the regional differences in resources that I described earlier in this chapter. Against the background of globalization, coastal areas in eastern China have benefited from their geographical advantages (large populations, excellent natural harbors, and proximity to the ocean) to become leaders of the world economy. This is one reason why some islands and coastal areas that were relatively poor in their natural resources have become economic powerhouses.

Appropriate exploitation of natural resources is necessary to achieve a resource balance and permit sustainable human interventions in nature. Because natural resources don't exist independently of each other, exploitation of one sometimes leads to inefficient use or no use of an associated resource. The unused or underutilized resource may be discarded as a waste product. For example, the production of iron from iron ore creates a large amount of rock waste. In addition to the inefficiency of this approach, such wastes may cause environmental damage and seriously harm society. Therefore, an essential first step in planning resource development and utilization is to learn about all resources affected by the proposed exploitation and all wastes that will be generated (including a range of externalities) so that planners can take steps to protect residents of the resource area and its ecological environment and thereby permit sustainable development. Many cultures have some form of saying that one person's garbage is another person's treasure. Thus, when we plan to develop and utilize a resource, we must consider how to use it most efficiently and how to utilize any "waste" generated by that use to prevent environmental damage and other adverse consequences (e.g., loss of a resource that will prove to be valuable in the future). This approach will contribute greatly to achieving a resource balance that will sustain society.

More and more research demonstrates that each region has its own unique resources (Cao, Li, et al., 2015). The primary factors that restrict the development of a region's resources are knowledge that such resources exist, the techniques and technologies required to exploit them, the funding required to apply those techniques and technologies, and a market for the resources. From this perspective, a lack of socioeconomic development results from our ignorance of how to exploit the resources that are available to us, not from a lack of resources. The natural resources that are available in different regions differ primarily in kind and in quantity, and trade is the means by which one region's surplus can fill another region's shortage. Rather than trying to dominate trade to create a zero-sum game in which there must be a winner and a loser, resource balance theory suggests that cooperation will produce better results, since this approach makes it possible for both participants in a game to be winners (for different resources). From the perspective of this theory, the common feature of the world's poor and underdeveloped areas is political instability and a lack of funds to adopt suitable techniques and technologies, and not a lack of resources. This returns us to what I said earlier in this chapter: poverty is first and foremost a political problem and only secondarily an economic problem. To solve the poverty problem, we must first build a political system in which everyone receives equal treatment by a government that emphasizes an equitable distribution of social wealth.

Chapter 7

China's Rise

Since 1978, China's economy has maintained an average annual growth rate of nearly 10%, and the country has undergone radical socioeconomic changes, rapidly transforming China from a state of poverty and weakness to one of the most powerful countries in the world (Song et al., 2011; Xu, 2011). At the same time, China's national infrastructure has grown astonishingly. High-speed railroads and expressways, which were nearly nonexistent in 1978, have grown to 30,000 km and 1,430,000 km, respectively (China Statistics Agency, 1979–2020). These changes have included remarkable new technologies and new educational achievements. China began its lunar exploration program in 2013, with the landing of the Chang'e 3 lander, and built the world's fastest computer in 2015, with a computing speed of 2.6×10^{15} operations per second (Thibodeau, 2016). On August 16, 2016, China launched the world's first quantum communication satellite (Gibney, 2016), and in 2019, Chinese universities (including specialized colleges) graduated 8.3×10^{6} people, which is almost 50 times the value in 1978. In addition, Chinese technology has advanced rapidly, leading to the launch of China's first space station in 2021.

In 2013, China's total imports and exports reached 25.8×10^{12} RMB, replacing the United States as the world's top trading nation (China Statistics Agency, 2014). China produced 1.2 Gt of steel in 2019, accounting for more than 50% of the global total. Also in 2019, China's gross domestic product (GDP) and per capita GDP reached 99.1×10^{12} RMB and 71,000 RMB, respectively, which were 269 and 184 times the 1978 values (China Statistics Agency, 1979–2020). After 40 years of development, China has transformed itself from an economically irrelevant country to a world power, setting historical records for the largest scale, fastest economic growth, longest growth duration, and largest beneficiary population in history (McMillan & Naughton, 1992; Zhu, 2012).

China's impressive socioeconomic achievements have not been achieved under easy conditions but rather in the face of a steady stream of natural and human disasters. These include the financial crisis that hit the Asian economy in 1997, the worst flooding in China since meteorological records began in 1998, the 9.1 magnitude earthquake in Sichuan Province in 2008, and the subprime mortgage financial crisis in the United States in 2008 that caused enormous economic harm worldwide (Baker et al., 2020; Ozili & Arun, 2020). Since 2020, COVID-19 has

A New Stage of Civilization: Striving for the Great Harmony, 177–203

Published under exclusive licence by Emerald Publishing Limited
doi:10.1108/978-1-83708-258-220251008

swept through more than 200 countries and regions around the world, killing millions of people and causing a disaster for humanity. Nonetheless, the fact that China has always managed to turn danger into success by recovering from disasters is one of the most important success stories in history.

China's rapid rise is undoubtedly one of the major events in contemporary society (Zhai, 2019). Never before in the history of civilization has such a large region been able to develop as fast as and for as long as China has done, despite the abovementioned disasters. This success has mystified researchers around the world. Scholars have proposed a range of explanations, but traditional economic explanations such as factor endowments (Henri, 2019; Hilmawan & Clark, 2019), human capital (Fleisher et al., 2010), competitive advantage theory (Porter, 1991), and institutional economics (Acemoglu et al., 2004), among other ideas, have failed to adequately explain China's rise. Some have even suggested that the Chinese model is unique to China and cannot be learned by other countries (Zhang, 2017).

In this chapter, I propose an explanation that previous researchers have missed: that although all of the abovementioned factors have contributed to China's success, China has found a new development path that differs from traditional economic models and that is quietly changing the trajectory of society. In a recent paper by my research group (Cao et al., 2022), we found that China is transforming a private property system that has lasted for thousands of years and the communist system that followed it, which lasted for only a quarter-century, into a novel system that combines the capitalist concept of private property with the socialist concept of shared (collective) ownership of resources. If this innovation can be understood and adopted by other countries, it seems likely to lead to a whole new era of civilization. Understanding the roots of China's rise will not only allay fears about its rise (Grzywacz, 2020; Mearsheimer, 2001) but will also provide lessons that can guide other nations to explore their own paths toward the evolution of a more pro-social civilization. To help readers understand China's socioeconomic rise in a way that differs markedly from previous explanations, I will describe how China has learned from the experiences of developed countries and used this knowledge to develop an innovative new system.

7.1. Learning from International Experience

Property rights are the legal expression of economic ownership relationships, including the right to own, possess, dominate, use, benefit from, and dispose of legal property (Coase, 1959). The definition of property rights is the basis of economic cooperation, since some countries own resources that other countries need. The resulting imbalance between demand and supply was probably the basis for early trade activities and the earliest definitions of private property (North, 1990). However, the identification of private property rights did not solve all the resource-distribution problems encountered by society, such as the widening gap between the rich and poor caused by the *failure of property rights to ensure equitable resource allocation*. There are also problems with the public (collective) property system, such as the "tragedy of the commons" (Hardin, 1968), which is also known as the "free-rider problem." History has repeatedly proven that *neither private property rights nor public property rights alone can solve the problem of the distribution of benefits*. Determining how to solve the distribution problem will be necessary for society to move to a more advanced stage of civilization, and this remains a core problem for global institutional change.

The concept of *division of labor* refers to the tasks or roles undertaken by individuals with different skills and responsibilities within the production processes of an industry or enterprise. The principle is that an individual who specializes in a given task will be better at that task and more efficient than an individual who lacks that specialized expertise. When the efficiency and quality of the work are important, a division of labor offers clear benefits. This is not a new realization. Xunzi (313–238 BCE) said nearly 1,800 years ago that humans survive better through the division of labor because there are no "part-time skills." With the development and rise of industries composed of specialists with divided responsibilities, the pace of industrial progress accelerated, particularly during the Industrial Revolution. Today, any complex product is produced from parts designed and manufactured by dozens or even hundreds of companies, none of which could produce the whole product itself. This industrial development has promoted the progress of society at an ever-accelerating rate (Cochran & Harpending, 2009).

On the one hand, the industrial division of labor can effectively utilize the different strengths of individuals, which improves production efficiency; on the other hand, it makes full use of the differences in natural resource endowments between regions or countries, which effectively reduces production costs (Christopherson, 2006). To ensure a smooth division of labor, society uses contractual relationships (institutions) guaranteed by contracts (formal or informal) that maintain orderly trade. When the exchange between two individuals requires trade across time and distance, a contract guaranteed by a third party (such as government officials or judges) or by a legal system constrains the economic behavior of individuals by creating a sense of trust and of penalties for violating that trust. Such contracts sustain a society's commercial transactions. Although contracts in various forms have existed for thousands of years, their economic value was not widely recognized by economists until the publication of Steven Cheung's *The Theory of Share Tenancy* (Cheung, 1969).

Because different regions have different natural resources that can be used as production factors in an industrial process (i.e., different factor endowments; Crossman et al., 2013), market transactions to exchange factors between such regions are the basis of cooperation and an important driver of the evolution of civilization. Heckscher and Ohlin (1933) described this as follows: First, the production of goods requires not only labor input but also other production factors such as capital, land, and raw or semi-finished materials, and different goods require different allocations of these factors. Second, differences in factor endowments between regions and differences in the intensity of the use of these factors in the production of various goods are the basis of international trade. Third, a country should export products produced from its relatively abundant production factors and import products produced from its relatively scarce production factors. (This is closely related to the division of labor I discussed in the previous section, with extraction of different raw materials becoming the different areas of expertise.) Fourth, as international trade develops, the prices of production factors will tend to equalize across countries.

Since the mid-1980s, the "labor force" has become one of the important elements of the new economic growth theory (Romer, 1990). Romer (1990) proposed the endogenous growth model of technological progress, which bases economic growth on "endogenous technological progress" (i.e., technological innovations produced within a system). This model of technological progress is based on three assumptions: technological progress is the core of economic growth; most technological progress is the result of conscious behavior stimulated by market incentives; and knowledge goods can be used repeatedly without additional costs, and their only cost is the cost of the initial production and development of the knowledge. The latter assumption provides the theoretical basis of the innovation economy. The population is not only an important source of labor but also the source of consumption of the output from an economic activity (Dasgupta & Ehrlich, 2013; Elvidge et al., 1997). Today, economists recognize the importance of human capital, and promoting higher education and technical training (including lifelong education) have become an important part of economic activity (Barro, 2001; Čadil et al., 2014).

7.1.1. Market Competition

There are many ways to stimulate economic development, and trade is one of the most important. Through the "invisible hand of the market," scarce resources (including workers) can be effectively allocated by trading with countries or regions where the resources are more abundant, thus promoting socioeconomic development for both trading partners and compensating for the harm caused by resource shortages. China's total import and export trade increased from 35.5×10^9 RMB in 1978 to 315.505×10^9 RMB in 2019, an increase of 8.9 times in only four decades, which is 3.3 times the growth of GDP during this period (China Statistics Agency, 1979–2020). That is, trade's contribution to China's economy grew much faster than the domestic economy. China is rich in many resources, including land, but must buy scarce resources such as oil and iron ore through the international market, while exporting resources in which China is rich, such as rare earth elements. The economic gains from international trade accounted for more than 35% of the total GDP in 2008 (Qiang, 2017). Trade has not only contributed to China's rapid economic growth but has also promoted the development of international commodity markets to supply China's needs. At the same time, trade has been an important means of international cultural exchange and political interactions between China and its trade partners, which also help to explain China's rise.

Markets play an important role not only in exchanges between countries but also between people and between businesses. Since China's reform and opening up to the West in 1978, the country's domestic market has expanded rapidly. In 2019, the retail sales of consumer goods in China totaled 41.2×10^{12} RMB, which is 264 times the value of 155.86×10^9 RMB in 1978, and China had become the world's largest trade market (China Statistics Agency, 1979–2020). The free exchange of goods and materials has simultaneously facilitated the rapid development of China's private sector economy, which complements the public ownership system; the power of this combination is analogous to adding another engine to a car. For example, the private sector's share of China's economy has grown from nothing in 1978 to 83% of the economy in 2019, simultaneously creating jobs for more than 80% of the population (China Statistics Agency, 1979–2020). Undoubtedly, the private sector and the associated trade have been essential for China's economic growth.

7.1.2. Industrial Specialization

Industrial specialization gives full play to the strengths of different individuals and different regions and is an effective means to improve a society's economic efficiency. With the emergence of industrial society, the rate of industrial specialization has continued to accelerate, and most modern technologies (e.g., cars, computers) are built from parts manufactured by hundreds of specialized enterprises that perform tasks it would be difficult for a single company to perform. The efficiency permitted by this specialization has accelerated economic growth and social change (Cochran & Harpending, 2009; Obach, 2003). If the cost reduction permitted by industrial specialization is greater than the increase in social transaction costs, industrial specialization will continue. For example, the industrial park in Shenzhen, China, covers less than 5 km^2, yet is home to thousands of enterprises that jointly produce the parts for a given product (e.g., a mobile phone), and the government's support for such specialization has been an important reason for China's rapid rise. A good global example of this kind of cooperation is the synergy that has arisen between American computer engineering skill and Chinese manufacturing skill (Crouch, 2013).

After the 1970s, the extreme planned-economy model represented by the former Soviet Union gradually became less influential as its flaws became increasingly apparent, and most communist and socialist countries abandoned the development model of a state-controlled economy and opted for the capitalist model of a market economy. The exception was China, which has moved toward implementing the capitalist concept of a market economy without fully rejecting the socialist concept of a centrally planned economy (Gong & Cortese, 2017).

In this model, increasing investment by the government, combined with private and overseas investors, has driven China's rapid economic growth. In 2019, China's total fixed asset investment was $55{,}147.8 \times 10^9$ RMB, which equaled 827 times the total of 66.67×10^9 RMB in 1978; in particular, private investment and foreign investment grew rapidly, from nothing in 1978 to $311{,}159 \times 10^9$ RMB and 939×10^9 RMB, respectively, in 2019, accounting for 56.4 and 1.7% of the total investment (China Statistics Agency, 1979–2020). The Chinese government has invested massively in transportation, communications, and other infrastructure, and this nonprofit government action has greatly reduced transaction costs and facilitated trade growth (Tsui, 2011). The investments and programs from the private sector, foreign investors, and China's government have undoubtedly contributed greatly to China's socioeconomic growth. Guo et al. (2022) found that foreign and domestic investment have together contributed as much as 17.6% to China's GDP growth over the past 40 years.

7.1.3. Innovation and Industrial Upgrading

Innovation highlights the importance of introducing new combinations of production factors and conditions that were not available in the past into the modern production system (Fritsch, 2017). According to Schumpeter (1912), innovation includes the adoption of new technology and production methods, the creation of new markets and economic organizations, and the expansion of new sources of raw materials or semi-finished products. The contradiction between the rapidly increasing demand of the world's growing population and the limited capacity of the Earth's resources to meet that demand has led to one ecological crisis after another. (I will discuss this in more detail in Chapter 10.) It has also been one of the major causes of wars (Cao et al., 2007). Although one way to solve these problems is to reduce human demand, that may not be possible in many cases. The solution must then be to improve production efficiency and a region's resource carrying capacity through technical, technological, and institutional innovation (Cao et al., 2007).

Innovation can not only improve the utilization efficiency of existing resources; it can also reveal new valuable resources and new ways to meet human demand (e.g., new industries). For example, most Western industries switched from coal to oil because oil's higher energy density decreased production costs. Now that the severe human and environmental costs of oil have become apparent, economies are transitioning to renewable energy sources such as hydroelectric power and wind and solar energy. Other forms of institutional innovation, and especially innovations related to property rights, can improve the motivation of individuals to work, reduce social transaction costs, and increase production efficiency through new benefit-distribution relationships (North, 1990). Such cultural innovations can find common ground for the interests of different groups of people, which satisfies the human need for social contact; on the other hand, innovations can promote communication and cooperation among groups, ease the growing conflicts among groups of people, and maintain peace and social stability (Cao, 2016a).

Trade, investment, and innovation are the three engines that promote socioeconomic development. In 2019, China invested $2{,}214.36 \times 10^9$ RMB in technological innovation and experimental research and development, which is 419 times the value of 5.29×10^9 RMB in 1978 (China Statistics Agency, 1979–2020). According to the annual World Intellectual Property Indicators report of the World Intellectual Property Organization (WIPO, 2019), the number of patent applications worldwide in 2019 exceeded 3.22×10^6, of which 1.4×10^6 were received by the State Intellectual Property Office of China, which ranked first in the world. At the same time, China's higher education has grown by leaps and bounds. The number of students enrolled in China's universities and colleges increased 29.9 times, from an initial value of 274,000 in 1978 to 8.2×10^6 in 2019

(China Statistics Agency, 1979–2020). Specialized education has given the labor force more skills, and the effective allocation of these trained workers with different skills has greatly contributed to socioeconomic development and an improved standard of living. It has also begun to mitigate the shortage of the skilled workers that are required by many enterprises in this era of rapid technological progress and economic growth, thereby permitting ongoing continuous industrial upgrading and transformation. Although I noted in Chapter 3 that China's scientific research and higher education programs have many problems compared with the systems of developed states, the improvements since 1978 must nonetheless be recognized.

Economic activities are production processes that aim to meet the material and other needs of a growing population. When society's basic needs are met, the force driving economic development weakens until other needs (or desires that resemble needs) become apparent, creating new demand that stimulates new economic development. These new needs promote industrial upgrades that lead to economic growth that prevents economic stagnation. For example, history suggests that industrialization in most countries began with labor-intensive industries such as the textile industry that met basic needs, followed by industries that met different needs, such as manufacturing of home appliances and automobiles, eventually leading to high-tech industries such as the computer and communications sectors (Cao et al., 2007).

Because no country exists in complete isolation, industries in developing countries begin to compete with a developed country's industries, until eventually all global demand is met, leading to stagnation of those industries. For a developed country to keep developing, it must innovate to either produce better products that compete more effectively against the products of other countries or new technologies that drive additional development. Because technological and institutional innovation is not a linear growth process, most countries experience periods of rapid economic growth due to early technological progress (such as the United States and Europe after World War II, Japan in the 1960s, and South Korea and Taiwan in the 1980s). When that progress slows, a country is likely to enter a sustained period of stagnating economic growth until new technologies stimulate new growth by creating new demand.

7.2. China's Experience with Economic Development

Political economics scholars generally agree that economic growth is the basis for social progress and political stability (Cao & Ren, 2019; Ip & Law, 2011). Therefore, how to achieve economic growth has been the focus of individuals, enterprises, and governments. The results of panel data calculations suggested (Guo et al., 2022) that the top factors driving China's per capita GDP since 1978 were trade (23.5%), development of a market economy (22.7%), fixed asset investment (17.6%), science and technology innovation (7.5%), and increased employment (7.0%), which is logical. However, because statistical data do not reflect the complete picture for all socioeconomic variables, and especially factors such as price discrimination, government control, and natural and human-caused disasters that are difficult to fully represent in monetary form, the calculation results are necessarily incomplete. As a result, econometric methods cannot fully reflect the intrinsic dynamics of economic growth, and politicians must rely on logical reasoning and empirical judgment to explore the logical relationships behind the econometric data.

Unfortunately, this approach can lead to wrong judgments, particularly for inexperienced analysts. For example, the high return on capital investments in China's coastal areas and big cities seems to be an attractive goal, but it ignores factors such as increased pollution and an increased cost of living that makes it difficult for many workers to afford to live in these areas. If the government, like the private sector, only pursues a high economic rate of return, this may lead them to ignore undesirable consequences such as a widening regional development gap and social unrest, which are not visible in the economic statistics.

7.2.1. Causes of China's Economic Growth

Government and cultural institutions play key roles in socioeconomic development (Wang, 2006). History shows that economic systems based on a single inflexible approach don't always work, especially when such systems ignore the realities of economic development (Gong & Cortese, 2017). This is exemplified, for example, by the comprehensive rejection of the traditional capitalist market economy in many communist countries, including China in the early years after the communist revolution. This slowed the economic development of China under Mao Zedong and led to millions of deaths from 1949 to 1976, as well as to the failure of centrally planned economies such as the former Soviet Union (Cao & Ren, 2019; Murrell, 1993). On the other hand, purely capitalist systems also fail because they provide no inherent way to protect the rights of society as a whole. When a capitalist system is inadequately monitored and constrained, it leads to economic disasters such as the Great Depression in the United States and the 2008 global financial crisis (Cao, 2016a).

In contrast, a diverse system, such as China's combination of central planning with a market economy, is an effective way to maintain stable economic growth. China's success shows that markets and central planning can both be important components of an improved socioeconomic system (Ansar et al., 2016; Jefferson et al., 1992). Since 1978, China has been supporting and expanding the development of a market economy while developing and implementing one five-year plan after another and also providing institutional safeguards such as government-funded health care and education for children that stabilize China's social environment and promote economic growth (Berger et al., 2013; Kwon, 2009; Li, 1998). Statistical calculations over the past 40 years also indicate that the development of a market economy has provided 22.7% of China's growth of per capita GDP (Guo et al., 2022).

Unlike the reforms in the former Soviet Union, China has never relinquished government control of its economy. This control includes the formulation and implementation of five-year economic development plans every five years, accompanied by government investment, government-directed individual and foreign investment (Xu & Yan, 2014). It also includes government intervention in the market to prevent or mitigate problems that resulted from excessive market competition (e.g., overheated investment in a particular sector), excessively high exchange rates, and shortages of commodities (e.g., food and energy security). As a result, China has been successful in avoiding the cyclical fluctuations of market economies, including the periodic economic crises that occur in pure capitalist systems (Fan et al., 2017). The Chinese government's successful experience in controlling markets and developing a market economy shows that active and effective government intervention can reduce market risks, maintain social stability, and achieve sustained economic growth. The Chinese government's approach is consistent with the requirements of Keynesian economics and provides an example for the capitalist world to follow.

Since the 2008 financial crisis, the sluggish world economy has forced China to reduce its dependence on international markets, so domestic trade (what the Chinese government calls the "domestic demand-driven economy") has become one of the most important forces that is driving China's economic growth. In 2008 and 2020, China's GDP was 31.92×10^{12} RMB and 101.36×10^{12} RMB, respectively, and the total import and export volumes were 20.43×10^{12} RMB and 32.42×10^{12} RMB, respectively (China Statistics Agency, 2009–2021). International trade was equivalent to 64.0% and 32.0% of GDP, respectively, in those years. China has a good mixture of industrial sectors, and its huge domestic consumer market provides a clear advantage for its economic development; that is, increasing domestic sales generate profits that can be invested to improve the production amount or efficiency and that can fund an enterprise while it tries to penetrate foreign markets or compensate for decreasing foreign sales. The expansion of the domestic market can help to reduce external shocks such as the trade war between China and the United States and to increase China's economic resilience. The importance of population growth is supported by the fact that China's huge population and the huge market created by its increasingly affluent people are becoming important forces for China's economic growth. However, some of this resilience is undermined by misguided demographic policies in the past (e.g., the "one child" policy), which were intended to reduce China's population to a more sustainable level but have instead led to a rapid decline in the birth rate that has created demographic problems that must be solved. (I will discuss these problems in Chapter 11.) If China's population decreases too rapidly, this could potentially trigger an economic recession, threatening China's success.

The increased employment that has resulted from China's industrialization and urbanization has largely solved the problem of surplus rural labor and has increased the per capita income and improved the livelihood of the Chinese people. However, GDP growth itself does not equate to improved livelihoods. Over the past 40 years, China's disposable income growth has lagged behind not only its GDP growth but also government revenue growth, and this has constrained the growth of the Chinese people's consumption power, which in turn has slowed the growth of China's economy.

Science, technology, and education play an important role in economic growth, and the higher the economic level of a region, the greater the contribution of science, technology, and education to its economic growth (Guo et al., 2021). However, China's government has not recognized the importance of these factors for driving growth. Because of government control and bureaucratic management of universities and research institutes (Cao et al., 2020), there are concerns about the ability of Chinese universities and research institutes to promote innovative research and researchers (Lagrotteria & Besescheck, 2012; Loyalka et al., 2021). I discuss this problem in Chapter 3. In 2010, China surpassed Japan to rank second in the world in terms of GDP, but its per capita GDP lags far behind the world's advanced economies. China appears to have completed its industrialization and urbanization processes, or will soon do so, and therefore must move to a new development path, such as innovation-driven economic development.

From 1978 to 2017, science and technology innovation contributed only 7.5% and 6.3% of China's growth of GDP and disposable income, respectively, and the Chinese government's massive higher education efforts do not seem to have affected these contributions (Guo et al., 2022). If the Chinese government continues its current education policy and is unwilling to adopt market-based reforms for scientific research and higher education, China will find it difficult to continue its rapid development after the industrialization process is complete, and it will become unable to outperform the capitalist world in key indicators such as labor productivity. This may lead to an economic slowdown similar to what has occurred since 1990 in Japan.

7.2.2. China's Financial Expansion Strategy

Capital shortages can become insurmountable obstacles to the transition from a subsistence farming economy to an economy based on industrial mass production in developing countries. Building factories, improving the national infrastructure, and achieving urbanization and development each require huge investments. The capital accumulation that resulted from heavy taxation of agriculture during Mao's era did not turn out to be the desired goal. After more than two decades of effort, China's urbanization rate increased from 12.5% in 1952 to only 17.9% in 1978, an average annual increase of 0.2 percentage points (China Statistics Agency, 1952–1979). China's recent history suggests that relying on the accumulation of agricultural capital to achieve industrialization and urbanization does not work, especially since developed countries can control global agricultural prices through price discrimination and other economic measures, further weakening the ability to accumulate wealth through agriculture.

After 1978, China opened to the outside world and developed its economy through the introduction of foreign investments, which required the government to invest more in infrastructure development. Statistical data show that from 1983 to 2020, China's actual use of foreign investment was US$2.5 × 10^{12} (China Statistics Agency, 1978–2021). To address the capital shortage for infrastructure development, the Chinese government embarked on a program of generating funds for infrastructure by expanding the money supply. In 2010, China's gross industrial product reached 69.8 × 10^{12} RMB, surpassing the United States for the first time as the world's largest industrialized economy.

7.2.2.1. China's Urbanization Experience

To obtain more capital to support urbanization and infrastructure development, the Chinese government expanded the money supply. For example, China's 2017 GDP was 6.5 times the 2001 GDP, versus 9.6 times for the M2 component of the money supply. (M2 represents the broad money supply, which includes cash circulating outside the banking system plus corporate deposits, residential savings deposits, and other deposits, and it includes all forms of money that may become real purchasing power.) This financial expansion strategy effectively addressed the capital shortage. In 1994, China transformed for the first time from a traditional capital importer to a globally important capital exporter, exporting 1.1×10^{12} RMB in Chinese capital in 2017, which is 1.2 times the value of 907.2×10^{9} RMB for foreign investment (imports; Cai et al., 2019). During this period, China's consumer price index grew by an average of only 2.6% annually (China Statistics Agency, 1994–2018), representing one of the lowest inflation rates in the world; during the same period, investment contributed 13.7%–17.6% of China's economic growth (Guo et al., 2021).

Issuing too much money is a common model of economic development that has been pursued globally, and this model is only feasible if the expected benefits continue to outweigh the risk associated with financial expansion (i.e., the possibility that expansion will turn to contraction). To increase future government gains, the Chinese government has issued excess currency to fund infrastructure development in transportation, education, health care, energy production, and other requirements of citizens. This contrasts with many developed capitalist countries, which issue excess currency for residential consumption. The infrastructure construction has reduced social transaction costs in China and contributed to the country's rapid socioeconomic development, thereby creating a virtuous economic cycle of expansion and development. For example, urban housing prices in China increased from 2,112 RMB/m^2 in 2000 to 7,892 RMB/m^2 in 2017 (3.7 times the 2,000 value; Cai et al., 2019). During the same period, the per capita disposable income of urban residents increased by 4.1 times, from 6,280 RMB to 25,974 RMB (Cai et al., 2019). The rapid growth of per capita disposable income partly alleviated the harm caused by inflation, thereby providing a buffer that gives the government time to intervene by means of financial regulation to reduce inflation. At the same time, rising housing prices have provided capital for local governments, who use the "land finance model" to sell land-use rights to finance their construction of urban infrastructure and industrial parks (Li, 2011). In 2017, local government revenues from land sales in China reached 520.59×10^{9} RMB, which is 4.0 times the value of 129.6×10^{9} RMB in 2001. The urban population grew by 79.2% from 2001 to 2017, and the total real-estate area grew by 3.1 times (Cai et al., 2019).

The value of money depends on the credibility of the issuer (Balvers & McDonald, 2021), which follows the basic principles of contract theory, in which issuing money is safe as long as the issuer has sufficient material wealth or sufficient profitability to guarantee the value of the money. Economic growth increases a government's fiscal profitability, and the positive interaction between urbanization and increasing real-estate values has provided a favorable environment for the Chinese government's land finance program. However, urbanization cannot go on forever; eventually, there will be no more land to sell and no more people to purchase or rent urban real estate. An additional problem is the risk of creating a real-estate bubble, such as the bubble that occurred in Japan from 1986 to 1991 (Bekiros et al., 2017).

When that bubble burst, Japan's economy entered a long period of stagnation as the government looked for ways to recover. China has benefited greatly from the land finance model but must learn from Japan's example to avoid suffering the same fate. Unfortunately, the housing sales market in China has remained sluggish since 2019. In 2022, the Chinese government issued another 28×10^{12} RMB to cope with the sluggish Chinese economy (China Statistics Agency, 1978–2023). However, the glory years of the real-estate market are now past. If China cannot find new and larger sources of income to replace the real-estate economy, the Chinese economy is at risk of falling into long-term stagnation like Japan did.

7.2.2.2. Basic Principles of Financial Expansion

Currency is not only the representation of wealth but also reflects the reputation of a national government. If a government's currency is recognized in the international market, the issuer can continue to create more of the currency until the supply equals the market's demand. According to the traditional theory of monetary economics, productivity determines the total price of goods and therefore determines the amount of currency that should be issued by a country (Friedman, 1968). If a country's central bank issues too much currency, and the economy's production does not increase accordingly, the currency will depreciate. On this basis, a country's total money demand (M_q) can be calculated as follows:

$$M_q = \frac{\left(\sum_{i=1}^{n} V_{i-1} + \sum_{i=1}^{n} \Delta V_1\right) \times \Delta S}{12} + \sum_{i=1}^{n} \mathrm{MS}_i + \sum_{i=1}^{n} \mathrm{MI}_i \tag{7.1}$$

where $\sum_{i=1}^{n} V_{i-1}$ refers to the total national commodity value in the previous year ($i - 1$) for analysis during a period of n years, $\sum_{i=1}^{n} \Delta V$ refers to the total increment of national commodity value in the present year (i), ΔS refers to the currency circulation cycle (months), 12 represents the number of months in a year, $\sum_{i=1}^{n} \mathrm{MS}_i$ refers to the total amount of national savings in year i during a period of n years, and $\sum_{i=1}^{n} \mathrm{MI}_i$ refers to the international demand for the nation's currency in year i during a period of n years.

When currency is issued, there is a time lag between the date of issue and the time when the currency is consumed to purchase something, so the actual amount of currency issued is often greater than the actual amount of money needed. In this context, how can a country use the time-lag effect to control the amount of money issued and to increase the government's profits that arise from the gap between issuance of the currency and spending it? From the practical experience of various countries (Amarasekara, 2009; Hume, 1994; Liu et al., 2019), the quantity of currency that is issued (M_s, the total money supply) is calculated as follows:

$$M_s = M_q + M_t \tag{7.2}$$

where M_q refers to the total amount of money actually needed (the demand in Equation 8.1), and M_t refers to the total amount of money that has been issued but not yet spent.

The higher the credibility of the currency issuer, the greater the desire of investors to hold the currency and the longer the time lag that is permitted. The "time-lag currency" (Liu et al., 2019) refers to the amount of money issued by the government from the time when the currency is issued to the time when it is absorbed by the market. This amount of money can be estimated using the following equation:

$$M_t = M_q \times \frac{\Delta t}{12} \tag{7.3}$$

where M_t is the total potential supply of money with a time lag, Δt is the time lag between issue and spending of the money (months), and 12 represents the number of months in a year. If the longer time lag that can be achieved, the greater the opportunity for the currency issuer to profit. After China's reform and opening up, international investors believed that China's economic development prospects were bright, and this provided an opportunity for the government to create a national debt by issuing large amounts of money.

The size of the time-lag currency is affected by the market's judgment of the issuing government's profitability and also by the sensitivity of depositors and financial investors to inflation. In general, if a country's economy is in a state of continuous growth, consumers will not engage in panic-buying and may even save money, and the time lag before the currency is spent will be increased. The time-lag currency can be judged from a country's historical monetary inflation cycle. Amarasekara (2009) found a monetary policy time-lag of 26–38 months for Sri Lanka. The same time-lag exists between expanding the M2 supply and the resulting price and output effects, and this time-lag is about 6–7 months in China (Zhang & Luo, 2016), and to take advantage of this delay, China's government has issued more than 100×10^{12} RMB of time-lagged currency since 1978. This time lag offers a huge opportunity for currency speculation, which creates a certain risk of sudden devaluation of the currency, but governments justify this risk because it represents an effective way for them to achieve financial expansion. Although China's government has a reputation for printing money indiscriminately, cleverly utilizing the time-lag currency to fund national infrastructure construction or improve the livelihoods of impoverished people in poverty-stricken areas may continue to be a good strategy.

China's experience (Liu et al., 2019; Zhang & Luo, 2016) shows that it will take more than six months for the price of raw materials to rise after the government issues money to fund infrastructure construction and for that price signal to be transmitted to the market, where it increases the price of consumer goods. If the amount of money issued by the government is less than the total increase in the amount of social profits during the time lag, the issuance of the money will not obviously harm the market economy. That is, the longer the time between the initial investment and terminal consumption (i.e., the longer the time lag), the greater the profit earned from issuing the currency. This explains the funding source for China's investment in infrastructure construction, in development of raw material or natural resource extraction (under China's Western Development Plan), and in replacement of old industrial parks (under China's Northeastern Revitalization Plan). Because China's excessive money supply is not used in the consumption sector, but rather in the investment sector, the money is safer from speculation. The success of this method explains why China has issued the largest amount of currency in the world, but its consumer price index has grown at an average annual rate of only 2.6% (China Statistics Agency, 1978–2021).

If currency time-lag seems confusing, consider it as following a principle similar to financial leverage. Financial leverage refers to the ratio of a bank's outstanding loans to its reserves. If we assume that a bank has 10×10^{12} RMB of assets (i.e., reserves), then a 5× leverage can sustain 50×10^{12} RMB of loans, whereas 10× leverage would sustain 100×10^{12} RMB of loans. Once the loans are recovered on schedule, the virtual currency issued to fund the loans disappears (i.e., because it has been replaced by the loan repayment). Of course, if the loan is not repaid, there's a risk that the bank will go bankrupt. This approach increases the amount of time-lagged currency so that the time this currency spends in circulation increases leverage. For example, if China's actual annual demand for currency is 100×10^{12} RMB, and the time-lag for currency issuance is six months, then the government can issue an equal amount of short-term loans to enterprises after issuing 100×10^{12} RMB of normal currency. After six months of loan recovery, the excess 100×10^{12} RMB will disappear. If the economy is expanding, such repeated operations can stimulate economic growth without much risk. The risk and leverage of the currency time-lag are the same, and it becomes dangerous if the currency cannot return to the issuing bank as scheduled. This suggests that time-lag currency can only be issued during periods of economic growth. If the economy is shrinking, time-lag currency must instead be withdrawn from the market so that the excess currency can disappear before it affects interest rates. In practice, few governments reverse the process and withdraw the currency, and this may be one reason why governments in many countries cannot sustain themselves and are at risk of a financial collapse.

Although governments sometimes indiscriminately issue currency to avoid making difficult choices about managing their money supply, this does not prevent the application of time-lag currency as an effective means for a government to expand its economic scale. Since 1978, the issuance of money by the Chinese government has been offset by the increased supply of time-lag currency. For example, in 2020, China's M2 was 218.7×10^{12} RMB (China Statistics Agency, 2021), of which the time-lag currency amounted to 110×10^{12} RMB – more than half of the total (Zhang & Luo, 2016). However, this large amount of currency was not used to support spending by Chinese consumers. As a result, inflation has remained relatively low and savings have continued to increase. China's use of this strategy to support infrastructure construction (such as roads and communications infrastructure) rather than directly distributing the currency to individuals to support consumption, as is done in capitalist countries, has strongly supported its economic development. However, in the long run, continuing to issue currency will inevitably lead to inflation and (potentially) to devaluation of the currency. If such inflation affects the normal livelihood of citizens, social unrest is inevitable.

Excessive issuance of currency is an invisible tax levied by the government on citizens, since the money represents an obligation that the government (thus, citizens) must eventually repay, and this has huge political risks. If a country's government is unstable, and the benefits produced by the currency expansion are less than the expected benefits, financial expansion will exacerbate both international and domestic distrust of the government, increase the risk of social unrest, and possibly jeopardize the government. China's experience suggests that the strategy of excessive currency issuance should work for as long as the country's economy and the disposable income of its residents grow faster than the rate of inflation (Liu et al., 2019). So far, this has been the case. However, inflation also creates opportunities for currency speculators, and when information asymmetry exists (i.e., if the rich have access to better knowledge), the rich can profit more than the poor, which can lead to further widening of the gap between the rich and the poor and increasing social unrest (Chen & Li, 2011). Starting in November 2013, President Xi Jinping spared no effort to implement poverty alleviation programs that have (thus far) successfully resolved these social conflicts in China. However, the income gap between the rich and the poor remains a problem, as I discussed in Chapter 6.

Historical experience shows (Cao et al., 2007) that there is an uncertain relationship between population growth and benefits such as economic development, an increase in the population's education level, and an increase in the urbanization rate. Population growth provides workers who will drive socioeconomic development by both producing and consuming products, but if the rate of population growth exceeds the rate of economic growth, the surplus workers will be unable to find jobs, thereby reducing domestic consumption, and this will slow socioeconomic development. At the same time, the urbanization rate cannot increase forever, and when it reaches a certain threshold, the prices of financial assets such as land and buildings will shift from inflation to deflation. For example, land prices in Japan rose rapidly in the early 1990s, creating a real-estate bubble, but this "frenzy" lasted only about five years. After the real-estate bubble burst, Japan fell into a prolonged recession (Miller et al., 2010). China is currently experiencing a real-estate bubble that resembles Japan's bubble sufficiently to raise concerns about China's future (Wang et al., 2014). Unfortunately, to the best of my knowledge, nobody has studied these concerns.

7.2.2.3. Financial Risk Control

Expanding investment has been an important strategy for industrialization and urbanization in China (Cao et al., 2008), but this approach is a double-edged sword that brings huge risks to the future society while benefiting present society. There is no perfect strategy, but financial expansion can be acceptable if this issue is properly addressed (i.e., if governments take steps to minimize the risk). For example, as China's urbanization goals are achieved and migration between urban and rural areas gradually slows, the real-estate market is bound to become saturated. To account for this change, the direction of investment in financial expansion must change; that is, the Chinese government should slow its expansion of the money supply or even start to reduce the supply and must do this before the market is saturated to avoid a market shock. China has a vast territory with highly uneven development between regions, and effectively addressing regional development by redirecting investment to western and central China offers new opportunities to continue China's economic growth. For example, there is a severe water shortage in northwestern China, leading to drought and environmental degradation. As I will suggest in Chapter 10, diverting investment funds from over-developed eastern provinces to bring water from other regions to the northwest to promote industrial and agricultural development in that region could mitigate the risks associated with the real-estate bubble and ensure that China's economy moves steadily forward.

In the long run, scientific discovery and technological innovation are fundamental forces of socioeconomic development, and industrial upgrading triggered by scientific and technological progress as well as increased social production efficiency created by institutional innovation are fundamental drivers of economic growth. Innovation is a fundamental path for development in modern societies (Xia et al., 2023), and the huge market formed by China's vast land area and large population can certainly support innovation. The lessons from Japan's experience show that the failure to create new industries to drive economic development after the bursting of land or financial bubbles can slow or reverse economic growth. Japan's stagnation will continue if they cannot find an innovation that represents a breakthrough for their high-tech industries. This is a lesson that China and the rest of the world should learn.

Today's Chinese government seems to have not yet realized the problem with their traditional industrialized economic growth model, which relies on the benefits China has gained from the economic development of foreign trade in the Pearl River Delta, Yangtze River Delta, and Yellow River Delta since 1990. The new round of economic stimulus plans that have been implemented since 2008 once again focused economic attention on these regions, such as the establishment of the Commercial Aircraft Corporation of China in Shanghai to promote manufacturing of large aircraft and such as implementation of the "Guangdong–Hong Kong–Macao Greater Bay Area" development plan for the Pearl River Delta in 2019. High-tech development relies heavily on investments in worker skills and knowledge rather than the access to maritime transportation required by eastern China's coastal industries, and this offers the provinces in eastern China a large advantage for international trade. However, focusing this investment in Shanghai is questionable, since the talent pool in China's inland regions, including Xi'an, Chengdu, or Shenyang cities, is higher than that of Shanghai in the field of aircraft manufacturing. These inland cities were the technological centers of China's aviation and aerospace industry as early as the 1960s in Mao Zedong's era. At the same time, the Pearl River Delta investment provides money for an area that is already highly developed instead of allocating the money to other areas that would benefit more from the investment.

Despite this pool of expertise, economic planning since 2008 has failed to account for opportunities to use this talent to diversify the economies of central and western China and has ignored key principles such as the fact that high-tech industries don't necessarily require direct access to China's seacoast to succeed or the fact that the new China Railway Express network provides efficient land-based transport to markets in Europe and the Middle East along the New Silk Road route. Choosing the wrong economic development plan, as in the two examples I provided, will further widen the wealth gap between coastal and inland areas, posing greater risks to the stable development of the economy and stable leadership.

7.3. Institutional Innovation in China

Since 1978, a series of economic reforms and initiatives to open China to the West have contributed to China's rapid rise in many social and economic fields and its increasingly important role in international affairs. However, the Chinese government has always insisted on its unshakable adherence to the socialist path, resulting in what has been called the "China paradox" (Zhai, 2019): How did China achieve such great economic success without fundamental changes in its political system? Since 1978, a great deal of research has been conducted to answer this question by foreign scholars (Fleisher et al., 2010; Grzywacz, 2020; Henri, 2019; Hilmawan & Clark, 2019; Mearsheimer, 2001; Porter, 1991; Robinson et al., 2005). Unfortunately, none of these studies have yielded convincing results, and deciphering the mystery of the Chinese system remains a major challenge for political economics research.

Unlike traditional capitalism and the former Soviet Union's communism, China is exploring a new development path accompanied by a new social system. China's reform and opening up have retained the effective elements of a centrally planned economy and the socialist collective property rights system while absorbing the capitalist market economy and the private property rights system. In doing so, it has created new production relationships that combine capitalism's approach, which rewards individuals for hard and innovative work, with socialism's approach, which uses society-wide ownership of property to protect society from antisocial behavior by individuals. One particularly interesting innovation is an approach in which an employer shares the benefits of their enterprise's success with the knowledge workers who are responsible for that success. However, unlike the Western approach based on rewarding workers with shares of their company, the Chinese approach only provides benefits for as long as the worker remains employed by the company. I call this the *shared property rights* system. The effective combination of the old and new systems has avoided political turmoil similar to what occurred during the reform period in the former Soviet Union, has maintained social stability, and has promoted both economic growth and social development. Through inheriting the benefits of the older institution (central planning and collective ownership) and of innovation, China has gradually entered a new stage of social development that differs from traditional capitalism and Soviet communism. The Chinese miracle has been based on a new system of planning, markets, and new production relationships.

The new system proved to be very effective in agriculture, high-tech enterprises, and the knowledge economy, all of which have driven China's rise. China's institutional change is a major evolution of social production relationships, marking a new stage of development for society. Although China's institutional changes are not yet complete, the effectiveness of the new system is already evident. The replacement of manual labor with mental labor and the replacement of the traditional industrial economy with a knowledge economy appears to be an inevitable trend in the development of society (Cao et al., 2022). If all countries follow China's example and promote the development of the knowledge economy through institutional innovation, the evolution of society will greatly accelerate.

7.3.1. Early Examples of Shared Property Rights

The definition of property rights and changes in this definition are essential components of social evolution (Coase, 1959) and a sign of civilization. Unlike the revolution that led to the formation of the People's Republic of China in 1949, China's reform and opening up in 1978, led by Deng Xiaoping (1904–1997 CE), was a gentle and elegant process. Because it was so peaceful, both domestic and foreign scholars have tended to underestimate the magnitude and importance of this change. In fact, China's reform and opening up represents a revolution for the 7,000-year-old civilization based on private property, as it resulted in a new system that successfully solved the problem of how to reward the intellectual labor that is the driving force behind modern society.

China's institutional transformation is the result of a series of changes in the definition of property rights, including the partial restoration of the private property rights system that Mao abolished in the private sector, the maintenance of collective property rights (i.e., state ownership of key resources) and of government programs in the public sector (especially for government monopolies), and creative reforms based on the shared property rights system in the high-technology sector. This complex combination of systems has been progressively advanced through trial and error, achieving the goals of both political stability and economic growth.

7.3.1.1. Partial Restoration of the Private Property Rights System

In 1978, Deng Xiaoping learned from the failure of the people's commune system during the Mao era and allowed peasants to operate autonomously on arable land by signing a contract with the government; though he retained state ownership of natural resources such as land, the farmers were allowed to choose their own crops and management and benefit fully from their production (except for a small share of the crop that they gave to the government to build food reserves in case of famine). This system effectively restored their status as tenant farmers, but their use of the land was protected by the government. Although this system seemed to be retrogressive on the surface, it actually corrected the mistakes of the Mao-era people's communes, which were too costly and inefficient. For example, the government no longer imposed target crop yields, which had encouraged peasants to lie about their production, and no longer sold the crop on behalf of the farmer and retained all of the profits. As soon as the new system was implemented, government-appointed managers such as accountants, cashiers, custodians, village chiefs, and secretaries disappeared, and the cost of agricultural production fell; at the same time, crop yield and profits increased, making the reform a success from the outset.

In contrast to a traditional feudal society, Chinese farmers were no longer forced to pay rent to a landlord after paying their agricultural taxes. During China's feudal period, which lasted until 1949 CE, the agricultural tax was approximately 10% of the crop yield. Before the Communist Party took power in 1949, tenant farmers not only paid the same state income tax as other workers but also paid 10% of their crop to landlords as land rent. Therefore, the burden on farmers under the new (post-1978) system was lower than that under previous sharecropper systems. After paying the state income tax, all the surplus went to the farmers, which motivated them to be more productive. As a result, China quickly increased its food security and provided a stable social environment in which the central government could carry out reforms in the industrial sector.

After this successful reform of rural land management, the Chinese government allowed unemployed urban people and migrant farmers to start their own businesses in the cities, gradually expanding from the commercial sector (e.g., restaurants and shops) to the industrial sector. The 1980s saw the emergence of private enterprises such as workshops and small companies. The private sector has accelerated the development of the market economy and driven the progress of the market. The private sector has therefore grown rapidly. It did not exist at the start of 1978, but by 2019, it comprised 25.3×10^6 registered individual businesses nationwide that employed 263×10^6 people in the urban private sector, accounting for 82.8% of urban employment and 60.0% of total employment (China Statistics Agency, 2020). The GDP of the private sector's industrial output in 2019 was 86.1×10^{12} RMB, accounting for 87.0% of the national GDP. The private sector has therefore been a major force in China's economic growth.

7.3.1.2. Reform of State-owned Enterprises

To dispel suspicions of the private sector within the Communist Party, Deng Xiaoping delivered a speech in Shenzhen in January 1992, affirming the achievements made by Shenzhen in market-oriented reform and clearly stating that the private sector economy is an important component of the socialist economy (Brodsgaard, 2010; Hasan et al., 2009). The Third Plenary Session of the 14th Central Committee of the Communist Party of China, held in November 1993, adopted the policy *Decision on Several Issues Concerning the Establishment of a Socialist Market Economic System*, which clearly defined the idea of establishing a modern enterprise system with clear property rights, clear powers and responsibilities, separation of government and enterprises, and scientific management as the directions of the reform.

The rise of the private sector not only accelerated development of China's economy but also competed effectively with the traditional public sector (state-owned industries), causing a large number of state-owned enterprises to lose orders and even go out of business in increasing numbers after 1993; as a result, a large number of workers for state-owned enterprise were laid off. From 1993 to 2000, there were 27×10^6 laid-off workers in state-owned enterprises nationwide (China Statistics Agency, 1994–2001). Most of the laid-off workers (more than 70%; China Statistics Agency, 1994–2001) were rehired by the private sector. Except for monopolistic industries such as power generation and national security, the public sector gradually withdrew from economic activities in competitive areas.

Competition from the private sector has continuously decreased the proportion of the GDP contributed by the public sector (China Statistics Agency, 1952–2020). In 1985, the private sector accounted for only 3.0% of the national industrial and commercial tax revenues, but by 2019, this value had reached 56.9%. In 1980, the private sector accounted for 13.1% of the social fixed asset investment, and in 2019, the private fixed asset investment accounted for 60.3% of the total. In 1978, the number of private enterprises totaled 150×10^3, accounting for less than 1.0% of the total. By 2017, the number of enterprises nationwide was 18.1×10^6, with private enterprises accounting for 97.0% of that total.

7.3.1.3. Spread of the Shared Property Rights System

To complete China's industrial upgrading more quickly, the Shenzhen Science and Technology Bureau, which was short of capital, promulgated the *Provisional Regulations on Measures of the Shenzhen Special Economic Zone on the Administration of Share-Holding Through Technical Achievements* and the *Provisional Regulations on Technology Dividend in Shenzhen Special Economic Zone* in 1994 (Zhou, 2021) to encourage scientific and technological personnel to participate in innovation activities by means of receiving shares of an enterprise's profits (Zhou, 2021). The goal was to promote industrial upgrading through institutional incentives rather than government financial support. Since then, *property rights incentives* have become an important driving mechanism for innovative development and have become a popular strategy throughout the country. The new system builds on the older systems of public and private property rights. As I noted earlier, I call this the *shared property rights system* (Cao et al., 2022).

Shared property rights refers to a new benefit-distribution system in which knowledge workers and managers share the enterprise's profits in addition to earning their wages. However, unlike the shares in a capitalist market, these shares cannot be transferred or inherited and automatically return to the enterprise after the employee leaves the company. Unlike the traditional shareholding system in which the dividends are a reward for past work, the shares function as an incentive for future work, since these workers must work harder and more innovatively if they want to receive more dividends than their salaries. Because the dividends come from new profits in the future, they don't affect the employer's present capital stock. Because the owners of the enterprise can increase their future profits by expanding their business to take advantage of the innovations of their employees, the new system is widely supported by both the workers and the business owners.

For state-owned public resources such as the land that is cultivated by farmers, the system is somewhat different. Those who use and manage the public resource, under a government contract, are entitled to earn a profit from managing the resource. However, the resource remains the property of the state, and when the management contract ends, ownership returns to the state. The former user of the resource is responsible for restoring the resource to its original condition or a better condition. This is similar to the Western concept of *usufruct* (Ghijsbrecht, 2021). For example, in Canada, the federal government owns more than 90% of the forested land and licenses the right to harvest that land to the forest industry. The government earns taxes on the forest industry's income and charges the industry a "stumpage" fee equal to a fixed rate per cubic meter of wood harvested and uses that income to reforest the harvested sites. However, in contrast with the Chinese system, employees of the forest industry generally do not benefit from their innovations in the form of a share of the enterprise's profits, although they may receive different rewards for innovations, such as stock options and promotions to more responsible jobs. Obviously, the corporate management systems of Western countries are fundamentally different from those of Chinese enterprises.

The new Chinese system has successfully solved a key problem with the traditional compensation system, in which mental labor cannot be measured by time invested or a piecework rate. The result is that engineers are rewarded for the quality of their work, in addition to their hourly wage, and have considerable freedom to choose the time and place of their work according to their needs. This more flexible working environment provides room for individuals to innovate and develop their ideas, which greatly improves their motivation and the efficiency of their work. This approach recognizes that the incentives for manual labor differ from those for mental labor and reflects the fact that the new era for work requires new thinking about how to reward workers. At the same time, the traditional way of work and benefit distribution for workers and managers can also be transformed by the new system, and there is no reason to confine this practice to knowledge workers and their managers; as this system evolves, more workers will be able to share the dividends of their enterprise.

This represents a radical departure from the past, since the owners of enterprises (in the private sector) or of resources such as land (in the public sector) retain that ownership but share the enterprise's profits or the income gained from using a resource with the workers who create those profits or that income. As this innovation spreads, it will mark the emergence and evolution of a new social group and new production relationships. From now on, knowledge workers are no longer simply wage earners in the traditional sense but rather "shareholders" who can participate in the decision-making and management of enterprises.

In this new society, traditional manual laborers can upgrade their skills through independent learning or workplace training, and because they can leave their employer if they are dissatisfied, they have gained the power to negotiate with owners of an enterprise on a more equal footing. This changes them from sellers of manual labor or brain power who have no voice in an enterprise's operation to masters who directly participate in the decision-making and management of the enterprise and are compensated with a share of the profits. This represents a major change from traditional capitalism, in which the surplus value was enjoyed exclusively by owners. I will discuss surplus value in the next section.

7.3.2. Economics of the Shared Property Rights System

In a capitalist production relationship dominated by private property rights, the value of a product reflects the enterprise's costs and profit:

$$V_c = \sum_{i=1}^{n} C_i + \sum_{i=1}^{l} \mathrm{NB}_i \tag{7.4}$$

where V_c refers to the product value under a capitalist production relationship, $\sum_{i=1}^{n} C_i$ refers to the enterprise's total production cost, including n costs (such as wages, raw materials, losses, taxes, and transaction costs), and $\sum_{i=1}^{l} \mathrm{NB}_i$ refers to the enterprise's profits (net benefits), including various profits of the enterprise engaged in l economic activities. Since workers cannot share in the enterprise's profits under this model, Karl Marx (1818–1883 CE) called the profits gained by capitalists the "surplus value of workers' labor" (Marx, 1859).

Unlike the capitalist mode of production, the system of shared property rights, though based on the capitalist system, accounts for the surplus value and therefore motivates employees to improve the enterprise's production efficiency and profits by sharing some of those profits. Thus, along with the traditional profit ($\sum_{i=1}^{l} \mathrm{NB}_i$), the enterprise obtains a new surplus innovation profit ($\sum_{i=1}^{l} \mathrm{SB}_i$).

$$V_S = \left(\sum_{i=1}^{n} C_i + \sum_{i=1}^{l} \mathrm{NB}_i \right) + \sum_{i=1}^{l} \mathrm{SB}_i \tag{7.5}$$

where V_s refers to the product value under the production relationship under a shared property rights system, and $\sum_{i=1}^{l} \mathrm{SB}_i$ refers to the new surplus innovation benefit obtained by enterprises through the shared property rights system. The surplus innovation benefit is a new value beyond the capitalist production relationship and represents a dividend earned by knowledge workers and managers beyond their traditional wages and by capitalists beyond their traditional profit, so the new system has gained the support of both enterprise owners and knowledge workers.

Although capitalism has not been eliminated under the new system, its share of the economy has gradually decreased. For example, Ren Zhengfei invested 210×10^3 RMB in a small private company that he named Huawei in 1987, and in order to turn it into a high-tech company, he introduced a shared ownership system in which all engineers and managers became equity owners of the company.

By 2021, the company had grown into a major multinational telecom company with 195×10^3 employees, of which 131.5×10^3 skilled workers and managers were entitled to share in the company's profits (https://www.huawei.com/en/); Ren Zhengfei only held 1% of the company's equity. In 2021, the company achieved annual revenues of 636.8×10^9 RMB and a profit of 113.7×10^9 RMB; employees who were eligible for shared property rights received a total of 61.4×10^9 RMB in dividends, which amounted to 467×10^3 RMB each. The income from dividends was much higher than their salary income (an average of 241×10^3 RMB per person).

Since the 1970s, the Internet economy has been spreading rapidly around the world, which has given rise to a new technology economy and has been accompanied by a wave of globalization (Kogut, 2003; Romm et al., 1999). The shared property rights system has greatly accelerated the pace of technological innovation and renewal, which in turn has contributed to rapid socioeconomic development. For example, China's Huawei became a leader in technological innovation by distributing 99% of its property rights to its employees in the form of shared property rights. As a result of this system, Huawei has had one of China's fastest rates of technological progress (Ma et al., 2025). According to WIPO data, Huawei submitted 5,405 international patent applications in 2018, an increase of 34.3% compared to 4,024 in 2017, setting a new record for the number of international patent applications submitted by a company and becoming the company with the fastest global technological progress (Cao et al., 2022).

Huawei is not an isolated case; the *shared property rights* system emerged in Shenzhen in 1994 and quickly spread across China, especially in privately owned technology companies. Ma et al. (2025) analyzed the annual financial reports of 904 Chinese companies that are listed on the Chinese stock exchange from 2009 to 2021 and found that the profitability (return on assets) of companies with a shared ownership system (52.3% of the total) was an average of 2.1% higher than in traditional companies, and the innovation and product development ability of these companies has continued to improve, with corresponding increases in economic efficiency (Bennett et al., 2017). Although this number may seem small, it's worth noting that the companies Ma et al. (2025) surveyed retained more than two-thirds of the traditional shares; if that proportion decreases to the 1% of shares held by Huawei's owner, it seems likely the return on investment will increase.

In 2018, the total size of China's digital economy reached 31×10^{12} RMB, which accounted for 34.8% of the country's total GDP for that year (China Statistics Agency, 1979–2020). In 2016, there were only 35 "unicorns" (*fast-growing companies younger than 10 years old and that have a market value of more than US\$1 × 10^9*) in China and 96 in the United States; in 2020, the figures were 233 and 227, respectively (Table 3). China is replacing the United States as the new global leader for technological innovation. However, China still trails behind the United States in scientific innovation, as I noted in Chapter 3.

Like trees growing new branches in the spring, new institutions emerge from the old institutional environment and coexist with those old institutions. China has neither rejected capitalism nor overthrown socialism but has instead developed an

Table 3. List of Countries with the Most "Unicorns" from 2016 to 2020.

	China	United States	United Kingdom	India	Korea	Germany	France	Japan
2020	233	227	24	21	11	10	7	3
2019	206	203	13	21	6	7	4	2
2018	205	149	15	13	6	8	3	1
2017	59	109	14	10	2	3	2	1
2016	35	96	3	5	–	6	–	–

innovative shared property rights system that has grown out of the old system. As Buzan and Cox (2013) point out, China's shared property rights system represents an example of peaceful economic competition and cooperation (i.e., coopetition), a gradual change that has been co-evolutionary rather than revolutionary. Today, the southeastern coastal region of China, represented by Shenzhen, is rapidly developing high-tech industries with the shared property rights system as the core, and this system is being nurtured and is growing. This change has been gentle and elegant. This is why China's institutional change provides a good example for other countries to follow. I propose that this model is not a unique Chinese experience; rather, it can be learned and used by other countries.

Although the system of shared property rights is only in its infancy in China, its power is already evident. If such an economic system matures and enters the political sphere (through a mechanism such as increasingly scientific governance), society would rapidly enter an incredible phase of more efficient government and greater prosperity, particularly as the system spreads to workers outside the knowledge industry sector. With the development of a technological and knowledge-based economy, more new industries and more effective economic systems will emerge. Thus, the system of shared property rights is not the end of China's current evolution but rather one more step in the evolution of social production relationships, and it will be only one part, not the only part, of future society. Through the effective combination of different production relationships in the same era, Chinese society can respond to the requirements of different social and economic groups that together maintain the diversity and stability of society.

7.3.3. Institutional Change in China

Some scholars argue that China's economy has grown rapidly but that its political system has not progressed (Brodsgaard, 2017; Gallagher, 2002). However, this perception ignores major changes in the way the Chinese Communist Party has governed the country. In fact, China's reform efforts began first in the political sphere, with the publication by Deng Xiaoping of "Practice Is the Only Criterion for Testing Truth" in the *Guangming Daily* on May 11, 1978, in which he proposed that rather than basing policy development and implementation on theory or the opinion of a single person, such proposals must be tested to ensure that they work (Cao, 2016b). This represented a major ideological change from the Mao era.

The new ideology profoundly altered the content and foundations of the political system. As a consequence of this change, the central government has begun a process of decentralization that has gradually increased the authority of provincial governments to test innovations that take advantage of local strengths to see if they can improve the efficiency of local markets. Provinces have also been given increased authority to generate their own income from taxation and other mechanisms, such as land sales. By this delegation of authority, the Chinese government has completely abandoned the political philosophy of "class struggle" and the "dictatorship of the proletariat" and has given more power to provinces, counties, and cities. They have even allowed Hong Kong and Macau to follow the path of capitalism, at least in part. The traditional centralized political system is being replaced by a decentralized federal economic system (Cao & Ren, 2019), resulting in an increasingly diverse political and cultural environment. The central government also emphasizes cooperation rather than confrontation and strives to build a new commonwealth society. This diverse political and cultural environment provides a more relaxed political environment that nurtures innovation.

Unlike the former Soviet Union, China's political reform is not a simple move from socialism to capitalism but rather a move to create a new and more effective system by drawing on the beneficial elements of both socialist and capitalist systems. For example, the Chinese government took the initiative to accept the capitalist market economy system and abolished the people's commune system while retaining national-scale economic development planning through five-year plans. Although these plans define national targets (e.g., for pollution reduction), provinces are free to determine how they will meet those targets. The government has also eagerly encouraged international investment and has tried to learn from Western management experience and technology to further develop the economy (Wei & Liu, 2011), while maintaining state control over key economic sectors such as transportation to ensure social stability (Christiansen & Maher, 2017). This is political wisdom worth learning by all countries.

Shared property rights have also led to a major revolution in production relationships. When an employee owns a part of the company, their identity is transformed: they are no longer workers for a capitalist owner but rather part owners of the company who work for themselves. This kind of relationship motivates workers more strongly, thus making their company more competitive and profitable. In the new stage of society that is beginning to emerge, state ownership, private ownership, and traditional stock ownership can coexist with shared property ownership, and all four types of ownership may even coexist in the same enterprise. The industrial sectors that worked well under the old system will not be eliminated, but will continue to exist in the new society, and will slowly change as their economic environment changes.

The reform of China's political system has activated all aspects of its economy (Cao & Ren, 2019), which has seen unprecedented growth. Rapid economic development has increased pressures on global resources, as in the case of China's transformation from an oil exporter to an oil importer in 1993, with oil imports reaching 506 Mt in 2019 and accounting for 12.9% of global oil production

(World Bank, 2020). China has also become the world's largest importer of major raw materials such as timber, grain, and iron ore. China's economic development is one of the biggest drivers of global economic development and the growth of international trade. The products that China provides to the world improve the lives of the world's people and promote socioeconomic development.

Unlike the capitalist world, China's primary means of addressing resource shortages has been trade, not war (Abraham & Van Hove, 2005; Cao & Yu, 2019). China's goal is win–win cooperation, not a "China first" policy. As the Chinese saying goes, "if you want to get something, you must first help to produce it"; that is, if you want to get help from others, you must first actively help them. This is a marked contrast to the "America first" attitude that has arisen in recent years, which will bring disaster, not good fortune, to the United States. Whereas China has engaged primarily in international economic development, the United States has engaged in a series of expensive and ineffective wars that have caused much human misery, with little or no gain for Americans. In response to the US policy of containment and the trade war launched by President Donald Trump, the Chinese government has not chosen to respond with ships and guns but has instead launched the "Belt and Road" initiative. Its goal is to avoid direct conflict with the United States in the Pacific by routing travel through eastern Europe and western Asia in an effort to maintain both its international trade and international peace and tranquility (Aoyama, 2016). This reflects the wisdom of a Chinese culture that has lasted for more than 5,000 years and provides a lesson for all of humanity.

Although the shared property rights system has been effective in promoting technological innovation, it has only been implemented in private enterprises and even though it has been more than 30 years since shared property was first tested by the private sector, the Chinese government has not allowed it to be tested in the education and research system. As a result, Chinese academic innovation has suffered (see Chapter 3). Past scholars have studied China's institutional change based on an economic perspective, rather than a political or social science perspective, by focusing on economic utility rather than on the evolution of production relationships (Hilmawan & Clark, 2019; Pu, 2017). It has been wrongly assumed that China has neither completed its socialist revolution (Herrmann-Pillath, 2006; Whyte, 2009; Zhao, 2006) nor fully embraced capitalist institutional arrangements (Grabowski, 2007; Meinzen-Dick, 2007), and as a result, many researchers believe that what I've described in this chapter is specific to China and has no universal value.

However, the information I've presented suggests that China has found an effective way to combine the strengths of the capitalist and socialist systems to mitigate each system's weaknesses. In so doing, China has created a new system that has driven its rapid rise. The new system is the result of institutional evolution rather than revolution and has therefore also minimized social unrest. People usually see and understand the world based on one or a few perspectives, and that limited perspective hinders their understanding of the complexity of the evolutionary process of society. Some see China using the simple label of "communism" or "socialism" and thus ignore the capitalist aspects of modern China;

others ignore the socialist nature of China and focus only on its economic growth, assuming that the Chinese miracle is purely the result of capitalism (Hachigian & Peng, 2010). In reality, neither perspective provides a full understanding, and it's necessary to combine the two perspectives to understand China's rise. If old approaches continue to work well in some industries, such as public safety and transportation, they do not need to adopt this new model. The coexistence of a range of ownership models is a fundamental feature of civilization, and the new step in society's evolution that appears to be happening in China does not require repudiation of the old private and public ownership systems.

The concept of shared property rights borrows aspects of both capitalist and communist ideology but is not absolutist like either ideology; on the contrary, the new institution does not exclude the possibility of private ownership and free market economics. Just as the Industrial Revolution did not wipe out agriculture, and instead replaced manual farming with mechanized agriculture, China has demonstrated through its own experience that evolution toward a pro-social society (i.e., Confucius' *great harmony*) does not necessitate the elimination of capitalism but rather will lead to the harmonious coexistence of capitalism and socialism in the same country, or even in the same enterprise, through technological and institutional innovation. Confucius said that those who live within the areas bounded by the four seas are all brothers. The shared ownership system reflects Confucius' belief that by emphasizing cooperation and coexistence, rather than strife and war, the Chinese experience offers a win–win solution for achieving world peace. The changes seen in China today are only the beginning of a long process of evolution of the system of shared property rights, but China's rise will not be sustainable if the new system is not applied to other areas of society, such as government administration, scientific research, and higher education.

Chapter 8

The Theory of New Social Groups

As a system, capitalism has existed for at least several hundred years, with recognizable forms of capital and its use to support international trade dating to at least the Renaissance. Nonetheless, compared with the long history of humanity, such a short time is not enough to call capitalism the mature condition of a civilized state. Therefore, it may be more appropriate to understand capitalism as a transitional stage toward a new form of civilization. Indeed, since the word *capitalism* first entered common use, its status has been widely debated by scholars. In particular, the publication by Karl Marx (1818–1883 CE) and Friedrich Engels (1820–1895 CE) of the *Communist Manifesto* in 1848 suggested the beginning of a new stage (i.e., communism) that they expected would be gradually replaced or absorbed by capitalism.

Marx, the spiritual leader of the Communist movement, predicted that the working class would become the gravediggers of the capitalist system, presciently predicting the movement's vigorous growth during the following century. More than 150 years have passed since this manifesto, however, and capitalist society has flourished while communist practice has declined and even collapsed in most countries. Nevertheless, capitalism has shown many problems in both developed and rapidly developing countries, such as financial crises, ecological damage, the development of a large income gap between the rich and the poor, and social unrest. Just like any other system in history, capitalism has gone through a series of historical phases, with rising dominance, prosperity, a growing recognition of the system's failures, and a rising sense of the need to improve or replace the system. As you will see in the rest of this chapter, we are currently in the last of these stages. How should we understand capitalism and its role in the progress of civilization, as well as the laws that govern its rise and fall, in the contemporary international political environment dominated by American and European capitalism? This important question must be answered now that there are signs that society must prepare to move into a new stage of civilization.

From a historical perspective, the rapid progress of science and technology has led to the emergence of new industries and new social groups, and new ways to distribute the benefits of these changes to adapt to the impacts of the new

A New Stage of Civilization: Striving for the Great Harmony, 205–231

doi:10.1108/978-1-83708-258-220251009

industries and new social groups. This has enriched society and promoted social evolution, which are both ongoing phenomena. History shows that any stage of civilization is temporary, and that irresistible changes imposed by forces within and outside a society, as well as changes resulting from a society's continuous innovation, are eternal phenomena. Nowadays, various new social forms that may replace capitalism are beginning to emerge, and the signs of change are becoming increasingly apparent. Unlike Marx, I don't believe that capitalism will be destroyed by any competing social system. Rather, I believe that capitalism is changing in response to both internal and external pressures that are leading it to evolve toward a new and higher stage of civilization. In other words, capitalism is not dead, but society is fast moving to modify it or replace it with a better system that will define the next stage of civilization. The new stage of civilization may be the *great harmony* advocated by Confucius.

In this chapter, I'll discuss the lessons learned from capitalism and the changes that are occurring that may lead to its evolution or replacement in a future civilization.

8.1. Lessons Learned from Capitalism

In 1765, Anders Chydenius (1729–1803 CE), a member of the Finnish Parliament, published *The National Gain* (Chydenius, 1765), which first proposed the concept of free trade and free industry and advocated the principles of liberalism. In 1776, Adam Smith (1723–1790 CE) published *An Inquiry Into the Nature and Causes of the Wealth of Nations* (Smith, 1776), in which he proposed that the pursuit of maximization of personal interests was the motivation for people to engage in economic activities. Smith believed that if governments don't interfere with the economic activities of individuals, then the "invisible hand" of the market's price mechanisms will lead people to not only maximize their personal economic interests but will also maximize public interests and social and economic development. In 1789, the French Revolution led to *The Declaration of the Rights of Man* (www.britannica.com/topic/Declaration-of-the-Rights-of-Man-and-of-the-Citizen), which removed the last ideological obstacle to the replacement of feudal modes of production by a capitalist system.

In contrast with a feudal system based on inherited privileges and a rigid social hierarchy, capitalism is based on the right of all citizens to participate in commerce and enrich themselves. In this system, everyone has the right to participate, and their success depends on their skill and wisdom, not on their social class or conditions of birth (although the latter two factors may determine whether they have enough money to participate equally). Capitalism replaced feudal theocracy as the dominant Western ideology and affirmed human rights and, in that sense, represented a big step in the progress of civilization. Economically, capitalism is dominated by the private-sector economy, often (but not always) accompanied by a free trade economic model with little or no government intervention. Politically, capitalism arose within the context of a democratic political system and completely rejected the hereditary system based on the "divine right of kings."

The concept of a free market promotes a trade environment of near-anarchy without government intervention. Although such a system works well for successful capitalists, it works less well for many others, particularly because it tends to trigger periodic financial crises. (Here, *financial crises* refers to market failures due to various factors, including periods of overproduction that lead to price collapses and unemployment.) Some of these crises can be severe and last many years. For example, the Great Depression of the 1930s, an economic crisis that originated in the United States and spread throughout the capitalist world between 1929 and 1933, hit the capitalist economic system hard and lasted for more than a decade. With the relatively recent development of economic globalization, recessions and other economic shocks have repeatedly swept through the global economic system (Dobbin, 1993).

Since the early 1900s, capitalist countries have undertaken a series of reforms in an effort to prevent or mitigate recurring economic crises. Unlike Germany and Japan, which changed their economic systems by declaring war on the rest of the world, American president Franklin Delano Roosevelt's (1882–1945) "New Deal," a series of economic policies that centered on what became known as "the three Rs" (relief, recovery, and reform), increased government intervention in the economy and was a great success in the following decade (Burnham, 1969). *Relief* was aimed at supporting the poor and the unemployed, *recovery* was about restoring the economy, and *reform* was about reforming the financial system in an attempt to prevent another Great Depression.

8.1.1. Failure of Private Property Rights

Friedrich Engels believed, somewhat erroneously, that the emergence of private property institutions represented the beginning of civilization (Engels, 1884). In fact, the concept of "institutions" (standardized social structures that guide human behavior) preceded the development of specific institutions such as private property. Institutions arose as societies became larger and more complex, since they made social and economic interactions more predictable and efficient. Institutions as different as the free market of capitalism and the planned economy of communist countries required such institutions to function. All such institutions relied on a formal or informal definition of the difference between public and private property. Unfortunately, once the concept of property evolved, conflicts arose over who would have access to that property.

8.1.1.1. Control of Land and Dynastic Succession

Although the history of the feudal Western world is long, it has been longer in China: China's privatization of land gained legal status and the sale of land was approved by the government after the Shang Yang (395–338 BCE) reforms. As time went by, some livestock owners or farmers who were better at management than others produced surplus production, which they traded or sold to others in exchange for ownership of the land; those who profited most therefore became increasingly wealthy landlords, while the poor and the bankrupt had to lease their land and became tenant farmers. The resulting gap between the rich and the poor continued to widen. When enough property was accumulated by a few individuals, a formal feudal system and related institutions arose based on land ownership by a limited number of owners. This division of property ownership, in this and other forms, is the basis for the relationship between capitalists and workers in today's capitalist society. The main difference is that the development of an agricultural society and its economy was slow, and the concentration of land in the hands of a small number of owners required several generations to complete, so the intensification of social differences similarly took decades or even centuries to accumulate. In contrast, industrial society moves much faster, so the widening gap between the rich and poor in capitalist societies became serious within a short time in some cases.

This process led to monopolies or oligopolies. These forms of management of a society's resources are not unique to modern capitalist society. For more than 2,500 years, landlords in China have been hoarding land and expanding their operations by leasing the land to peasants. However, landlords have repeatedly failed to learn the lessons of history: when the ways they asserted their ownership became sufficiently painful to their tenant farmers, and particularly during social crises such as famines, the farmers rebelled and killed or displaced the landlords. Although they initially shared the land they liberated from the landlords, the same process of property accumulation soon began again. China's history has alternated between periods with increasingly powerful emperors and periods dominated by anarchic peasants. After the establishment of each new dynasty, the most wealthy or powerful became the new landlords, and the peasants who eventually seized the land through violent revolution once more became tenant farmers. Such recurring crises have disrupted Chinese society for more than 2,500 years.

From the perspective of economics, the competition in a free market is undoubtedly efficient. However, due to information asymmetry, differences in individual ability, and collusion between governments and the rich to control prices (as well as other illegal behaviors), the gap between the rich and the poor inevitably widens and social conflicts intensify. At the beginning of a Chinese dynasty, the strong government was able to control its people and respond effectively to natural disasters such as famine, but by the end of the dynasty, the government had weakened sufficiently that it was unable to resist the hungry and angry rebels who eventually overthrew it. The wiser landowners understood this threat and opened their granaries to the people to win them over and strengthen their power. However, greed was often stronger than wisdom. Politicians have long recognized the dangers of selfishness that generates anger or resentment, and the damage to society caused by the failure of markets to mitigate these pressures, but they have often been unable to address them. This demonstrates the failure of systems based exclusively on a free market that ignores the needs of society's poorest individuals. The current approach for governments around the world is generally to provide relief to the poorest people through government subsidies in order to relieve their frustration and anger, thereby reducing the risk of rebellion. However, if the underlying problem is not addressed, this approach only delays conflicts, as it doesn't resolve the market failure that created a gap between the rich and the poor and the resulting social tension.

8.1.1.2. Market Failures and Economic Crises

In an ideal free market environment, all economic decisions emerge from market forces rather than external forces. The results are determined by individuals exchanging, negotiating, cooperating, and competing with each other. The government may act to prevent market participants from using coercion, but it generally does not actively intervene in specific market transactions so long as they are legal. However, products take time to move from producers to consumers, and inadequate information about the demand that will exist when a product is available for consumption can lead to under- or overproduction. Moreover, information asymmetry often develops in ways that let those who have the best information profit before others can act; the former therefore become richer than the latter, but their purely selfish actions can have socioeconomic consequences. As in the example of Chinese dynasties that I have described throughout this book, private ownership alone cannot prevent market failures, particularly in the context of an unregulated (free) market. With the continuous and increasingly rapid development of a market economy, the cycle of economic crises may occur more rapidly (Dovern & Zuber, 2020).

In reality, perfect and perfectly symmetrical information does not exist in the free market, so it is impossible to achieve the ideal of "perfect competition." The seemingly inevitable result is discriminatory pricing, the development of monopolies, and other adverse consequences such as employment disruptions (because capitalism treats workers as production factors rather than as people). For example, when there is high unemployment, workers must compete for the available jobs, and capitalists can generally hold down wages to reduce production costs, leading to a widening gap between the rich and the poor. At the same time, not all economic resources are private property. When the government does not take measures to protect public property, which they nominally manage in the best interests of the public, market mechanisms that drive producers to minimize their costs to maximize their profits look for shortcuts that will improve their profits. These shortcuts often harm society. For example, actions such as failing to invest in pollution control create serious externalities, such as environmental pollution, whereas failure to pay workers a fair wage or a government's failure to implement socialized medicine and education lead to inequity in medical treatment and education. Obviously, some activities function best as natural monopolies, such as electricity, communications, and water supply, since these industries may represent unprofitable activities with high costs, and a nonprofit structure is necessary to ensure that they serve their social function. Such services cannot function through free competition, since a private monopoly always attempts to maximize profits rather than provide the best possible services in ways that might reduce their profits. Therefore, from the beginning, capitalism has represented a one-sided institutional arrangement based entirely on profit, with no sense of social responsibility unless that sense was imposed externally by a government.

Markets have always been, and can only be, one of the several social institutions that a society requires to function smoothly, but markets have existed throughout history. However, free trade cannot solve all the problems encountered by society, such as the environmental problems that totally unconstrained industrial activity creates for public goods such as the atmosphere and such as the difficulty of providing public services as a natural monopoly when governments forget that their role is to serve the people. Capitalism's greatest weakness, and thus, the harm it can cause, arises from its "survival of the fittest" ideology. Although the French Revolution's 1789 *Declaration of the Rights of Man and of the Citizen* is undoubtedly laudable, because it holds that all individuals should have equal rights, that the sovereignty of the state belongs to the people, and that private property is sacrosanct, it fails to account for the social attributes of individuals. For example, capitalism allows more effective competitors' unconstrained amplification of their private rights. The extreme development of the "everyone for themself" ideology inevitably leads to extreme behaviors that harm society. *Individual freedom cannot be prioritized over the rights of society as a whole if we hope to overcome these problems. Civilization cannot allow individuals to endanger others or society for the sake of their individual freedom. These aspects of human behavior are essential for the survival of society*. Unfortunately, the richest and most powerful capitalists are motivated to ignore these beliefs, even if this will eventually lead to social collapse.

Given that selfishness and a desire to become more powerful seem to be inherent human characteristics, and given that legal constraints on such behaviors are generally delayed until governments recognize a problem and take action, creating laws is not sufficient to constrain individual behavior, particularly in new fields such as high technology that evolve faster than the law can evolve. "Everyone for themself" cannot produce individuals who are willing to sacrifice their needs to benefit society. Capitalism provides little or no incentive for capitalists to fight famines and unpredictable natural disasters; rather, it encourages them to take their property and money and flee. The extreme selfishness that capitalism encourages will surely lead to the demise of current societies. Obviously, capitalism can improve the utilization efficiency of economic resources, but without external constraints, it cannot save people from suffering. It is therefore an extreme, limited, and imperfect social system. The *Communist Manifesto* that lies at the root of communism provides an alternative, though it too is not without its flaws, as we will see in the next section.

8.1.2. Reactions Against Capitalism

When society advances sufficiently that people have leisure time to engage in philosophy and sociology, philosophers and sociologists begin to perceive and discuss social problems. For example, during the more than 500 years of China's Spring and Autumn period and Warring States period (770–221 BCE), the feudal system established by the Zhou Dynasty (1046–256 BCE) began to collapse. Chinese sages engaged in a protracted debate that ended with widespread acceptance of Confucius' philosophy that the world was the property of the common people. Although this philosophy did not fundamentally curb the selfish control of China's resources by emperors, it played an important role in constraining the behavior of the Chinese people, and the Chinese empire (i.e., the series of dynasties) encouraged the people to accept the emperor's rule for as long as the emperor did not abuse his power beyond the people's ability to accept. As a result, the Chinese form of dynastic rule lasted more than 2,000 years.

Similar philosophical revolutions have occurred outside of China. For example, as Europe's feudal society began to lose its influence over society, the Renaissance of the 14th century, accompanied by anti-feudal and anti-church ideologies, led to the Enlightenment of the 17th and 18th centuries. These cultural movements, which at least partially liberated the people from feudal and theocratic rule, lie at the roots of the capitalist system. Soviet Russia had a different experience. After World War I, the people of the Soviet Union established the world's first communist state through the October Revolution (Mayer, 1993). (In this book, I have made the distinction that *communism* refers to a political system based on Marxism, which emphasizes the concept of struggle among society's classes in the context of historical change; in contrast, I define *socialism* as a political system that emphasizes the needs of all the people rather than just the wealthy and that may or may not involve class struggle.) The former Soviet Union largely escaped the effects of the Great Depression and, in so doing, became an example for global politicians who no longer trusted capitalism, and 39 countries adopted a communist or socialism system during the next few decades (Cao & Liu, 2020). More than 160 ruling or non-ruling parties joined the Socialist International.

Although communism was originally intended to be a philosophy that promoted the interests of the working class, it has evolved in ways that differ from Marx's intentions. For example, what some countries call "communism" or "socialism" is really a system controlled by a dictator or a system that uses the name to suggest that it is an approach designed to secure peaceful prosperity, as in the case of the "national socialists" of Nazi Germany under Adolf Hitler (1889–1945), who embarked on a path of centralized control and imperialism in the name of communism, which led to World War II. Unfortunately, the ideology of class struggle has not brought peace and progress to society. Rather, it has led to violent conflicts between countries and constant struggles among a nation's people, leading to poverty and death and threatening the progress of civilization. It has also led to political collapse, as in the case of the former Soviet Union, which had (before its collapse) been more of a stumbling block than a pathway to a superior civilization. This collapse undermined trust in communism and socialism until fairly recently, when China implemented market-oriented reforms that were intended to adopt some of the policies of a capitalist system in China.

From a philosophical perspective, Marx recognized the important role of an economic foundation for the development of human society and recognized that class division also conformed to the dialectical philosophical principle of "unity of opposites"; this is similar to the Western philosophical concept of thesis, antithesis, and synthesis. However, Marx's theory of "class struggle" emphasized opposition between classes and ignored the possibility that classes could work together to achieve class "unity"; as a result of this omission, Marx ignored history, including the fact that it was the cooperation between the proletariat and capitalists that eliminated feudal society and led to capitalism. As a result, communist regimes around the world wasted time, money, and lives by trying to eliminate capitalism rather than finding a way to cooperate with it. When communist governments succeeded in eliminating the bourgeoisie, and should then have assumed the role of a referee or coordinator for the distribution of interests between different groups of people, they instead replaced the bourgeoisie with new and more powerful exploiters: corrupt government officials. The negative consequences (increasing inequality of income between the rich and the poor) and even death were inevitable.

To justify government policy and exploit the people under the cover of an attractive slogan, Mao Zedong and his colleagues promoted the idea that poverty was beautiful and aggressively encouraged the people to become more beautiful. Unfortunately, even today, nearly 150 years after Marx's death, many political leaders have not realized his mistake, leading to predictable disasters when communist dogma was applied blindly, without accounting for how this could easily enrich corrupt regimes. In the next section, I will propose some new ideas on how to avoid this mistake and guide human social and political institutions down a more ethical and effective path.

8.2. A New Social Group Theory of Institutional Change

As discussed in Chapter 1, Marxist theory has serious flaws. However, Marx's and Engels' overall understanding of the essence of capitalism is correct, because capitalism never stops seeking to increase profits and tends to replace traditional social ties that strengthen a society with economic ties that are more often neutral or negative. Such a change will commercialize social systems, weaken the differences in traditional culture and lifestyle between countries and regions, and increase the vulnerability of social development (Marquand, 2011). Therefore, capitalist private ownership and the associated requirement for society to protect private ownership can restrict the development of society (Thompson, 2007). To solve this problem, the capitalist system itself must change.

8.2.1. The Emergence of New Social Groups

Society is constantly evolving in terms of both time and space, and this evolution depends on the complex relationships among many factors such as environmental change, population growth, evolution of an ideology, culture, and history (Butzer & Endfield, 2012). Under the pressure of population growth and increasing demand for resources by that population, individuals constantly seek new resources and try to develop new technologies to exploit those resources. The development of new technologies and exploitation of new resources has given birth to new industries and corresponding new social systems (Cao et al., 2007). For example, the Industrial Revolution created a new class of factory workers, and their needs for protection against abuses by their employers led to the evolution of trade unions and protective government regulations. When a new industry gradually becomes a dominant factor in social development, it will have an impact on older industries, forcing those industries and the systems in which they exist to adapt through competition and improved operating efficiency (Cao & Yu, 2019). Competition between industries and between political regimes forces social institutions to evolve in a new direction and thereby creates new social groups.

Around 12,000 years ago, ancient humans abandoned their hunter–gatherer nomadic lifestyle in favor of a sedentary or semi-sedentary agricultural lifestyle, which became increasingly dependent on the development of social and trading networks (Bar-Yosef, 2000; Hellenthal et al., 2014). This agricultural revolution and the resulting food surplus were key factors in the emergence of civilization, and a thriving agricultural economy laid the foundation for additional population growth (Weiss & Bradley, 2001). This feedback mechanism forced societies to seek ways to protect their assets from external encroachment, thereby leading to new institutions such as armies to protect a resource against invaders (Cao, 2015).

The emergence and development of new industries will lead to imbalances in the old socioeconomic system, and those who could profit from these imbalances will promote social change and create a new institutional environment (North, 1971). For example, in China during the Spring and Autumn period and the Warring States period (770–221 BCE), the use of iron tools greatly increased labor efficiency, which increased agricultural productivity, leading to population growth that further amplified agricultural production (Cao, 2016b). At the same time, this created new social groups such as miners who obtained iron ore, smelters who extracted the iron from the ore, and blacksmiths who forged the iron into useful tools. These new social groups and the relationships among them changed the structure of society. They also created a new source of revenue for governments through taxation of the new wealth these groups created.

If the development of new industries depends on new production relationships, the people who depend on the new industries for their livelihood tend to form new social groups, some of which may have never before been seen; for example, there is no historical precedent for the social groups created by computer software. With the development of society, new groups continuously arise and replace or coexist with older groups. The Western Industrial Revolution in the 18th century and the subsequent development of modern capitalism accelerated the development of Western democracies (Bowles, 2012). The new working class generated from the Industrial Revolution and the capitalists who hired them jointly formed the dominant social groups of that era. Together, they buried the feudal society, which contradicts the predictions of Marx and Engels, who claimed that the bourgeoisie would bury feudal society with no help from other groups.

The emergence and development of new industries create the basis for the birth of new social groups, and the new social groups will, in turn, become the basis for the development of a new civilization. However, because these groups evolve from a unique set of social and economic conditions, a government that attempts to blindly create these groups in their own country is likely to fail. For example, after World War II, many developing countries copied the political systems of developed countries, but because their political, social, and industrial structures were not well suited to this form of socioeconomic development, neither the democratic system nor a market economy achieved the desired results (Cao & Yu, 2019). To create a market economy where one did not already exist, trading rules and mechanisms, as well as investment funds and market competition rather than monopolies, are necessary for the market to efficiently provide goods and services to consumers (Jo, 2013).

Today, with the rapid development of technology, disruptive technologies such as printing presses, assembly lines, and personal computers have not eliminated capitalism. On the contrary, they have been absorbed by capitalism and become part of it. Because technology itself is neutral, it can become a tool used by capitalist "gravediggers" but cannot itself become the gravedigger (Thompson, 2007). In contemporary society, the application of science and technology has continuously promoted industrial development and even triggered industrial revolutions, such as the "computer revolution." Technological innovation such as more powerful and efficient machines and new techniques permitted by scientific innovation, such as replacing steam power with electricity, and new organizational innovations, such as refinements of accounting and taxation, have facilitated the development of capitalist enterprises such as manufacturers and other businesses and of social institutions such as bureaucracies and hospitals (Fafchamps, 2011).

New industries do not necessarily produce new social groups. If the underlying economic system of the new industry does not change, it will maintain its stable operation. If there are new changes in the production relationships among people within the new industry, and a new and more efficient system for distributing benefits arises, the people who participate in the new and more efficient system can become a new social group. Of course, an institutional innovation must be more efficient or attractive before it replaces the older system, and only in this way can the new groups survive and grow despite sometimes fierce competition from older groups. New social groups that arise in society's economic sectors often spread to the political sector as they grow strong. This process may be peaceful and friendly at the beginning but may become contentious or even violent if it disrupts or threatens existing power structures. Because the appearance of a new social group potentially increases the government's fiscal revenues (through taxes on the new industry), the process is welcomed by the government until the new social groups attempt to influence political opinions.

When a new social group becomes the leader of social development, the old system will also change to ensure that all people can continue to benefit under the new system (Cao, 2016b). This process attracts the attention of philosophers and other scholars, who attempt to persuade politicians to accept new approaches and avoid unnecessary struggles that create social turbulence. (I will discuss this in more detail in Chapter 9.) In the new environment, the old industry still exists, and the systems that adapted to the old industry will also continue to exist until a more efficient or attractive system evolves to replace them. Even if a new social group attempts to exert a political influence, it does not inevitably need to eliminate all the old systems; rather, through dialog with the old groups, it may encourage the old systems to change so as to improve social and economic efficiency. For example, when agricultural societies transitioned to an industrial society, agriculture typically embraced a parallel large-scale industrial transformation.

Such processes tend to be evolutionary (slow and peaceful) and tend to lead to a gradual and orderly transition.

From a historical perspective, new systems tend to evolve from the existing system, rather than arising from nothing and completely overturning the original system, although there are certain examples of revolutionary changes. As a result, peaceful evolution such as reform is more likely to succeed and have a longer impact. This evolution is often spontaneous, rather than the product of elaborate designs by governments or social movements. At first, the new system produces its products under the old system's environment and then gradually grows; after its social system has become dominant, elements of the old system that continue to work well in the new environment can continue to exist, whereas elements that are no longer effective either choose to change, or are eliminated (Cao, 2016a). Ideally, new and old institutions continue to coexist to take advantage of a more diverse social system. One advantage of the coexistence of old and new systems is that the hybrid system can generally better meet the needs of different groups than the single older system (Cao, 2015). Diverse systems offer several advantages, including the ability of different system components to meet different needs, greater flexibility to respond to challenges such as global climate change, and the possibility that additional new groups will arise from the currently new system. Therefore, the diversity formed by the coexistence of old and new institutions can potentially promote the long-term existence of society.

Not every ruler is wise, especially when a ruler develops an inflexible ideology. Political representatives of the old era often fail to recognize or accept a new ideology, leading to institutional lock-in or even violent revolution, as in the case of the French and Chinese revolutions. History has repeatedly shown that governments that cannot learn the need to evolve as society evolves cannot last long. Similarly, leaders who don't understand culture and who are unfamiliar with history cannot understand the continuity of society, and although they can delay the birth of new systems, they cannot stop the evolution of civilization, particularly since that evolution often follows unanticipated twists and turns. The Soviet Union provides a good example because it ignored the lessons of history, and specifically the need to evolve, and therefore collapsed rather than adapting and surviving.

8.2.2. China's Experience

Because the emergence and application of every new technology will disrupt the existing equilibrium, technological change will induce institutional innovation, and this will promote social and economic development. This, in turn, will promote new technological innovations that trigger a new round of institutional evolution. The long history of civilization has shown that new technologies create new opportunities for profit and upset the social equilibrium of the old system. The emergence of the new system may force the evolution of the old system or may lead to coexistence of the old system in competition or coopetition with the new system (Beddoe et al., 2009). For example, technological innovations that increase food security can promote population growth, which in turn promotes urbanization and the emergence of related industries such as public transportation and waste management.

Unlike economic institutions, which can evolve rapidly in a competitive environment, political institutions may not evolve until social institutions or economic institutions have accumulated sufficient energy to drive the change (Cai & Treisman, 2006; Chan et al., 2015; Shi, 2019). This energy includes the desires of a numerically superior new social group, pressure by economically dominant industries, and society's growing frustration with a problem the government is unwilling or unable to solve. The evolution of political institutions often begins with the development of a new ideology or the revival of an old one. Philosophers and other scholars patiently describe the benefits of the ideology so that more people understand it and believe in its significance, and so that politicians understand the ideology's relevance for governance in terms of the potential benefits it brings. Although most philosophers love peace, political change often begins as a peaceful evolution and ends as a disruptive or even violent revolution. In the rest of this section, I will discuss these processes in the context of Chinese history.

8.2.2.1. Institutional Changes in the Last Years of the Zhou Dynasty

In China, during the Zhou Dynasty (1046–256 BCE), every emperor distributed land to his sons and to meritorious officials and governed the country in a manner similar to Western feudalism. Feudal lords, in turn, redistributed their land to their subordinate nobles, who then divided the land into 3 × 3 grids of cells in which the central cell belonged to the nobles themselves, and the surrounding eight blocks were allocated to the people for farming. The nobles did not cultivate the land but instead survived by taxing the production of their subordinate people. Those people were required to prioritize the needs of the nobles. After meeting those needs, they were allowed to cultivate the land to support themselves. Because the nine pieces of land formed the shape of the Chinese *jing* character, historians called this the *jing* field system.

By the end of the Zhou Dynasty, iron farm tools began to be widely available. These superior farm tools made it much easier for farmers to complete their cultivation work, thereby reducing labor requirements and making it easier to support the noble's needs. The increase in labor productivity meant that each farm required less labor to accomplish the same amount of work. Moreover, the growing farmer population permitted by the increased food supply soon began to exceed the ability of individual farmers to feed everyone from the limited amount of land that was available. Many of the farmers abandoned their land and moved to land outside the boundaries of the noble's land. Although all farmland in China was the property of the king, or of officials who had been granted rights to the land by the king, there were still areas of uncultivated land available for reclamation. These newly reclaimed lands were called *private farms*, and the corresponding populations were called *homesteaders*.

These homesteaders formed a new social group. Their departure from the traditional system threatened the economy of the noble landlords, and the feudal lords sent armies to suppress the farmers. However, the large number of homesteaders made it prohibitively difficult to suppress them militarily, and the feudal lords gradually lost their power over the land and were forced to compromise and recognize the legitimacy of the homesteaders. In return, homesteaders paid taxes to the feudal lords based on the number of people and the amount of land they actually cultivated. The flight of peasants left the noble's land uncultivated. To solve this problem, they developed a new innovation: they leased their land to the farmers, who became tenant farmers with a new relationship to the landlords. Tenant farmers paid for their lease with a share of their crops but were free to sell their surplus products after paying their rent and relevant taxes. Landlords and homesteaders could also buy and sell land as a commodity.

During the feudal period, landowners divided their people into groups and worked collectively, and the whole process needed special supervision by the lord who owned the land. After the new system emerged, the tenant farmers had no relationship with the landlord except to pay rent. Therefore, as long as the rent was paid, the landlord did not need to supervise their work, and the social cost of this labor was reduced. At the same time, because of their personal freedom, the farmers were willing to work harder, so the production efficiency also increased and the government earned more tax revenues. Obviously, the new system was not only more efficient but also represented a win–win institutional arrangement that was equally welcomed by the rulers and the people.

The evolution of this economic system and the expansion of the homesteaders eventually induced changes in the political system, which had endured for hundreds of years. According to records from the reign of King Wen of the Wei (472–396 BCE), the Wei state was the first to recognize the legitimacy of homesteaders through political reforms, and this approach made the state prosperous. In 361 BCE, Shang Yang (395–338 BCE) carried out political reforms in the Qin state to reward military service by depriving the aristocracy of their hereditary status and land and awarding farmland to successful or distinguished soldiers. In this way, everyone (including homesteaders and slaves) could gain land, wealth, and political status by fighting in the army. Shang Yang's reforms brought an end to the feudal system in China. At the same time, the nobles were transformed into landlords, so their economic interests were not greatly harmed.

The Qin state unified China in 221 BCE. Subsequently, the Han Dynasty (202 BCE–220 CE) started a new system for the selection of government officials, in which local officials identified talented individuals within their jurisdiction and recommended that they be hired by the central government. In 621 CE, Emperor Yang of the Sui Dynasty (581–618 CE) established the imperial examination system. This made it possible for ordinary people to enter the government by demonstrating their mastery of the skills that were believed to make someone a good imperial bureaucrat. This system continued to exist until the Qing Dynasty, which abolished the system in 1905.

8.2.2.2. China's Rural Reforms in 1978

In 1949, the Chinese Communists gained power through a violent revolution and then confiscated the land owned by landlords and distributed it to the tenants.

This increased the enthusiasm of the farmers to work harder, and China's agricultural output developed rapidly. However, in 1958, China embarked on a radical reform of public property rights, expropriated the land allocated to the farmers, and forced them to work in collective villages to meet government production targets. Private property rights were completely eliminated and replaced by state ownership. Apart from significant differences such as modern mechanization techniques, this situation was tantamount to returning to the feudal system described earlier in this chapter. Moreover, government monitoring of the agricultural communes increased the number of unproductive management posts such as accountants, cashiers, village heads, and secretaries, and the cost of agricultural production increased. As a result, from the start of the people's commune movement in 1958 to the end of the cultural revolution in 1976, China's agricultural economy stagnated.

Moreover, the farmers who lost their land had no other income except the rations and a small amount of cash provided by the government, and many of them became destitute. By 1978, the annual per capita disposable income of Chinese farmers was only 133.6 RMB (China Statistics Agency, 1979), making them the poorest farmers in the world. China also experienced terrible famines in the 1960s that forced impoverished farmers into risky behavior just to survive. For example, some villages launched a rural land contract system that allowed individuals to use collective land. However, after the famine, Mao Zedong quickly banned this system. In December 1978, during Deng Xiaoping's reforms, the farmers of Xiaogang Village in Anhui Province took the risk of signing a similar agreement again, with the village contracting (leasing) its collectively owned land to farmers for operation.

The new agreement stimulated the enthusiasm of farmers to work. Xiaogang Village produced 66 t of grain in 1979, equivalent to the total grain output of the previous five years (Cao, 2016b). Edible oil production reached 17.5 t, equivalent to the total output of the previous 20 years. In addition, it gave farmers more flexibility in their choice of crops, thereby allowing them to improve their income by meeting the need of consumers. The behavior of Xiaogang Village was approved by the government and promoted throughout the country. By June 1982, 82.6% of the villages in China had implemented this form of land lease management. The per capita grain output of rural residents increased three times, from 385.7 kg in 1978 to 1,177.0 kg in 2019, and the per capita disposable income of rural residents increased 119 times, from 134 RMB in 1978 to 16,024 RMB in 2019 (Cao, 2016b).

Social systems are complex. Small institutions and informal institutions can accumulate energy through slow changes and use that energy to induce large institutions and formal institutions to change when that energy reaches a certain threshold. After the older, larger system changes, a small system that works well does not need to be changed or may only need to be partially changed. In China, for example, land is nationalized and controlled by the central government but is leased to farmers for cultivation, and farmers operate similar to how they operated in the ancient historical examples I described earlier except that they pay rent to the government rather than to feudal landlords. Although the change was small, replacing landlord rent with government leases reduced the burden on farmers, thus improving their enthusiasm and productivity.

8.2.2.3. China's Urban Reforms

To catch up with Western developed countries, Mao Zedong adopted a radical high-tax policy, which unfortunately confiscated almost all products of the farmer's labor except the rations needed for survival and the seeds needed to grow next year's crops. This approach resulted in low investment to improve agriculture, exacerbated by low motivation for farmers to produce more crops. The result was decreased food production, with farmers living in a state of long-term famine because they could not provide themselves with enough food. From the beginning of the people's commune movement in 1958 to the end of the cultural revolution in 1976, China's gross domestic product (GDP) grew by 6.1% annually. During this period, China's population increased from 540×10^6 to 930×10^6, an increase of 72%. The rapid population growth offset some of the results of economic growth in per capita terms, to an average annual growth rate of only 4.4%. China's economic growth rate was lower than the government expected and was lower than that of capitalist countries such as Japan and South Korea and lower than that of capitalist regions such as Taiwan, Macao, and Hong Kong (World Bank, 1958–1976).

Since 1978, China's market-oriented economic system reform has promoted vigorous development of the private sector economy, and the number of people employed in the private sector has increased rapidly. In addition to the overall privatization of activities such as agriculture in rural areas, the urban private economy has also developed rapidly. In 2019, the number of urban private sector employees (excluding self-employed workers) in China reached 263×10^6, accounting for 82.8% of the total employment in 2019, up from 0.02% in 1978 (China Statistics Agency, 2020). The development and expansion of the private sector economy have promoted the rapid development of China's economy. At the same time, the factory owners and workers responsible for development of the private sector economy have formed new social groups that did not exist in China during the Mao Zedong era and have earned their living through new production relationships. With the development of these social groups, group members were no longer satisfied with only economic interests and began to seek political freedom and greater political power. On June 4, 1989, the student movement for freedom, human rights, and democracy organized protests throughout China. Students even erected a statue of the "goddess of liberty" in Tiananmen Square.

Although the 1989 protests ended in failure, they also demonstrated that changes in economic institutions could become a driving force for new political institutions in the future. Unlike young students and most scholars in 1989, Deng Xiaoping did not aspire to follow the capitalist road; rather, he wanted to find a new development path through a process of trial and error that he called "walking and looking" (i.e., taking a step and observing the results). In other words, he did not give up his original ideal of eliminating capitalism. After the 1989 protests, Deng did not stop China's market-oriented reform because he believed that a more efficient social system could be built on the shoulders of capitalism.

8.2.2.4. The Emergence of New Chinese Social Groups

Since the 1990s, new social groups have emerged in China. In 1997, the Internet and the digital economy were unknown to most Chinese citizens and Internet sales were almost nonexistent, but by 2016, 52.9% of the people in China were using the Internet (China Statistics Agency, 2017). This phenomenon has contributed to rapid socioeconomic change. For example, in 2020, Internet-based sales reached 11.8×10^{12} RMB, accounting for 54.6% of the total retail sales that year (China Statistics Agency, 2021). This dramatic change is also driving a shift in the way the Chinese government views and uses Internet technology. In March 2015, the third plenary session of the 12th National People's Congress declared that developing the "Internet Plus" economy was China's top priority. This represented a new form of economic and social development in which Internet innovations are deeply integrated with all sectors of the economy and society – a new type of economic and social development with the Internet as the key infrastructure and driver of innovation. The emerging Internet sector has created a new breed of entrepreneurs, such as those who create or provide Internet services. A large number of engineers joined this industry and became shareholders either through traditional stock ownership methods or through the shared property rights system, gradually forming a new social group. New industries also provide 2.4×10^6 job opportunities for Chinese college and university graduates each year (Cao & Yu, 2019).

The combination of new technology and high profits has made "Internet Plus" a major driver of China's social and economic development. Those who have benefited have also gained political influence. For example, Jack Ma, the founder of Alibaba, China's largest Internet company, spoke at the World Internet Conference in Wuzhen, China, on November 17, 2016. When American president Donald Trump tried to raise tariffs on Chinese products, Jack Ma immediately visited the United States and met with him on January 9, 2017, successfully delaying the start of a trade war between China and the United States (Cao & Yu, 2019).

As I noted in Chapter 7, the Shenzhen Municipal Bureau of Science and Technology implemented the *Provisional Regulations on Measures of the Shenzhen Special Economic Zone on the Administration of Share-Holding Through Technical Achievements* and the *Provisional Regulations on Technology Dividend in Shenzhen Special Economic Zone* in 1994 (Zhou, 2021). These regulations stipulated that knowledge workers (including engineers and technicians) could use their technological innovations to earn shares in their enterprise. (In this book, I will define technical innovation as an improvement of techniques rather than technology. For simplicity, I will use the phrase "technological innovation" to refer to both technique and technology.) These regulations represent China's first institutional documents that attempted to balance the institutions of private property rights and shared property rights. This system is, to the best of my knowledge, different from all previous systems. Unlike state ownership in communist countries, employees are able to hold shares in their company, and unlike shareholding in Western countries, the shares are only held while a worker remains an employee. Unlike traditional skilled workers, engineers who hold shares can receive both the wages of a traditional skilled worker and a share of the enterprise's profits by participating in decision-making. However, unlike Western stock owners, they do not own a share of the enterprise and must return their shares when they leave the company. They therefore represent a new social group.

Because the knowledge economy appears to be the future development direction of society, the shared property rights institution represents a promising candidate for a major form of future production relationships. Under this system, the capitalists who own the enterprise do not pay their knowledge workers extra (e.g., overtime) unless these workers create innovations that increase the enterprise's profits; they therefore share the risks of innovation with the capitalists who own the enterprise. These workers not only obtain additional income if their innovations succeed but also improve their political status by participating in corporate decision-making either personally or through representatives. Since the shares these workers receive cannot be inherited or taken with the employee when they move to another enterprise, the children of these workers cannot get something for free, unlike the children of capitalists. This interrupts the intergenerational transmission of wealth, and particularly the wealth represented by shared property rights, and thereby narrows the social gap between the rich and other individuals that begins at birth. The fairness of society seems to have improved. Although the new property rights cannot be inherited, as described in the Huawei dividend case I described in Chapter 7, the new system brings higher benefits to each participant compared to the old system. As a result, the new system has been widely welcomed by knowledge workers, capitalists, and governments and is becoming increasingly widely adopted. It represents a promising win–win path for the wealth represented by shared property rights and thereby focuses on the evolution of a prosocial civilization.

The evolution of an economic system often results from local, casual, and small changes that are difficult to discover. The path of these changes is more likely to be harmonious and friendly than in the case of more radical changes. Therefore, society has enough time to adapt to these changes and incorporate new institutions into the existing institutional system (Petr, 1986; Roland, 2004). In this process, the new and old systems develop in concert to form a win–win solution, so that both systems can share the benefits with a lower cost. New technologies and systems can also improve old industries and make them more efficient. Technological progress eliminates old jobs while creating new ones to replace those that were lost. For example, between 1999 and 2010, technological progress in the European Union (EU) region increased employment by 1.9% (Gregory et al., 2016), with a positive effect in 27 countries. Over time, "new economy" industries may replace old industries, and employees in old industries may find new jobs, integrate into new industries, and generate new revenues.

The basic feature of institutional evolution is that technological progress produces new industries, but also, and more importantly, it produces new institutions adapted to the new industries and a new life for people who live under the new institutions. The development and expansion of these new groups will inevitably lead to a new system, possibly with feedback loops. For example, the industrial revolution in Europe and North America was made possible by the emergence of capitalism, and its economies in turn facilitated the development of capitalism. Although the evolution of capitalism has produced many negative effects, such as environmental pollution and the exploitation of child labor, it has also promoted the maturity of Western democratic systems (Bowles, 2012).

Technological innovation is a necessary condition for a new system, but it is not sufficient. Not every technological innovation leads to institutional change. If new technologies and industries work well in the old institutional environment, the old institution will function more efficiently without changing its essential nature, so new institutions do not need to be created. Progress more often results when new technologies create new industries (Mabogunje, 2000). Both for technology and new systems, high efficiency is attractive and can persuade people to adopt a system. The resulting spread of the innovation can lead to a major transformation of society. Today, the shared property rights system is quietly spreading in China's high-tech sector, licensed and supported by local governments, due to its efficiency and potential for increasing tax revenues (Ma et al., 2025). This suggests that the innovation may spread outside of China, since governments are likely to be strongly attracted by increased revenues.

8.3. The Next Stage of Civilization

It is human nature to strive to improve the quality of life and pursue a better life. However, capitalism confuses quality of life with consumption, as it treats the growth of resource consumption and GDP growth as proxies for improvement of the quality of life or as a proxy for social progress. This ideology and the system itself are inherently hostile to sustainable development because they don't accept a need for environmental protection and social progress; as a result, the benefits of this form of capitalism have been questioned by scholars in the fields of sociology and ecology (Beddoe et al., 2009). To encourage production and meet the ever-increasing demand for consumption, capitalism emphasizes competition rather than cooperation. Such an ideology ignores the social value of individual existence within a group and encourages unethical behavior disguised as market economics. The result is that the ideology encourages antisocial behavior disguised as competition, harms the public interest, and makes collective action more difficult. It sacrifices the power needed to build a harmonious social system (Fafchamps, 2011). Therefore, market-oriented capitalism is inherently immoral (Gorodnichenko & Roland, 2011).

When early communists considered how to correct the defects of capitalism, they overestimated the moral power of individuals and ignored the existence of selfishness, thereby making the concept of selflessness for the greater good of society an unattainable utopia. The tragedy of the commons, in which public goods are abused due to a lack of social constraints on antisocial behavior, prevented the socialist dream from becoming real and made the evolution of society slower and more painful than it needed to be. Fortunately, society has not been destroyed by such difficulties. The continuous technological revolution and China's attempt to promote social progress through trial and error have made it increasingly clear that the basic outlines of the next stage of civilization will require that we find ways to overcome selfishness and achieve more harmonious development by promoting prosocial behavior.

8.3.1. The Failure to Constrain Capitalism

Modern society has taken advantage of communication, trade, finance, technological cooperation, arms transfers, international exchange, and other forms of cooperation intended to achieve globalization, which is claimed to be promoting the progress of society. However, globalization has also produced a series of complex social problems such as ecological degradation due to overexploitation of natural resources, as well as military conflict, global climate change, and their interactions (Giesen, 2004). Despite international institutions such as the United Nations (UN), the current capitalist society has not developed effective mechanisms for coordinating action to support global interests, and this magnifies the seriousness of international problems that require large-scale cooperation to solve. On the one hand, capitalism's emphasis on satisfying the needs of individuals undermines the sense of a cohesive social identity that would promote efforts to achieve the good of society as a whole. On the other hand, the nature of private ownership tends to discourage cooperation, which ultimately weakens the ability to improve a society's public utility (Buchan et al., 2009). In international affairs, capitalism emphasizes obtaining benefits rather than sharing benefits or making efforts to minimize adverse consequences associated with these benefits. Where an international agreement proves to be inconvenient for capitalists, they seek ways to escape those agreements. For example, Donald Trump's withdrawal from international organizations and treaties such as the Paris Agreement is a dramatic manifestation of the flaws of the international political system.

Continuous technological improvement in the fields of transportation and communication have shortened the effects of distance and eliminated the time lag in communication, thereby reducing the cost of communication and increasing the probability of cooperation (Hoffman et al., 1996; Whitt & Wilson, 2007). Mutually beneficial international interactions further increase the power of large-scale cooperation (Buchan et al., 2009). If cooperation were to be applied to the whole world and most relationships between nations, all nations would take responsibility for preserving the world so that everyone, everywhere in the world, could share the benefits of this action. To achieve this goal, it will be necessary to establish an effective system that ensures international cooperation and to remove unfavorable systems such as tariff barriers and religious conflicts that restrict global cooperation (Thompson & Smith, 2009). Although the UN has provided the world with a model for resolving international disputes and helping all nations to work together to achieve shared goals, old institutions (national sovereignty) impede the UN's efforts.

It may be possible to support these efforts by promoting a consideration of both the past and the future.

8.3.1.1. The Role of Promoting Institutional Progress

Both Marxist and capitalist scholars have recognized that knowledge and the acquisition of knowledge will lead to the development and expansion of the group of knowledge workers (Thompson & Smith, 2009). Most employees in modern societies work with computers or automated equipment (Felstead et al., 2002) rather than hand tools, leading to the evolution of new classes of workers, such as the growing ranks of knowledge workers (e.g., data analysts) and service personnel (Nolan & Slater, 2003). The development of these skills is both liberating and empowering (Smith, 2013), as it leads to the creation of new institutions that will further challenge the traditional principles of capitalism (Moore, 2010). If these challenges succeed, knowledge workers may even become the gravediggers of the capitalist system that Marx predicted (Cao & Yu, 2019). But they may also become the gravediggers of communism, since (as I noted earlier in this chapter) that ideology also has flaws that knowledge workers want to solve.

Social institutions are a collection of interdependent cultural norms and rules (Beddoe et al., 2009; Ostrom, 2005), including the universal structures that are present in all cultures, such as kinship, economics, religion, politics, and education (Tainter, 2000; Turner, 2003). Any new system must evolve from the existing system and must (at least initially) coexist with the older system rather than completely replacing it. This evolution preserves the existence of older social groups even as it leads to the emergence of new groups (Cao, 2015). Globalization is an institution that constrains the economic activities of nations through free trade agreements and other international treaties. Such institutions transcend the limits of national sovereignty, so politicians have been forced to expand their scope of action from the national level to the international level (Giesen, 2004).

Over time, institutional evolution is likely to create new social groups based on new industries and new production relationships, and these groups will grow and seek new social status. Trade federations such as the EU and Association of Southeast Asian Nations (ASEAN) are an example of institutional groups that have arisen from globalization. Institutional diversity helps maintain the status quo and protects the interests of older groups (Piketty, 2007). However, the diversity provided by new institutions can make a society more robust against internal and external pressures. When different institutions overlap, they may evolve into a relationship of coexistence (i.e., complementarities) or competition (i.e., replacement of one or more aspects of an institution by others), with a risk that competition may evolve into turmoil or even violence if it becomes too aggressive (Fafchamps, 2011). In most cases, technological progress and institutional evolution will break the balance among old political powers, which will seek to strengthen their own power (Butzer & Endfield, 2012). This can exacerbate power imbalances between the new and old political groups, resulting in shocks to society. However, these shocks can also disrupt a rigid system and make it more responsive to the need for change.

8.3.1.2. The Evolution of a System That Accounts for Both the Past and the Future

New institutions generally evolve from or in response to old ones, usually as a result of intense debate and competition in the "political marketplace." Such competition can lead to institutional changes that promote the improvement of social, economic, and resource utilization efficiency (Zhao, 2006). In such cases, the better solutions to social problems are retained, whereas inefficient or ineffective solutions are gradually eliminated (Hou & Hou, 2002). Because there is no pre-set model for how a nation works, early politicians learned by doing (Ostrom et al., 1999) and often found solutions to problems through trial and error. At the same time, successful local trials of a solution can help governments and leaders build prestige and confidence that encourage others to emulate their solution and work with the people to find subsequent solutions. Central governments often understand that local governments know local conditions best, and this encourages the adoption of decentralized management (Qian & Weingast, 1997). This, in turn, allows a certain degree of local government autonomy. This approach has an additional benefit: it can promote competition among local governments to innovate and implement more effective systems.

Of course, nations don't exist in isolation; that is, they don't have a "hard shell" that protects their society from external influences (Krasner, 2011). In particular, they cannot prevent the invasion of competing ideologies or eliminate impacts from external politics, economic systems, or even military interventions, all of which can affect a nation's institutional arrangements. For example, the Chinese Democratic Revolution led by Sun Yat-sen (1866 to 1925) in 1911and the founding of the Communist Party of China in 1921 resulted from ideologies imported into China from outside. Within a nation, fierce competition between and within political parties or the threat of violence from someone whose security is threatened can also change a nation's institutional arrangements. The central government and its national governance model may not be accepted by the people's representatives but may be adopted indirectly through the competition between political parties or political opponents within a party (Myerson, 2011).

Stability is the top priority of national governance and a prerequisite for national economic development. Because no single system can manage shared resources fairly, efficiently, and sustainably in all situations (Ostrom et al., 1999), society must accept complex institutional arrangements to ensure that when one system fails, another system may succeed and restore the system's stability. It is wise for politicians to choose institutional diversity to support this flexibility (Cao, 2016a). As a result, leaders are most willing to accept the right of competing ideologies to exist when those ideologies don't threaten the nation's stability. Unfortunately, ideological and political changes are often not as successful as economic changes because they threaten a leader's power, whereas economic reforms may be more likely to succeed because they enrich both the leader and the people. Especially in feudal or dictatorial systems, where the king or dictator prioritizes remaining in power, the leader may refuse to change. In such cases, revolution is inevitable.

Unlike evolution, in which changes are most often slow and gradual, and allow the coexistence of multiple institutions, revolutions completely replace one institution with another, as in the case of the French Revolution overthrowing the royal government. When a revolution is successful and the nation grows rapidly because of the efficiency of its new institutions, the new system will spread as the nation expands. If the leaders or monarchs of other nations refuse to accept the new system, their citizens who embrace the new system may launch their own revolutions to establish a new regime that will adopt the system. In other cases, the nation could be annexed by another nation. For example, after the Western Industrial Revolution was introduced into China at the end of the 19th century, the rulers of the Qing Dynasty not only refused to accept the new idea but also killed reformers such as Tan Sitong (1865–1898 CE) who tried to implement the new system. This resistance proved futile, as the Qing Dynasty was overthrown by Sun Yat-sen (1866–1925 CE) during the 1911 Revolution.

History shows that successful institutional evolution is typically gradual, at least initially, and that it is difficult or impossible to reach a society's ultimate position in only one step due to constraints such as the limitations of human cognitive ability and the human resistance to change. China's institutional transformation seems to be cultivating gravediggers for both traditional socialism and traditional capitalism and may eventually form a hybrid institutional system that inherits the historical and cultural traditions of both ideologies in ways that combine the beneficial aspects of capitalism and socialism while discarding or compensating for their harmful aspects. This is analogous in some ways to Georg Wilhelm Friedrich Hegel's (1770–1831 CE) system of thesis, antithesis, and synthesis. If this happens, the gravediggers will not be the destroyers described by Marx but rather will be the inheritors and builders of civilization. If China cannot reconcile its new and old systems through reform of its systems, this will decrease social stability and may even create pressure that leads to revolution, whether peaceful or violent. Deng Xiaoping repeatedly stressed the importance of experimentation to identify changes that both work and maintain social stability, not only to retain the useful elements of the old system but also to provide opportunities for observation and space for new systems to grow. Innovative achievements from local governments will be popularized by the central government to encourage their adoption elsewhere in China.

8.3.2. The Next Stage of Civilization

The Soviet Union disintegrated in 1991, and the world communist movement almost completely failed. The Occupy Wall Street protests swept across the United States as a protest against capitalism (Cao & Yu, 2019). Growing protests against capitalism have created a growing pressure to reform the system around the world, and that pressure may herald the birth of a new system, possibly in the form of a people's revolution. Because the capitalist system is an extreme consequence of the private property institution, the evolution of a new system may be based on the desire to replace private ownership with a new system that prioritizes people over profits. Obviously, overthrowing a private property institution that has lasted for thousands of years is a huge challenge, and this revolutionary activity will not be completed quickly. Nonetheless, in the following sections, I will describe some of the potential factors and processes that may lead to a new society and a new stage of civilization.

8.3.2.1. The Future Roles of Capitalist and Socialist Ideology

The cores of capitalist and socialist ideology are exactly opposite: "personal freedom before social responsibility" and "social responsibility before personal freedom." For individuals, survival comes first, and on that basis, it's hard to criticize the capitalist ideology. However, there is a broader and more important basis for individual behavior: as John Donne (1572–1631 CE) noted, "no man is an island," and humans cannot survive entirely on their own, particularly in today's complex world. Humanity comprises many groups, large or small, and individuals can only thrive if their group survives. In contrast with capitalism, socialism recognizes this interdependence and places the group above the individual. Although selfless dedication to the group is laudable, individuals must first earn enough money or gain enough resources to survive before they can contribute to their group's success. Neither ideology is sufficient by itself.

In practice, every individual must seek a balance between caring for themselves and caring for their group. On this basis, perhaps the two ideologies should be merged in a form such as "do well yourself so that you can then do well for society." Everyone should work hard to maximize their own value, but even as we are realizing ourselves, we must not forget society as a whole. Without society, the individual's needs for survival cannot be met, and we owe society a debt for providing conditions that let us thrive. Individuals who excel should be rewarded for their effort but not before they accept some responsibility for the success and stability of the society that created the conditions for their success. Truly excellent individuals must understand their social responsibilities and help society overcome its challenges so that society can evolve into something more equitable for all citizens.

About 2,300 years ago, the Chinese sage Mencius (372–289 BCE) wrote that those who are unsuccessful should focus on their own affairs to cultivate a highly moral character and work hard to improve themselves, but that once they achieve riches, they should change their focus to how they can benefit the people of their society. This would be a laudable ideology to guide future society, but it must be added that when individuals are poor and weak, they should accept the assistance of the society with dignity and integrity so that they can together achieve a better future society. On this basis, I would rephrase the words of Mencius as follows: change yourself when you don't succeed and help others when you do.

8.3.2.2. The Future Economic System

The economic essence of a capitalist system is that capitalists earn surplus value through activities such as mass production in factories, as I described in Chapter 7. Under this system, workers do not have the right to share an enterprise's surplus value, even though their labor produces this value and they account for the majority of the population. Marx and Engels considered this an unfair and exploitative system. Whether or not their logic is correct, the growing gap between the rich and the poor and cycles of overproduction and shortage seem to be inevitable consequences of the capitalist economic system. Socialist economic systems attempt to eliminate these problems through central planning that is intended to benefit society as a whole. This planning potentially provides an effective mechanism to avoid the blindness of the market and the economic crises that result from this blindness, as well as from excessive competition that threatens the economic order and social stability. But the drawback of this system is that planners cannot see or predict everything, and careless or corrupt central planning can lead to disaster for a socialist society. Socialist societies are no different from capitalist societies in terms of their vulnerability to oppressive hierarchies, corruption, excessive taxation, price discrimination, and other government actions that drain the people's enthusiasm to participate and enrich government officials rather than the society they should be protecting. Socialism cannot lead humanity into the future if these problems cannot be overcome.

Fortunately, Deng Xiaoping's trial-and-error approach seems to have worked in China and is therefore worthy of careful study. At least two things can be learned from China's experience: First, both free markets and central planning are important economic institutions. In a competitive economy, market competition not only brings efficiency but also stimulates and promotes innovation in technology and in economic models. On the other hand, some sectors of activity benefit from monopolies, such as a central government that provides public services (e.g., transportation and medical care). In those cases, central planning is an effective strategy to solve the tragedy of the commons and address the widening gap between the rich and poor that arises from market oligopolies or monopolies. Second, both markets and planning can be inefficient, or even ineffective, particularly for groups with unique characteristics, such as knowledge workers. Because the time and intensity of effort invested in knowledge work cannot be easily measured (e.g., an observer cannot tell whether a scientist who is gazing into the distance is asleep or carefully exploring a potentially brilliant idea), managers cannot know how to compensate the scientists for their activity. Similarly, it can be difficult to predict whether knowledge and technological innovations in previously unexplored areas of knowledge will have potential economic value in the future. Since scientific discovery and technological innovation have gradually become the main driving forces behind social and economic development, neither capitalist free markets nor socialist central planning can solve the problem of rewarding knowledge workers appropriately while protecting society.

By letting knowledge workers participate in an enterprise's decision process and benefit from their efforts through receiving a share of the enterprise's profits, the shared property rights system provides both the incentives of capitalism and the responsibility to the group promoted by socialism. Because knowledge workers, capitalists, and governments all share in the benefits of this approach, it represents a win–win–win situation. The workers and the capitalists who own enterprises share both the risks and the benefits. In this approach, the enterprise is no longer the private property of the capitalist, because the capitalist no longer independently decides the actions and the fate of the enterprise. Similarly, the knowledge workers don't change their status as employees, and their share of the profits ends when they leave the company and are no longer contributing to the welfare of the group. In this approach, the independence of the knowledge workers is sublimated to become part of the larger group that collectively benefits or suffers from a lack of innovation or hard work.

However, the shared property rights system cannot solve all social distribution problems. Because manual laborers don't participate in the decision-making process and management of enterprises, the private property system of capitalism (e.g., the ability for these workers to purchase shares in the enterprise) cannot be eliminated before manual labor is eliminated or before manual laborers can be included in the shared property rights system. In addition, whether for private enterprises or governments, effective management requires careful thought by individuals, implemented in the form of plans for the future. Without such plans, enterprises and governments both fly blindly into the future. Thus, careful planning by knowledge workers and managers will be required both for enterprises and for governments. As the old saying goes, just because capitalism and socialism have problems, we shouldn't "throw the baby out with the bathwater."

8.3.2.3. The Future Political System

Although scientific and technological innovation are important driving forces for improving society and standards of living, adopting these innovations must account for human nature and the possibility of negative consequences. For example, the economic and political system must maintain the enthusiasm of all workers but particularly of the knowledge workers who are responsible for these innovations. The system must also account for the possibility that some innovations, such as mechanization, will eliminate the role of manual laborers. Government supervision will be necessary to ensure that workers can negotiate on an equal level with capitalists to prevent exploitation of the workers. For example, future political systems must protect the right of workers to create trade unions that let them negotiate with capitalists on a more equal basis. At the same time, governments should provide forms of welfare such as unemployment insurance to support those who lose their jobs to a new technology until they can obtain a new job.

Through improved access to education, many of the working class have evolved from manual laborers into knowledge workers and from a lower class exploited by capitalists to workers with a role in decision-making, management, and dividend distribution. Of course, not all workers can complete this evolution (whether because they lack the learning skills or because there are insufficient jobs for everyone to become a knowledge worker), and those who cannot must be supported by the political system so that they too can seek a good quality of life. As society changes and new social groups emerge, the ideology that gave rise to older political systems must change from a dogma that slows society's progress to a new ideology that promotes this progress. The central government, which is ultimately responsible for the health and stability of a nation's society, must accept this need for change and seek ways to protect those who do well for themselves while encouraging them to contribute to society. This should become both a societal moral standard and an activity that is embraced by all citizens. We should not only encourage the pursuit of wealth but also punish selfish and anarchic behaviors such as tax evasion and evasion of social responsibilities. We should make contributing to society a conscious behavior of the rich; for example, measures must be devised to ensure that the rich pay their fair share of taxes.

Since capitalism and various forms of socialism (including early forms of communal ownership) have existed for hundreds of years, their influence is deeply rooted and will not disappear overnight. I predict that a future political system that has evolved to account for shared property rights will modify a nation's constitution and laws to protect and promote this system. If the approach works as well as I believe it will, it will spread throughout the world. Regimes that don't account for this social evolution and that try to preserve traditional capitalism or communism will compete less effectively and will therefore lag behind more advanced countries, leading to unrest and possibly even revolution. This change will take decades at least. The system I've described will not be a purely socialist society nor a purely capitalist society, and governments will remain the highest power as the representatives of the people. Governments should therefore supervise their own activities through decentralization (to limit the power of individuals) and development of a system of checks and balances. The *people's supervision* that I proposed in Chapter 5 would be an effective way for people to govern the country. The shared property rights system is a continuation of both the capitalist system and the socialist system. As a result, it may let a nation finally achieve the status of a true "people's state."

The people often see more clearly than their government. In January 1990, McDonald's opened its first restaurant in Moscow. To cool the people's desire for this capitalist luxury, the Soviet government declared that "every meal of McDonald's is equivalent to sending a bullet to the enemy to the Soviet Union." Despite this warning, the enthusiastic Soviet people accepted the risk of American bullets. In winter temperatures of –15°C, people lined up for 2 km to wait for their turn (Egorov, 2019), thereby setting a new record for 1-day sales. In an unusual historical parallel, the Allied forces of Britain, the United States, France, Germany, Russia, Japan, Austria, Hungary, and Italy invaded China on May 28, 1900. On August 14, they occupied Beijing. When the invaders entered Beijing but could not enter the Forbidden City, Beijing's citizens volunteered to lead the invaders through the system of drainage channels and entered the Forbidden City without firing a shot. History has proven time and again, sometimes painfully, that the people are the true masters of their country. Governments that go against the people's needs and desires will incite the people to overthrow their regime, sometimes with the help of invaders. Guided by wisdom and compassion, the future world can become the people's world, and future countries can become their people's country.

Humans are weaker and more fragile than nature. As I will note in Chapter 10, infrequent but severe natural disasters can cause severe loss of life and property.

Such disasters have occurred frequently during the long history of society, and this means we should not be complacent and believe that they will never again occur. To protect humanity against the most severe disasters, such as climate change and the impact of an asteroid such as the one that caused the extinction of the dinosaurs, humanity must unite into a federation in which all nations work together in response to a disaster. Achieving Confucius' *great harmony* would be a large step toward achieving this goal.

Chapter 9

The Path for Institutional Innovation

An *institution* represents a series of rules that guide or restrict human behavior and includes formal systems (e.g., governments), informal systems (e.g., barter networks), and mechanisms that define the operation of these systems. *Formal* systems refer to a series of rules enforced by laws and regulations and that are clearly defined by the government or other authorities. *Informal* systems refer to a series of behavioral norms formed by people during long-term social interactions and include personal ethics, cultural customs, and ideologies, which rely on social (rather than legislative) pressure to enforce suitable behavior and encourage noncompulsory behavior through morality.

Institutions operate within a larger social system. They can be understood as a philosophical approach to solving problems. For example, they may be a combination of solutions for implementing government policies, institutions for dealing with interpersonal problems, and institutions for the interactions between governments, citizens, and the environment. They also represent a cultural background that shapes how people deal with problems. With the rapid progress of technology during the past century and the resulting rapid changes in the social environment, the balance of interests among social groups has become stressed and may even be broken. Thus, society must solve the resulting problems and form a new balance through institutional reform (North, 1971). Trying to design a system that can balance the interests of many individuals, organizations, and social groups is more like an art than a science (Ruttan, 1999). Therefore, political actions that attempt to rebalance the interests of all stakeholders are a complex blend of art and science.

Institutional innovations that change the overall social system are among the main means by which society deals with the various conflicts caused by resource shortages, alleviates the influence of various constraints on social development, and solves the imbalance of interests among groups (Alchian & Demsetz, 1973; Argandoña, 2004; North, 1971). Given the complexity of society and the difficulty of identifying, facing, and solving society's problems, different levels of government, as well as individuals and nongovernmental organizations, must work together to account for these challenges (Berkes, 2007; Mabogunje, 2000).

A New Stage of Civilization: Striving for the Great Harmony, 233–260

doi:10.1108/978-1-83708-258-220251010

As institutional evolution has changed the balance of resource allocation and the balance of political power structures and interests (Bridgman, 2008), the power differences among stakeholders inevitably affect the establishment and evolution of the networks of relationships among the components of a social system.

Society has repeatedly experienced institutional evolution, with the winning institutions preserved and the losing institutions eliminated or relegated to a secondary role. Since the 1950s, communist countries such as the former Soviet Union carried out a series of economic system reforms. Due to a lack of effective strategies, most of these reforms failed (Meinzen-Dick, 2007). The Soviet regime collapsed in 1991, followed by those of Yugoslavia, Czechoslovakia, and other Eastern Bloc countries. Similar turbulent periods have been common throughout history, and together, they illustrate the extremely high risk and cost (human and economic) created by institutional reform. Therefore, it is essential that we find a safer and less expensive path for institutional change.

China provides an example of one possible path. Since the late 1970s, China has successfully reformed its economic system and has achieved rapid economic growth for more than 40 years. Moreover, China has made great progress in reforming its political system (Cao & Ren, 2019). Compared with the sluggish economic development of Eastern European countries and the repeated international financial crises that have affected capitalist countries around the world (such as the South American debt crisis from 1970 to 1980 and the global economic crisis in 2008), China's impressive political and economic achievements demonstrate that institutional evolution can be achieved peacefully and with relatively minor social disruptions.

Western economists have been eager to explain China's miracle from traditional economic perspectives, with the proposed explanations based on the competition between local governments (Lin, 2002; Zhao, 2006), on overcoming the obstacles created by a political system (Grabowski, 2007), and on the role of culture in social stability (Herrmann-Pillath, 2006). These explanations have been unsatisfactory, and the international community misunderstands and worries about China's new institutional arrangements. Therefore, they have framed their response more in terms of "responding to the challenges of China's rise" instead of "sharing the opportunities brought about by China's rise."

Unlike during the French Revolution that began in 1789 and the socialist revolution in the Soviet Union led by Vladimir Ilyich Lenin (1870–1924 CE), Deng Xiaoping's (1904–1997 CE) leadership of China not only retained aspects of the traditional socialist system such as collective property rights but also restored the system of private property rights that was eliminated during the Mao Zedong era (1949–1976 CE). During China's institutional reforms, there were none of the riots or revolutions that were widely experienced during previous major social institutional changes and few incidences of social disruptions (e.g., the Tiananmen Square protests of 1989). Instead, different systems were allowed to operate in different social and economic contexts, creating the possibility that the most effective system would be revealed and adopted, thereby achieving a win–win goal of institutional reform combined with economic growth and providing a reference for peaceful and sustainable institutional evolution both in China and elsewhere.

9.1. The Principle of Balanced Institutional Evolution

Since 1978, China has gradually transformed from an exclusively centrally planned economy into what has been called a socialist market economy (Lin, 2002). The key characteristics of this transformation are that central planning has been retained so that the government can define a series of national goals for the upcoming five-year planning period, but provincial governments have considerable freedom to choose how to meet those goals, such as reinstating the concept of private property and creating a vibrant private sector economy. Today's China is a laboratory for the evolution of social systems. The country's comprehensive economic, social, and political changes have not marked a transition from socialism to capitalism but rather a transition from a rigidly hierarchical society that resembled a feudal monarchy to a new stage of civilization that combines a planned economy, a market economy, and an economy based on shared property rights. China's political and economic reforms have been one of the biggest political events in modern history.

The economic reforms of the past 40 years show that maintaining a dynamic balance among the political and economic systems has been one of the keys to China's success. Chinese leaders hope to combine the centrally planned economy with the traditional capitalist development path and constantly innovate new institutional arrangements to improve the flexibility of the social and economic systems. For example, the shared property institution combines the benefits of capitalism's economic incentives with the benefits of collective ownership of a production resource. The goal has been to surpass the capitalist world and realize the "Chinese dream" of leading the future development of society. As in the evolution of a natural ecosystem, the institutional evolution of socioeconomic systems also follows the principle of survival of the fittest, with the most suitable solution becoming dominant over or eliminating less effective solutions (Hou & Hou, 2002). History shows that neither a single economic system such as a market economy nor a single centrally planned economic system controlled by the government can solve all the development problems faced by society. Therefore, more effective solutions must be found. China's ongoing model of co-evolution between the political and economic systems provides an example that can guide future global innovation and development.

9.1.1. China's Political Reforms

After the Communist Party of China (CPC) came to power in 1949, the private ownership system was gradually eliminated, and the industrial output value of Chinese private enterprises decreased from 55% of gross domestic product (GDP) in 1952 to 0% in 1962 (Li, 2004). This change was supported by Mao Zedong's ideology that "being rich is shameful" and "being poor is glorious." After Deng Xiaoping became China's leader in 1978, he immediately launched a nationwide discussion of changing from Mao's ideology, which suggested that communist principles determined reality, to an ideology that *practice is the only criterion for testing the truth* (Table 4). Deng Xiaoping's practice has been described as the

Table 4. Institutional Changes in China's Economic Ideology Since 1978.

Political Reform		Social and Economic Reforms	
1978	The editorial "Practice is the only criterion for testing truth" was published in May 1978 in the *Guangming Daily*. The article declared that economic effectiveness was the only criterion for formulating policies	In December 1978, the Third Plenary Session of the 11th Central Committee of the CPC declared that economic development was China's top priority	1978
1979	In July 1979, the central government selected four cities (Shenzhen, Zhuhai, Xiamen, and Shantou) to test reforms of the economic system based on a market economy	In February 1987, Deng Xiaoping pointed out that both the market and central planning must be components of the socialist economy	1987
1980	In September 1980, the central government adopted the household contract responsibility system, thereby replacing 26,000 people's communes with contracts that gave responsibility for managing the land to individual farmers.	In April 1988, the central government announced that a private sector economy was an integral part of the socialist economy	1988
1981	In September 1981, Defense Minister Ye Jianying announced that if Taiwan Province agreed to become a part of China again, it would be allowed to retain its autonomy and local democratic rights	In December 1993, the central government adopted financial reforms that linked the performance appraisal of local officials to their ability to generate fiscal revenues	1993
1982	In September 1982, Deng Xiaoping announced that a policy of "one country, two systems" would be used to define the future of Hong Kong; that is, Hong Kong would be an integral part of China but would be allowed to retain some of its older systems	In September 1999, the Fourth Plenary Session of the 15th Central Committee of the CPC proposed a market-oriented reform plan for state-owned enterprises	1999
1983	In April 1983, the central government gave Hainan Province certain rights to self-determination to develop a market economy	In November 2013, the Third Plenary Session of the 18th Central Committee of the CPC declared that the market would play a decisive role in future economic development	2013

"two cats theory"; that is, it doesn't matter whether the cat is black or white, so long as it can catch mice. This evolved into a broader ideology that "getting rich is glorious" (Li, 2004).

Because ideologies play a crucial role in politics and changes in ideology require changes in political practice, Deng Xiaoping's reforms should be seen as starting from a political perspective in the very beginning, which contradicts the claims by some scholars that China has only paid attention to reforming its economic system and has paid insufficient attention to reforming the political system (Zhang, 2017). For example, the ideology of Mao Zedong's era was a powerful obstacle to the development of private enterprises (Lin, 2002). The Deng ideology that practice was the only criterion for testing truth eliminated the ideological barrier that blocked the development of a market economy and gradually led to the evolution of a market economy as an important component of the socialist economy and a market-oriented socialist market economy with Chinese characteristics (Ip & Law, 2011). China's reform process has been more like the process of removing political obstacles to the development of a market economy.

In the 1980s, China's reforms targeted many of the weak links in society. For example, in September 1980, the central government adopted the household contract responsibility system, in which contracts gave responsibility for managing the land to individual farmers after abolishing more than 26,000 people's communes. As a result, hundreds of millions of Chinese farmers were liberated from the more oppressive aspects of the centrally planned economic framework (Zhao, 2006). This change of the power structure was a major political breakthrough and is a typical change to the political system (Cao & Ren, 2019). This reform of the rural political system has enabled farmers, who accounted for 82% of the country's farmers in 1982, to have the right to plan their use of the land and sell surplus products in the market. The implementation of this system rapidly improved the agricultural production efficiency (Zheng et al., 2009), with crop yields increasing by 123% for China as a whole from 1978 (300×10^6 t) to 2020 (669×10^6 t) (China Statistics Agency, 1978–2021), and solved the hunger problem that plagued the Chinese people during Mao's era. The subsequent reform and opening up to the West has further increased the power of Chinese citizens. Compared with the Mao Zedong era, Chinese citizens finally have the right to decide their employment, housing, schooling, marriage, leisure, and so on and can travel freely both at home and abroad (Cao & Ren, 2019). These powers are obviously political powers with economic repercussions.

With the continuous progress of rural reform, China has simultaneously implemented several key political reforms. In 1979, Shenzhen, Zhuhai, Xiamen, and Shantou were selected as "special economic zones" and given considerable autonomy for developing a market-based economy. They became experimental fields for reform of China's economic system and tested various economic innovations, such as joint ventures with Western enterprises, to test whether they worked before expanding the practice to the rest of China. Similarly, in 1983, Hainan Island was granted the right to test the feasibility of reform that incorporated a market-based economic system, including the right to establish a free-trade zone with no tariffs. In September 1981, former Minister of National Defense Ye

Jianying (1897–1986 CE) announced that if Taiwan Province agreed to return to the motherland, it would be allowed to retain its autonomy and local democratic rights (Lin, 2002); Taiwan did not accept this offer. In September 1982, Deng Xiaoping announced that the "one country, two systems" approach would be used to define the future of Hong Kong and Macao. In 1997 and 1999 (respectively), Hong Kong and Macao returned to China and, at least initially, retained some of their former autonomy. This series of political reforms, which continue today, have laid the political foundation for China's economic miracle.

In 1993, China introduced fiscal decentralization by granting local governments more rights to collect taxes and plan regional development. For example, local governments now have the power to approve investments and market access, to collect tax revenues, and to manage public expenditures, although these activities must still be performed within the context of national five-year plans. By controlling local state-owned enterprises, local governments can provide a wide range of social services, including education and medical care (Li, 2011). Because local governments know the local conditions better, they are better able to create efficient new systems that account for local constraints, and the ability of each province to collect taxes and reinvest them in socioeconomic development promoted the rapid development of their local economy (Montinola et al., 1995; Qian & Weingast, 1997). For local governments, it is more important to improve local economic efficiency and increase local fiscal revenue than to implement the central government's policies, so the macro-influence of the central government on economic regulation has dropped sharply (Weingast, 1995). However, the central government's influence has not been eliminated completely, since provincial governments must still meet the overall goals specified by national plans. With the emergence of a federal system (i.e., provinces acting together in a federation rather than entirely controlled by the national government), obvious differences in the systems have evolved among the provinces, and this has promoted economic growth and evolution of the national and local political systems (Ji et al., 2014; Li, 2011).

Based on these changes, China is gradually developing into a market-oriented federal political system that unites the provinces in an economic federation in which the provinces compete with each other (Ip & Law, 2011). Different regions have chosen different development models and have also obtained different results. For example, Shandong Province chose an economic development model that combines government control with market competition; Guangdong Province actively promoted market economy reforms and embarked on a free-market development path. In 1978, the per capita GDP of Guangdong Province and Shandong Province was 370 and 316 RMB, respectively. In 2020, this figure became 88,521 and 72,619 RMB, respectively. GDP therefore increased by 239.2 and 229.8 times, respectively, in 42 years (China Statistics Agency, 1979–2021).

Finally, institutional change itself is a political event. It's not wrong to say that China's reforms have not been completed, but to claim that China's economic reforms are ahead of the political reforms isn't a fair description of the current system. In fact, many of the economic reforms cannot be separated from the political reforms that allowed them to occur.

9.1.2. Balanced Evolution of the Economic and Political Systems

China's political and economic system reforms are advancing at the same time, so it's difficult to determine which of the two systems is the cause and which is the result. With the ideological emancipation provided by the government's testing of a market economy and a series of supportive policies, a federal economic system gradually appeared in China, and both market mechanisms and a planned economy were accepted as functioning at the same time. During the second wave of reform, from 1985 to 1992, state-owned enterprises became the main target of market-oriented reform. Under these reforms, they gained the right to operate independently of the government and the right to participate in market competition with the private sector. At the same time, the vigorous development of township-level enterprises and village-level economic entities absorbed rural surplus labor, and a large number of Chinese farmers migrated to cities to find employment opportunities (Zheng et al., 2009). As a result, China's urbanization rate is rapidly increasing, at a rate of 1 percentage point per year. Because the monopolistic state-owned enterprises were not very competitive, they were quickly defeated by emerging private sector enterprises, including township-level enterprises, village-level economic enterprises, private enterprises, and foreign-funded enterprises that were allowed to establish joint ventures with Chinese enterprises. The competition among enterprises is becoming increasingly fierce (Ding & Knight, 2009), and this is driving increases in efficiency and productivity. Note that the market-oriented reform of state-owned enterprises was not caused by national policy but rather by the need of these enterprises to survive in a competitive market (Zhao, 2006; Zheng et al., 2009).

Since the 1980s, the abovementioned reforms have allowed China to gradually develop from a centralized planned economy to a national market economy that combines central planning with political decentralization (Montinola et al., 1995; Qian & Weingast, 1997; Weingast, 1995). To increase fiscal revenues, local officials help local enterprises to compete in the market by mobilizing local resources and changing rules, and as a result, these enterprises can compete better with enterprises in other regions (Lin, 2002). To develop the local economy, the local governments constantly introduce new policies, recruit talented individuals from elsewhere in China and around the world, and allow capital investments from outside China. Competition among local governments has promoted population migration and the associated flows of talent and capital (Montinola et al., 1995; Zhou, 2012).

Since the reform and opening up to the West, private enterprises have developed rapidly due to the less-restrictive management environment. The number of private enterprises (excluding self-employed individuals and farmers) increased from 0 in 1978 to 19.812×10^6 in 2019, which promoted the rapid development of the national economy. Statistics show that the proportion of the national gross industrial output accounted for by private enterprises increased from 2% in 1985 to 34% in 1997. In 2019, the gross industrial output of private enterprises was 88.1×10^{12} RMB, accounting for 87.0% of the national GDP (China Statistics Agency, 1979–2020). The number of employees in private enterprises increased from 150,000 in 1978 to 263×10^6 in 2019, and the proportion of the total employed individuals employed by these enterprises increased from 0.2% in 1978 to 82.8% in 2019 (Cao & Ren, 2019).

9.1.3. Significance of Balanced Evolution

Maintaining stability is the primary goal of governments. However, in contrast with this political goal, the economic system is more active, as its primary goal is to develop the economy. But economic development should not only meet the needs of individual survival; it should also improve the quality of life (Hou & Hou, 2002). This requires evolution of institutions and the systems in which they operate. Informal systems such as values, beliefs, and social ethics are gradually evolving, whereas formal systems such as laws, regulations, and policies don't often change. Only when sufficient pressure is exerted from inside or outside can formal systems change rapidly. China's current institutional changes are the result of parallel changes in the political and economic systems (i.e., balanced evolution). This is inconsistent with one school of thought in mainstream political economics: that the political and economic systems evolve separately (Li, 2004; Roland, 2004).

From the perspective of sociology, political and economic systems are two aspects of a single problem, since they are both essential components of a social system. Therefore, when they evolve synchronously, there is a dynamic balance between them that results from their interactions and mutual adjustments. During balanced development, the political system and economic policy complement each other to achieve mutual benefits and produce more social and economic benefits. This balance can also reduce the total cost of national defense, domestic and international trade, and institutional change. This balance can be achieved if a series of systems that can improve efficiency and flexibility are implemented (Zhao, 2006). Cultural diversity promotes the interaction between cultures, and the increasing cultural integration that has occurred during thousands of years of Chinese history provides a large cultural reservoir that can drive institutional innovation (Cao, 2016a).

The monopoly power of local governments is small compared with that of the central government. Because economic development determines the tax revenues available to local governments and the political future of local officials, government officials in different regions compete fiercely for capital, workers, technology, and other resources to develop the local economy (Zhou, 2012). Competition among local governments has become a major form of market competition in China (Zhang, 2017). This kind of competition forces local governments to learn faster and better from successful experiences both domestically and elsewhere, to try to prevent local enterprises from migrating to other regions, and to ensure that they win in the competition between regions (Zhao, 2006).

Similar to the importance of biodiversity for the stable existence of ecosystems, institutional diversity is very important for the long-term stability of social and economic systems (Cao, 2016a; Ostrom et al., 1999). In a complex social system, it is almost impossible to find a single best rule for the operation of all components of the system. Therefore, one important advantage of the Chinese model is that it enables different regions to develop their own self-management mechanisms and explore the best options through competition among institutions, including between different regional institutions. Although this does not eliminate the possibility of making mistakes in a certain area, it reduces the overall risk of catastrophic mistakes that affect the whole country simultaneously, which was always a risk with strong central control. At the same time, regional innovations that fail allow the regional government to learn from the experience of successful areas and mitigate the deficiencies of the failed innovations (Lin, 2002; Ostrom et al., 1999). China's federal system allows and encourages the coexistence of different political systems, such as socialism in mainland Chinese and capitalism in Hong Kong and Macao, with different economic systems (planned and market economies, respectively) and different property rights systems.

Just as plants grow new roots, stems, and leaves from pre-existing tissues, new systems also develop from older systems. During the reform of a system, some older systems find new development opportunities and try to coexist with newer systems, thus avoiding conflicts and providing a degree of institutional diversity (Cao, 2012b). In the early stages of China's reforms, the communist heritage provided a stable social foundation for the development of the new socialist market system. Today, 40 years after the reforms began, aspects of the communist heritage such as five-year plans still exist, whereas others (e.g., agricultural communes) have been abandoned or adjusted (Cao & Ren, 2019). The flexibility of China's institutional evolution creates an ability to promote social innovation. This flexible mechanism can adapt to the changing social and economic conditions, as well as to technological, population, and environmental changes by learning from the successes and failures of other regions, and can promote sustained economic growth (Davis, 2010). (In this book, I will define technical innovation as an improvement of techniques rather than technology. For simplicity, I will use the phrase "technological innovation" to refer to both technique and technology.) Just as the diversity of natural ecosystems increases the ecosystem's long-term stability, institutional diversity promotes social and economic development in rapidly changing modern society by increasing social stability and flexibility. The liberalization of China's economic system has therefore been a positive factor for economic growth right from the start of Deng's ideological revolution (Cao, 2016a; Zhang, 2012).

9.2. The Win–Win Principle of Institutional Evolution

When institutional evolution affects the interests of individuals, then even if these changes are beneficial to society as a whole and promote economic development, some people will resist the changes (Berkes, 2007). If people find that institutional changes have harmed or are about to harm their own interests, they will use their resources to fight the changes. The greater the resistance to institutional change, the greater the difficulty of implementing the change and the smaller the net social benefits (Goldberg, 1974). Institutional change that creates fear in the people affected by the change is often accompanied by fierce political and social resistance, leading to conflicts and even revolutions (Acemoglu et al., 2011). Therefore, it is important to explore methods of institutional change that can ensure that every stakeholder benefits from the institutional change or at least does not suffer (Argandoña, 2004).

Institutional change often involves interactions between institutions at the same level in the same system (e.g., between provincial governments) as well as interactions between levels (Berkes, 2007). The complexity of the social and economic system requires politicians to find quick and effective solutions, such as taking advantage of the government's power and favorable information asymmetry during institutional changes, to quickly solve problems of public concern. However, acting in this way without fully understanding the consequences can replace one problem with another. Because governments can't always fully understand the context in which change occurs and therefore can't coordinate the demands of different stakeholders, such as nongovernmental organizations, enterprises, and individuals, institutional changes often produce uncertain results (Ruttan, 1999).

Both in theory and in practice, society has not found a path for institutional evolution that will be accepted by all people and that will simultaneously improve social and economic development (Acemoglu et al., 2011; Bridgman, 2008). Therefore, it is necessary to construct and develop a new theoretical framework that will let everyone easily understand the essence of a proposed institutional change and work together to build a fairer social system. When institutional change is resisted, this is usually because it produces adverse results for some individuals or groups. Seeking a win–win approach, in which everyone benefits or nobody is harmed, seems likely to be the solution. Throughout history, there are countless examples of conflicts and wars caused by institutional changes that had unacceptable consequences (Bridgman, 2008). Therefore, it's necessary to adopt a new perspective that lets us explore a path of institutional evolution that has the goal of maintaining both economic development and social stability, thereby avoiding social conflicts by meeting the needs of all stakeholders. That is, the goal is to seek win–win solutions.

9.2.1. Looking for a Win–Win Solution

Both institutional evolution and institutional stagnation have costs. The difference is that change may bring benefits, whereas stagnation can (at best) maintain the status quo. Therefore, when the change happens, people will not resist for long if their personal situation seems likely to improve. A society's institutions are generally recorded in laws such as a national constitution, as this approach is intended to safeguard the long-term development of the interests of those who drafted the legislation (North & Thomas, 1971). When new industries and new social groups appear, the authorities who maintain the existing system will resist their influence until they realize the benefits of the new system. For example, the Shang Yang agricultural reforms in 361 BCE that I discussed in Chapter 8 involved a major social change, from a situation in which farmers were effectively slaves of landowners to a situation in which farmers rented land from landlords and after paying a small rent (about 10% of their crop), they were free to sell any surplus. This created a direct connection between how hard they worked and how much they earned and greatly stimulated agricultural production. This represented a win–win solution because landlords also gained increased stability (farmers had less incentive to move elsewhere) and increased profits from their land.

Although the old system will eventually accommodate the new system, changes of political systems tend to be very slow in the absence of a revolution, and it usually takes several generations before a political system can change fundamentally (Petr, 1986). Deng Xiaoping shrewdly avoided both revolution and long delays for his reforms by freeing China from the shackles of the old political system; however, by maintaining key aspects of the old system alongside the new, he gave the two systems time to gradually establish new relationships through the trial-and-error path of "try and see." In contrast, it took more than 400 years from the 13th century to the 17th century for land privatization in England to be legally recognized (North, 1971), and the language of the old feudal land law was not removed from the modern property rights law until the 1920s (North & Thomas, 1971).

The United States considers itself to be the most democratic country in the world, but it took nearly 200 years after its founding before it became a true democracy with the enactment of the Voting Rights Act of 1965 to give most adults the right to vote. This democratic process began with the arrival of the first slaves in the United States in 1619, took nearly 250 years before the abolition of slavery, and took another 100 years before the descendants of liberated slaves received the right to vote (Bowles, 2012). Although China has successfully achieved rapid political and economic changes during the past 40 years, including the implementation of a socialist market economy, the CPC still announced at the 18th National Congress in November 2011 that it would never take the capitalist democratic road.

9.2.2. Creating New Opportunities

Personal economic interests are often reflected in the form of wages, rents (income earned from the use of fixed assets), and shares and may be promoted by exchanges of money, materials, or services that can be directly used or exchanged in various markets to obtain needed goods and services. However, only by solving social problems such as population growth and the resource shortages it creates can individuals maximize their personal interests. To effectively deal with social problems, society requires institutional innovation and changes based on that innovation (North & Thomas, 1971). With the development of society, new ways of exchanging goods and services to satisfy individual interests are constantly emerging, the transaction costs are constantly decreasing, and the advantages of traditional systems for exchanges of labor and goods are gradually disappearing (Schneiberg, 2005). When the marginal cost of protecting old assets is greater than the marginal revenue growth brought by an improvement of production efficiency, a new system will emerge. North (1971) noted that the institutional change represented by the new system is an effective way to reduce transaction costs and increase corporate profits.

China's institutional evolution has always been accompanied by the growth of innovative new industries, such as manufacturing of home appliances in the 1980s, manufacturing of vehicles and sales of real estate in the 1990s, the emergence of a services industry and cultural industries (such as the production of television programs) in the 2000s, and the development of tourism and aerospace industries in the 2010s. Since 1978, the production of TV sets, air conditioners, houses, and vehicles has increased by 23.2×10^3, 695.7×10^3, 30, and 869 times, respectively (Fig. 12). The continuous emergence of new industries has provided new opportunities for the growth of private institutions, while the rise of private enterprises has also provided new tax sources for the government and new employment opportunities for surplus rural labor. The continuous industrial upgrading provides space for everyone to benefit, and this win–win situation provides new opportunities for the emergence of new systems.

China's experience shows that the emergence of new industries and the resulting evolution of the economic system have promoted rapid economic development by bypassing the constraints of the old system and by adopting new systems such as shared property rights; as a result, they have improved the distribution of benefits among the government, individuals, and new social groups (e.g., knowledge workers). The development of new systems and new industries has forced the old system to gradually change to adapt to the new economic environment and improve its production efficiency. This kind of evolution aims to achieve

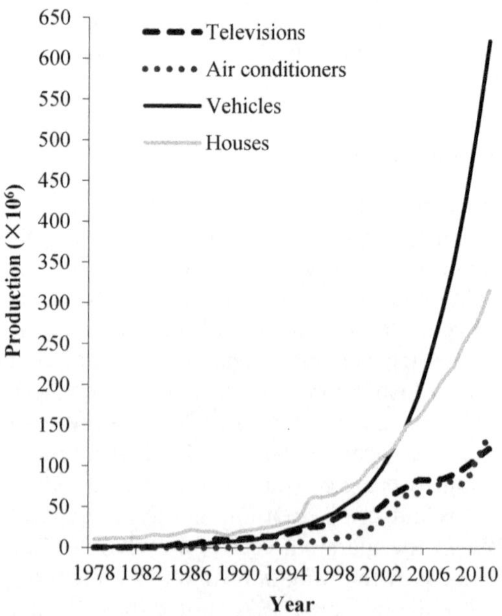

Fig. 12. Production of Televisions, Air Conditioners, Houses, and Vehicles in China from 1978 to 2011. *Source*: The figure is created by the author.

the win–win goal of institutional evolution by increasing the future benefits of stakeholders.

Historically, the redistribution of benefits has inevitably led to conflicts or resentment between the winners and the losers (Zheng et al., 2014). This results in a win–lose system rather than the more desirable win–win system. Without an innovation to resolve this conflict, strong political power is needed to force stakeholders to accept the redistribution and permit a smooth institutional evolution. One solution was the shared property rights system. As I noted in the previous section, China's change from a pure centrally planned economy to a socialist market economy has been accompanied by active reform of the political system to promote balanced evolution of the political and economic systems, thereby permitting a win–win solution for both systems. In the next section, I will focus on the social aspects of this evolution.

9.2.3. Escape Institutional Lock-in

"Lock-in" describes a situation in which a particular institution provides clear benefits to the people who are responsible for maintaining that institution, who therefore have no incentive to change the institution and a strong incentive to resist change. When the institution is efficient and effective, this may be a good thing, but when technological or social change makes the institution less effective or ineffective, lock-in creates strong barriers to necessary change.

9.2.3.1. The Significance of Competition

Since 1978, China's reforms to decentralize fiscal and taxation planning have made local governments more like independent enterprises, and because government officials are rewarded for improving their fiscal and taxation performance, this has stimulated the enthusiasm of local officials for economic development (Lin, 2002). Competition among local governments is a form of market competition and forces local governments to improve their economic policies, protect the development of local enterprises, and prevent the outflow of capital or enterprises to other regions, with the goal of increasing local tax revenues and employment (Zhao, 2006). Competition makes local governments sign contracts with local enterprises to specify that they will receive certain incentives to encourage hiring of more employees from the local population (North, 1990). Competition will also motivate governments and enterprises to consider alternative property rights regimes, such as shared property (Goldberg, 1974; Schneiberg, 2005; Zhao, 2006).

The political decision-making structure in a region can be changed through internal consultation or external pressure (Tilly, 1990). Often, powerful countries interfere in the internal affairs of other countries, prompting the weaker party to adopt a system similar to that of the more powerful country (Krasner, 2011). This kind of dramatic change took place in China's Spring and Autumn period and Warring States period (770–221 BCE) and in other civilizations in areas such as Mesopotamia, Central America, Peru, Egypt, and the Indus Valley, particularly from 500 to 300 BCE (Bowles, 2012). These changes are not exclusively a phenomenon of ancient history. After the French Revolution in 1789, the subsequent institutional changes in Europe (e.g., a widespread move away from feudal government) were some of the factors that brought about economic prosperity, and under the strong deterrent of force, European powers began to impose their political model on other countries through trade and colonialism. Other countries were forced to accept this European ideology to preserve their sovereignty and territorial integrity, and not all nations were able to achieve this. After World War II, the United States imposed its own ideology on every corner of the world. Pickering and Peceny (2006) showed that from 1946 to 1996, the United Nations and the United States conducted military interventions in five and three countries, respectively. These interventions led to socially damaging and irreversible changes in the systems of some countries (Mabogunje, 2000).

9.2.3.2 Lock-in of Systems

The win–win path of institutional reform is commendable but difficult to achieve. Whether in historical Europe or modern China, people see only the result of redistributions of power and wealth after institutional evolution; they generally don't see the internal mechanisms that lead to institutional change. Because information is always asymmetric, some groups gain benefits, while others lose benefits or receive fewer benefits whether the system changes or remains unchanged (Goldberg, 1974). (Asymmetric information refers to a state in which some participants in social, political, economic, and other activities have information that other members lack. In economic markets, this results in differences in the understanding of relevant information by the participants. Those who have sufficient information have a more favorable position than those who lack essential information.) When decision-makers face multiple choices, they will maximize their own interests (Zhao, 2006). Because this situation favors those who have an advantage, they will be reluctant to change, and this can lead to lock-in.

Because changes in the institutional rules cause the redistribution of wealth and power, and there is a time lag between decision-making and its effects, it is difficult for people to predict the outcome of institutional evolution. When they cannot see the benefits, or when the benefits appear to be too distant in the future, institutional change leads to dissatisfaction, which may in turn lead to power struggles and other forms of conflict. Such conflicts may eventually increase social benefits, but at least initially, they have significant adverse consequences (Argandoña, 2004). Policy developers generally have a strong motivation to use institutional changes to strengthen internal cooperation within a nation or socioeconomic system, but over time, the system may become locked-in (Argandoña, 2004). This may occur because governments and other social organizations have a strong motivation to collect monopoly rent (Olson, 1993) and fear disruption of the system that provides that rent. In Chinese history, most political powers have carried out institutional reform (e.g., political reform) soon after they acquired power, but when they exercised this power clumsily, without accounting for the impacts on the people, the result was political disintegration that led to the fall of the government. Shang Yang's agricultural reform in 361 BCE and Deng Xiaoping's reform and opening up to the West in 1978 are rare Chinese examples of successful national-scale institutional change.

Any form of institutional lock-in is intended to safeguard the interests of certain groups, not to strengthen overall social stability, optimally allocate resources, improve social and economic benefits, and achieve other social goals. Unless the agent of change has a strong motivation to benefit the society through their proposed institutional change, it is difficult for them to change the locked-in system, and when the lock-in is sufficiently strong, the agent may be unable to change it through gradual evolution; this can lead to violent changes such as a revolution (Goldberg, 1974; North, 1971). Although China's socioeconomic development has been very successful in the last 40 years, it has been accompanied by corruption, a lack of innovation, and other unpredictable consequences that are increasing dissatisfaction among the people and may lead to future conflicts (Whyte, 2009). A new system will only be effective when it is accepted and adopted by the majority of government officials and the people. If governments refuse to learn from the successful experience of other governments or of enterprises and refuse to accept the need for change, civil conflicts become difficult to avoid.

9.2.3.3. The Error of Shock Therapy

Scholars have increasingly helped us to recognize the important role of institutional evolution in promoting social and economic development. As a result, institutional reform, especially in socialist countries, has become a major political trend. Some government officials, such as former Soviet leader Mikhail Gorbachev (1931–2022 CE), accepted the necessity for shock therapy (Essers, 2013; Papava, 1996), since the economic development that occurs in the initial stage of institutional change is slow, whereas shock therapy forces more rapid changes that bring benefits to stakeholders faster (Gérard, 2004; Schneiberg, 2005). Unfortunately, shock therapy often fails, as in the case of the collapse of the former Soviet Union and subsequent collapse of communist governments in Eastern Europe, which I have discussed in several chapters. As these failures show, shock therapy can fail dramatically, suggesting that it is not a good path for institutional change.

Most resources in modern society are nominally controlled by the central government. Such a government tends to maximize its own interests by designing a system to protect its own interests (Lin, 2002). They frequently try to promote reforms that improve their own interests and resist or prevent reforms that reduce their own interests, which eventually leads to lock-in of the system. To prevent government officials from using their power to gain the benefits of institutional reform for themselves, the Chinese government established the *National Economic System Reform Commission* in 1982, which was responsible for formulating and reviewing national policies. As a neutral institution, the commission did not participate in the implementation of policies, thus it was more difficult for members of the commission to benefit personally from the proposed system reforms.

During Deng Xiaoping's tenure from 1978 to 1996, the Chinese government began to fulfill its true purpose of serving the people, and the proportion of the gross national income accounted for by government fiscal and tax revenues gradually decreased from 40.7% in 1978 to 17.7% in 1996 (China Statistics Agency, 1979–1997). After Deng Xiaoping resigned from all of his roles in 1996, the *National Economic System Reform Commission* was immediately dissolved by the Chinese government because ambitious politicians found that the commission was blocking their efforts to benefit from their roles in the government (Cao, 2016b), and each subsequent administrative department not only gained the right to formulate policies but also gained the right to implement them. This created a powerful incentive to create policies that benefited the national government rather than the people. The Reform Commission was not replaced by a new institution that would review the behavior of policymakers and correct any abuses. As a result, the proportion of gross national income accounted for by government fiscal revenues expanded rapidly, reaching 35.0% in 2011, and it was only after Xi Jinping took office in 2012 that this trend was reversed.

China's experience tells us that the powers of policy formulation, implementation, and supervision should be separated. The policymakers should not implement policies, and those who implement policy should not participate in policy formulation, since combining both forms of participation can lead to the concentration of power in too few hands. An independent group that neither proposes nor implements policy can then more effectively supervise policy development and implementation groups to detect and correct abuses of their power. This supervision can also reduce the risk of lock-in, since it prevents abuses such as modifying the system for personal benefit.

9.3. Selection of a Path for Institutional Evolution

Institutional evolution is an adaptive response of society to social and economic pressures such as resource shortages, population growth, cultural changes, or an economic crisis. History shows that an institutional change that leads to unfair resource distribution will decrease the income of citizens and promote conflict between groups that benefit from the unfair distribution and groups that suffer. Therefore, exploring a more fair and effective (win–win) solution is a wiser path for institutional evolution. Evolution that benefits all stakeholders, or that at least does not harm any stakeholder, is the best path for institutional reform because it avoids shock therapy. Improving an old system, improving the fairness of resource and benefit allocation, and promoting economic growth through institutional innovation are key elements of successful institutional reform.

In the rapidly changing modern economic environment, the ability of a government to optimize its institutions is crucial for maintaining economic growth, improving citizens' welfare, and maintaining social stability. However, it's human nature to distrust change when the current institutions seem to function adequately, so it can be difficult to convince institutional stakeholders that reform can bring benefits. The failure to persuade stakeholders and the failure to produce the promised benefits have mostly led to institutional reforms that ended in failure. To avoid such a failure and the social disorder caused by system evolution, Deng Xiaoping chose the gradual reform path of "try and see" to reduce the perceived risks of change and increase the likelihood that the change will be successful. In this approach, Deng proposed that a new system should be tested in a small area before it is widely implemented. The advantage of this approach is that, on the one hand, it shows the benefits of the new system to the public in a real-world demonstration; on the other hand, it can minimize the risks and costs of failure, and because the approach is inherently gradual, it avoids the disruptions caused by "shock therapy."

9.3.1. Smoother Policy Implementation

When an existing system can't effectively deal with social and economic problems, revising the system or developing a new system can solve the problems (North & Thomas, 1971). Based on the win–win approach, the government should intervene gently in the system's evolution by carefully and meticulously following a step-by-step approach that benefits every stakeholder or at least does no harm. This can avoid or mitigate conflicts, reduce resistance to the change, reduce the costs of change, and smooth the road to change. The trial-and-error method of "try and see" advocated by Deng Xiaoping has undoubtedly been an effective way to follow this path.

9.3.1.1. Persuasion

Economic development and political progress are closely related. When interest groups perceive no danger to themselves (e.g., acting illegally and getting caught), they often seek rent (i.e., income gained by allowing the non-consumptive use of some resource in exchange for a payment) and try to influence decision-makers, thus reducing the flexibility of the political and economic systems (Davis & North, 1971; Grabowski, 2007). Even though institutional evolution can be beneficial in the long run, insufficient information and uncertainty of the results of a reform motivate some interest groups to protect the present institution, which creates obstacles to success of the institutional reform (Heinemann & Tanz, 2008). Changing this resistance to cooperation requires persuasion.

For successful institutional reform, policymakers must cooperate with scholars to obtain strong evidence of the need for and benefits from the reform so that they can persuade all stakeholders, especially government officials and the public, to try something new (Sachs & Reid, 2006). Because governments have provided citizens with little reason to trust them or their motives, the task of persuading citizens to participate in the reform and cooperate with the system change can only be accomplished by rebuilding the lost trust. Scholars can help, since many have reputations for unbiased, objective evaluations. When all stakeholders know the potential benefits of change and trust the government to provide those benefits, the resistance to change will be reduced, and it will be easier to persuade them to cooperate.

People who have received more political education are more willing to participate in policy development and implementation (Goldberg, 1974). Therefore, encouraging stakeholders to participate through education is an effective method of persuasion. Because scholars also make mistakes, education is not the only way to get support for change, and other measures are equally important. For example, public debates between scholars and between scholars and officials were very popular in ancient China. It was during the Spring and Autumn period and the Warring States period (770–221 BCE) that Shang Yang (390–338 BCE) examined the problems faced by Chinese society at that time and found effective strategies to deal with the problems. In addition to agricultural reform, Shang Yang carried out a series of military, government, and judicial reforms. These reforms succeeded because his ideas accounted for the needs of his nation.

Many Chinese philosophers, including Laozi (571–471 BCE), Confucius (551–479 BCE), Mencius (372–289 BCE), and Zhuangzi (369–286 BCE), spent their lives arguing with the ruling class about the need for institutional changes. For example, Confucius' advice that only the best scholars should become government officials formed the basis for the imperial examination system of ancient China, which increased the likelihood that the most capable individuals would be selected. Similarly, to change China's policy focus from class struggle in Mao Zedong's era to the modern focus on economic development, Deng Xiaoping led a discussion of economic system reform in 1978, resulting in the ideology that "practice is the only criterion for testing truth" (Lin, 2002). To change the egalitarian thought of the Chinese people in Mao Zedong's era, which encouraged them to hate wealth and oppose private property, Deng proposed that "getting rich is glorious" (Li, 2004). After Mao's death, Hua Guofeng became the government leader and proposed no change from the previous practice of policy evaluation by the government's leader. However, Deng Xiaoping published several articles in *Guangming Daily* and *Renmin Daily* that opposed this institution: in its place, he proposed that only practice can reveal the truth, and that only facts can liberate the mind and encourage people to work together effectively. His proposals gained considerable public support and provided a theoretical basis for China's subsequent market-oriented reform.

Ideologies tend to become rigid and are harder to change once they become locked-in. Although society relies on ideology to make decisions efficiently, instead of having to "reinvent the wheel" for each new situation, this requires an ability to make logical judgments based on correct information; sometimes, a new wheel will be necessary. Therefore, before citizens will accept an institutional change, they want to obtain a trustworthy proposal that clearly describes the reform and want to believe that if any problem arises with the reform, the government will promptly solve the problem. Further reassurance is provided if the government promises to accept monitoring by the people who are affected by the reform to ensure that the innovation will be beneficial to them and will minimize the risk of losses. History has repeatedly shown that changing an ideology through persuasion should be the first step and that it is most likely to successfully promote institutional reform.

9.3.1.2. Institutional Diversity

In this book, I repeatedly emphasize the need for cultural and institutional diversity, since diversity not only maintains the stability of the social system but is also the source of social innovations that will lead to the *great harmony*. It is the key to a country's long-term survival (Cao, 2016a). The concept of private property has existed throughout history, but because it rewards the wealthy and powerful and penalizes everyone else, its long-term fairness and its resource-allocation efficiency (i.e., its ability to stabilize society) may be lower than those in other systems (Ostrom et al., 1999). It can also lead to failures such as the tragedy of the commons. Conversely, state ownership of resources protects those resources for the good of all citizens but can lead to corruption of officials if they act in their own interests and to low efficiency if the state is unwilling to change in response to changing circumstances. The shared property system that I have described attempts to combine the best aspects of both private and state property institutions. The coexistence of the three systems creates institutional diversity that allows a society to respond more flexibly to changing circumstances.

By not trying to eliminate an old system, governments can reduce the resistance to a new system, enhance social stability, and maintain more stable economic and social development during the transition period (Cao, 2016a). Confucius' *great harmony* must be a stage of civilization that is more harmonious and that differs from previous institutions. In particular, it must encourage an attitude in which people respect each other's choices, even if they don't understand them, so long as the choices cause no harm to others. Unlike the concept of private property, which encourages people to seek more property because such behavior is clearly rewarded, the *great harmony* demands mutual respect and an acknowledgment that some property must be shared by all citizens, thereby greatly reducing the probability of social conflicts.

China's reform and opening up started more than 40 years ago. The new approach actively encouraged market-based economic activities (such as family-operated farms, private enterprises, free trade, and joint ventures with foreign enterprises) that were prohibited by Mao Zedong yet also retained many elements of the planned economy to provide stability (Whyte, 2009). China's social and economic prosperity since 1978 has not only been due to the continuing reform of the socialist market economic system but also due to the retention of the old centrally planned economic system and correction of market failures through government plans. For example, the Chinese government allows private capital to be invested in competitive industries such as textiles, household electrical appliances, vehicles, and houses, thereby encouraging economic development through market competition. However, national control has been maintained in industries that would benefit from a government monopoly, such as transportation, electricity, communication, and urban services. This control is particularly important in core areas related to social stability, such as food security, energy security, military security, and financial security. This ensures social stability despite the pressures created by economic growth (Cao, 2016b). Similarly, the government's *Precision Poverty Alleviation and Rural Revitalization* project has upheld the interests of Chinese society's poorest individuals and shows both political wisdom and foresight.

A nation that relies exclusively on a single system may not last long if it faces strong internal or external pressures that are beyond the system's ability to resist.

For example, the Soviet Union (1922–1991 CE) pursued a single economic institution (i.e., a centrally planned economic system) and collapsed after less than 70 years because it could not compete with the capitalist system. To establish a pure communist country in 1949, Mao Zedong tried to eliminate both any traces of capitalism and the influence of traditional Chinese culture (e.g., Confucianism) on China and launched the Cultural Revolution to accomplish these goals from 1966 to 1976 (Lin, 2002). Because the resulting society was based on a single institution (communism) and did not account for human nature, it was inflexible and could not adapt to the rapidly changing world. As a result, it failed, as did various alternative forms of Soviet and Chinese communism around the world. As I noted in Chapter 3, Chinese higher education, under the control of the Chinese government's single centrally planned curriculum, has deprived students of academic freedom and has therefore failed to promote innovation. It has therefore reduced academic flexibility and diversity.

The traditional communist centrally planned economic system appears to lead to resource waste, disappointing economic performance, and even national disasters. For example, in the 1950s, the Chinese government confiscated private property nationwide (Li, 2004). By 1962, all private enterprises were nationalized. The Great Leap Forward, which was intended to revolutionize Chinese agriculture from 1958 to 1962 by implementing the commune system, combined unrealistic policies with three years of natural disasters (primarily drought). This resulted in famine from 1958 to 1960, causing millions of deaths from starvation and the descent of hundreds of millions of people into poverty (Yang, 2006). Simultaneously, the national economy fell into a severe depression (Whyte, 2009). Fortunately, the single centrally planned economy lasted for less than 30 years. In 1978, Deng Xiaoping implemented an institutional reform that saved China and the Chinese people by allowing farmers to reject the agricultural commune system, thereby giving them the flexibility to choose more appropriate crops and cultivation methods; it also allowed the development of a market economy, funded in some cases by investments from outside China (joint ventures). However, the central government continued to control the national economy to protect citizens from the consequences of this change. These and other historical examples show that when it becomes necessary to correct an imperfect or outdated system, complete elimination of the old system to replace it with a single new system violates the goal of institutional diversity and the goal of avoiding risky shock treatments.

9.3.1.3. Compromise and Consensus

When an institution changes, people fear that others will gain more than they do or that they will be worse off after the change is complete. This creates resistance to change, and unless those who suffer from the change are compensated for their loss, they are not only unlikely to participate in the change (North, 1971) but will also use their resources to oppose the change. To gain the support of those who may lose something (e.g., wealth, power) due to the change, it's necessary to find a compromise solution that will compensate them for their loss. For example, before Deng Xiaoping eliminated the old Maoist system of lifelong work for members of the Chinese Communist Party (the "iron rice bowl"), he set up the *Central Advisory Committee* in 1982, so that powerful individuals who had enjoyed certain privileges during Mao Zedong's era could retain their power by serving on the committee. This not only earned them higher wages, but it also gave them power to guide government policy. All they had to do to obtain these benefits was to support the new system. As time went by, most of the committee's members died, and the committee was eventually dissolved in 1992 (Cao, 2016b). Similar changes have occurred elsewhere in the world, including a change in the king's role in England under the Magna Carta and the change of the role of the Japanese emperor in the late 19th century. These examples demonstrate the effectiveness of an ability to compromise during the reform of a system by retaining elements of the old system. Recognizing that it may not be possible to achieve the best solution immediately, planners can make an effort to achieve a win–win solution that balances the needs of stakeholders through negotiation. In this institutional environment, compromise that leads to consensus is an acceptable solution and will produce an acceptable or even optimal result.

Because the compromise is based on justice (i.e., equity of outcomes for all stakeholders), it has a low social cost compared with alternatives such as power struggles or revolutions. It works because it attempts from the beginning to balance the power of the old and new systems and because it offers all stakeholders benefits that encourage them to be patient until the reform is fully implemented.

9.3.2. The Trial-and-Error Path

In the past 40 years, the Chinese government did not have a single rigid approach to reform. Instead, they emphasized trial and error (i.e., testing a policy to ensure that it worked before implementing the policy throughout China), and each successful policy was implemented slowly and gradually (Herrmann-Pillath, 2006; Lin, 2002). Based on Deng Xiaoping's "try and see" approach, most reform measures started in a single county or province, which served as a policy "pilot study." At the same time, the government maintained the traditional centrally planned economic system, while local governments were allowed or even encouraged to test new economic activities, such as family-owned workshops, private enterprises, self-employment, foreign investment, and joint ventures with companies from outside China.

9.3.2.1. Pilot Studies

As I noted earlier in this chapter, the central government explored the feasibility of a socialist market economy in 1979 by giving Shenzhen, Zhuhai, Xiamen, and Shantou permission to test reforms based on a socialist market economy (Hasan et al., 2009). Although the pilot tests were successful, the Chinese government remained cautious because it feared that the results of the small-scale pilot studies would not be achieved after expansion to a national scale. As a result, they gradually extended the reform to the eastern coastal provinces, and it was not fully implemented nationwide until 1992 (Brodsgaard, 2010). The experience gained from the pilot projects provided reference data for policy design, reassured other regions that the approach was feasible, and avoided the risk of problems with the new system by allowing provinces to test the implementation to ensure that it worked under their unique combination of local constraints.

There are several reasons why this approach was highly effective. First, small-scale failures could not damage the whole social system, and this allowed implementers to maintain social stability and reduce the risks and costs of this institutional evolution. Second, through small-scale trial-and-error observations, implementers could explore their experience and the experiences of other regions before wide-scale popularization and application of the new approach, thereby revealing any blind spots that might jeopardize the reform. Third, the new system was transformed from an abstract concept into a tangible model that provided an example that subsequent adapters could imitate and learn from, thereby reducing fears, suspicions, and resistance, and increasing the smoothness of system evolution. Fourth, new implementers were given the freedom to modify the approach to account for their unique local constraints and advantages. People from any culture fear taking collective risks even when there is no alternative. Deng's cautious approach mitigated this fear and accounted for the Chinese people's cultural emphasis on stability and respect for tradition. Small-scale experiments and demonstrations are effective strategies to mitigate or eliminate risks and convince people to be willing to try the new approach. This cautious approach gives stakeholders enough time to understand the risks and benefits of the new system, adapt to the new system's operating rules, and minimize the risk of institutional change and public resistance, thereby minimizing resistance (Lin, 2002).

In contrast with the endless debates and voting in democratic systems and the blind or highly subjective individual decision-making of authoritarian regimes and dictatorships, the approach based on small-scale experiments and demonstrations is more efficient and effective. As a result, the probability of accepting the new system is much higher than in a democracy or a dictatorship. And because the approach is tested and demonstrated to work, it reduces the risk of serious errors such as those of Mikhail Gorbachev, who presided over the collapse of the Soviet Union. Interestingly, societies are reluctant to learn from history, particularly when (as in the case of the United States) they have been dominant for so long that they have forgotten the need for change. Capitalist societies have much to learn from China's recent experience with reform. Failure to learn may validate Marx's and Engels' prophecy that communism would become the gravedigger of capitalism.

9.3.2.2. Technology Demonstrations

In China, the application of new technology and new techniques (i.e., new systems) almost always starts with small-scale demonstrations and then slowly spreads, similar to how a single spark can start a prairie fire. For example, in 2000, China's Transportation Ministry introduced the concept of near-natural greenway roads, which are popular in Europe and North America, to solve the problem of damage to the ecological environment during road construction. At first, this plan was strongly opposed by local governments who feared that the additional environmental protection costs would have a negative impact on local economic development (Xu et al., 2011). To alleviate this fear, researchers adopted a small-scale experimental demonstration method to reveal the benefits of the new scheme. In 2003, the Ministry of Communications took the lead in building two demonstration highways with lengths of 94 and 99 km in Jiuzhaigou, Sichuan Province, and in Xishuangbanna, Yunnan Province, respectively. After the highways were completed, the researchers organized tours for local government officials to encourage them to visit and study the results, and as they became convinced of the method's validity, they were able to promote its adoption step by step (Cheng et al., 2015).

To promote the development of a tourism economy, Hubei Province's Communications Department planned to invest 2×10^9 RMB to build a 53-km expressway around the Shennongjia World Natural Heritage Reserve. When China's Ministry of Communications was informed of this plan, they invited the leaders of Hubei Province's Communications Department to visit the Jiuzhaigou demonstration highway. After their visit, they abandoned their original plan and adopted a greenway road construction plan that would be less damaging. Moreover, the new plan was less expensive, with a cost of only 38×10^6 RMB, which is only 2% of the original plan's cost. The new approach discourages highly damaging measures such as digging through mountains and crossing rivers when alternatives were available, thereby respecting nature, protecting the environment, and promoting more harmonious coexistence with nature. The highways are instead integrated with nature, and nature is protected to the greatest extent possible, giving both drivers and passengers who are traveling on the highway a sense of nature's beauty. Compared with traditional roads, the disturbance of soil and rocks and the damage to vegetation decreased by 46.0% and 52.4%, respectively (Xu et al., 2011).

The beautiful highway also attracted more tourists. In the three years after completion of the highway, the average number of tourists per year increased by 48.2%, greatly increasing local tourism revenue, the regional GDP, and government tax revenues (by 96.0%, 54.5%, and 76.0%, respectively). The number of road traffic accidents decreased by 50%, and the number of deaths, injuries, and economic losses caused by traffic accidents decreased by 74.1%, 7.4%, and 84.6%, respectively (Cheng et al., 2015). The success of these demonstration projects has promoted the rapid development of China's transportation and environmental protection projects. By the end of 2007, 30 demonstration highways with a total length of more than 2,000 km had been completed and opened to traffic in various provinces. By the end of 2021, China had built more than 80,000 km of greenways nationwide (Hongyu, 2022). This experience confirms that experimental demonstrations are an effective path for promoting the adoption of technological innovations through institutional evolution and have been effective measures to convince people to participate in innovation by making the benefits tangible and visible. This novel Chinese approach can be adopted with little revision by the rest of the world.

9.3.3. Chinese Wisdom

There is no panacea for all problems, so trying to solve all the problems encountered in real life by using a single method is bound to end in failure (Olsson et al., 2008). Despite this, some politicians insist on trying a single method in all situations and are unwilling to adapt when the context changes (Beddoe et al., 2009). The failure of communism in the Soviet Union stemmed from its complete rejection of the capitalist system. The subsequent collapse of the Soviet regime resulted from its blind acceptance of the capitalist system without recognizing that this solution was inappropriate given the country's social and economic contexts and without recognizing the need for testing. In contrast, China has succeeded because it recognized the need to adapt the capitalist market system to a new context and the need to test that adaptation to confirm it would work.

Because of the interaction of policy development at the national level with the relationships between higher levels of government and local governments, society faces complex institutional problems (Berkes, 2007). If a system that evolved to deal with the constraints in a specific context is transplanted to a different social and economic context, the system is unlikely to succeed without at least some adaptation (Meinzen-Dick, 2007). Therefore, instead of setting unrealistic expectations of success, as occurred in the former Soviet Union, it is better to acknowledge that the new system will produce different results and must be tested to determine whether those results are acceptable or require modification of the system (Mabogunje, 2000).

9.3.3.1. Deng Xiaoping's Philosophy

China's process of testing and gradual reform provides a flexible model that can cope with a wide range of situations and explicitly acknowledges the possibility of failure. Even if the reform fails in a certain region, China can handle the related consequences, and the reform can be modified and tested again to see whether the modification was successful. Before large-scale implementation, small-scale experiments in small areas can reveal serious problems and provide time to modify the development model. The Chinese government not only encourages such institutional learning but also provides sufficient time and space for planners to adapt the institutional reform (Meinzen-Dick, 2007). Because this approach resembles exploration rather than blind application of a formalized approach, it resembles art more than engineering (Karouni, 2009).

In contrast with sudden, widespread, and direct institutional or policy reforms, China has provided a reform path that is gentler because it both preserves and works with the old system that may be replaced by the new institution. This path maintains the stable operation of society and the economy while the new system comes into effect and thus avoids the problems created by solutions based on shock therapy. Those who doubt or oppose the innovation can continue to take advantage of the old system until they become sufficiently confident in the new system to adopt it. On the other hand, advocates of the new system can perform small-scale trials to identify and control the risks and reduce the risks and costs of failure during subsequent implementations. Therefore, China's path reduces the resistance to institutional change and makes it easier to succeed.

The effect of a new technology and policy may not appear immediately, since it takes time to transform an existing institution (i.e., there is a time lag). For example, the effect of the near-natural greenway road construction scheme described earlier in this chapter would only be gradually revealed after the road was built, so it was inevitable that traditional road builders would be suspicious of and oppose the innovation before the road was built. Gradual testing and adoption of the new method avoided the shock that would have been created by banning the old methods, while also reducing the risk of institutional change and increasing the sustainability of the reform. Through local experiments, followed by gradual expansion of the approach to other parts of the country, the smooth implementation process avoided the risks of unexpected accidents and encouraged adoption of the new approach.

In a complex social system, any change may harm the interests of one or more groups, so it is difficult to make political decisions that meet the needs of all groups (Shi, 2004). Rigid behavior and path dependence (i.e., results that vary depending on the paths that lead to a decision point) are common obstacles to institutional change and the development of public policy (Olsson et al., 2008). Due to the lack of sufficient information to judge the benefits of a new system, people are reluctant to abandon even an unsatisfactory old system and are therefore reluctant to accept the risks of reform. This is particularly serious if the effects of the reform are not obvious in the short term, and if there is strong path dependence (Meon et al., 2009). The origin and characteristics of a culture, such as the Chinese people's philosophical preference for harmony and stability, and the nature of a country's political process, such as the contest between democratic and autocratic regimes, influence a culture's response to reform and determine whether and how fast a system can evolve over time (Meinzen-Dick, 2007). Because different regions have different political, economic, cultural, and environmental characteristics, it is difficult to successfully apply a policy that was shaped by the unique characteristics of its original region and culture in other regions and cultures (Chapin et al., 2006).

Thus, the design of any new system should account for the interacting factors described earlier in this section. The reform should be promoted by overcoming each stakeholder's fear of failure and encouraging stakeholders to take the initiative in shaping the proposed change. The use of pilot programs provides evidence that the reform is likely to be successful and shows the willingness of implementers to ensure that they are meeting the interests of stakeholders; it also explicitly acknowledges the need to modify an approach to account for the unique constraints in other regions. Only by enhancing the cooperation between managers and the social groups their innovations will affect, by increasing public attention to environmental issues, by including a wider range of stakeholders, and by gaining political support for the reform can the manager's goals be achieved (Olsson et al., 2008; Shi, 2004). Policymakers can't simply import a new system to an area that differs greatly from the region where the system originated but must instead ensure that the advantages of the existing system are preserved and must try to integrate the new and old systems to adapt the new system to its new environment. To test the success of this system integration, policymakers must first test the proposed reform through a pilot project before attempting to implement it on a larger scale.

9.3.3.2. An Incremental Path

Institutional change is an incremental process in which society gradually adapts to economic and technological progress. As a result, it is more like social evolution than revolution, and the resulting process is gradual and almost non-destructive (Petr, 1986; Roland, 2004). The system's evolution should benefit all stakeholders or at least ensure that they experience no losses. Only by following such a win–win path can the reform succeed. Under normal circumstances, a few people often receive most of the initial benefits of a new institution, and most other participants receive relatively few benefits and bear the corresponding costs before the institution matures (Heinemann & Tanz, 2008). For example, the development of urbanization has increased the value of land, improved the fiscal revenue of local governments, and increased the profits of real estate developers and banks. However, the majority of ordinary people in China who have obtained urban residency rights bear enormous costs from the high cost of renting an apartment and the high cost of mortgages to fund purchases of a place to live; as a result, they obtain far less benefits than the government and businessmen (Cai et al., 2019; Zheng et al., 2014).

If there are more potential losers than winners, institutional reform will usually not succeed unless the winners are sufficiently powerful to impose the reform on the losers. In contrast, the win–win method starts from the old system, thereby preserving benefits for those who benefited from the old system and revises the social and economic systems to promote the emergence of new institutions, such as the birth of new industries and the related social groups. With the passage of time, the new institution gradually grows enough to complement or replace the old institution and then the two institutions reach a mature balance. This is one of the greatest contributions of modern Chinese culture to the world. The evolution of a system lets new people gain new social status, as in the examples of farmers who gained the right to manage their own land at the end China's agricultural commune system and the examples of the private sector entrepreneurs and self-employed people who gained legal status after Deng's reforms. These rights are the key forces that were needed to realize the system reform. Similarly, the social forces generated by the Industrial Revolution and the increasing development of capitalism in the 18th century accelerated the development of Western democratic politics (Bowles, 2012). In contrast, the lack of new industries and the lack of growth of new social groups has led to slow adoption of the democratic system and market economies in many developing countries such as those in Africa (Mabogunje, 2000). Only when the economy and key outputs such as food exceed the basic living needs of the producers can a market economy develop.

To promote the development of the new system, it is necessary to develop new industries that lead to the emergence and growth of new social groups who depend on the new industries to make a living and who therefore desire to promote the development of these industries. As shown in Fig. 12, the constantly emerging new industries not only promoted rapid economic growth in China but also created new social groups (e.g., knowledge workers) and new systems (e.g., shared property rights). Due to their high efficiency, these new social groups and systems are increasingly becoming the main components of the future social economy. Promulgating a new law by the government can be completed overnight, but people's ideas change much more slowly. Before we can propose an acceptable compromise, we must first understand people's wishes and needs, as well as the influence of a society's ideology on institutional evolution. In particular, we must seek an effective way to convince people who are opposed to our own views to work with us to avoid lock-in.

In the rapidly changing modern socioeconomic environment, a country must constantly adapt its institutions to maintain economic growth and increase the welfare of its citizens (Heinemann & Tanz, 2008). However, the adaptation of social and economic systems is relatively slow, and people may be unwilling or unable to adapt to the pressure caused by rapid changes. Most institutional changes have failed or only partially succeeded because those who proposed the changes blindly imitated the successful experience of other countries or regions without accounting for the social and cultural conditions of the regions where the innovations evolved or without understanding the difficulty of transplanting the innovation to a new context; as a result, they failed to consider the difficulties in the implementation of the transplanted method (Cao, 2012b).

Although the evolution of cultural knowledge is slow, the huge amount of cultural knowledge that accumulates over time can support institutional innovation and help both the government and the people it represents adapt to an institutional reform (Roland, 2004). To increase the odds of success, policymakers must understand that different stakeholders need different forms of communication to ensure that they understand the proposed change and different reassurances that their interests will not be harmed. For example, experts and scholars prefer research data, rich stakeholders want economic data to ensure that their wealth will be protected, and poor stakeholders want to ensure that they directly benefit from the institutional change and improve their quality of life. Because these needs and desires differ, a compromise approach is generally necessary. The compromise may not achieve the best results for all stakeholders, but it can at least aim to achieve a win–win situation so that all stakeholders believe that they will receive sufficient benefits to justify the risk of change. Demonstrating the effect of institutional innovation to stakeholders through small-scale pilot projects can reduce resistance to the innovation when stakeholders see the safe operation of the new method. Implementers and planners should adopt flexible and diverse methods that are adapted to local conditions and the needs of local stakeholders. China has shown the effectiveness of these methods during 40 years of reform of its economic policies, and their ability to reduce or eliminate unnecessary obstacles to change.

9.3.3.3. Unfinished Business

The emergence of a federal system (i.e., a federation of provinces), market-oriented reform, and the shared property rights system has greatly promoted

China's economic growth. However, China's transformation is not yet complete. The centralized politics that result from a planned economy still provide opportunities for local officials to abuse their power (Heinemann & Tanz, 2008; Ip & Law, 2011). At the same time, increasing social injustice (e.g., the income gap between the rich and the poor) and environmental crises that result from mismanagement of the environment (Knight, 2013) jeopardize China's achievements. The problems are exacerbated by rising relative poverty (Li, Cai, et al., 2021), widespread corruption (Dong & Torgler, 2013), increasing commercial disputes, protest movements, rural poverty, and the spread of infectious diseases such as COVID-19 (Ip & Law, 2011; Whyte, 2009; Yang, 2006), which are threatening China's achievements. China's reform process will be restricted by the lack of an electoral mechanism that lets citizens express their preferences to representatives who will act on those preferences, by the lack of an independent judicial system that can enforce China's laws, regulations, and social conventions to punish the corrupt behavior of government officials and enterprises, and by the lack of an independent system in which policy designers don't participate in policy implementation and in which the activities of both designers and implementers are carefully monitored by the people. If the central government wants to continue its successful social and economic reforms, it must develop a political structure in which the people supervise government and enterprise behavior, must use an independent judicial system to prosecute antisocial behavior, and must weaken the administrative monopoly on power by transferring this power from the national level to the local level. That is, China must practice the idea of a people's republic rather than a republic that exists for the benefit of the powerful. To achieve this, the government must serve all of the people, not just some of them.

China's market-oriented reforms have promoted its rapid economic growth, but the abuse of power by governments and their officials has increased social injustice and social instability (Cao et al., 2014). To promote more effective and fair institutional change, it will be necessary to limit the power of government departments, prevent government departments from using institutional evolution to maximize their own interests, and ensure that citizens, not just government officials, can also benefit from the new system. In particular, it will be necessary to introduce competition mechanisms in Chinese universities and research institutions to give students and researchers freedom to innovate, independent of government desires; that is, universities and the government officials that control their policies must embrace institutional diversity. It is impossible for a country that lacks innovation to become a leader in the evolution of civilization.

China's approach is not comprehensive, because it has failed to solve a series of social problems such as corruption, the income gap between the rich and the poor, and a lack of innovation. This indicates that additional institutional reforms will be necessary and that solving the abovementioned problems will continue to require a cautious trial-and-error attitude and an approach that accounts for China's culture and history.

Chapter 10

The Relationships Between Humans and Nature

The global economy's rapid recovery after World War II rekindled the dream of conquering nature. Slogans such as the statement that man is destined to triumph and conquer nature resounded (Reynolds, 1974). In the 1950s, nature was seen only as an object that humans conquered and controlled, rather than a living environment that needed to be protected and lived in harmony with. It was not until the 1962 publication of *Silent Spring* (Carson, 1962) by Rachel Carson (1907–1964 CE) that humanity was gradually brought to its senses. Humans finally understood a simple truth: nature can exist without humans, but humans cannot survive without nature (Cao et al., 2007). In contrast with the 1950s, environmental protection is now one of the biggest political issues faced by society today, and the need for this protection has created one of the strongest social movements of our time – perhaps the greatest legacy of Rachel Carson.

Silent Spring is a masterpiece that helped give birth to the global cause of environmental protection. Carson noted that because of the excessive use of pesticides and fertilizers, humanity may face a future world without birds, bees, and butterflies. The resulting rise of ecological consciousness brought environmental issues to the attention of the world's governments. Since 1962, various environmental protection organizations have been established around the world, including government organizations such as the United States Environmental Protection Agency (in 1970), and this prompted the United Nations to hold the Conference on the Human Environment in Stockholm, Sweden, from June 5 to 16, 1972. The resulting *Declaration of the United Nations Conference on the Human Environment* (Handl, 1972) was signed by 114 countries, led to the creation of the United Nations Environment Programme, and further promoted the cause of environmental protection.

With the awakening of society's environmental protection consciousness, scientists gradually accumulated evidence that environmental problems are long-term social problems that arise from the evolution of civilization. Supposedly civilized people who were more eager to conquer than to preserve nature have

A New Stage of Civilization: Striving for the Great Harmony, 261–286

Published under exclusive licence by Emerald Publishing Limited
doi:10.1108/978-1-83708-258-220251011

damaged every corner of Earth throughout history, leading civilization to the brink of collapse again and again. The ecological crisis that we face today is just one more repetition of the historical cycle of ecological crises. The first step for environmental protection is to understand the roots of this repeated crisis by understanding the history of the relationship between humanity and nature.

10.1. The Historical Cycle of Ecological Crises

The environment is a natural entity and a natural context in which humans live. For as long as there have been humans, environmental problems have emerged. Although most people now have at least a basic understanding of our dependence on the environment, disharmony between humanity and nature has existed throughout humanity's long history. Today's environmental problems are simply a reappearance of this ancient problem (Wilkinson, 1973). From a historical point of view, the relationship between humans and the natural environment has evolved and become increasingly complex. Society has repeatedly experienced a transformation from harmonious coexistence to a disharmonious game between humans and nature, followed by evolution from discord to a harmonious state again.

Due to the increasing human impact on global ecosystems, the importance of the close relationship between humans and the environment has become increasingly prominent because of its impacts on human health, economic development, social justice, and national security. Thus, the concept of sustainable development has attracted increasingly widespread attention (Lubchenco, 1998). The United Nations National Research Council of Science and Technology interprets the goal of sustainable development as reducing hunger and poverty and maintaining the stability of the global ecosystem while ensuring that the needs of the world's future population can be met. Research on ecological economics has similarly taken environmental sustainability and the environment's human carrying capacity as central parameters for measuring the consequences of economic development (McMichael et al., 2003). Thus, the basic concept that underlies sustainability is that both current and future generations must be protected.

However, there are several forms of sustainability with different ecological consequences: *Strong sustainability* assumes that humans and natural capital are not interchangeable, and that the environment must be preserved in a state as close as possible to its natural state to provide future generations with the same benefits as the current generation. *Weak sustainability* assumes that human and natural capital are interchangeable and allows natural resources to decline so long as human needs continue to be met. *Agrowth* is a form of sustainability in which the economy is maintained at its current level to prevent additional development-induced damage to the environment but assumes that nature can recover by itself. Finally, *de-growth* assumes that it is possible to reduce the size of the economy and, thus, its impact on nature. Although de-growth may be theoretically possible by taking advantage of greatly improved technology, it is likely to be at best difficult to achieve in practice.

From an evolutionary perspective, history is a long process in which the natural environment, production activities (e.g., agriculture, industrialization), and social institutions are mutually constrained (Butzer, 2000). Nature has nurtured humans, but human activities have increasingly changed the natural environment. The inappropriate behaviors of humans combine with the wastes we discharge to create a need for environmental purification, since environmental problems become increasingly severe when the rate of accumulation of our wastes exceeds the environment's capacity to eliminate them (Diamond, 2004). Unfortunately, early humans did not recognize the limitations imposed by environmental carrying capacity because their populations were too small to cause severe environmental damage that would have revealed these limitations. However, ignoring these constraints led to the repeated occurrence of ecological crises that caused the collapse of many ancient civilizations, sometimes accelerated by natural disasters such as earthquakes.

10.1.1. Ecological Crises and the Origin of Civilization

Early humans thought that they lived on a vast and endless space and that unknown lands could always be found beyond the area of human habitation. For thousands of years, there were no limits to their discovery of new land. Whenever they encountered a problem with the natural environment or the social structure of their community, they could always move somewhere else to escape the problem. Because populations of hunter–gatherers were low and they were sparsely distributed, their consumption needs rarely exceeded the environmental carrying capacity. At this stage of society, human survival depended entirely on the natural environment because humans had little ability to transform the environment to better meet their needs. When the resources available to a group (mainly edible animals and plants obtained from the natural environment) could not meet the needs of a growing population, it was easy to migrate to other areas to continue their traditional lifestyle of hunting and gathering the necessary resources. Due to the slow population growth during this period, society remained largely unchanged for tens of thousands of years, except for changes related to continuous migration of growing populations.

About 1 million years ago, humans learned how to create fire. This discovery transformed society and the relationship between humans and nature. Cooking food often made the raw materials easier to digest and (in some cases) less toxic. Cooked food is not only easier to chew but also easier to digest and absorb, leading to improved nutrition and health. This is likely to have reduced disease severity and increased life expectancy. Humans also learned to use fire to hunt and prevent attacks by predators. As a result of this technology, the food supply increased and the chance of being injured or killed decreased. Improved nutrition also improved a mother's health and the quality and quantity of her milk. Because of these changes, Earth's population increased more rapidly. Simultaneously, humans changed from a somewhat rare and endangered animal to consumers at the top of the food chain. As population growth accelerated, the growing population eventually exceeded the local environmental carrying capacity and triggered the first ecological crisis.

When a region's population density was low, migration was an effective way to access new resources and let the old environment recover from human pressures. However, at some point, there were no new areas suitable for colonization, and the resulting lack of food may have represented the first ecological crisis in history and may have forced humans to find new ways to survive. The use of primitive but increasingly sophisticated tools that made it easier to acquire or process food contributed strongly to solving this first ecological crisis. The use of tools and collective hunting further increased the human food supply, which in turn facilitated social interactions and population growth. About 10,000 years ago, the number of humans reached about 5×10^6 (Cao et al., 2007). The hunter–gatherer approach could no longer provide enough food to feed this many people, even with the new tools, and this led to the second ecological crisis. The solution to this ecological crisis was the invention of sedentary agriculture.

Agriculture opened a new era in the relationship between humans and their environment. In a sense, the origin of agriculture represented a new way of life in which humans actively altered the environment to promote their survival under environmental and population pressures. Under such pressures, humans were forced to recognize the growth and development requirements of animals and plants and would gradually begin the process of domestication (breeding of wild animals and plants). Sedentary agriculture (also known as "grain agriculture") increased the food supply and helped humanity escape this second ecological crisis. For the first 5,000 years or so after the birth of agriculture, agricultural practices were probably dominated by nomadic farming. During this period, humans were constantly reclaiming new land, then abandoning it after a few years of crop cultivation led to decreased soil fertility, resulting in a migratory, nomadic, and pastoral agricultural lifestyle. With the continuous advancement of medicine and agricultural technology, survival of illnesses and increased food production increased the population rapidly, while the land available for migration kept decreasing. To ensure that a local population protected its limited land resources against encroachment by others, groups of people declared their sovereignty over the land and prepared to defend that sovereignty when necessary. Where the sovereign population and invaders disagreed over the land ownership, this sometimes produced an exchange of resources (i.e., trade) but also led to wars over control of the land.

Around 4,000 years ago, the people of China's Yellow River Basin entered a third ecological crisis. The legendary "fight for the throne," a large-scale war between the three dominant tribal alliances (Huang Di, Yan Di, and Chi You), was a large-scale conflict caused by the shortage of land resources and the development of a long-term drought in the Yellow River Basin. After years of continuously increasing population, violent plundering of land and possessions by neighboring tribes became the norm, and to preserve their own property against foreigners and win wars, centralized bureaucracies and state systems evolved to unite and efficiently distribute a tribe's resources, as I described in Chapter 4. From these disputes and wars, it's likely that the concept of private property (here, owned by the social group rather than individuals) emerged. As sedentary populations continued to grow, agricultural production technology continued to progress, with breakthroughs such as replacing stone tools with metal tools (especially iron tools), manure application to improve soil fertility, and application of agricultural irrigation technology that greatly improved production efficiency. As a result, society increasingly freed itself from the insecurity of relying solely on nature for food. The available evidence (North, 1990) suggests that technological progress and institutional innovations tended to start from a specific population in a specific region and then gradually spread to other populations over a long period.

Due to geographical differences in climate and environmental resources such as soil, the time for a society to reach an ecological crisis and solve it by adopting sedentary agriculture varied widely. For example, the civilizations of Egypt's Nile River Basin and the Tigris–Euphrates River Basin entered a sedentary civilized state more than 2,000 years earlier than societies in China's Yellow River Basin (Cao et al., 2007). Tribes that did not invent or adopt agricultural technology and centralized power would be eliminated in future conflicts with more advanced civilizations. Although this form of civilization offered many benefits, including a flourishing of the arts and writing, it also created concentrations of resources that promoted conflict and warfare to control those resources. It's interesting to speculate that civilization is not so much the product of human wisdom as it is the product of responses to an ecological crisis.

10.1.2. Ecological Crises and the Evolution of Civilization

Once humans settled down, farming and domestication of livestock gradually became the main sources of livelihood, and because of their high productivity, the population grew at a faster rate. However, the acceleration of population growth further shortened the time between ecological crises. However, in addition to ongoing and gradual improvements of agriculture, a sedentary lifestyle promoted the development of technology improvements that, in turn, permitted breakthroughs such as steam power that both improved agricultural technology and permitted a major change in society: the Industrial Revolution. Compared with agricultural civilization, the emerging industrial civilization further accelerated the pace of social development. Although it greatly mitigated the problem of producing sufficient food to feed a large population, it also triggered a new and greater crisis: exploitation of distant lands (e.g., colonialism) to gain access to precious resources, including the seabird guano fertilizer that was an important component of industrial agriculture (Salvado, 2017).

Since there was much competition among nations for access to this resource, and since owners of the resource were reluctant to simply give it to another nation, this self-interest and competition among consumers of the resource led to increasingly violent conflicts. The Industrial Revolution also increased worker productivity far beyond the environment's ability to supply the necessary inputs and process the wastes produced by this consumption. The resulting unsustainable resource utilization inevitably exceeded the environmental carrying capacity and aggravated famines, wars, plagues, and other threats to civilization; in extreme cases, this prevented further population growth or even decreased a country's population (Kates et al., 2001). Unfortunately, we humans seem unable to anticipate such crises, or when we do, we delay action until it may be too late, as in the current case of global climate change. In most cases, technological and institutional innovations are not completed before the crisis arrives; on the contrary, many major inventions and innovations represent forced responses to a crisis (Cao et al., 2007). Prior to the emergence of new technologies and social regimes, societies, like natural ecosystems, repeatedly experienced cyclical fluctuations between boom and bust. Just as trees grow, die, and are replaced by new trees, most civilizations have experienced a similar historical cycle (Odum & Odum, 2001). After the establishment of a new social regime, the civilization expanded through the consumption of resources, the accumulation of wealth, the promotion of population growth, and the support of technological progress and then became unsustainable, resulting in varying degrees of collapse and often the replacement by a new civilization.

Just as trees absorb the nutrients formed when dead vegetation enters the soil, new civilizations rise in the same areas as prehistoric civilizations. During a civilization's decline, the forests and soil and other environmental resources that it exhausted have time to recover and to support a new round of growth. For example, the ancient Roman Empire started from a small country in the corner of Europe (similar to a small tree) but gradually expanded to rule most of Europe and the Mediterranean basin (similar to a forest) and then collapsed and was replaced by other European and Mediterranean civilizations. Today, a strong industrial civilization has risen again in Europe, accompanied by serious environmental problems such as land degradation and air and water pollution. At rates restricted by moisture and temperature, nutrients are released relatively rapidly by the decay of organic matter and more slowly by weathering of the mineral soil. These nutrient-release mechanisms provide ongoing cycling of materials and energy in natural ecosystems. Through evolution, an ecosystem adapts to survive by exploiting the available soil nutrients and recycles them within the ecosystem. This slow cycling maintains the ecosystem's stability, with the ecosystem gradually reaching a balance with the soil's carrying capacity.

A similar process should be possible for humans if we can learn to live within our means (i.e., to not exceed the environmental carrying capacity). Unfortunately, society has not evolved an effective mechanism to maintain a balance between the population and the environmental carrying capacity. Because humans are conscious beings, we can consciously choose to use natural resources at a rate that exceeds their production by the environment, and we usually do. This inevitably leads to degradation of the ecological environment. Because modern society is not limited to the use of local resources and can temporarily escape carrying capacity limits by importing resources from other regions through trade, it seems that modern civilization can develop more rapidly while remaining sustainable. However, this only delays the next crisis, since this approach occurs at the expense of unsustainable resource consumption in other regions. The gradual depletion of soil nutrients and the increase of atmospheric greenhouse gases represent the effects of slow, cumulative processes, and the environmental problems are already very serious by the time the harm they are causing becomes apparent; even if society finds an effective solution to the problem, it still needs time to heal the wounds. Therefore, whether the ecological crisis occurs or is prevented, a long time will be required before ecosystems begin to recover, and this time lag effect delays our ability to respond to the crisis and increases the extent of the damage. Historically, ecological crises have caused cyclical fluctuations of the global population growth rate, and with accelerating socioeconomic development, the cycles appear to be becoming shorter and the fluctuations appear to be becoming more and more dramatic (Fig. 13; Boserup, 1981; United Nations Population Division, 2024).

Ancient China also went through similar cycles, with one dynasty after another rising to power in a small area of China and then expanding to rule or influence most of China and East Asia and even some parts of Europe for a time; the most famous examples are the Tang Dynasty (618–907 CE) and the Yuan Dynasty (1279–1368 CE). Due to the lack of sufficiently advanced technologies and systems to expand the environmental carrying capacity, China has frequently been unable to feed its large population and has experienced repeated changes of dynasties in response to food shortages during the past 2,000 years. The war and anarchy caused by the collapse of each Chinese dynasty greatly reduced the population, and stability was not restored for many decades.

The population theory of Reverend Thomas Robert Malthus (1766–1834 CE) suggested that populations always grow faster (exponentially) than our ability to acquire the resources needed to feed them (linearly), and that this would inevitably lead to famines, wars, and plagues. His suggested solution was to greatly reduce the birth rate. Although his theory was cold and unsympathetic, it was not

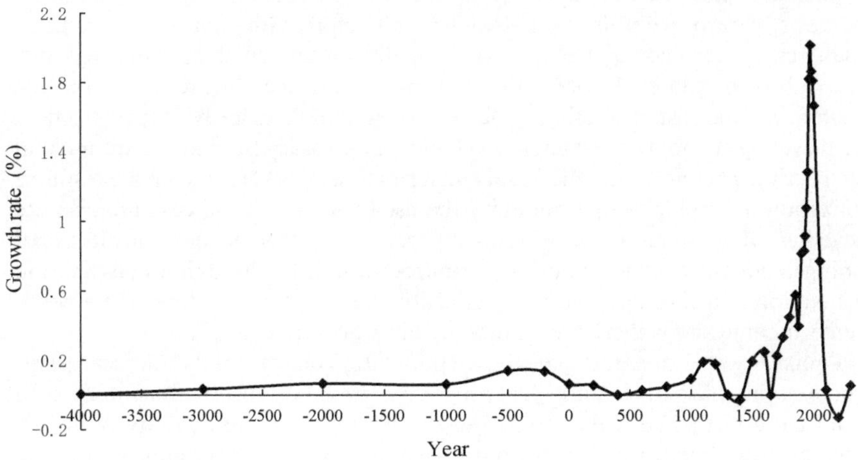

Fig. 13. Cyclical Pulses in Historical Global Population Growth Rates.
Source: The figure is created by the author. *Note*: Years to the left of 0 represent BCE dates; years to the right represent CE dates.

necessarily wrong, although he did not account for the effects of technological and social change on the two growth rates. Early societies were blocked from expanding by other societies, mountain ranges, rivers, and oceans, so crises occurred at different times in different regions. Therefore, the overall changes of global population growth shown in Fig. 13 don't provide a good picture of the extent of the damage caused by regional ecological crises. For example, the Manchu army slaughtered the civilians in Yangzhou after overrunning the city in 1645 CE, with only 3 of the 800,000 citizens surviving. Similar tragedies did not stop until organizations such as the United Nations proposed a law to protect civilians against harm by both sides during a war. Unfortunately, the conflict in Ukraine in 2022 and others in many other parts of the world shows that this protection is incomplete and inadequate.

The natural pattern of population growth is also applicable to other life forms. For example, the number of carnivores will increase rapidly with an increasing number of prey and will then rapidly decrease as the number of prey decreases (Odum & Odum, 2001), ultimately maintaining a delicate balance between species (an ecological equilibrium). Fortunately, the population will not completely disappear during such fluctuations but will instead adapt to the fluctuations through continuous self-adjustment. For a human example, consider how a society can reduce the pressure on the environment through migration, through adapting to environmental changes by redesigning social structures, through developing symbiotic relationships by improving a nation's political and economic systems, through improving resource efficiency through technological innovations, or through finding new resources to sustain socioeconomic development (Dillehay & Kolata, 2004). (In this book, I will define technical innovation as an improvement of techniques rather than technology. For simplicity, I will use the phrase "technological innovation" to refer to both technique and technology.)

Societies have generally operated on the basis of economic efficiency, not on the basis of resource utilization efficiency. Therefore, although the recycling of resources is more conducive to environmental protection than using new raw materials (Iranpour et al., 1999), the economic cost of recycling resources is often greater than the cost of wasting resources, so few countries are willing to promote the recycling economy as strongly as would be necessary from an environmental perspective. Therefore, scientists and engineers must work hard to create resource utilization technologies that minimize the use of natural resources and promote recycling while simultaneously reducing costs. Another effective institutional arrangement to regulate the use of resources would be through a combination of taxation and subsidies, but this institutional arrangement reduces the government's income and is therefore ignored by most governments.

Unlike the situation during historical population changes and ecological crises, modern scientific and technological progress is providing effective technologies to control the birth rate while improving the Earth's carrying capacity. With the emergence and maturity of birth control technology and further improvement of women's status by education and economic development, more and more women have reduced their number of children, and some have even chosen to have no children (Cao et al., 2010). Therefore, it is reasonable to believe that populations will stabilize or decrease, thereby mitigating or eliminating the curse of the ecological crisis cycle. Nevertheless, if the growth of personal consumption exceeds the dividend brought by the population reduction, an ecological crisis will occur once more. On the other hand, a certain minimum population may be required to promote sufficient economic development to move society forward and prevent a societal collapse. I will discuss this in more detail in Chapter 11.

10.1.3. Environmental Problems in Modern Society

The birth of sedentary (grain) agriculture strongly promoted the development of society. With the progress achieved by agricultural science and technology and the use and improvement of metal tools (especially machinery), the land's crop production efficiency has rapidly improved. Especially after World War II, with the acceleration of agricultural mechanization, increased use of synthetic fertilizer, and breeding of superior crop varieties, the global agricultural economy has developed rapidly. However, due to improved medical technology and nutrition, the survival rate of newborn babies and the human lifespan have increased, leading to continuing growth of the world's population. The rapidly increasing population creates a risk that the demand for food will outpace technological progress, creating a risk of another environmental crisis. This risk is exacerbated by the increased pressure on land and the environment created by modern agriculture, possibly causing history's fourth major environmental crisis. Furthermore, climate change is increasingly leading to a risk of crop failures that can place large populations at risk of starvation (Kornhuber et al., 2023).

The main characteristic of historical environmental crises was intensification of a series of natural and social contradictions caused by the insufficient supply of food to meet basic demand. The modern environmental crisis is not only manifested by local or regional food shortages but also by global shortages of energy, minerals, and arable land. There is no new virgin land to which people can migrate. That is, unlike the conditions in any previous ecological crisis, it will be impossible to move to a new land without first subjugating or eliminating its inhabitants. Thus, the current ecological crisis is unprecedented and devastating because it may lead to extinction of whole civilizations that are unable to adapt to climate change. If we cannot overcome the crisis through technological and institutional innovations, global civilization will face the risk of extinction.

Most developed countries have exhausted at least some of their soil and forest resources after centuries of land reclamation for agriculture or urbanization. During the past two centuries, urbanization (the movement of rural people into cities) has proceeded rapidly, and although this has relieved some of the pressure on natural land, it has been accompanied by rapidly increasing resource consumption accompanied by low efficiency and a large waste of resources (Dasgupta, 2004). Today's humans must face the risk of accelerating species extinction during the 21st century. With the continuous expansion of human activities, the living space available to wild species has been greatly reduced, and this is leading to extinctions of species (Rosenzweig, 2001). Industrial development has led to the disappearance of more than 50% of mammals, and the rate of species reduction is the fastest in areas where human activity is most frequent or severe (Ceballos & Ehrlich, 2002). By 1990s, the forest area in Mexico was decreasing at a rate of 500,000–800,000 ha per year (Mez-Pompa & Kaus, 1999); at the same time, 26×10^6 ha of coral reefs worldwide were destroyed or on the verge of disappearing, representing about 58% of the total area (Odum & Odum, 2001). To feed their rapidly growing population, the Chinese people have historically redirected rivers by building dikes and reservoirs and have used the newly exposed soil to grow food. Nowadays, more than 300×10^6 people live in areas that were originally part of river floodplains, so it is not difficult to imagine that the annual losses due to flood disasters in these areas are large (Chou et al., 2018; Su et al., 2012). Fortunately, China has a population of 1.4 billion, and local disasters can be quickly resolved through the support received from people elsewhere in the country.

10.2. Cycles in the Relationships Between Humans and Nature

Modern people live in an era of rapid scientific and technological development accompanied by conflict, violence, economic turmoil, and widening inequality. Citizens of most developed countries generally feel insecure about unemployment, economic risks, terrorist attacks, and environmental pollution (Fei & Vahid, 2023). Even if we ignore serious dangers such as nuclear proliferation, we cannot avoid the increasingly serious environmental challenges that we face (Serageldin, 2002). As I described in Chapter 4, all political crises stem from an imbalance between society's demand for consumption and the supply of consumable resources defined by the environmental carrying capacity. Whenever consumption exceeds the limit imposed by the environmental carrying capacity, an ecological crisis will arise, and sometimes, it will be accompanied by political and military threats such as a trade war, an economic recession, military warfare, and other forms of conflict.

Scholars of economics understand that there are short-term fluctuations and long-term cycles of economic growth and stagnation, and that economic cycles in the capitalist world appear to be characterized by cyclical fluctuations over periods ranging from 5 to 50 years or more (Wallerstein, 1984). Historical records show that there are important internal social mechanisms, such as cyclical fluctuations in population growth rates as well as the regime changes that have occurred in China roughly every 70 years over the past 2,500 years (Cao et al., 2007; Fei & Vahid, 2023), that have caused societies to evolve from prosperity to decline, and that are responsible for long-term cyclical fluctuations (Odum & Odum, 2001). To achieve sustainable development, we must first understand the factors that drive these periodic fluctuations.

When a nation's economy enters a recession and traditional economic strategies such as reducing interest rates are ineffective (as in the case of Japan), this leads to frustration throughout a society. For example, the recessions in China from 1959 to 1978, in Japan after the 1980s, and in Eastern Europe and South America after the 1990s (Cao et al., 2007) are just a small sample of many such economic disruptions. It's important to understand the laws that govern these changes and that can, in some cases, lead to an ecological crisis so that we can seek ways to prevent the crisis and so politicians can make the necessary interventions.

10.2.1. Periodic Fluctuations

When the population is relatively small and growing slowly, renewable resources can meet society's demand, but non-renewable resources will be increasingly exhausted; when human demand exceeds the environmental carrying capacity, the renewable resources will also be gradually exhausted (Cao et al., 2007). If these circumstances continue, an ecological crisis will be unavoidable. A mature economic system is similar to an ecosystem, with the exception that economic systems seek continuous growth, not equilibrium. For example, in a well-developed mature forest, losses of mature trees are balanced by recruitment of young trees, biodiversity is stable, and the use of soil nutrients and other resources is balanced with their availability. In contrast, governments desire their nation's economy to grow continuously, both in terms of the quantity of money and the complexity of the structure, until the rate of resource utilization exceeds the rate of supply (Odum & Odum, 2001).

10.2.1.1. Cycles of Climate Change

Researchers have confirmed that the greenhouse gas content in the atmosphere has increased rapidly during the past century, and the scientific community almost universally believes that this increase has been driven by human activities (Dietz & Rosa, 1997). Meteorological records and satellite observation data confirm that the global tropospheric atmospheric temperature has increased by about 0.6°C in the past 100 years (Oram et al., 2017; Walther et al., 2002). However, when we use a longer time scale to evaluate environmental change, global climate change reveals periodic fluctuations. The paleoclimatic record suggests that the changes being observed in present-day climate change processes resemble the changes during the transition between cold and warm climates around the end of glacial periods (Overpeck & Webb, 2000). Long-term historical studies confirm that even without human intervention, the climate is variable and will alternate between cold and warm periods (EPICA, 2004). This doesn't mean that modern climate change is benign; on the contrary, the changes that occurred around glacial periods had catastrophic consequences for life on Earth.

From a long-term perspective that covers large areas, natural small-scale oscillations are often seen as random and uncorrelated "noise." Nonetheless, large-scale processes such as typhoons and tsunamis that occur as sudden pulses are often accompanied by huge energy transfers that cause disastrous consequences for small-scale systems such as ecosystems, leading to dramatic reorganization or even disappearance of small ecosystems (Odum & Odum, 2001). Economic systems can undergo similarly abrupt changes, as in the example of a price bubble that bursts (Xing, 2020). Over the past millennium, equatorial eastern Africa has experienced alternating warm and cold climate changes, such as the warm and dry climatic period between 1000 and 1270 CE, followed by a relatively wet climatic period with small glaciers at high elevations between 1270 and 1850 CE (Verschuren & Cumming, 2000). Similar phenomena have occurred in other parts of the world. The long-term periodic changes in nature are obviously stronger than those caused by human influences. The periodicity of climate change is often accompanied by a similar periodicity of natural disasters and social, political, and economic fluctuations (Zhang et al., 2007).

Natural disasters have been particularly serious for civilizations. For example, a huge tsunami triggered by an earthquake flooded most low-lying areas of eastern China with saltwater around 4,000 years ago, rendering them no longer suitable for agriculture, causing the relatively advanced Liangzhu Culture and the Longshan Culture to suddenly disappear (Azzam & Kong, 2021; Yu, 1997). A similar phenomenon occurred 1,500–2,000 years ago, when a huge tsunami inundated most of China's coastal areas. Historical records confirm that sea level rise inundated the ocean coast of eastern China from 2 to 57 CE and from 465 to 527 CE, and that there was almost no human activity in areas below 4 m above sea level between 2 and 600 CE (Yu, 1995).

Natural disasters this severe are closely related to social crises. Large natural disasters such as regional drought that is sufficiently severe to cause crop failures can cause huge social crises, leading to wars, the collapse of political power, sharp population reductions, and other disastrous results. For example, the two tsunamis about 1,500–2,000 years ago may have caused the collapse of the Han Dynasty (202 BCE–3 CE) and may have led to the most chaotic and bloody period in Chinese history, the Northern and Southern Dynasties period (420–589 CE). During the Han Dynasty, a time of relative peace and stability during a period with a stable and agriculturally suitable climate and no major destructive natural disasters, China was relatively stable and the population grew from 13×10^6 to 67×10^6. Subsequent climate disasters, including drought and exceptionally warm or cold temperatures, led to a chaotic usurpation of power by Wang Mang (3–25 CE), the Three Kingdoms period (220–280 CE), the chaos of the Eastern and Xijin Dynasties (265–420 CE), the Five Hu rebellions (also called the Northern and Southern Dynasties period, 420–589 CE), and other wars. China's population plummeted to 12×10^6 (from a peak of 67×10^6). In the following 300 years of relatively peaceful development during the Tang Dynasty (618–907 CE), a period with a stable and beneficial climate, the population recovered to 90×10^6 (Table 5). At present, more than 500×10^6 Chinese people live within 100 km from the coastline (Wang et al., 2016), which increases their exposure to natural disasters such as tsunamis (Liao, 2004; Morabia, 2009).

One of the most important historical books in China, the *Zizhi Tongjian* (*History as a Mirror*), records the history of China from 403 BCE to 959 CE and reports 41 occurrences of a "great famine," which represents an average of one occurrence every 33 years. Episodes of "human cannibalism" caused by famine occurred a total of 33 times, with an average of one occurrence every 41 years. Clearly, famines are not rare incidents. The History of the Yuan Dynasty (1271–1368 CE) recorded 21 periods with cannibalism, and the History of the Ming Dynasty (1368–1644 CE) recorded 23 periods. More than 2,000 years have passed since the last dynasty-ending tsunami, and the economic focus of China and other parts of

Table 5. Population Changes During Key Chinese Historical Periods.

Dynasty	Time Period	Population at the Start of the Period (×10⁶)	Population at the Time of Peak Prosperity (×10⁶)
Xihan	202 BCE–3 CE	13	67
Tang	618 CE–907 CE	12	90
Song	960 CE–1279 CE	32.1	126
Yuan	1279 CE–1368 CE	70	93
Ming	1368 CE–1644 CE	60.5	112
Qing	1616 CE–1911 CE	85	436

the world is mostly concentrated in coastal areas at low elevations. Governments of these areas have not planned how to respond to natural disasters so severe that they occur only once in 2,000 years, such as the two huge tsunamis that struck eastern China 4,000 and 2,000 years ago. Moreover, the highly urbanized region is extremely vulnerable to such a disaster due to its high population density. The COVID-19 epidemic that was sweeping the world while I wrote this book is only a once-in-a-century natural disaster (the last similarly destructive disease disaster was the 1918 influenza pandemic); a once-in-2000-year natural disaster would be far more destructive than anyone has imagined.

10.2.1.2. Cycles of Social Development

The development of society is inevitably affected by cyclical processes such as the seemingly inevitable decline of a civilization after it reaches its peak (Odum & Odum, 2001). History suggests that the society of a given area shows cyclic fluctuation, with civilizations collapsing and being replaced by new civilizations. However, unlike natural cycles, which tend to fluctuate around a consistent level, human cycles have tended to show a cyclical but overall upward trend. For example, after the gradual depletion of a resource leads to a crisis, new innovations mitigate or solve the crisis, thereby establishing a new balance between humanity and nature and allowing the society to recover. The repeated environmental crises that I described earlier in this chapter therefore seem to be one of the characteristics of social development. The history of succession from one stage of civilization to another suggests that after each environmental crisis (Cao et al., 2007), society has shown great technological progress and institutional innovation – but has also promoted population growth that will trigger new, future crises. Modern society is nearing the end of the metal age and the early knowledge age, and this suggests we are beginning another key period in which society must solve the fourth major ecological crisis: climate change.

Since the rates of social and economic development and the growth of human demand have always exceeded the historical rate of technological progress and institutional innovation, pessimistic scholars attribute the root of ecological crises to human self-indulgence (i.e., the unwillingness to consume less) and have proposed the concepts of zero growth or low growth, since both approaches can potentially delay or even prevent a future environmental crisis (Goffin et al., 2010). History has shown how difficult it is to account for the human desire for increased consumption (Cao et al., 2007). This may be linked to the institution of private property, since the essence of this system is an institution of indulgence in which each person considers only his own interests. If we cannot eliminate the greed that leads to increased consumption, we can at least attempt to achieve the ideology of a prosocial society, in which everyone feels responsible for helping each other and for working together to preserve society. This can also lead to an attitude in which people and nature coexist harmoniously.

Innovation appears to be cyclical. Breakthroughs in new technologies or social institutions often rely on the accumulation of knowledge over a long period of time, and it is not until the new knowledge is successfully applied to create innovations and directly affects socioeconomic development that its significance for social development becomes apparent. As I described in Chapter 3, this process takes a long time. For example, society has depended on fossil fuels for more than a century, and even though nuclear fusion technology (the "artificial sun") has been promised for most of that century, the required breakthrough has not occurred; as a result, our reliance on fossil fuels continues, and this is increasingly endangering the sustainable development of society. Similarly, as I described in Chapter 9, a formal institutional system will not change until society's informal institutions change sufficiently that the cumulative economic and other pressures for change grow too strong to resist. The accumulation of incremental knowledge alternates with major technological and institutional revolutions that result from the mutual interactions and respective evolution of social progress and environmental cycles.

The relatively small prehistoric human population let social groups repeatedly find new living space when they outgrew the old space's ability to sustain them. However, as the population increased, this approach became increasingly unfeasible, and it is now impossible. Unfortunately, the attitude that we can always move on to a new environment after destroying the old one persists. Historians of nature have noted that "civilized" people walk across Earth's surface and leave a wasteland wherever they leave their footprints (Cao, 2001). This plundering of the land is one reason why civilizations have collapsed in some areas and emerged in other areas. Social progress changes the relationships between humans and nature in a range of ways, but this progress has not yet let us escape the cycle between environmental crisis and a period of harmony between humanity and nature.

We must remember that although Earth has passed through many periods of severe environmental change (e.g., ice ages), modern civilization has never before faced one of these periods or at least has never faced an environmental crisis as threatening as global climate change; we should therefore not blindly continue our past behavior and hope that a technological solution to our problems will magically appear. The historical fact that most ancient civilizations on Earth have become extinct suggests that we should not be too confident in our ability to survive future disasters.

10.2.2. Relationships Between Society and Nature

History shows that an ecological crisis can sometimes be solved by obtaining access to new resources or by improving the utilization efficiency for existing resources (Odum & Odum, 2001). For example, new resources become available when we invent new technologies and new processes and also when we improve the efficiency of resource utilization through improved extraction and production processes. Social progress responds to challenges through active innovation, as in the case of water conservation and irrigation through the Chinese canal system I described in Chapter 2. Such engineering innovations can bring water from where it is abundant to where it is deficient, thereby improving crop yield. Societies can also benefit from passive innovation, in which they adopt technology and institutional inputs that were developed elsewhere. After a region finds effective strategies to deal with a crisis, the successful strategies can be adopted by other regions. For example, Western democratic institutions and industrial technology have been continuously exported to the rest of the world for centuries, with varying degrees of success.

Changes of the environmental carrying capacity result not only from ecosystem degradation and restoration but also from scientific and social innovations that increase the efficiency of resource use and waste treatment (Loomis & Connor, 1996). Environmental pressure is mainly caused by population growth (Butzer, 2000) and by the associated increased demand for consumption and a better standard of living. It is also caused by phenomena such as natural and anthropogenic climate change. When the environmental carrying capacity is greater than human needs, citizens of a society will become comfortable, but when the environmental carrying capacity is less than human demand, the imbalance disrupts this comfort as certain desired resources become less available and more expensive; this will inevitably lead to crisis if balance is not restored. All urban civilizations seem to follow a cycle of birth, growth, development, and demise; this has occurred for the great European and Mediterranean civilizations of ancient Egypt, Greece, and Rome; for the great South American civilizations such as the Aztec, Inca, and Maya; and for the great Asian civilizations such as the Cambodian and Chinese cultures. However, after enough time has passed, each of these fallen civilizations has recovered and begun a new cycle.

Ecosystems that have evolved over millions of years survive because they have developed an ability to live within the constraints imposed by the environmental carrying capacity and repair themselves and the environment that sustains them when they become damaged, thereby maintaining a state of dynamic ecological equilibrium. Human systems lack these self-repair and self-stabilization mechanisms. The application and development of new social systems can, on the surface, reduce pressure on the environment and improve the relationship between humanity and nature. However, such changes don't necessarily mean that the relationship between man and nature becomes more harmonious. For example, the Industrial Revolution improved the lives of many people but also harmed many workers and created serious long-term environmental damage that continues to accumulate today. As our understanding of and ability to transform nature have grown, we have increasingly damaged the natural processes that maintain an ecological balance. Because the damage takes a significant amount of time to develop (i.e., there is a time lag between a cause and perception of its effect), scientific discoveries and technological progress often mislead people into believing that there is no problem, and this optimism delays action until the severity of the consequences can no longer be ignored (Woodwell, 2002).

In a market economy, the price of resources is determined by the scarcity of the resources rather than by their role in maintaining social or environmental health, which are treated as externalities. Thus, changes in the price of a resource fail to reflect the impact of consuming the resource on the natural environment. When the output of natural ecosystems is high, the resources represented by this output are easily accessible and less expensive than the cost of their formation and acquisition. The greater the supply of cheap resources provided by the environment, the lower the price of products produced with these resources as inputs and the smoother the economic development (Odum & Odum, 2001). In early societies, resources were easy to obtain and therefore cheap, so everyone had access to abundant real wealth (material wealth) and a high quality of life. However, as populations grew and societies developed, the cost of access to resources remained low, particularly when technological innovations made resource extraction and processing easier and less expensive. This situation provided little motivation for society to improve the efficiency of resource utilization. The low price also led to excessive use of resources, since there was little incentive to use them efficiently, resulting in waste of resources and environmental pollution that foreshadowed a coming crisis.

The price increase caused by a resource shortage creates and intensifies competition for the resource, and in a perfectly competitive market economy, the high price drives resource developers to sell more resources (to increase their profit) until the resource is depleted. The resulting low supply of the product and the rising price caused by the resource scarcity drive the market to increase production efficiency, which in turn leads to faster utilization of the resource and further accelerates resource depletion (Loreau et al., 2001), creating a vicious cycle. At the same time, rising prices increase the cost of products produced from the resource until few people can afford to buy them. As overuse of resources begins to create a resource scarcity, market mechanisms drive up the price of the resources and society's poorest individuals become unable to buy these resources, exacerbating their poverty and leading society toward a state of crisis due to a growing wealth gap and a risk that those who can still have the resources will become unable to sell them at a profit because nobody else can afford to buy them (Myers, 2000).

The resulting lack of demand exerts a downward pressure on prices, potentially creating a situation in which production exceeds demand, leading to decreased prices and the risk of bankruptcy of producers who cannot sell enough of their products at a high enough price to cover the production costs. Even with higher resource utilization efficiency, the resource supply may be unable to support the required production, thereby decreasing production precipitously when resources are depleted. This is exemplified by the steep decline in the Atlantic cod catches off the eastern coast of North America between the 1960s and 1990s (the fishery has still not recovered) and by China's need to ban timber harvesting to protect its remaining forests (Liu & Diamond, 2005). Uncontrolled population growth has led to irresponsible and excessive resource consumption and waste generation, and the demand for resource consumption and environmental services continues to increase. At the same time, growing social affluence is increasing the demand for a better quality of life, further increasing per capita resource consumption and waste generation (Dietz et al., 2003). Although technological progress and institutional innovation can mitigate the problem, they can also exacerbate the problem by promoting demand. For example, the increased survival rate of newborn babies and the extension of lifespans permitted by improved nutrition and medical care have increased the global population, thereby increasing demand. Because exploiters of resources tend to consciously overestimate Earth's self-recovery capacity after resource extraction, demand tends to exceed the environmental carrying capacity despite technological and social progress (Woodwell, 2002), leading to a continuing series of ecological crises.

10.2.3. Lessons Learned from Our Experiences

The evolution of systems from simple to complex and from low to high sophistication has occurred throughout history. History has repeatedly proven that the relationship between humanity and the natural environment has evolved from harmonious coexistence to a cycle of ecological crises and recovery from these crises (Cao et al., 2007). Recovery has benefited from technological progress and from institutional innovation. These changes have promoted social evolution again and again, leading to increasingly sophisticated societies with an increasing standard of living.

Scientific, social, and technological advances can sometimes delay or prevent a crisis, including both environmental disasters and warfare, as in the examples of improved agricultural production that I described earlier. Social changes can also alleviate the pressure that would otherwise lead to a crisis, as in the cases of agricultural reforms that gave farmers more control over their life and of ownership reforms such as the shared property rights system that I described in Chapters 7 and 8. Innovation has always been a core driver of social development (Haas et al., 1993; Hayami & Godo, 1998). If technological progress and institutional innovation cannot occur sufficiently fast or if increases in the environmental carrying capacity cannot meet growing demand, the risk of conflict (ranging from trade wars to military warfare) will increase. Unfortunately, war is rarely a long-term solution, since it doesn't solve the resource scarcity problem, and it creates anger and resentment that may lead to additional wars.

After the Shang Yang reform from 356 to 350 BCE, social stability was restored for a time. However, with the food problem solved, China's elites focused on literature, art, entertainment, and other recreational activities that improved their quality of life, and little progress occurred in society, the economy, the political system, and science and technology. This lack of progress was accompanied by a growing gap between the rich and the poor, which led China into repeated cycles of warfare and peace for thousands of years. Crisis and innovation have also shown cycles. The interactions between humanity and our environment have changed global ecosystems, and these changes have shown cycles, with the time between changes seeming to be decreasing. At the same time, climate change and other natural and anthropogenic environmental changes have affected society and its historical changes. Short-term events such as tsunamis and earthquakes can also have long-term impacts on society. Consider, for example, the collapse of civilizations in China's coastal regions nearly 4,000 years ago.

History has repeatedly shown that technological advances, such as the adoption of iron tools, have played an important role in exploring the path toward sustainable development (Merk, 1998). For example, advances in agriculture (iron tools), trade (steamships), and energy sources (fossil fuels) have increased a society's access to resources, often solving environmental constraints, at least temporarily (McMichael et al., 2003). Since society is a complex system that is strongly affected by its interactions with nature, the economic impact of environmental protection differs among social groups and regions and is often unfair (Butzer, 2000). Therefore, environmental issues are not only scientific issues but also political and economic issues. As I described in Chapter 9, institutional lock-in can block opportunities to prevent or respond to crises. When lock-in occurs, a specific system is closely intertwined with other systems and the cost of incremental reform of the system becomes too high. Because the future benefits provided by institutional reform are uncertain, the distribution of such benefits among a society's social groups is difficult to predict, and the losses suffered by groups that already receive a large share of the benefits are obvious, so the resistance to reform is usually strong; in contrast, there is only weak support for the change (Argandoña, 2004; North, 1971). As a result, the old locked-in system exacerbates the crisis or delays any proposed solution and finally exacerbates the ecological crisis.

Overpopulation is a major cause of ecological crises, but this doesn't necessarily mean that smaller populations are better. Because individual humans are weak, we tend to form social groups that are large enough to ensure our survival. When war or natural disasters such as plagues, earthquakes, floods, and climate change decrease the local population density below a certain threshold, the population may no longer be large enough to sustain itself or to function efficiently through a rational division of labor and through cooperation among individuals. At that point, the economic foundation for maintaining the social structure will collapse, and the society will collapse. For example, from 1800 to 1300 BCE, the Kayenta Anasazi people in the Long House Valley of the Black Mesa area in northern Arizona, the United States, went through a period of decreasing population. When the population was no longer large enough to maintain the local social structure, the people abandoned their valley (Axtell et al., 2002), and the associated civilization disappeared.

10.3. The Challenges Facing Current Society

Urbanization (migration of residents from rural to urban areas) has historically been an important phenomenon that defined the nature of a society's economic and social development and that has been a particularly important force in regional economic growth (Cai et al., 2019). Urbanization promotes the development of economies of scale by forming industrial agglomerations that are made possible by population clustering and specialization of skills that permits a division of labor. By providing access to public services, urbanization can improve the production and living conditions of residents, thereby improving human welfare. It can also reduce pressure on the environment, since concentration of people in the urban area permits economies of scale for processes such as waste treatment. Because of these benefits, governments pursue development based on urbanization. However, problems such as degradation of the city's ecological environment, resource shortages, a widening gap between the rich and the poor, and unbalanced regional development inevitably occur during urbanization (Li, Ma, et al., 2021). These problems have seriously hindered the sustainability of economic and social development and have created serious political, economic, social, and environmental risks that must be addressed.

China is the largest developing country in the world, and its urbanization process has developed at an unprecedented speed since the reform and opening up to the West began in 1978. Especially since the 1990s, the government's efforts to expand domestic consumption have relied on accelerating urbanization as the main goal of social and economic development (Shin, 2015). More than 15×10^6 rural residents migrate to cities every year, resulting in the disappearance of 550 km^2 of arable land every year due to the conversion of cultivated land into residential land (Cao et al., 2014). From 1978 to 2019, China's urban population increased from 172×10^6 to 848×10^6, and the urbanization rate increased from 17.9% to 60.6% (China Statistics Agency, 1979–2020). This urbanization has become an indispensable part of China's economic miracle. In 1947, only 69 Chinese cities had a population greater than 500,000, but this increased to 223 in 1980 and 669 in 2007; in 2007, 89 Chinese cities had a population greater than 1×10^6, compared to 37 in the United States and 32 in India (Normile, 2008). Peng (2011) estimated that China's urban population would reach 926×10^6 in 2025 and 1×10^9 in 2030.

10.3.1. Urbanization in China

Industrialization has been the main driving force for urbanization. However, traditional industrialization causes great damage to the ecological environment and seriously challenges the government's ability to sustainably develop the urban economy (Tan, 2017). Since most of China's cities rely on industrial development to sustain their economy, it's not possible to abandon the road of economic development through industrialization, and this has inevitably caused a series of intractable ecological and environmental problems. The key to solving these problems lies in technological progress (to improve production efficiency and reduce or recycle wastes) and industrial structure upgrading (to promote low-pollution industries), thereby avoiding the old path of economic development and environmental destruction by reducing the pressure on the environment, creating more jobs, and improving the ecological environment during urbanization (Cheng et al., 2015). However, China's long-term implementation of an export-oriented industrial economic policy has led the Chinese government to drive economic development through the export trade. As a result, China's inland population continues to migrate to the southeastern coast, which is the source of China's exports and China's economic center, resulting in a huge regional development imbalance and equally huge environmental pressure. As I described in Chapter 6, the government has accelerated the migration of China's rural population to cities and the migration of the Western population to the east by offering incomes sufficiently high to offset the costs of social benefits such as medical care and education (which are not provided free of charge to rural immigrants) and by controlling the prices of agricultural products and mineral resources. These unfair government and market actions together distort social and economic development, and the increased economic, social, and environmental risks have not been sufficiently addressed by economists and government departments (Cao et al., 2014).

The geographical distribution of China's population (Abramson, 2019; Li et al., 2018) shows that China's population center of gravity is near Henan and Hubei provinces, whereas the economic center of gravity is in the middle and lower reaches of the Yangtze River and the Yellow River, especially for the high-tech industry that doesn't depend on access to a seaport for transportation and whose development relies on engineering and technology workers trained by colleges and universities. However, the Chinese government promotes foreign trade through tax reductions and tax rebates for export enterprises, and under this policy, the coastal areas naturally become concentrations of industrial activities and population. Such policies not only hurt the development of high-tech industries, but more importantly, they have accelerated the consumption of limited resources by lowering the price of resources and giving tax rebates to enterprises based on foreign trade, thereby ignoring the potential ecological costs. The flaws with this geographical distribution of industries have greatly increased the threat to coastal industries through natural disasters such as tsunamis and hurricanes, while also increasing the potential damage from earthquakes due to the concentration of large populations in small areas.

As a result of overpopulation and misguided industrial development policies, China's environmental problems are becoming more and more serious. Much of China's food is grown in northern China, and pressure to increase production in this region is growing as migration to cities has reduced the population of farmers and increased the population of urban consumers. Unfortunately, in many arid and semi-arid regions of northern China, there is significant over-exploitation of groundwater resources to support agricultural irrigation, and groundwater levels are rapidly declining (Cao et al., 2011). As a result, the Chinese government had to implement the large-scale South-to-North Water Diversion Project to solve the water shortage problem in northern China, and the resulting ecological risks are not clear. Today, China is the world's largest consumer of steel, cement, aquaculture products, home appliances, textiles, automobiles, and other industrial products, as well as the world's largest fertilizer consumer and largest real estate market. The result is that environmental problems such as air, soil, and water pollution are becoming increasingly serious, with China ranking 133rd in a 2005 assessment of 146 countries worldwide for environmental sustainability (Liu, 2010). Among the 519 Chinese cities that China's State Environmental Protection Agency monitored in 2008, only 21 met the air quality standards of the World Health Organization, and among the 669 large and medium-sized cities, 400 faced a water shortage, with the shortage in 100 cities having a serious impact on the lives of their residents (Chen & Cao, 2013).

China's unbalanced urbanization strategy has led to the excessive growth of megacities, while neglecting the development of small cities, towns, and villages. Compared with large- and medium-sized cities, these small cities, towns, and villages are relatively poor and underdeveloped. If the rapid growth of the urban population continues to exceed the resources available to support the city, urbanization will inevitably face great risks (Cao et al., 2014), and by dominating resource consumption, larger cities will have a negative impact on residents in other parts of China and even elsewhere in the world. Megacities face greater but unpredictable disaster risks and may even collapse when they exceed the maximum sustainable scale (Seto et al., 2010).

10.3.2. Risks Created by Population Aggregation

Industrialization, especially of agriculture, has greatly improved production efficiency. Although the problem of overpopulation cannot be solved by traditional agriculture, the increased production permitted by modern agricultural techniques has prevented this problem from becoming a crisis. In other industrial sectors, the emergence of synthetic materials and rapid urbanization have caused an unprecedented environmental impact in terms of the quantity and characteristics of the pollution. At the same time, the construction of infrastructure such as roads, railways, and airports, combined with the expansion of industrial and commercial parks and the widespread agricultural use of pesticides and fertilizers, has increased the risk of environmental hazards such as land degradation, air and water pollution, and biodiversity loss. Because these risks are associated with China's rapid industrial, commercial, and trade development, urbanization is facing serious social, economic, and environmental problems, such as the increasingly serious shortage of water resources, increased air pollution, decreased quality of life, increased risks to human security, and accelerated species extinction (Chen, 2007). Accelerating global urbanization is resulting in environmental problems at scales ranging from local to global (Seto et al., 2010), and this has caused unprecedented harm to the sustainable development of society.

To reduce transportation costs and improve the efficiency of commodity and information exchange, societies have undergone urbanization throughout history. In 2020, 55% of the global population lived in cities, and this number is expected to reach 70% in 2050 (Cai et al., 2019). However, even though this kind of social development model looks favorable from an economic perspective, it conceals serious risks that few people have considered. For example, the risks created by natural disasters increase exponentially with increasing population density (Zhang et al., 2007). At the same time, the environmental impacts of industrial wastes and of urban construction may exceed the self-healing capacity of ecosystems, leading to long-term degradation of the ecosystems. Humans are products of nature, and civilization cannot exist without the natural environment. Short-term climate change (such as droughts and cold periods) and sudden disasters (such as volcanic eruptions and pandemics) can have a huge impact on social development. Population aggregation through rapid urbanization has led to an increase in per capita resource consumption, which has eroded the resilience of societies against climate change and natural disasters, while globalization and the resulting long-distance trade of resources have further increased the vulnerability of societies (Lenzen & Peters, 2009) by making supply lines more vulnerable, as we learned during the COVID-19 pandemic.

When a region's society exceeds the local environmental carrying capacity, it must import resources from its trading partners to maintain its own development, and this dependence on resources the society doesn't control will inevitably increase its vulnerability to supply disruptions (Cao et al., 2007). Because urbanization means that the limited land that is available is prioritized for development of infrastructure such as housing, workshops, business parks, and streets, cities cannot produce enough necessities such as food and become excessively dependent on external resources. Due to the high dependence of life on freshwater resources, most cities have been built near bodies of water, which increases their vulnerability to flooding by heavy rainfall or (in coastal areas) a tsunami (Chen & Cao, 2013). Cities also develop frequently along rivers due to the high nutrient content of the silty soil deposited by repeated flooding and the lower cost of obtaining irrigation water; as a result, farmers choose to accept the risks of flooding.

Modern cities are highly concentrated and heavily dependent on resource imports to maintain their operations and are therefore increasingly vulnerable to anything that disrupts their supply chains, including natural and man-made disasters. With global warming, the sea level will continue to rise in the future, thereby increasing the risk to populations in low-lying areas near the coast. At present, more than 100×10^6 people around the world live in dangerous areas along the coast with an elevation of less than 1 m above sea level (Seto et al., 2010), and global trade has accelerated the pace of coastal development. This coincides with the rising global sea level (Pilkey & Cooper, 2004), and even if cities are not at risk of being inundated by rising water levels, they still have to face the threat of water-driven inland by hurricanes and tsunamis, as well as slower and subtler problems such as saltwater intrusion. For example, the Indonesian tsunami on December 26, 2004, killed at least 170,000 people, and the 2011 Fukushima earthquake and the resulting tsunami caused at least 15,878 deaths and displaced more than 340,000 people (Wang et al., 2016).

Desertification continues to expand around the world due to climate change and unreasonable land use patterns (Cao et al., 2011). History shows that the expansion of desertification will damage and eventually break the balance between society and its environmental support system; this has led to the disappearance of ancient civilizations in many regions of the world (Diamond, 2004; Takács-Sánta, 2004). Although many believe that technological progress and institutional innovation will eventually solve such problems (Cao et al., 2007), there is no guarantee this will occur; many historical regional civilizations collapsed before innovation could save them (Odum & Odum, 2001). The selfish and self-serving ideology of a civilization based solely on private property ownership has encouraged people and governments to choose short-sighted and unsustainable development models, and we cannot lead humanity to a sustainable path if we cannot persuade governments to find an alternative to private ownership (Guan et al., 2011).

From a historical perspective, population aggregation increases the risk of long-term natural disasters in exchange for short-term economic benefits, and large cities are exposed to greater risk from unpredictable environmental hazards and will inevitably collapse during a crisis if the population grows beyond the ability to sustain the city (Odum & Odum, 2001). The high population density of large cities also increases the death toll when a disaster occurs. For example, the magnitude 7.8 earthquake in China's Tangshan City on July 28, 1976, caused 240,000 deaths, and the magnitude 8.3 earthquake in Xi'an, China, on January 23, 1556, killed an estimated 830,000 people (Wang et al., 2016). If we ignore the impacts of environmental damage, natural disasters, hidden taxes (costs such as a lack of support for rural workers who migrate to cities in search of employment), and other factors, and rely solely on market prices to calculate the economic return from urbanization, the associated hazards are easily ignored.

The huge population in cities is also placing increasing pressure on the urban environmental infrastructure, such as the water supply, drainage, and waste treatment, and both the shortage of water resources and temporarily excessive supplies of water, such as during intense rainstorms, have sounded the alarm bell (Sun et al., 2020). For example, the heavy rainstorm in Zhengzhou City on July 20, 2021, killed 380 people, affected 14.786×10^6 people, and caused 53.2×10^9 RMB in economic losses (Wei et al., 2023). Unfortunately, this is not an isolated case, as similar problems associated with urban development have affected many of China's cities. Because artificial structures such as urban streets and roads prevent infiltration of rainwater into the soil, unlike land in its natural state, the expansion of cities leads to increasing flows of rainwater down streets and roads until it accumulates in low-lying areas, causing increasingly serious urban flood hazards. In recent years, the uncontrolled expansion of cities has made flood disasters increasingly common in China's inland cities, far from seashores, and this has made "going to inland cities to see the sea in summer" a popular online joke (Zhang et al., 2021).

The spread of disease is another large risk of urbanization. The high population density decreases the distance between individuals, and this increases the spread of pathogens. Since 2020, the global spread of COVID-19 has been far more frequent in large cities than in small- and medium-sized cities (Zerbo et al., 2020). For example, since 2020, the current coronavirus pandemic has led to the temporary closure of 10 Chinese cities, including 6 cities with a population of more than 10×10^6, accounting for 60% of the number of cities that were locked down. At the same time, urban crime, traffic congestion, air pollution, and various environmental problems have become global problems, and the higher the population concentration, the more dangerous these problems become because of the large number of people placed at risk. The continuous growth of cities has exacerbated these problems, creating obstacles to the sustainable development of modern society (Guo et al., 2021). When the city size exceeds a certain threshold, the city's operating costs will increase due to the increase in environmental costs with increasing population (Zhang et al., 2021). China's experience shows that excessive urbanization creates an obstacle to sustainable development, and that maintaining the simultaneous development of rural areas and small- and medium-sized cities provides a simpler and less risky path to urbanization.

10.3.3. Predictions and Possible Solutions

As a result of globalization, both imports and exports are often transported over long distances, and water-based transport is an efficient and relatively inexpensive way to transport these goods. Many aspects of life, such as agriculture, industrial activities, and marine transportation, would be impossible without good access to water. This is why populations continue to concentrate in areas that are rich in freshwater resources, which are often low-lying areas. This inevitably increases the risk of natural disasters. Market-oriented development, industrial upgrading, government subsidies, price discrimination, market failures, and government failures jointly promote the migration of workers to these high-risk cities, and society's vulnerability to natural and economic shocks continues to increase. Excessive population aggregation not only increases the pressure on the environment but also increases the consequences of natural disasters. Some of these risks, such as flooding beside rivers, are highly local, but others, such as pandemics and climate change, are global.

I have already mentioned the risk of coastal flooding, but floods can also occur in inland areas. For example, rainfall in mountainous or plateau regions can cause severe flooding in downstream reaches of rivers that flow from these higher elevations. This flooding can also significantly decrease food production in the large agricultural areas along these rivers, thereby jeopardizing both local and global food security. Because the world's human population continues to increase, more agricultural land will need to be reclaimed, but most of the world's arable land has already been reclaimed, and the remaining areas that will be most suitable (e.g., with fertile soils and ample light) often lie in areas at risk of flooding or drought caused by global climate change. One solution that has been proposed is to capture floodwater that would otherwise not be used and transport it to agricultural areas that have insufficient water (Suo et al., 2023). This would simultaneously solve two problems: it would mitigate downstream flooding and it would provide water to drought areas. This would improve global food security and improve the ecological environment in the arid areas. The alpine climate of the Qinghai–Tibet Plateau is not suitable for large-scale grain production, but the arid Hexi Corridor in western China that lies downstream from the plateau has vast areas of potentially arable land that lack water (Zhang et al., 2016). Thus, transferring the floodwater to the Hexi Corridor and increasing the cultivated area seems like a viable strategy (black line, Fig. 14). However, there are many risks involved in transferring water from the plateau (Suo et al., 2023).

In addition to the Tibetan Plateau water resources, Heilongjiang, on the border with Russia, has rich water resources, with an annual runoff of 370×10^9 m^3 (Fu et al. 2015). In addition, Russia's Lake Baikal contains 23.6×10^{12} m^3 of freshwater. The transfer of water from the upper reaches of Heilongjiang and from Lake Baikal to northern Xinjiang via the China–Mongolia border (red line, Fig. 14) would provide a constant water supply to support industrial and agricultural production in northern China. This route has several advantages over water diversions from the Qinghai–Tibet Plateau, including more stable geological conditions, easier construction at lower elevations, and the ability to supply electricity powered by local wind or solar energy systems, as well as low maintenance and management costs, and thus appears to be the best route for water transfer to northern China.

In this project, a canal will be built between the Black Sea and the Caspian Sea in southern Russia (thick red line, Fig. 14) to divert water from the Black Sea to the Caspian Sea. This would raise the Caspian Sea's level (which is currently 14 m below sea level) and expand the area covered by the Caspian Sea. The evaporating water from the Caspian Sea should increase precipitation in the downwind arid regions of Eurasia and improve their climatic conditions. Most importantly, transportation created around this route would shorten the land route between western China and Europe and increase the strategic economic value of China's

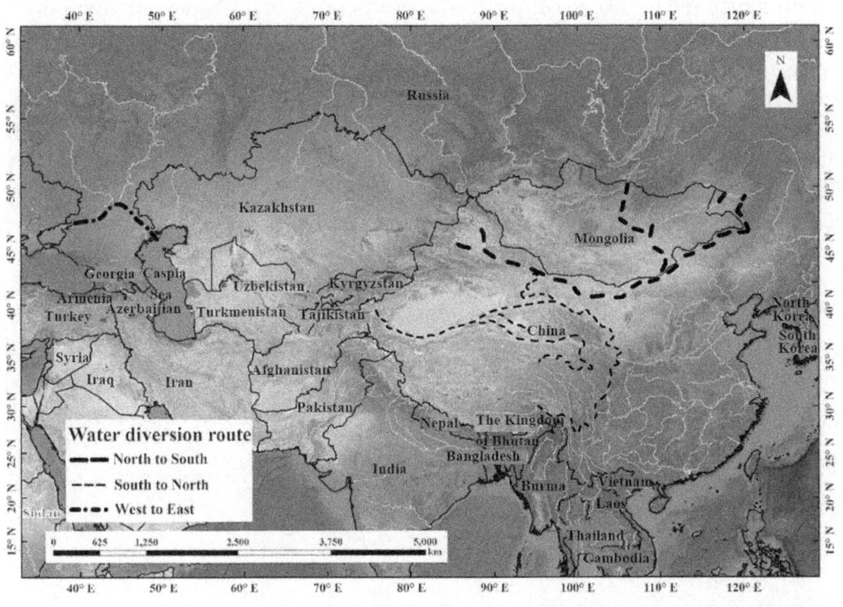

Fig. 14. Schematic Diagram of China's Proposed West-to-East, North-to-South, and South-to-North Water Diversion Projects. *Source*: Dr Suo Xinhao.

New Silk Road initiative. This project therefore appears to be an attractive alternative and deserves careful study.

Cross-regional resource allocation will have a significant impact on the economy and ecology of the source and destination regions, and such major resource allocation projects will cause disputes among the countries that are currently sharing these resources. Therefore, scientific demonstration projects to demonstrate the project's feasibility and coordination between countries and regions will be very important. One of the preconditions for carrying out the abovementioned water transfers will be research to predict the possible problems in the allocation of water resources in Eurasia. Goodwill between the affected nations and a desire to work together to find an equitable solution will be important. It must be emphasized here that the primary goal of the water transfers I have described is to deal with the food shortage facing much of Eurasia. Although the proposed projects have enough problems that they cannot provide a perfect solution, the number of people at risk of starvation means that we must consider proceeding with the projects despite their problems. The majority of people in the world who face the challenges of poverty and food insecurity have neither the ability nor the time to worry about natural disasters that occur once in a thousand years; they face much more immediate challenges to their survival even in the absence of a disaster. Politicians are willing to ignore the truly catastrophic natural disasters because they believe the disaster is unlikely to occur while they are in office. Ongoing annual disasters such as spring floods are harder to ignore, and politicians should accept their responsibility to mitigate or solve such problems.

Humanity must find solutions to the problem of the world's growing population, who must be fed and kept safe from disasters. This responsibility becomes increasingly challenging as the population grows. One of the most famous contemporary ecologists, Eugene Pleasants Odum (1913–2002) noted, in his book *A Prosperous Way Down: Principles and Policies* (Odum & Odum, 2001), that capitalism is a civilized process based on the consumption of natural resources. Once the Earth's resources are exhausted, capitalism will inevitably decline. Politicians should look at problems from a comprehensive perspective and not be swayed by the one-sided views of scholars who focus on a single discipline such as economics or ecology. Resource allocation is not only an economic issue but also a political and social and environmental issue. Some difficult choices may need to be made; they will be easier to make if we identify the choices we must make and develop ways to make the choices easier to survive. The essence of this political problem is the choice between life and death, not between more or less. Now the challenge will be to use what we have learned from several thousand years of Chinese history to improve our future history.

Chapter 11

Evolution of the Population System

A nation's people are the driving force behind its production and consumption activities, and population issues not only constrain the social and economic development of a society but also determine whether the society survives or fails (Otovescu & Otovescu, 2019). In the 1970s, the population explosion became the focus of global demographic research due to fears of what Stanford professor Paul Ehrlich (1968) called the "population bomb." In 1978, the United Nations Population Program predicted that the global population would reach 6.2 billion in 2000 and 14.9 billion in 2100 (UN-DESA, 1978), which appeared likely to seriously exceed the carrying capacity of Earth's environment. Therefore, demographers and governments began to emphasize the need to reduce population growth.

Thanks to the unremitting efforts of governments and other factors such as increasing education and prosperity, the global population growth rate has dropped miraculously, from 20.6‰ in 1970 to 11.1‰ in 2019, and the United Nations changed its original forecast. Their 2019 World Population Prospect projected that the global population will rise to 9.7 billion in 2050 and gradually decrease after peaking at 11 billion by 2100 (UN-DESA, 2019). The widely used fertility control technologies that were developed in the 20th century were an effective way for women in Western society to control their fertility and limit population growth. In most developed countries, the population explosion that was permitted by sedentary agriculture and subsequent industrial development has been replaced by population shrinkage, although not in all countries.

Although it's necessary to reduce the global population to reduce the burden on Earth's carrying capacity, achieving this goal will require careful analysis and planning. The need for this arises from a demographic problem: to reduce the population growth rate, fewer children must be born, but if the birth rate drops below the replacement level, there may not be enough adults of working age to feed and support the older generation. The current replacement birth rate that will produce a stable population is 2.1 children per woman. In countries where the birth rate is below this level, maintaining a stable population (if this is a desirable goal) will require finding ways to increase women's willingness to have children.

A New Stage of Civilization: Striving for the Great Harmony, 287–311

doi:10.1108/978-1-83708-258-220251012

People have dual attributes as producers and consumers. If the Earth has too many people, the available resources will not be enough to meet humanity's consumption needs, increasing the risk of conflicts between countries for access to the scarce resources and even the risk of wars, thereby threatening the stability and development of civilization. On the other hand, when the population is insufficient, the society will lose its producers of goods and services and its creators of wealth. The harm caused by a population shortage may even equal the harm caused by overpopulation (Cao, 2015). For this reason, it is necessary to try to maintain the population at an economically and environmentally sustainable level so that society can survive and continue to develop (Liu et al., 2016).

It's easy to understand that the population problem is the starting point of all other social problems, since if there are no people on Earth, all social problems will (by definition) disappear. From the description in Chapter 4, it can be seen that the emergence and development of a civilization based on the institution of private property is, in part, the response to a resource shortage created by overpopulation; at the root, most of society's problems can be seen as the derivatives of population problems. Whether or not you believe that population, per se, is the problem, it clearly contributes strongly to the problems faced by humanity. Therefore, to understand the evolution of social institutions, we must start by understanding how populations are produced, which relies on the evolution of institutions such as marriage that determine how people come together to create families and ensure the survival of children.

11.1. Historical Evolution of Society's Population System

Social systems that control reproduction have evolved to determine how and when children are produced and how they are subsequently raised to ensure their survival. These systems may represent one of the earliest social systems (Flowers, 2013). We govern our reproduction through conscious development of a complex system of constraints such as compulsory formal institutions (e.g., marriage) or non-compulsory institutions (e.g., customs) that control reproduction for a whole society rather than exclusively for small social groups. The population system is further complicated by the fact that different social groups impose different constraints on their members.

11.1.1. The Historical Institution of Marriage

The emergence of the private property institution may have been caused by constraints on the supply of natural resources, and this institution led to rapid and substantial changes in society, including (in many cases) an evolution from a matriarchal social structure to today's widespread patriarchal structure (Horowitz, 2006). To ensure that a parent's personal property can be inherited by their children, the private property system requires a stable definition of the family and group, and this definition was often achieved through marriage institutions.

Marriage is a complex institution that evolved to meet many needs, including inheritance of private property and elimination of competition for a spouse between stronger and weaker individuals. Protecting reproductive rights through the constraints of marriage was an early step to promote social cooperation. In matrilineal societies, daughters inherit their mother's property. However, after patrilineal society became dominant, possibly due to the increased power provided by the normalization of war and conflict to determine ownership of property such as land, patrilineal inheritance became dominant and the personal wealth (property) of men soon surpassed that of women and was inherited by male descendants. Although powerful individual men often had multiple wives, monogamy was probably more common because it simplified inheritance. Marriage institutions that reduced conflict among individuals over access to a spouse (for reproduction) or over property (for inheritance) promoted this cooperation and provided a social structure that constrained marital relationships.

Social systems gradually evolve in response to socioeconomic development, and marriage systems are no exception. The driving forces for evolution of a society's marriage system go beyond the need for cooperation among individuals and for property inheritance to include mechanisms that balance the supply of and demand for people. In the rest of this section, I will describe the most common marriage institutions and their social and economic implications.

11.1.1.1. Group Marriage

The institution of marriage would have had a significant social function even in early societies. Initially, it was probably intended to form strong social bonds between individuals, including bonds of affection and mutual support during child-rearing, and by protecting the married couple from interference by other individuals, it would have maintained harmonious relationships among the members of a social group and possibly even served as a prototype for later political alliances between nations, which were often formalized through intermarriage between the ruling families.

Group marriage appears to have been an early marriage institution that was intended to further strengthen social bonds. The most common form today is a marriage among three or more individuals. In a matriarchal society, this was often between one woman and multiple men. In a patriarchal society, it was often between one man and multiple women. Another form was "exogamy," in which individuals were encouraged to marry individuals from a different social group, with the goals of promoting harmony between the groups and possibly avoiding the damaging effects of excessive inbreeding. Although group marriage is a very old marriage system, it is still popular in many regions today such as southwestern China, Africa, and the South American rainforest.

The walking marriage, in which a man and a woman establish relations after the man's nocturnal visits to the woman, has been observed within China's Mosuo ethnic group, who generally live in Yunnan and Sichuan provinces (Xinhua, 2016). However, this relationship is unstable because the men may not visit a second time, and multiple men may visit on different nights. In early societies or in specific regions where populations were sparse and resources were abundant, sexual activity with different men maximized a woman's chances of conception and bearing a healthy baby, thereby increasing the birth rate and maintaining population growth. Especially in the Paleolithic era, when humans were still an endangered species and maintaining the population was the first priority, such a loose marriage system may have been helpful for population growth.

The institution of group marriage undoubtedly evolved to improve protection and survival of children, while also reducing inbreeding when the institutions promoted exogamy. This institution was often strengthened by both formal institutions such as religious restrictions on who could marry and informal institutions such as cultural customs that prohibited incest. However, even ancient cultures often violated social proscriptions against incest. For example, Empress Lü Zhi (241–180 BCE) of the Han Dynasty (241–180 BCE) forced her son to marry her granddaughter, and the ancient Egyptian royal family was perpetuated by brother–sister marriages. In addition, members of a group often "cheated" by having sexual relationships with someone who was not sanctioned by their group's customs or laws. As societies evolved and populations grew, other forms of marriage were adopted.

As I noted earlier in this chapter, many marriage institutions evolved to increase the production of children with genetic contributions from outside the mother's group, which produced children who were more likely to survive a range of environmental stresses. Where sexual relations were not restricted to a specific pair of individuals, this created a potential problem in the context of the private property institution: although a child always knew who their mother was, it became more difficult to know who was the child's father and thus which children would inherit the father's property.

11.1.1.2. Pair Marriages

As local populations grew and resource constraints emerged, conflicts often arose between social groups over control of the resources. Since men have historically provided most of the warriors who protected a group's resources, the increasing power of men (and their increasing wealth from the spoils of war) created pressure for evolution from a matriarchal society toward a patriarchal society. The marriage institution would have evolved to adapt to these new conditions, leading to a gradual change from group marriage to pair marriages. Pair marriage refers to a relatively stable relationship between a husband and a wife, but in contrast with monogamy (which I discuss in the next section), the relationship did not always exclude extramarital sexual behavior and therefore represented a transitional form between group marriage and monogamy. In a pair marriage, the relationship between men and women is closer than that under group marriage, but looser than that under monogamy, and represents a kind of consensual, relatively unconstrained but slightly fixed form of cohabitation.

In the late matriarchal period, daughters naturally became the heirs of their mother's property, and the practice of a man marrying into his wife's family gradually developed. Because of the stability and clarity of these bonds, it was easier to establish paternity, and men were more willing to maintain a long-term relationship with a woman and work for her to ensure that their children received the resources and protection they needed to thrive, while also ensuring access to the corresponding inheritance. However, in periods of growing (often military) conflict between groups, soldiers (mostly men) would have acquired wealth through plunder, and their social status would gradually strengthen, creating pressure for the marriage system to evolve. This would have been one factor responsible for the gradual shift from a man marrying into a woman's family to a woman marrying into the man's family, and a shift from the daughter inheriting her mother's property to the son inheriting his father's property. I will not discuss the additional complication of dowry systems in this book, as they don't directly affect reproduction.

In the matriarchal system, women had a high status and could marry one or more husbands if they were sufficiently wealthy. In contrast, the man had the higher status in the patriarchal system, and men could have multiple wives. In modern Tibet and Nepal, both forms of marriage are still very popular.

11.1.1.3. Monogamy

In China, strict monogamy emerged during the Song Dynasty (960–1279 CE). Because the population was not only a source of labor but also a source of both agricultural workers and soldiers, the Chinese government before the Song Dynasty encouraged married women who were not yet pregnant to stay out at night during the spring Qingming Festival to become pregnant and increase the population. For example, the ancient Chinese sage Confucius (551–479 BCE) was conceived during the Qingming Festival.

Many Chinese sages knew their mother but did not know who their fathers were. Other examples include Laozi (also known as Li Er, ca. 571–470 BCE) and Gui Guzi (also known as Wang Xu, 400–320 BCE). Such a fertility strategy was also popular in the Tang Dynasty (618–907 CE). For example, the Tang Chancellor Yang Guozhong (716–756 CE) was forced to work away from home for a year, during which time his wife became pregnant and gave birth to a son named Yang Fei (732–755 CE). Not only did her husband not take offense, but emperor Li Longji (685–762 CE) of the Tang Dynasty approved of the son's birth and married his daughter, Princess Wanchun (732–770 CE), to Yang Fei.

After nearly 400 years of warfare in China from the Three Kingdoms period (220–280 CE) to the Northern and Southern Dynasties period (420–589 CE), China's population decreased sufficiently that the Tang emperors urgently needed to encourage women to have children to increase the population, so the chancellor and the emperor needed to set an example for the people. However, as society stabilized under the Song Dynasty (960–1279 CE), the population grew sufficiently that it became necessary to prevent pregnancies before marriage and prevent infidelity after marriage. The Qingming Festival in China was changed, by law, from the traditional "Valentine's Day" festival that encouraged promiscuity to the "Ancestral Festival," which was dedicated to remembering ancestors. Non-marital pregnancy became much less common.

11.1.2. Mechanisms Behind Evolution of the Institution of Marriage

The marriage system is an effective strategy to control the population through the ethical and moral restraints imposed by society. In the early days, when the number of people on Earth was small, encouraging fertility and preventing population extinctions were the primary problems faced by society. Therefore, the status of women, who were the creators of new people and therefore represented the strongest constraint on population growth, was higher than that of men. Chinese legend states that the goddess *Nüwà*, the world's first mother, shaped the first girl with mud, worried about her loneliness, and used her ribs to shape a boy. This creation myth was strengthened by the fact that during the early hunter–gatherer period, when hunting tools were still relatively primitive and hunting was probably dominated by men, most nutrition would have been provided by women gathering fruits and vegetables and excavating plant roots, particularly during a food shortage. Therefore, the women who labored to feed their families and give birth to and raise children made the greatest contributions to the group's survival. They were the most capable people, the highest leaders, and undoubtedly the key producers of society. The Chinese people's worship of Nüwà subsequently evolved into the Chinese people's worship of ancestors and respect for mothers.

The behavior of the Tang dynasty's prime ministers and emperors in encouraging pregnancy was not an isolated case. The introduction of Buddhism to Tibet in the fifth century CE promoted monogamy, thereby decreasing the population in Tibet (Li, 2013). More than 100 years later, the sexual relationship between a man and a woman came to be seen by Tibetans as the duality of wisdom and compassion in the context of dharma (compliance with one's divine duty) and was referred to as *Mandkesvara* (also referred to as Yab-Yum), with the man and woman facing each other during copulation as they become a single being. In the temples of Tibetan Buddhism (Lamaism), sculptures of a man and woman copulating are enshrined at the highest position in a temple (Li, 2013) and may even be emphasized more strongly than Śākyamuni (623–544 BCE), the founder of Tibetan Buddhism. Larger Buddhist communities elsewhere in China don't recognize or emphasize *Mandkesvara*.

In the harsh high-elevation environment of the Qinghai–Tibet Plateau, with its intense ultraviolet radiation, cold climate, and low oxygen concentration, the natural birth rate and infant survival rate are lower than in other parts of the world. In an environment where the natural population growth rate is low, sexual abstinence will reduce the chances of conception, and the resulting decreased birth rate could lead to local extinction of a population if other pressures (e.g., natural disasters, wars) become significant. Preventing this outcome is one reason why Tibetan Buddhism encourages sexual activity. In contrast, in other parts of China, where overpopulation is a problem, a cultural concept has evolved in which "lust is the first of all evils" and customs are intended to encourage abstinence to reduce the risk of conception and an increased population; that is, institutions that restrict sexual behavior have evolved to control population growth.

Individuals have dual attributes of a producer and a consumer, and maintaining an appropriate population size in a region with limited resources is required to balance these two roles so that society will survive and social and economic development can continue. With the continuous increase of a regional population, it becomes necessary to restrain population growth to maintain the population within the environment's carrying capacity and to maintain the regional ecological balance. This need can guide the evolution of a society's marriage system. For example, during the Southern Song Dynasty (1127–1279 CE), China's land area was only 2×10^6 km^2, equivalent to one-fifth of China's current land area, yet the population was as high as 80.6 million and how to feed the growing population was one of the most difficult problems faced by governments of that time. To mitigate the problem, governments implemented a system to deny the legal status of any births that occurred outside of marriage, and it was not until 2001 CE that Chinese women once again had the right to have children without marriage.

Institutions have always been the core means for the development of society because they constrain behavior to meet society's needs. The relationship between population and resource carrying capacity has been an important factor in the evolution of China's marriage institutions. In 1980, China's population reached 974 million, and overpopulation once again became a cruel problem that the Chinese government had to face. To control population growth, the Chinese government introduced the one-child policy, which allowed only one child per couple, resulting in the abortion of hundreds of millions of fetuses and the forced sterilization of tens of millions of women (Liu et al., 2016). I'll discuss this in more detail in the next section.

11.1.3. Historical Turning Point for the Population Problem

Before the 1970s, demographers generally paid most attention to overpopulation because its effects (e.g., starvation) were obvious and serious, but with the rapid development of the global economy, a new problem emerged: improved access to birth control technology, combined with economic development, the improvement of education, and improvement of women's status have led more and more women to reduce their number of children or even to have no children (Cao et al., 2010). In many countries, this has led to a decreasing population, which has the demographic consequences discussed earlier in this chapter. In the early 1960s, the world's population growth rate reached 2.2% and then began to decline (Myrskylä et al., 2009). This is because of the problem of replacement-level fertility: not every child survives to adulthood or becomes fertile, so on average, parents must have more than two children so that each parent will be replaced. Without this level of fertility, the population will decrease. On this basis, demographers define 2.1 children per woman as the replacement level required to maintain a constant population, although this number depends on many factors (e.g., a country's maternal and child mortality rates). In 1960, the fertility level of five countries was lower than the replacement level. By the 1970s, the number of countries with reproduction rates below this level increased to 14; by 2000, the number had increased to 64 (Cohen, 2003), and in 2021, 112 countries had fertility lower than the replacement level (Yang et al., 2022).

Different countries achieved different reductions. For example, it took France 77 years to reduce the birth rate from 30‰ to 20‰, versus only 5 years for China (Table 6). China's total fertility rate was only 1.05‰ in 2015, and the *United Nations World Population Prospects 2015* (https://population.un.org/wpp) predicted that by 2100, China's population could decrease to only 600–700 million and could possibly decrease by half again in the next century (Liu et al., 2016). Of course, this would create a demographic crisis, so there are strong reasons to believe that China's government will take effective measures to prevent this problem. However, empirical evidence suggests that the effect of fertility incentives may be limited (Cao et al., 2010; Prettner et al., 2013). After all, economic development, increased educational attainment, and the elevation of women's status seem likely to be outcomes of the current social trends, and compulsory fertility regimes will not be well received by modern women.

Today, the world's most populous countries (China and India) have joined the fast track of economic development. However, China's population began to decline after reaching a peak in 2021 (China Statistics Agency, 2022), and despite India's relatively large population, there is likely to be an unavoidable decrease in birth rates accompanying its rapid economic growth, and the global population is expected to begin to decrease rapidly in the coming century. During China's rapid social and economic development, the willingness of Chinese women to bear children has continued to decrease (Wang & Chen, 2016; Zakaria et al., 2017). The birth rate dropped from 21.1‰ in 1990 to 10.4‰ in 2019 (Wang, 2019). Although the Chinese government abolished the one-child policy in 2015 and allowed women to have a second child, the fertility rate has not improved, except for a brief increase in Shandong Province (Yang et al., 2022). Global demographic research supports the view that social and economic development, accompanied by increasing income and education levels, are causing increasing numbers of women to have fewer or no children, and the global birth rate continues to decrease (Liu et al., 2016; Prettner et al., 2013). China's government claims that from 1980 to 2016, the one-child policy reduced the number of births in China by 400 million (Cai, 2013). As a result, the labor force aged 20–60 will continue

Table 6. Years in Which the Birth Rate Decreased from 30‰ to 20‰ Around the World.

Birth Rate (‰)	**Year in Which the Established Birth Rate Was Reached**							
	France	**Sweden**	**Belgium**	**United States**	**Japan**	**Germany**	**Korea**	**China**
30	1832	1880	1886	1897	1938	1910	1971	1972
20	1909	1922	1924	1929	1955	1926	1985	1977
Time interval (years)	77	42	38	32	17	16	14	5

to decrease. Simultaneously, China's economic growth rate has decreased below 10% and continues to decrease, in part because of a growing labor shortage (Guo et al., 2022).

Because the life expectancy of China's population continues to increase, it will take a few decades for the population to reflect the birth rate decrease, so the risks created by the population reduction are easy to ignore. However, governments cannot afford to ignore this time lag effect. As they formulate policies for the coming decades, demographers and government officials should account for the predicted changes in the birth rate and the expected labor demand in 20–30 years rather than making decisions primarily based on the existing population. The decrease of China's birth rate has been serious since the end of the last century, but government departments have formulated policies based on the assumption that the total population will continue to increase (Cao et al., 2010), resulting in an increasingly serious future demographic problem in China. China's government still hasn't accepted that the total population has started to decrease, and there is a famous joke circulating on the Internet: "Chinese women have no desire to have a child, but government departments are still meeting to discuss whether to allow women to have a third child."

11.2. Causes and Consequences of the Population Decrease

Due to the environmental and social risks created by overpopulation, people once believed that reducing the global population would be a good thing, but they did not fully consider the risks created by a decreasing population, which can lead to serious social problems. In response to their fears, the problem of population reduction has gradually become the focus of governments and scholars around the world. Research has shown that economic growth, education, urbanization, and unemployment are the main factors responsible for the decreased desire of women to have a large family (Cao et al., 2010; Yang et al., 2022). The population reduction and sustained trend of an aging population caused by increasing lifespans and the decreasing fertility rate will lead to a series of social and economic problems such as an insufficient labor supply and possibly an economic recession as consumer demand decreases.

China's population-reduction policy has greatly eased the environmental pressure created by society, and this will be a good contribution to solving the overpopulation problem. However, the decreased labor supply that will result from a continuing population decrease will jeopardize China's future economic development (Prettner et al., 2013), especially if the rate of the population decrease is greater than the simultaneous increase in worker productivity permitted by improved education and improved production technology; if this is combined with decreased demand from the smaller population, an economic recession is likely. Therefore, it is important to determine the most appropriate target population that will both protect the environment and preserve socioeconomic development. Historically, social unrest and other negative social phenomena have often resulted from an economic recession (Cao et al., 2007). The consequences of a severe recession should therefore not be underestimated.

China's population problem is representative of the situation in many other countries, and the predicted population reduction will have a negative impact on both local and regional economic development and political stability (San Juan Mesonada & Sunyer Manteiga, 2020). Demographic imbalances such as fewer children combined with aging parents will seriously undermine the demographic dividend for China's economic development that was created by China's huge population and domestic market (Wang, 2019). To identify the most appropriate measures to achieve a sustainable population, China will need to identify the key factors responsible for the population decrease and begin seeking remedial measures.

11.2.1. Willingness of Chinese Women to Give Birth

To learn the reasons for China's decreasing birth rate, Cao et al. (2010) surveyed 4,600 Chinese women of reproductive age in 2005 about their willingness to have children and clarified the relationship between the desired number of children and factors such as their income, age, education level, and working environment. The number of children Chinese women were willing to have decreased significantly with increasing income and with increasing education, and younger women were significantly less willing to have children than older women. Even if the Chinese government adopts the economic stimulus policies that have been popular in developed countries to encourage childbirth, the willingness of Chinese women to have children is unlikely to reach the replacement level of 2.1 children; in particular, young women aged 20–29 years desired an average of only 1.3 children when they paid for the cost themselves and 1.7 children when the government paid, and the difference was significant. Modernization has also been an important factor in discouraging fertility, since urbanization (a move of rural residents into cities in search of work) and underemployment also significantly decreased women's desire to have children (Cao et al., 2010). Because there is a significant positive correlation between education and income, it will be difficult to change the low fertility rate of Chinese women without finding ways to compensate them for their economic losses and losses of career opportunities from having a family. Thus, overpopulation may not be a problem in China for much longer.

In the agricultural age, children needed relatively little education, and the method of parents teaching their children the necessary skills was enough to enable each new generation to master basic production and life skills. Moreover, children were able to help their parents work even when they were young, and they remained as free labor for their family until they married and became responsible for their own family and land. Because the benefits of having children outweighed the costs, there was a widespread belief that "the more children, the greater the blessing." However, industrialization requires workers to master a greater range of skills (such as literacy and numeracy) but also to learn complex professional labor skills, especially for technological industries. Simultaneously, physical labor has been gradually replaced by machines, and intellectual labor has gradually become an increasingly important mode of employment. Both today and in the future society, children need a long education process from birth to employment, and by the time they enter the job market, it is around the time many are considering whether to start a new family. Because modern children rarely work in their parent's business, parents get less and less return from their investment in their children, and childbirth gradually becomes a high-input, low-return investment. Once the expected benefits no longer exceed the costs, people are likely to reduce their desired number of children or even refuse to have children, as this is the economically rational choice.

In summary, the survey showed that adult women with more economic opportunities and greater income and education are less willing to bear children because this requires a high cost until their children become workers like themselves; at the same time, the opportunity cost of raising children (e.g., loss of income and of opportunities for promotion) is higher than that for low-income women. This is an important reason why professionals such as teachers, civil servants, business managers, urban residents, and other high-income groups are unwilling to bear children (Cao et al., 2010). For low-income farmers, the unemployed, and manual laborers who move to a city, earning a living is difficult, and because they are often not eligible for benefits such as healthcare and education for their children, they are even less willing to consider having children. The younger generation has grown up after the population explosion of the previous centuries, and members of this social group have experienced the real-life hardships of overpopulation, such as difficulties in finding employment and difficulties in completing their schooling. Only when these practical problems are solved will it be possible to change their perceptions about starting a family (UN-DESA, 2019).

11.2.2. Econometric Analyses

The econometric results discussed in the previous section, though useful and reliable, are limited by the relatively small sample size (given China's enormous population). Other researchers have clarified the relationship between changes in social and economic indicators and demographic changes by performing statistical analyses over larger spatial and temporal scales (Sachs, 2002). They have found that population change results from many factors, including the mother's education level, women's rights, the labor market, access to modern birth control techniques, the infant survival rate, social and economic development, and a country's population policy (Lutz et al., 2001; Wilson, 2004). Measures such as women's education, female empowerment, market-oriented reforms, healthcare for the poor, and family planning services that are increasingly prevalent in modern societies are also important factors behind the significant decrease in global birth rates (Ehrlich, 2001).

To explore the factors that have affected the decrease of China's birth rate, Yang et al. (2022) calculated the impact of various factors on this decrease based on the panel data for social and economic indicators from 31 Chinese provinces from 1990 to 2019. The main causes of the continued decrease in China's birth rate were rapid marketization (i.e., implementation of a socialist market economy) and the rapid increase in women's educational attainment, with contributions of 21.5% and 18.2%, respectively. The developments of secondary industries (13.8%)

and tertiary industries (15.1%), which represent industries with better opportunities for women, were also important causes of the decreasing birth rate. Marketization has increased mobility as workers move to cities where better jobs are available, but the resulting local overpopulation has led to employment difficulties (e.g., competition for the available jobs, particularly among unskilled workers), industrial upgrading has led to inevitable structural unemployment (e.g., when manual labor was replaced by mechanized production), and the increasing burden of education that I discussed earlier in this chapter has increased the cost of childbearing (Lutz et al., 2001; Prettner et al., 2013); at the same time, social welfare has increased so that older people no longer need their children to support them during their retirement, but the government has also provided funding to support pregnant women and young mothers, thereby reducing the risk of low fertility (Adsera, 2004). Thus, a population decrease seems to be an inevitable consequence of the development of society, although there are offsetting factors.

An interesting result of the econometric analysis is that the improvement of medical services produced an initially surprising result: it decreased the birth rate, probably as a result of access to effective birth control and the legalization of abortion. The number of abortions in China reached 9.762 million in 2019, versus only 14.65 million births in the same year; the number of births dropped to 10.62 million in 2021, but the number of abortions remained high, at 9.5 million (China Statistics Agency, 2020). This suggests that if China prohibits abortion, the birth rate would increase significantly. However, the ethics of this approach are questionable, particularly if the prohibition is applied differently for different social groups.

If society wants to avoid the risks that accompany a decreasing population, it must first solve social problems such as funding children's education and promoting job training that will improve employment, while also accounting for risks such as famine and environmental degradation. Chatterjee and Vogl (2016) found that a 1 percentage point increase in per capita gross domestic product (GDP) decreased the birth rate by 0.45‰ for women aged 30–34 years; however, other researchers found the opposite results (Audi & Ali, 2016; Taher, 2020). Yang et al. (2022) showed that the impact of economic growth on women's willingness to bear children could be either positive or negative: in the economically underdeveloped western region of China, women are more inclined to seek to improve their livelihood through employment, so the higher the income, the higher the birth rate; this was also true in the highly developed eastern region. Because graphs of sociological data often show a U-shaped curve, women's intentions would be likely to change when their income exceeds a certain threshold. For example, the increasing demand for pets by the rich reflects the desire to care for another life but not a life as demanding as a child and suggests that such people may consider raising children as a part of their happiness in the future, thus maintaining a relatively balanced global population. However, unless couples can be encouraged to have more than one child, their fertility remains well below the replacement level of 2.1 children per couple. Thus, economic development may mitigate the harm caused by a population reduction, but it cannot eradicate the harm. Politicians must therefore do more to eliminate the threat of a population reduction.

11.2.3. The Harm Caused by a Decreasing Population

The success of a social policy depends strongly on the support of the people who are most strongly affected. The perceptions of these people are influenced by the characteristics of the policy and other factors (Cao et al., 2007). Against the background of long-term efforts to control population growth, 78.7% of the Chinese women that my research group surveyed in 2005 accepted and supported the Chinese government's one-child policy, and women who were younger, more educated, had higher incomes, and lived in larger cities where they performed "knowledge jobs" were more willing to accept the strategy (Cao et al., 2010). These results are consistent with those in developed countries (Ehrlich, 2001). In 2013, the Chinese government changed its family planning policy to allow Chinese women to have a second child, but the new policy has not been widely accepted by Chinese women. Subsequent research showed that only 60% of women of childbearing age were willing to have a second child (Yang et al., 2022). These results demonstrate that the new policy has failed to fundamentally change women's opinions and will therefore be unlikely to increase the birth rate in China, and that the potential harm of a future population decrease will become a fundamental feature of China's socioeconomic development if more effective measures are not taken to reverse this trend.

The shift from an agrarian society, in which more children is better, to an industrial or post-industrial society, in which most people prefer fewer children, has slowed the global population explosion but at the same time has created risks associated with a future population decrease. Because modern society has generally promoted development through urbanization, and this has improved women's education, provided more employment opportunities for women, and increased women's economic power (e.g., income), the impact of these changes on birth rates has exceeded the impact of policies that promote fertility (Cao & Wang, 2009). Therefore, population reduction is becoming a derivative effect of modernization and development, and if the impact of this trend exceeds the impact of economic growth, the aging of workers will lead to an economic contraction or even recession, which in turn will result in insufficient income to fund social welfare and in other social hazards (Cao et al., 2010).

If a country's population cannot be maintained at a sustainable level supported by the environmental carrying capacity, both overpopulation and underpopulation can harm economic development and social stability (Chu & Ching, 2001). During the past half century, the world's decreasing birth rate has led to aging of the global population (i.e., the mean age is increasing). Globally, the proportion of citizens who are more than 60 years old is expected to rise from 10% in 2000 to more than 20% in 2050 (UN-DESA, 2019). The lack of labor caused by retirement of these aging individuals will not only directly affect economic growth and decrease socioeconomic development (Jóźwiak & Kotowska, 2008) but will also increase the proportion of the population that will bear the economic burden to pay taxes to provide retirees with government social benefits (Cruces et al., 2012).

The impact of population growth on economic growth results not only from changes in human capital but also from changes in consumption, which is one of the main factors that drives economic growth. Economic analysis suggests that population growth during the second half of the 19th century accounted for 32.9% of global economic growth (Ricker, 1997). Sustained low fertility will not only inhibit economic growth but will also complicate economic difficulties caused by the aging population (Prettner et al., 2013). Even if society's future economic development can solve the social welfare problems that arise from the need to care for the elderly population, other social problems related to aging will be more difficult to solve (Henseke, 2011). For example, the shortage of workers will also affect the delivery of medical services (since there will be fewer health-care workers), social pension services, and social assistance and will reduce the number of citizens available to enter military service. Technology innovation may mitigate these problems but will not solve them all by itself.

The social pressure caused by population growth (Chapter 10), an insufficient supply of resources, and the increasing demand of people to improve their standard of living are driving social progress (Bettencourt et al., 2007; Gerland et al., 2014; Lee, 2011). However, these factors also create problems such as a decreasing birth rate that will change the traditional relationships between humans and nature. With a too-small population, a fair and effective social division of labor becomes more difficult to achieve, and in a smaller population, this decreases the probability that someone will innovate to develop new technologies, new industries, new systems, and other breakthroughs. A study of technological innovation showed that a reduced population density reduces the environmental pressure while reducing the impetus for innovation (Ni et al., 2020). For example, Japan has experienced a continuous population decrease during the economic transition it has experienced since the 1990s, and under the combined effect of multiple factors, its technological progress and industrial upgrading stagnated and its economy fell into a continuous recession. If a future global population decrease leads to a global economic recession caused by an insufficient labor supply, possibly combined with insufficient consumption demand, society will not only face social crises such as poverty and inadequate medical services but also may face challenges in producing the innovation that could solve these problems.

Curiosity can help humanity by leading thinkers toward discoveries that in turn lead to innovations. Is there a risk that people who are sufficiently comfortable with their lives will stop innovating? Anthropologists and sociologists should carefully consider whether this risk will be serious. Throughout history, most societies have collapsed when they encountered a crisis such as overpopulation, although many (including China) were subsequently and repeatedly reborn or replaced by a new and more innovative society. Capitalism represents a major change in how a civilization functions, but there is little evidence it will prevent this historical pattern from repeating.

11.3. Ethical, Institutional, and Feminist Evolution of Society

If we consider social change and the associated problems from the perspective of the long history of humanity, we would find that such change is not simply based on good will but rather depends on the relationships between individuals and between humanity and nature. As I described in Chapter 4, the emergence of a private property institution is based on the contradiction between population growth and an insufficient supply of resources (i.e., a limited environmental carrying capacity). From a short-term perspective, we would find that the relationship between people is the dominant factor that restricts social development; in contrast, from a longer historical perspective, we would find that the relationship between humanity and nature is a stronger constraint (Feng et al., 2019b). If population growth does not lead to a scarcity of resources, there is no need for a group or nation to declare their sovereignty over their territory to protect its resources by declaring it private property. Because disputes that could not be settled through negotiation were often settled through warfare, and warfare was a predominantly male endeavor, societies dominated by private property tended to be male dominated (Aranya et al., 1986).

Modern society is undergoing a series of revolutionary changes that are closely linked to the rapidly increasing population. Although many people still worry about global overpopulation, decreasing population is becoming common in developed countries and showing signs of appearing even in rapidly developing countries. In the coming century, we will see what is perhaps the first human-chosen global population reduction. If the reduction is sufficiently dramatic, the ecological crisis that we are now facing may be eliminated, and we will enter a new period of more sustainable development if we can avoid repeating our previous mistakes. Environmental constraints on society will ease as the population begins to decrease, and a new social system must arise to cope with this change. Good will is not sufficient to develop effective political strategies to solve our problems. We must also correctly understand them before we can propose solutions that will avert turmoil and disaster.

11.3.1. Ongoing Ethical Changes

New systems emerge in response to changes in our context that create pressure on old institutions. If the new institution is in the interest of the government, it is likely to be accepted and will be easily institutionalized by the government. If it isn't acceptable to the government, it will be prohibited, and if the people support it, this may lead to a confrontation that may even progress into a revolution. Because the government's interests are not necessarily consistent with the interests of the people, adoption of the new institution will be restricted by the government's prevailing ideology and the ability of government officials to change how they think. Sometimes this may occur even if the interests of the two parties are consistent. Such situations have been common throughout history. The development of society often shows alternating advances and retreats but overall has shown an upward spiral toward a progressively better and more advanced society. Some institutions are replaced and then return again, creating a sense of déjà vu. For example, childbearing outside of marriage was a basic institution many thousands of years ago and became less popular as population growth reached levels that threatened the availability of resources and as the social status of men continued to rise. It was not until 1968 that the US government issued a decree that recognized the legal status of unmarried mothers and of children born out of wedlock so that they could enjoy equal treatment (United Nations, 1968).

The legal status of births outside of marriage and the increase in the number of these births represent important institutional changes during the last half century; according to the World Child Trends Databank (Child Trends Databank, 2015), the global proportion of children born to unmarried women was 5% in 1960, rose to 32% in 1995, and reached 40% in 2014. Formally defining the legal status of these children created diversified family arrangements everywhere the institution was accepted, and non-marital cohabitation has become a particularly significant change in recent decades, particularly in the developed world (Kiernan, 2004; Sobotka & Toulemon, 2008). Today, the attitudes of the United States, the Netherlands, Sweden, and other Western developed countries toward unmarried mothers has changed from initial opposition to protection. For example, in 2007, more than 40% of Dutch babies were born, while their parents were not registered as being married, and more than half of Swedish children were born out of marriage (Grail, 2009; Meyer & Sullivan, 2010). The Chinese government first clarified the legality of unmarried childbearing in 2001 with the enactment of the *Population and Family Planning Law* (Xia, 2021). With declining birth rates and rising rates of unmarried cohabitation and divorce, the proportion of unmarried mothers and their children in China has grown rapidly, at a rate of 10%—13% per year (Liu et al., 2016), and childbirth outside of marriage has become a major force for sustaining population growth.

The evolution of social systems starts from the existing ideology (the standard values of a social group) and then a new institution gradually spreads until it becomes a formal system enforced by the government through laws and regulations. A system without public support cannot exist for long. In 2005, 46.9% of Chinese women supported the legal status of unwed mothers, and as the literacy and net income of the women surveyed increased and their age decreased, support for legalizing unwed motherhood increased (Cao et al., 2010). This result demonstrates that this institution will gradually become a major pathway for future Chinese population growth. In modern society, the rapid development of science and technology has been accompanied by increasing individualism (Sobotka & Toulemon, 2008), the improvement of women's employment and education opportunities, the availability of effective birth control technology, and improved medical services (Kiernan, 2004). Moreover, the mobility and instability brought by urbanization, the rising divorce rate, and other modern changes in social factors have prompted more and more young women to choose unmarried cohabitation (Oppenheimer, 2003). As more young women choose not to marry, unmarried mothers are becoming increasingly common and may gradually become the main mode of population production in future societies. This change will affect other areas of society (e.g., it will affect the demand for childcare during the workday) and will eventually cause major changes in social systems.

Similar to the pair marriages I described earlier in this chapter, unmarried cohabitation is a social system based on a looser relationship than in monogamous marriage. This is becoming so popular that it seems no one (not even the government) can stop it. If this practice continues to encourage pregnancies, it may mitigate the problem of inadequate future population growth and its economic and social consequences. In China, these changes have also been accompanied by a rise in the popularity of "sex parties" (gatherings of several individuals to have sex outside of marriage), "one-night stands" (sex outside of an ongoing relationship), and "open relationships" (long-term relationships in which the partners are free to engage in sex with others) (Liu et al., 2016). An important characteristic of all of these changes is that in most cases, they give women more agency than they would have in traditional monogamous relationships.

As the population stabilizes and then begins to decrease, the importance of childbirth (whether within or outside marriage) will increase (Basten & Jiang, 2014; Liu et al., 2016). Unmarried mothers who are willing to contribute to solving the problem of an insufficient population will have an opportunity to improve their social status and if children become a scarce resource, they may even acquire enough power or influence to lead society into a new feminist era. Some scholars consider marriage to be a form of private property institution in which the man controls all rights to a woman's body (Chused, 1992). Interestingly, this bears a strong resemblance to the private property institution but weighted entirely in favor of men. But as the marriage alternatives I described become more popular, marriage may evolve into something that more closely resembles a shared property rights system (Cao et al., 2022) in which the female participant controls her "property." This "property" not only includes women's reproductive rights but also includes all the material and spiritual wealth obtained by women who participate in the workforce. Under the new system, men must also bear certain responsibilities and obligations, because genetics technology makes it impossible for any man to deny they're a child's father and avoid the responsibilities and obligations of being a father.

Although population reduction will increasingly relieve the pressure on natural resources and reduce the risk of war and conflict over scarce resources (Cao, 2015; Carneiro, 1970) and will potentially give women more power in society, it will also bring the risks I described earlier in this chapter. Controlling the birth rate to avoid both over- and underpopulation can potentially keep the population within an acceptable and reasonable range, and women will play an essential role in achieving this state. The emergence of unmarried mothers and growth of their numbers provide new opportunities to solve the problem of a too-rapid population reduction. Although unmarried mothers are becoming an increasingly important component of population growth, their numbers are currently not sufficient to maintain a stable population. If the population begins to decrease, women will eventually become the scarce resource that limits social development, and this will give women power that lets them improve their social status and lead society into a future feminist society.

11.3.2. Emergence of a "Maternal Service System"

Although overpopulation is considered to be the most serious environmental problem facing civilization, decreasing the birth rate will eventually lead to a population reduction that will become a serious demographic challenge to future society (Bongaarts, 1998; Jensen et al., 2004; Myrskylä et al., 2009). The incentive plans to encourage pregnancies in developed countries (such as government-subsidized daycare for working parents) and the Chinese government's 2013 two-child policy failed to achieve the expected results. However, even if effective strategies are found to stimulate fertility, there will be a time lag before the adult population increases (Basten & Jiang, 2014). Thus, we cannot afford to wait until the global population decrease triggers the outbreak of social problems such as an economic recession, and research to guide current planning is becoming increasingly important and urgent. Population decrease is a direct consequence of the increasing number of women who have chosen to have fewer or no children (Reher, 2007). To reverse this trend, it will be necessary to find effective solutions to the problems that women face. One possibility is a maternal service system, in which bearing children becomes a highly respected and well-paid form of employment.

Compared to Europe, East Asian countries have experienced more rapid economic modernization and a faster decrease in birth rates (Table 6). However, this has led to changes in traditional systems, such as the responsibility of children to care for their aging parents. For example, this approach has been largely replaced by a government or private welfare system of care for the elderly (Shi & Zhang, 2008). Parents no longer need large families to support them, so it has become common to form smaller families. In developed countries, the potential adverse consequences of long-term fertility below the replacement level have been widely discussed, but few countries have taken effective measures to mitigate these problems (Wang, 2019; Zakaria et al., 2017) because lower birth rates are often balanced by immigration from regions with higher birth rates (Odum & Odum, 2001). For example, at the beginning of this century, 14.8% of the population in the western United States, 10.8% in the eastern region, 5.3% in the southern region, and 3.6% in the central and western regions were born in other countries (Liu et al., 2016). In China, the majority of Chinese residents have migrated away from their birthplace to seek work. For example, 68.8% of urban residents were rural residents who migrated from rural areas to cities from 1978 to 2017 (China Statistics Agency, 1979–2020).

The problem with this approach is that population migration is not a permanent solution. As more and more countries join the ranks of countries with a decreasing population, migration will eventually lose its significance. This suggests that no country will be able to escape the harm of population reduction forever. Exploring effective strategies to encourage women to give birth is the ultimate solution to the population reduction. To find an effective solution that will alleviate the future population reduction, some futurists speculate that technological progress can ultimately solve the problem, such as by creating an artificial uterus that frees women of the burden of pregnancy and childbirth (Liu et al., 2016). However, such a solution involves huge ethical problems. For example, if the machine replaces women, it will weaken the mother–child relationship, which is the basis for between-person relationships in any society. Another problem is that only the rich will be able to afford this solution at first, and this will give them an advantage over the poor in terms of access to the technology. Also, even when such technology becomes mature and reliable and affordable to most people, it is not clear whether people will accept it, as the social and psychological consequences are unknown (Simonstein, 2006). Thus, technological innovation is not, by itself, an effective solution in the short term, and to provide insights into what the solution may be, we should consider what we've learned from the evolution of other social institutions.

As I explained earlier in several previous chapters, institutions represent effective mechanisms used by society to regulate citizen behaviors and interactions. With a declining birth rate, a new institution should consider the impacts on social and economic development as well as the ethical challenges, and governments should seek solutions through relevant policy changes. For example, governments should increase subsidies for infants and mothers to reduce the burden of children on a family, provide longer maternity leave, give more education subsidies and living subsidies to the children, and give more subsidies to mothers (e.g., a salary to replace the earnings they lose while raising children). However, even though these strategies seem to protect the rights and interests of women and children, they have been opposed by some researchers who believe that this practice will force women to have children against their wishes (Jóźwiak & Kotowska, 2008). In practice, the best-of-both-worlds strategy is laudable but will be difficult to achieve and does not avoid the ethical challenges that arise if population growth becomes essential to a society's survival. Then, those who oppose forcing women to bear children may be silenced by louder voices who fear the consequences of a decreasing population. This may become particularly problematic if depopulation leads to a risk of extinction of minority ethnic populations. When the harm caused by population reduction is relatively minor, institutional evolution can be gentle, and multiple schemes can be tested, with different choices selected by different groups. However, when the threat is serious, institutional evolution may be too slow, and evolution may be forced to become revolution, with the solution forced upon everyone by the government. Those who do not accept the new institutional arrangement will be at best ignored and at worse severely punished.

Rewards must balance costs. For women to take on the future responsibility of maintaining the continuity of a stable society or even humanity itself, they must be given higher political and economic power and status to compensate them for this responsibility and should receive a corresponding amount of respect. In this approach, women will not be forced to take on the challenge of bearing children; rather, they will be offered sufficient incentives that they choose this profession voluntarily. The result will be a system in which having children will no longer constitute an economic, career, or other sacrifice. Obviously, it may be difficult to persuade the current male-dominated society based on a private property system to support this approach, so it seems likely the new system would only be adopted when depopulation threatens the existence of society, at which point the system of private property rights would be replaced by alternatives such as the shared property rights system described in Chapter 8, and the prosocial ideology that I proposed in Chapter 7 could become the dominant institutional form of society. In such a society, the respect for mothers advocated by Confucius will grow stronger.

Before society came to be dominated by men, it is likely that humans lived under a long period of matriarchy. Because men are, on average, stronger than women, men came to dominate society when the population grew large enough to require military conflict over the control of scarce resources. As I described in Chapter 4, the normalization of war and plundering gave strong male bodies an advantage both in warfare and during times of peace. On the one hand, men defended their community against invasions through warfare, and on the other hand, they plundered other people's property through warfare to obtain essential resources they could not produce themselves. Today, a new lesson must be learned: if a future population decrease threatens the existence of a society, women (as the only source of more people) must be empowered and rewarded for providing this service to society, and women's power may replace male power as the dominant force in society. (Of course, it's also possible that a cooperative power-sharing approach will evolve. Despite the stereotype of men and women competing for dominance, sometimes we cooperate well to achieve win–win solutions.) One interesting alternative arises from the concept of *prosocial society* that I described in Chapter 1. I call this the *maternal service system*. Many countries currently operate a national service system in which every citizen must choose a way in which to serve their country (https://en.wikipedia.org/wiki/National_service) and is compensated for the work they do. In countries that feel threatened by their neighbors, this is often achieved through military service. In other countries, other forms of service (e.g., performing socially useful work such as community service) are possible. For women, bearing children would be one option to serve their country, most likely in the context of some form of marriage and with the requirement (as I noted earlier) that the service should be well paid and strongly supported to compensate women for their difficult contribution.

Initially, governments should continue to develop policy options to encourage childbirth, such as free or subsidized child care, tax reductions for families with children, provision of paid parental leave, and social housing for young couples (Bongaarts, 1998). For example, in Canada, most provinces give mothers 6 months of paid parental leave, and some provinces give the father 6 months too, which can be shared with the mother (who could therefore receive 12 months of leave if the father doesn't take any paid leave). In addition, the woman's job is protected so that when the leave is over, she can return to her original job. Because there is little or no surviving evidence from pre-civilization eras, we can only speculate about how early societies attempted to encourage childbirth (Jóźwiak & Kotowska, 2008). The policy of encouraging but not requiring childbirth allows women to choose freely, rather than forcing them to bear children. This approach may be difficult to implement, as many people are selfish and don't believe they have any responsibility to their nation. Therefore, it is necessary to promote the concept of a prosocial society in which citizens accept the responsibility to protect and improve their society, thereby encouraging everyone to accept their social responsibility. For countries and ethnic groups with small populations, a significant and ongoing population decrease can threaten their extinction, and in those cases, a voluntary service system may not succeed, especially for poor and financially challenged countries and regions that cannot afford such programs.

These societies may instead choose compulsory maternal service that resembles the compulsory military service many countries require for their male citizens. Although this dystopian approach seems unrealistic, the rising number of nations in which authoritarian leaders are attempting to legally control the right of women to choose suggests that this approach is not implausible.

In a compulsory maternal service system, the government perceives a threat to the society's survival and issues a decree that healthy women must have at least two children to ensure that the national population is maintained within a safe and controllable range. Women who violate the regulations would be punished similarly to men who evade military service. Of course, this approach will be (and should be) strongly opposed, which will create social turmoil, and sufficiently strong opposition may even lead to a violent revolution. My hope is that researchers and philosophers will find an alternative that will maintain a woman's rights to choose when and if she will become pregnant.

Building a world based on Confucius' great harmony may be the only way to solve problems such as a decreasing population. In the utopian new world based on this ideology, there would be no differences in rights among races or countries and humanity would no longer need military service to maintain the existence of a nation's power. The world population would stabilize at a relatively low level, ensuring that humanity can overcome natural disasters through innovation and cooperation. Because the development of science and technology can extend human lifespans, while citizens awaken to the benefits of a prosocial society, people are likely to be more willing to assume their social responsibility and ensure the sustainable development of society. This will solve many of the world's problems.

11.3.3. A Vision for Future Society

Although technological progress has caused widespread environmental problems, it also offers a change to ease the tension between humanity and nature. We are increasingly recognizing that we are no longer the masters of Earth, nor do we need to be; rather, we can become allies or friends who live in harmony with nature. There is currently enough land and technology to feed everyone and meet their other living needs. There are even utopian predictions that future humans will not need to work for a living, as technology (e.g., robotics and artificial intelligence) may perform most or all of the work roles currently performed by humans. This suggests the possibility of a harmonious and prosocial life. However, reaching that goal will create several challenges for politicians.

11.3.3.1. Population Migration

In the first few hundred years of the social stage in which the world's population is decreasing, developed countries will attract talents and people from around the world through various policies designed to encourage immigration. This will be attractive to governments because there is no need for them to pay the cost of cultivating these talents (i.e., this has already been done by their original country).

The influx of talents from developing countries will promote the high-tech sector and offer the possibility of improving these talents by taking advantage of higher education in the developed countries. Unfortunately, this "brain drain" will impede development of the developing countries where these people were born and the economic gap between countries will widen. Although this will increase resentment in developing countries, it's not clear that this process can be stopped. If developing countries fail to achieve technological progress and industrial upgrading, their best talents will seek better opportunities elsewhere, even though this migration has become an effective path by which one country exploits another. A prosocial society could mitigate this problem by ensuring that the innovations and breakthroughs created by these migrants are shared freely with the whole world.

In a country with a large population, such as China, corruption and a lack of innovation in national politics provide a disincentive to great talents to remain, and many outstanding young people choose universities in developed countries to complete their studies. At the same time, the lack of employment in high-tech industries in developing countries has prevented graduates of foreign universities from returning home for employment and has encouraged them to stay in the developed country where they obtained their advanced education. As I described in Chapter 3, tens of thousands of Chinese students emigrate overseas every year and become contributors to the human capital of developed countries. This creates a vicious circle, in which their contributions promote their new home rather than their country of origin, thereby making their new home even more attractive to additional immigrants. The resulting imbalance in national development creates an international political order that will be difficult to change without the adoption of a prosocial society.

Due to the combination of ineffective population policies and economic development factors, China's population appears likely to decrease faster than in any other country in the world. Therefore, China will soon face a series of political problems such as insufficient workers to drive economic development, an aging population, a risk of economic recession, and social instability caused by the unbalanced population structure. A future population reduction means that the per capita social operating cost increases. Therefore, when the population decreases to a certain threshold for the rate of population reduction or for the population density, the society may no longer be able to fund government expenditures, leading to collapse or dramatic reconfiguration of the regime. Climate change and natural disasters will accelerate the migration process between countries, driven by global warming that makes some regions uninhabitable, which already appears to be happening in parts of Africa and the Mediterranean region (https://en.wikipedia.org/wiki/Little_Ice_Age).

Of course, environmentalists now generally agree that the Earth's population has exceeded Earth's environmental carrying capacity and that population reduction will therefore be beneficial to the future development of society. The core issue will be how to control the population so that it neither damages the environment to the point that civilization is threatened nor limits the economic development that will drive social progress. The examples of social collapse that I have described throughout this book suggest we should not dismiss the possibility that our own civilization will suffer a similar fate.

11.3.3.2. Collapse of Countries

People are a country's core resource for social and economic development, and when the labor force is in short supply, workers become the scarce resource that limits future development. What will happen to the institutional arrangement that we call a "country" when Earth's population is getting smaller and the population cannot be replenished through immigration from other countries? When the population decreases to a certain threshold, people become the scarcest resource, and efforts to capture this resource (whether through force or voluntary recruitment) will become the top priority of national governments, who are already competing for the greatest talents. Regimes that are willing to protect the interests of their people are more likely to gain the people's support and the net inflow of people to such countries will increase, whereas political systems, countries, and regimes that ignore the rights and interests of their people will be gradually eliminated. The speed of the birth rate decrease varies from region to region and will upset the political and military balance between regions, thereby increasing the risk of conflicts that include economic, trade, and military warfare. During the initial period of the future population decrease, various forms of conflict may continue unabated until regimes that disregard the rights and needs of their people are eliminated, or until politicians can no longer afford the cost of such conflicts.

With the further reduction of the population and a corresponding reduction of the pressure on the global resource supply, there will be less need for the private property institution, which will be replaced by more ethical and effective alternatives such as the shared property institution. Rather than basing their actions solely upon private property and a zero-sum game, nations will have an opportunity to pursue peaceful coexistence and seek win–win solutions that protect humanity from the threat of extinction due to problems such as global climate change. That is, the prosocial ideology may be increasingly adopted and extended beyond national borders to include the whole world. It is even conceivable that the frequency of war will gradually decrease, and war may eventually disappear. By 2100, countries with the fastest population reduction will be the first to find it difficult to conscript enough troops to support warfare, as was already occurring in Russia during the war between Russia and Ukraine while I was writing this book.

Countries with an ideology based on the private property institution prioritize the interests of their own people and lack the desire and motivation to explore the common good of humanity. Such a system that pursues individual freedom and ignores social responsibility will accelerate the demise of civilization if the global population cannot decrease to an environmentally and economically sustainable level and then stabilize at that level. Therefore, the capitalist system will need to change to avoid contributing to the demise of humanity. When a country's population decreases sufficiently, it will no longer be possible to sustain its previous economic level, and it will be necessary to accept reduced economic growth or a stable economic level. If a country can no longer sustain itself, calling it a "country" may become meaningless. Most people do not think about these issues or are indifferent to these issues. But if we don't pay attention to them now, it may soon be too late to remedy the situation.

Misfortune can have a positive side, and population migration is not always a bad thing. For example, migration can reduce the demographic pressure on developing countries. On the other hand, a strong international competition for talent can force developing countries to improve their national systems to train and retain these talents. Countries that fail to learn this lesson will continue to be depleted by the exodus of their population and will eventually fail if they cannot find ways to retain their population. In countries that are willing to change, their old system will be replaced by a superior and more efficient system through peaceful evolution to achieve a new institutional arrangement such as the prosocial society that solves the problem of scarcity of human resources.

When a country's population decreases sufficiently, humans will become the scarce resource that constrains future society, and military warfare (which depletes this essential resource) will become unsustainable and be replaced by peaceful competition for human resources. However, the darkness before this state is achieved may be the most dangerous time. Wars may intensify before the population decreases enough to make warfare unnecessary or infeasible, since warfare represents the last madness of societies based on the institution of private property. To shorten this period of conflict, politicians should work together to avoid the stupidity and madness of the warmongers and instead seek more effective and ethical solutions. Such periods are often referred to as storms, but fortunately, there is always a rainbow after the rain!

11.3.3.3. Ideological Change

While the population decrease continues, placing new stress on the world, the global population is aging, and the demographic problems faced by society will continue to increase. If we cannot solve these problems, we face a very real risk of losing our current civilization and possibly even a risk of human extinction. To avoid this fate, we must replace our current ideology of "everyone for themself" with an ideology based on cooperation to ensure humanity's survival. The shared property regime and a more feminist society are two important components of a possible solution, but both will require considerable institutional innovation.

In particular, we must reconsider the role of women in society. The fact that early matriarchal societies flourished for thousands of years before being overcome by patriarchal institutions tells us we can learn much from a more feminist approach. Because the future decreasing population will eventually make humans the resource whose scarcity jeopardizes society's ability to sustain its functioning and socioeconomic development, the women who can produce new citizens will become the most important individuals in society.

We must show our gratitude to these women for creating life, for sacrificing their health and careers to bear children, and for sustaining a more ethical and affectionate relationship among people. The great harmony proposed by Confucius will lead us into a future of equality, friendship, and harmony for all. It isn't a utopia that could only be achieved by saints; rather, it should be the shared vision of all humanity.

I hope that this book will be part of the solution that leads us into that better future.

Chapter 12

A Vision for Future Society

Civilization has struggled with conflict, hatred, and war since the first people tried to own private property and protect their property and its resources against other people. This phase of civilization has lasted for at least 7,000 years and probably much longer. As populations grew, thereby placing growing pressure on a society's resource supply, local resources gradually became unable to meet the needs of resource owners. To provide the necessary resources, societies established a complex set of political and social institutions to control how individuals could exploit the Earth, other nations, and other ethnic groups. This exploitation could be peaceful and conducted through resource sharing or trade, or it could lead to conflicts over control of these resources ranging from theft to warfare. Even in the absence of resource scarcities that led to conflict, the social and economic pressures that civilization has created have placed increasing strain on the institution of private ownership, which is showing signs that it must be replaced by something more modern.

Ideologies have been invented by most societies to create unity and consistent moral standards for their members to encourage prosocial behavior and discourage antisocial behavior. The institutions associated with this ideology encourage harmonious and friendly interactions (Cao, 2016a). Unfortunately, different groups may have different ideologies that will be compatible to different degrees. When ideologies are incompatible, this leads to conflicts and sometimes even warfare (Huntington, 1996). However, this isn't an inevitable outcome. As I've noted several times in this book, ideologies can coexist if those who follow them are willing to coexist with those who follow different ideologies; in fact, this coexistence resembles the coexistence of species in ecosystems, and like ecological biodiversity, human institutional diversity can make a social system stronger and more resistant to disturbance by (for example) natural disasters. The challenge becomes how to maintain unity within a social group and harmony between that group and other social groups; that is, the problem is how to achieve Confucius' ideal of the *great harmony* by using an appreciation for ideological differences to unite groups as a federation rather than tearing them apart.

A New Stage of Civilization: Striving for the Great Harmony, 313–336

Published under exclusive licence by Emerald Publishing Limited
doi:10.1108/978-1-83708-258-220251013

The *great harmony* that I have proposed in this book differs from the Chinese government's concepts of "harmonious development" and "community with a shared future for mankind," which are based on Marxist dogma. One flaw in the government's policy is that it relies on *fajia* rather than true Confucian ideals. Although *fajia* has been an efficient way to deal with wars and national emergencies, it gains this power by violating human rights, killing innocent people, and tolerating or even encouraging corruption. These flaws make it a stumbling block to the innovative development of Chinese society. Striving for the *great harmony* is impeded by a common human flaw: the desire to use binary thinking to divide phenomena into only two categories. For social institutions, these categories are often "right" and "wrong" or "us" and "them." It takes an effort and some education to understand that the world is more complex than simple binary categories can explain, that multiple possibilities can coexist, and that no simple explanation is likely to be fully satisfactory. The ideological confrontation between capitalism and communism after World War II is an example of unproductive and highly damaging binary thinking. Millions of people died or suffered unnecessarily because governments guided by the two ideologies could not see the possibility of cooperation and coexistence.

However, ideological conflicts are not the only problem. The private property institution creates an attitude in which trade between nations is seen as a zero-sum game in which one nation's power is threatened if they cannot "win." Today's confrontation between China and the United States, which is fortunately taking the form of a trade war rather than military warfare, is an example of how the private property institution can blind us to wiser approaches. Science is an institution that shows us an alternative way to look at the world: science works as a cooperative endeavor in which members of the group (i.e., scientists) compete vigorously over which worldview (theoretical framework, which is the equivalent of an ideology) is most correct, with consensus finally being reached, often without wholly eliminating one of the competing worldviews. This occurs because less successful worldviews sometimes explain aspects of the world that the victorious worldview fails to explain.

One of the key insights that I've tried to provide in this book is that rather than seeing communism and capitalism as incompatible ideologies that must inevitably compete in a zero-sum game, each offers some advantages that can compensate for the other ideology's problems. For example, the "everyone for themself" ideology of capitalism creates competition that rewards hard work and innovation, thereby leading to greater productivity and more efficient solutions, but at the cost of ignoring society's needs. In contrast, the communist ideology that society comes first discourages innovators because they cannot gain personal value from their innovation but does promote prosocial behavior in which everyone works together for a better collective benefit. Combining the two ideologies offers the potential for results superior to those of either ideology by itself (i.e., synergy), as we have seen in my descriptions of China's history. This approach may lead us to Confucius' *great harmony*, sustained by coexistence of and cooperation among competing ideologies. This harmony may be more familiar to many readers in the American concept of *e pluribus unum*: unity from diversity.

In this final chapter of this book, I will explore these concepts and their contributions to achieving the *great harmony*.

12.1. Lessons Learned from History

The invention of the steam engine in the 18th century launched the Industrial Revolution by accelerating production of goods and supporting a capitalist system adapted to large-scale production in large factories. However, when workers felt exploited and demanded better working conditions and a larger share of an enterprise's profits, capitalists rejected these proposals, as they were unwilling to reduce their growth or share their power with less their workers. The result was a series of conflicts that continue to this day and have greatly damaged society. The root of the problem is that capitalists tend to focus on their own interests and ignore the interests of society and particularly the interests of their workers and the consumers of their products. This problem can only be solved through an institution such as shared property rights.

The capitalist ideology of "everyone for themself" is an irrational, antisocial approach to social development, as its emphasis on the concept of private property ignores the needs of society as a whole. Capitalism encourages this approach and, by ignoring society's needs, leads to excessive consumption and neglects the environmental costs that arise from exceeding an ecosystem's carrying capacity and the social costs that arise from failing to account for the needs of future generations (Zheng & Cao, 2011). This problem includes aspects of the free-rider problem and the tragedy of the commons. An approach based solely on private property leads to shortsighted and unsustainable economic development that wastes natural resources while depleting and degrading these resources. This has led to the collapse of many civilizations throughout history, including the repeating cycle of failure by Chinese dynasties throughout China's long history (Cao et al., 2007; Odum & Odum, 2001). Today, the global climate change that has been produced by selfish, antisocial behavior such as unsustainable socio-economic development has created a social and environmental crisis that can no longer be ignored and that must be solved by all of humanity working together (Sachs, 2004). In Chapter 1, I advocated for replacing the capitalist ideology with a new ideology that I called *prosocial society*, which accepts the notion that one can act to benefit oneself first, then serve society as well out of gratitude for society's creation of conditions that allowed personal success. It's increasingly apparent that we must adopt this approach if we want to prevent the repetition of historical tragedies.

The capitalist worldview relies on private ownership of resources under the mistaken belief that unlimited growth of material production and consumption is possible (Beddoe et al., 2009; Vlek & Steg, 2007). At a national scale, emphasizing the concept of private property rather than shared resources that are the common property of humanity leads to a belief that nations have no responsibility to each other, leading to international conflicts and sometimes even world wars in which nations compete for exclusive access to resources rather than seeking ways to share these resources for the benefit of all of humanity. Moreover, the externalities associated with the utilization of natural resources and ecological services are only rarely "internalized"; that is, the beneficiary of the resource exploitation passes on the costs of that exploitation to the rest of society while retaining all the benefits. If humanity cannot modify capitalism to continue rewarding individual effort while instilling a sense of responsibility to society as a whole, it will be difficult to solve the contradictions between humanity and nature. If those contradictions cannot be solved, even the most promising scientific discoveries, technological advances, and social institutional innovations will not prevent us from repeating the same mistakes as past societies, leading to the collapse of our civilization and perhaps even the extinction of humanity if we cannot find a way to act together to cope with threats such as climate change.

Although capitalism does offer some effective strategies to overcome the world's environmental and social crises, such as the fact that it generates wealth that can be taxed to fund a government's operations, capitalists lack inherent incentives to share their wealth, although many wealthy capitalists do become philanthropists. To solve this problem, we must seek ways to encourage capitalism to embrace a collective ideology in which individuals can succeed through innovation and hard work but also share their success with the rest of society. That is, individuals who do well should share their success with the rest of society, who collectively created an environment in which individuals can prosper.

In the rest of this section, I will discuss three problems with capitalism that must be solved: political oligopolies and economic monopolies, excessive reliance on warfare as a solution, and competition.

12.1.1. Economic Monopolies and Political Oligopolies

Selfishness and greed are primitive but ubiquitous human psychological needs. Capitalism encourages individuals to strive to maximize their personal interests and uses competition between individuals to maximize efficiency and innovation in ways that can improve society (e.g., by paying taxes, by increasing the efficiency or effectiveness of products). However, the success of these mechanisms depends to a large extent on the existence of private property. Unfortunately, these mechanisms rely to some extent on the harm that results from information asymmetries and "everyone for themself" competition. Individuals differ in their access to information and their ability to take advantage of the information available to them. Those who have an advantage in the information they use can outcompete others with weaker access to information. In a completely free market (i.e., in the absence of government action), the result is the concentration of wealth and power in relatively few hands, leading to an evolution toward oligopolies or monopolies, resulting in further exacerbation of existing economic differences between individuals. The widening wealth gap between the rich and the poor creates resentment among the less-wealthy majority, and the resentment ultimately evolves into conflicts that can become violent revolutions. These processes are responsible for the social contradictions in the capitalist ideology and have led to political collapses such as the repeated dynastic changes in Chinese history. These collapses can be accelerated by natural disasters such as flooding and drought that reduce food availability, since capitalists rarely seem to look ahead to prepare responses to such crises that will benefit all of society.

Moreover, members of an oligarchy and monopolists tend to not be satisfied with the economic benefits brought about by their control of a resource or product or service. They inevitably seek to consolidate their interests by seeking political power, particularly if that can let them modify the political system (e.g., government regulations) to favor their activities (i.e., regulatory capture). This is often accomplished through seemingly legitimate means such as providing financial support to political candidates or through illegal means such as directly colluding with government officials and other businesses. The concentration of political power in the hands of an oligopoly has caused great harm to the equity of social and economic development of capitalist societies. Therefore, weakening monopolies and preventing their formation has always been an important task for the government. However, although this approach can be effective within a country, it can weaken enterprises when they compete to gain an advantage over their competitors in international trade, where large size provides a competitive advantage; as a result, governments around the world often take measures to strengthen domestic enterprises that must compete internationally, even though this creates a risk of monopolistic behavior. As long as there is competition between countries, the risk of a monopoly cannot be eliminated.

The acquisition of power is expensive in any system of the government, and this favors wealthy individuals in both democratic and authoritarian countries. This can lead to the development of political oligopolies or monopolies; for example, most democratic countries have only a handful of powerful political parties, whereas most communist countries have only a single political party. For example, in the 44th US presidential election, BBC News estimated that politicians spent nearly US$6 billion during the presidential election campaign (bbc.co.uk/news/magazine-19052054). Although such costs for regime change seem negligible compared to the human and economic costs of a violent revolution, most citizens lack the funds, the time, or the access to well-informed advisors that would let them rise to dominate a country's government. As a result, almost all the state powers in history have fallen into the hands of oligarchs or dictators, and the citizens they nominally serve become victims of the politician's self-interest. This is the biggest failure of a society based on private property, as it derives from institutional flaws that the private property institution cannot overcome, even in an advanced democracy. How to ensure that power remains in the hands of the people is therefore a core issue in political science research.

Oligarchs also seem to have unique talents for deception. Even as they shout political slogans such as "everyone is equal" and "serve the people," they are simultaneously engaging in collusion with businessmen and other special-interest groups exclusively for their personal benefit. The resulting economic and political corruption erodes the ideals of a democratic republic that exists to protect the interests of its citizens. Historically, there has been conflict between the wealthy, who would prefer that the government intervene as little as possible in the free market that made them wealthy, and the majority of a country's citizens, who are harmed by unrestrained capitalism. After the Great Depression that struck the capitalist countries in the 1930s, created in large part by inadequate government constraints on the richest and most powerful individuals, governments increased their intervention in the economy to control the worst abuses of capitalism. This was accomplished by measures such as the Glass–Steagall Act in the United States that was intended to reduce the risk of a future depression. This act protected Americans for more than 40 years, but the wealthy and powerful individuals who were constrained by the legislation worked tirelessly to undermine it. Those who benefited most from the neoliberal ideology that began to flourish in the 1970s eventually succeeded in having this act repealed (in 1999), thereby increasing the wealth gap once more and contributing to the 2008 world economic crisis. Global price increases, worker unemployment, and economic stagnation have become hot topics in major newspapers and magazines, but in practice, these phenomena hurt the wealthy far less than they hurt ordinary citizens; as a result, the wealthy have no incentive to change the situation and may even profit from the situation. The shadow of economic recession has fallen on every corner of the Earth, and political relationships between countries are becoming increasingly tense. The conflict between the rich and the poor seems to be gaining in strength again!

To correct the defects of the private property institution, the communist ideology proposed by Karl Marx promoted a prosocial ideology that was highly attractive to workers around the world; the ideology therefore spread rapidly. A civilization based solely on the communist ideology has several advantages, including the fact that it promotes a prosocial society in which the collective rights of society nominally outweigh individual rights. In this book, I have distinguished between communism, which I have defined as a doctrinaire approach based on the class struggle philosophy of Marx and his successors, and socialism, which emphasizes social welfare rather than adherence to Marxist dogma. Although this description is obviously somewhat simplistic, it nonetheless expresses an important distinction: that communism has tended to lead to authoritarian regimes that are antisocial rather than prosocial, whereas socialism strives to be prosocial and benefit society as a whole. However, as in the case of a capitalist civilization, communism has serious defects, some of which are shared by socialism to a lesser degree. These create barriers to achieving the *great harmony*.

Communist ideology doesn't tolerate the coexistence of other ideologies. As a result, it resembles a monoculture more than a rich ecosystem with high biodiversity that is strongly resistant to disturbance. Because all efforts are devoted to improving society, there are few rewards for hard work and innovation. Only obedience to the will of the government is rewarded. This sacrifices one of the greatest benefits of capitalism and private property: feeling that one's efforts are appreciated and rewarded. Although corruption is also a problem for capitalist systems, communist systems tend to lack the checks and balances that detect and punish corruption in a capitalist system. Communist systems also seem to encourage the development of authoritarian governments (often with a single dictator or small group of oligarchs). These systems also refuse to allow the existence of a free press, since reporters are likely to discover and reveal embarrassing behavior by government officials. As a result, there are fewer obstacles to corruption than under capitalism.

The communist ideology attributes the unfairness of social development to market failures. Communist governments therefore strive to comprehensively eliminate free-market competition; instead, the government controls the necessary socioeconomic activities, and the lack of competition discourages (or deliberately suppresses) scientific, technological, cultural, and artistic innovation. Socioeconomic development therefore stagnates, social progress is slow, personal goals cannot be realized, and a loss of citizen power becomes normalized. Deng Xiaoping drew inspiration from the Confucian concept of harmony among competing ideologies in his effort to create a socialist market economy, which has helped China to overcome the famine and poverty problems that had plagued the country for the 30 years before the implementation of his reforms. However, the corruption problem and lack of innovation caused by centralized politics and a centrally planned economy (subsequently exacerbated by government decentralization initiatives that gave the provinces more control of their own finances) continue to plague China's socioeconomic development, and China's institutional reforms still have a long way to go.

12.1.2. Excessive Reliance on Warfare as a Solution

In 1832, the famous military scientist Carl Philip Gottfried von Clausewitz (1780–1831 CE) posthumously published his pinnacle work, *On War* (von Clausewitz, 1832). In it, he claimed that war was a continuation of politics when politics failed to achieve a desired goal, and this belief became a political dogma in the Western world. However, this viewpoint has not been shared by the Chinese people. *Sima Fa*, one of the earliest Chinese military books, was published more than 3,000 years ago and noted that even though China is large, its regimes will inevitably perish if they are too belligerent, yet at the same time, the world is a dangerous place and governments must prepare for war. *The Art of War* by Sun Tzu, which was published during the fifth century BCE, summarized the lessons learned from China's domestic wars and emphasized that a nation that wants to survive must be prepared for war but should not seek out opportunities for warfare.

Unlike the Western world, China has continuously maintained a recognizable culture for thousands of years, and in its long history, invaders have only rarely conquered China. On the contrary, there have been many cases in which China defeated invaders not by military means but rather by absorbing the invader as a new component of Chinese culture. As society has advanced and become more sophisticated, there has been a growing recognition of the value of human life. Although this has not prevented small-scale regional wars, the sheer destructive power of modern nuclear weapons has discouraged warfare among the "great powers." However, even the countries with the most powerful armies have found it difficult to win a war of aggression without relying on nuclear weapons, even against much weaker countries. For example, the Soviet Union invaded Afghanistan from 1979 to 1989 and the United States invaded Afghanistan from 2001 to 2021, and both invasions ended in failure. Historically, wars have not solved many problems, although they have reduced the populations of the opposing countries and have occasionally mitigated pressures on one country's ecological environment if a successful war provided access to more resources. This leads me to conclude that war is futile, and that (to change the conclusion of von Clausewitz) diplomacy is the termination of war by wiser means.

There is a Chinese saying that the praying mantis consumes the cicada, but the sparrow consumes the mantis. In the context of warfare, this means that in most cases, both sides of a war are exhausted, allowing a third party to take the fruits of victory from the weakened combatants. Even if one party wins a military victory, its political and economic losses make it hard to justify the war. For example, from March 24 to June 10, 1999, the United States conducted large-scale air strikes on Kosovo, with zero casualties for American soldiers. However, after the defeat, Serbia joined neither the European Union (EU) nor NATO but instead became an ally of China (a third party). Similarly, the United States overthrew Saddam Hussein's regime in Iraq through military means, but the new Iraqi government established friendly relations with Iran (a third party), the enemy of the United States.

In ancient China, wars were often initiated by periods of famine, when starving people had no choice other than to launch a violent revolution. However, cunning politicians and other politically powerful individuals often moved aside to let the warfare finish, then stepped in to take control of what remained of the nation and launch a new dynasty. For example, in the late years of the Tang Dynasty (618–907 CE), a famine caused the Huang Chao Uprising (878–884 CE). After the peasant army overthrew the Tang Dynasty, there was chaos for several decades. Later, Zhao Kuangying (a third party) of the Song Dynasty (927–976 CE) unified China and established the Northern Song Dynasty (960–1127 CE). In 1644 CE, the peasant uprising led by Li Zicheng (1606–1645 CE) overthrew the Ming Dynasty (1368–1644 CE). The Manchus (a third party from northeastern China) took the opportunity to invade China and establish the Qing Dynasty (1644–1912 CE). In its long history, China has rarely launched a war of aggression in which they attacked other countries, although internal civil wars between dynasties were common. In addition to causing terrible losses of life, warfare creates hatred between peoples that endures for many generations and severely damages the economies of both participants in the conflict, while rarely providing enough rewards to justify the damage. The Confucian *great harmony* I have discussed in this book suggests there is a better approach: seeking common ground through cooperation while preserving differences is the best means to resolve political differences.

12.1.3. The Economic Significance of Competition

The biggest cultural heritage that the ancient institution of private property has given us is an understanding of the roots and correct application of competition. Competition is a confrontational behavior in which individuals or groups strive to determine who will control resources such as a piece of land or which of two competing solutions or ideologies will be adopted. Its positive effect is to inspire people, thereby promoting social and technological progress, as well as improving the production efficiency of workers (Xia et al., 2023). Competition is the driving force behind innovation and is therefore one of the main drivers of economic growth. It is precisely because of the competitive relationships between individuals, industries, regions, and governments that society has been able to continuously evolve and develop. However, competition must avoid zero-sum games and situations in which monopolies develop, in which competitors act illegally or seriously damage each other, and in which the resulting losses outweigh the gains.

Although I have criticized the private property system throughout this book, I want to make it clear that this system offers many benefits. In particular, competition among individuals or schools of thought strongly motivates workers to work hard and innovate because they know they will be rewarded for their effort, thereby creating both personal and social wealth and sustaining social progress in areas such as government, science and technology, the arts, and literature. These advances then become the shared property of all mankind. In addition, I have avoided the suggestion that the private property institution should be abandoned. As I have repeatedly emphasized in the book, new institutions are like new sprouts that grow from the tree that represents the old institution: the old system nourishes the new, and both coexist. Inheriting the effective components of the old culture and forming cultural and institutional diversity through continuous innovation and development is the institutional foundation for maintaining the existence and development of civilization. Similarly, I have criticized communist and socialist systems for failing to motivate hard work and innovation and for the failure of the rigid communism in the former Soviet Union and other countries to overthrow capitalism. But despite my criticism, I have not ignored how both communism and socialism remind us of the importance of contributing to society rather than focusing exclusively on one's personal desires. Confucian *great harmony* reminds us that two institutions can coexist, even when they are as different as capitalism and communism, so long as they compete in ways that bring out the best aspects of each system. One way to think of this is by analogy with how Olympic athletes compete: although they exert their utmost effort to outperform other athletes, they also recognize each other's value as humans, and sometimes even the most vigorous competitors are good friends after the competition ends.

As Charles Tilly (1929–2008 CE) famously said, "war made the state, and the state made war" (Krasner, 2011; Tilly, 1975). To avoid a zero-sum game, it is necessary to abandon the national institutions that require an opponent's defeat and instead embrace more cooperative approaches. One way to achieve this goal would be to build a global coalition of nations (i.e., a federation) whose primary goal is to achieve the *great harmony*. For example, the EU, NATO, and the Shanghai Cooperation Organization should act, first locally and then globally, to build on the lessons they have learned and promote the development of federal global cooperation, including tighter cooperation with the United Nations instead of independent action. Institutions such as the modern world order, which forces the world's nations to compete in a zero-sum game, cannot lead us into a better future. Instead, we must seek solutions that let us cooperate and improve the world for everyone, with competition promoting innovation and efficiency rather than creating winners and losers.

12.2. Lessons from History

China's rapid rise is one of the major events in contemporary history (Zhai, 2019). However, the reason for China's rapid rise has puzzled politicians and researchers from China and around the world, as previous research results have not provided satisfactory explanations (Cao et al., 2022). In Chapter 7, I reviewed how China's rise depended on learning from the experiences of other countries to develop a new type of production relationship, supported by embarking on a win–win path that reduced resistance to change. Unlike private and public property models, the new property rights model allows land users and knowledge workers to share benefits from the success of their labor without owning the land or their employer's enterprise, thereby increasing their enthusiasm for participating in economic activities. This model's success indicates that it has been crucial for China's socioeconomic development but also provides an important reference for other countries that have completed industrialization and hope to develop into a knowledge economy (Cao et al., 2022).

The main reason for the failure of reforms in communist countries such as the former Soviet Union was that they neglected the government's responsibility for supervision and management when they introduced a market economy system, leading to market failure. Most socialist countries have not abandoned government planning during the reform process, but China's achievements have been more prominent because China has created a new property rights model that mobilizes knowledge workers to work hard because they know they will be rewarded for their effort. Despite this success, we must also acknowledge the other social and economic problems that have accompanied China's rise. For example, as I noted in Chapter 3, Chinese innovation has been stifled by the government's unwillingness to accept new approaches to education, scientific research, and human rights, accompanied by a resurgence of Marxist dogma that casts a shadow over the future progress of China and human civilization. Summarizing these successful experiences and issues can not only increase society's knowledge content but also provide experience to guide global socioeconomic development.

There is no magical elixir that can solve all the world's problems. On the contrary, while we struggle to solve our old problems, we are busy creating new ones. To stop this vicious cycle, we must seek new institutions that can lead us toward the *great harmony*. Because the adoption of new institutions can create problems that are not immediately evident, a better approach to institutional change may be to adopt Deng Xiaoping's recommendation to "test and see": institutions that prove to be successful in a specific context can then be tested in new contexts with the necessary changes to account for new constraints and opportunities. As I described in Chapter 9, the cost of institutional change can be reduced by encouraging scholars to educate the public by demonstrating the benefits of changes, by identifying ways to compensate those who lose as a result of institutional change, by protecting institutional diversity, by allowing old systems that operate effectively to continue operating in the new environment, and by maintaining social stability through parallel evolution of political and economic systems. Society can actively and safely explore new development paths in this way.

Rather than waiting for a prophet to appear, governments should try many ways to promote innovation, and once an innovation is shown to work, they should promote its spread to all regions or sectors where it can provide benefits. The experience of the former Soviet Union and of China under Mao Zedong has shown that authoritarian governments fail because they sacrifice the benefits of institutional diversity by refusing to learn from the experience of other people and other countries. Avoiding this approach reduces the risks created by a lack of institutional diversity. Combining the two to produce what I have called a *prosocial society*, as China has begun to do with its socialist market economy, offers the potential for results superior to those made possible by the two competing ideologies, as we have seen in China's unprecedented socioeconomic development and the evolution of the shared property rights system.

12.2.1. The Chinese Experience

China's biggest recent contribution to humanity has been the results of its reform and opening up to the West since 1978. In particular, the results of this experiment have shown that innovation is a major driving force for the development of society. Humanity has evolved from hunter–gatherer societies to societies defined by sedentary agriculture, the Industrial Revolution, and now high technology and knowledge industries. The emerging new institutions have created new production relationships and new ways to redistribute the new wealth that has been created. The people who participate in the new production relationships form new social groups. The political demands of these new groups also promote innovation and evolution of the political system.

The traditional Western concept of property rights holds that resources and enterprises are privately owned and that this ownership is sacred and inviolable. In contrast, the Chinese government maintains the socialist principle of national ownership of property, while allowing property users and managers to share the benefits gained from their work. Many Chinese private enterprises follow a similar model: as long as knowledge workers are still employed by the enterprise, they will receive a portion of the enterprise's profits that are generated by their innovation. However, when they obtain employment elsewhere, they will return these rights to the company. The potential for increased income makes this model highly attractive to employees, but because employees automatically return their shares to the employer when they seek employment elsewhere, the new system is also attractive to employers (Cao et al., 2022).

Political changes have often taken the form of violent revolutions, which have been supported as an acceptable consequence by political philosophers such as Karl Marx and Mao Zedong. However, since 1978, China has followed a more advanced and less violent process of institutional evolution based on co-evolution of institutions rather than revolution (Buzan & Cox, 2013). This accounts for how new institutions and new industries often evolve from older institutions and industries, and that at the same time, new social groups also emerge from older ones. New industries have emerged, but the old industries have not disappeared. Instead, the new industries gradually increase their share of the social economy and ultimately become a major part of the new social economy. Similarly, the emergence of new social groups rarely eliminates the old ones, and the main change is the addition of new components to the old social system, with the more efficient or more attractive new elements gradually becoming dominant. In the evolving new society, old industries, old social groups, and old systems often continue to exist until they are transformed by new technologies or lose their social functions and are replaced or eliminated. Contrary to the beliefs of Marx and Engels, there appears to be no case in history where one class eliminated another. The gravediggers of the capitalist system appear not to exist; rather, social evolution seems to be seeking ways for capitalism to evolve in ways that make capitalism work for, not against, the workers; the shared property rights system is one such way that will increasingly change the production modes of both capitalism and socialism.

Because new groups and new industries gradually emerge from the old ones, new production relationships and new political systems that adapt to new industries and new social groups will evolve. Most often, this seems to be an unconscious growth process rather than the result of careful planning. Wise governments accept these new systems rather than fighting them and gradually promote their application after they have been shown (through careful study or successful pilot projects) to work and be worth exploring in other regions or sectors. This evolutionary approach avoids "shock therapy" (e.g., through violent revolution), which only occurs when the old system is so constrained by lock-in that it cannot change and leaders refuse to accept the new systems desired by the people. China's new approach, which attempts to combine the best aspects of the capitalist and socialist systems through mechanisms such as the shared property rights system, seems likely to succeed because the approach avoids lock-in and zero-sum games, particularly in the system that I have called a prosocial society, in which innovators and hard workers are allowed to benefit from their efforts, but are encouraged to "give back" to the society that created the conditions that let them succeed.

One recent study suggests that this approach is about 2.1% more efficient than the traditional capitalist system (Ma et al., 2025), and this partially explains why China's economic growth rate has been so much faster than those of neighboring countries such as Japan and South Korea during their older economic transformations. If you think that a difference of only 2.1% is small, remember that this is an annual difference, and thus compounds over time. In China's case, that compounding has occurred for nearly 30 years (Cao et al., 2022). For most of history, the annual global economic growth rate did not exceed 0.3% annually (North, 1990), despite the enormous social and economic changes that have led to our present global society. Since 1990, except for China, India, South Korea, Australia, and the United States, the average annual GDP growth rate of all other countries in the world was less than 2.1% (World Bank, 1990–2023). This demonstrates the enormous economic significance of China's new system.

12.2.2. The China Trap

Every new system emerges from the failure of an old system, but despite the new system's vigorous growth, the harm done by the old system doesn't disappear soon. This is not just a recent phenomenon. The centralized political control of most communist and socialist countries often resembles the *fajia* system under which regimes stretching from the imperial dynasties of China's distant past to the authoritarian Mao Zedong regime have harmed China for long periods. Their legacy continues to harm the Chinese people today. A common problem has been the selfish individuals who have surrounded the authoritarians. In their search for personal benefits, they have often provided rulers with incorrect information that led to decisions that harmed society and benefited only the selfish individuals. For example, the Ming Dynasty exempted government officials from agricultural taxes on their family land under the Hongwu Emperor (1368–1398 CE), leading to depletion of the imperial treasury, and this mistake was repeated under the Chongzhen Emperor (1627–1644 CE), who exempted these individuals from commercial taxes on their family businesses. The emperors of Ming Dynasty diverted essential income from the empire to the government officials, eventually leading to collapse of the empire when it could no longer afford to fund its operations, including defense against other peoples. There are signs that a similar scene is unfolding in China today. For example, there are many ways for wealthy individuals to avoid paying taxes, and Chinese law stipulates that when wealthy individuals who evade taxes are caught, they only need to pay their taxes and do not need to bear any other consequences (e.g., imprisonment) for their actions. This provides little incentive for the Chinese people to pay their taxes, and the failure to punish those who break the law is equivalent to robbing the national treasury – and thus, robbing the people.

To conceal their crimes against the people, authoritarian rulers often persecute dissidents and ethical individuals who try to report these crimes. They accomplish this through "literary inquisitions" in which books are confiscated and destroyed or by revising the state education system to prohibit teaching of the truth. It's a foolish strategy, as it forces the most excellent individuals, whose wisdom could greatly improve society, to hide in remote places or to rally domestic forces or even obtain aid from foreign political forces to overthrow their own government. Such cases are common in Chinese history but have not vanished from modern China. For example, China's government education and technology ministries strictly control what students learn and tightly control the innovations that are permitted. In addition, administrative officials view themselves as prophets and pressure professors and researchers in Chinese universities to seek evidence that supports the prophet's beliefs rather than seeking the truth. This not only leads to a loss of innovation skills in Chinese universities and research institutes but also leads to a significant loss of talent, since those who are prevented from innovating in China seek opportunities to innovate elsewhere in the world. Even when central and local governments introduce policies to attract talent, these policies fail if they don't attempt to disrupt the current locked-in system. (I describe this in more detail in Chapter 3.) Data from the United States suggest that 56% of China's top researchers have migrated to the United States, with 88% of Chinese PhDs in the field of artificial intelligence working in the United States (Morales, 2021). The technology war between China and the United States is essentially a battle between Chinese immigrants to the United States and Chinese residents living in their homeland. Therefore, despite having a large population and investing heavily in scientific and technological research, China has made few real contributions in new fields of science and technology.

These failures have large economic consequences. For example, China was unable to complete the development of the C919 aircraft, which was intended to provide an alternative to Western-designed aircraft. Despite 17 years of research and total expenditures of 170 billion RMB, China was unable to solve the plane's engine problems and was forced to rely on Western engines (Joane, 2023). This is not an isolated problem. China relies on imports for nearly half of its technology in fields such as biomedicine, computer software, industrial design, and precision manufacturing (Bajpai, 2022). As I noted in Chapter 9, China has achieved sustained economic growth over the past 45 years through continuous upgrading of industries such as textiles, home appliances, automobiles, and real estate. However, the old markets for such industrial products are saturated, and the new high-tech products needed to sustain China's continuing growth have not been developed in China, inevitably leading to slowing of the Chinese economy's growth. The annual growth rate of China's GDP has gradually shrunk from 9.7% in 2008 to 3.0% in 2022 (China Statistics Agency, 1978–2023), and it is expected to shrink further. China's current predicament repeats the historical examples of countries such as Japan and (to some extent) the United States. Any country that fails to innovate will inevitably lose its international power.

More than 150 years ago, political philosophers such as Marx and Engels proposed the theory of class struggle based on the belief that only opposition between the working class and the bourgeoisie was possible, with no possibility of working together. On this basis, they predicted that the proletariat would become the gravediggers of the capitalist system (Cao & Yu, 2019). From this perspective, they initiated the global communist movement, pushing the world toward opposition and division. The subsequent opposition between communist and capitalist ideologies has undermined world peace and endangered the development of human civilization. But as I've discussed throughout this book, history has revealed the shortcomings of both ideologies and demonstrated that this confrontation has provided no social benefits for humanity (Kornai, 2000). Marx and Engels seemingly failed to understand that cooperation and the search for win–win solutions is a more effective combination than class struggle, which assumes that one class must inevitably lose (i.e., a zero-sum game). Contrary to the understanding of Marx and Engels, Cao and Yu (2019) proposed that the emergence of new technologies and institutional systems is the driving force for society to move toward a new stage. Unfortunately, despite Shenzhen's successful experience, the shared property rights system and ideology have not been incorporated into the legal documents of the Chinese central government; On the contrary, we are increasingly hearing voices of hatred raised against capitalists and calls to prohibit freedom of speech, both of which are dangerous signals.

As Joseph Alois Schumpeter (1883–1950 CE) pointed out, innovation introduces a new combination of production factors and conditions that did not exist in the past within a production system (Fritsch, 2017). Historical experience has shown that higher education, scientific discoveries, and technological and institutional innovation are not only the original driving forces of economic growth but also a part of ongoing economic activities (Xia et al., 2023). If the Chinese government wants to continue increasing China's economic growth, it must learn from its experience with implementation of a competitive socialist market by challenging the status quo and thereby achieving innovation. Only this approach will let high-tech industries develop and replace traditional industries that are losing their importance for China. It will also replace the current land sales model being used to fund provincial governments, which has become a real estate economy that is producing a dangerous investment bubble. The stagnation that results from a lack of innovation has more than just economic consequences. China's long history of the rise and fall of dynasties shows how endlessly repeating the same mistakes inevitably leads to the same consequences: the fall of an empire, followed by the rise of a new empire that eventually makes the same mistakes.

The ability of a centrally planned economy to concentrate social forces to achieve a national goal is an effective strategy for many problems, but it relies excessively on existing knowledge and technology and has little ability to drive innovation by taking advantage of new knowledge. For example, a planned economy achieved significant success during the early stages of industrialization in the former Soviet Union, and this success attracted global attention. But after completing industrialization, planning errors caused by excessive reliance on individuals ("prophets") rather than on objective evidence undermined the modernization of the Soviet economy. The Chinese government fantasizes about replicating the West's new technology to surpass the Western world economically, but this cannot happen without government's willingness to encourage new scientific and technological research that challenges the status quo by producing breakthroughs. In effect, China is hoping to continue riding on the success of Western innovation rather than stimulating its own innovation. At best, this will cause China to follow the West rather than leading the West into the future. Perhaps more importantly, China's leaders must recognize that success requires more than scientific and technological innovation. China must also seek social innovations that will prevent a repetition of the cycle of dynastic rise, failure, and collapse, such as shared property rights and other characteristics of the *great harmony*. In particular, as China has learned from its experience with adapting a Western market economy, it must also learn from the Western example of free and innovative universities and research institutes, in which professors are given a motivation to change the course of their university, possibly through rewards such as a share of their employer's profits or being acknowledged for disrupting rather than protecting the status quo.

12.2.3. The Constraints Imposed by Nature

Scientific discovery and technological innovation have accelerated the development of society, but modern society remains ecologically unsustainable. However, two opposing forces are emerging that may change this: First, technological progress has increased the environmental carrying capacity, allowing the Earth to support an increasing number of people. Second, technological progress, combined with improvements in women's education level and social status, has reduced the willingness to have children, thereby slowing population growth (Chapter 11). If these trends continue, the world's human population will eventually decrease below Earth's carrying capacity, allowing the damaged world to begin recovering. On the other hand, this creates potential demographic problems that must be solved to avoid replacing one problem with a different problem. Decreasing the pressure of the world's population on the environment will not prevent natural and man-made disasters, though they may decrease in frequency or severity. On the other hand, industrialization and globalization have had a significant negative impact: they have accelerated the homogenization of society, reducing its diversity and making it more fragile in the face of external or internal crises.

Industrialization and globalization have also created complex supply chains that are highly vulnerable to disasters such as the COVID-19 pandemic and the grounding of the Ever Given cargo ship in the Suez Canal in 2021. As I noted earlier, nature imposes constraints on humanity through its finite ability to supply resources and ecological services. However, it also creates natural disasters such as hurricanes, drought, and flooding, which are likely to increase under global warming. One important consequence is that there is a large and growing need to find ways for nations to work together to respond to these disasters. Compared to the Earth, the human lifespan is very short, so we can only understand Earth's history from geological and archaeological evidence rather than personal experience. This makes it difficult for us to understand the destructive power of natural disasters with a magnitude so high that it occurs only once in every thousand years or even less frequently. Such a disaster will kill far more than the few thousand people that are killed by the disasters that have occurred in the past century. If a natural disaster with a once in million years frequency occurs, most of the Earth's population will die (Wang et al., 2016). It's also important to note that disasters are not necessarily sudden and dramatic; climate change is a slow-moving disaster that may result in the extinction of our species or at least the fall of most or all current societies.

Although we could not prevent a disaster of the scale that resulted in extinction of the dinosaurs, humanity could work together to mitigate the consequences of less severe disasters. Unfortunately, the current political system based on nation-states competing in a zero-sum game under a poorly regulated market economy are forced to pay more attention to short-term national or personal interests than to whether human civilization will survive a hypothetical future disaster. Governments find it challenging to prepare even for lesser disasters in earthquake zones and in flood-prone river basins and coastal areas, particularly when it's necessary to allow large populations to develop in these areas to support activities such as mineral extraction, fisheries, or farming. More and more cities and increasingly large populations are gathering in these dangerous areas. This is easily seen in satellite images of the Earth's surface at night.

Unfortunately, most people would rather believe the evidence of their eyes than the claims of experts ("seeing is believing"), and the majority of the population who have not personally experienced a disaster do not believe that such disasters will happen to them or their friends and loved ones. Politicians around the world generally belong to this group, thus have generally not realized the seriousness of the problem and have therefore not taken actions to mitigate the consequences. Chinese historical and archaeological research (e.g., repeated flooding of China's eastern coast by tsunamis) provides ample evidence that even a moderately serious disaster can result in the collapse of a civilization. Even if we don't believe we'll live to see such a disaster, how can we ignore the needs of our children and of the future generations who may experience the disaster? Building the *great harmony* would make it easier for nations to work together before a global-scale disaster occurs so as to mitigate the death toll and the cost to civilization.

12.3. Toward a New Stage of Society

The world of the *great harmony* pursued by Confucius is undoubtedly a beautiful one, based on the principles of serving humanity, rewarding hard work and talent, and prioritizing improvements in human lives rather than in profits. However, achieving this goal will be very difficult because governments must overcome greed, corruption, and the human tendency to seek dominance rather than cooperation. Unfortunately, we seem to be no closer to solving these problems. Failure to solve these problems has prevented previous global federations, such as the League of Nations and the United Nations that replaced it, from achieving their full potential. The problem has been exacerbated by the speed of technological progress, which has been unable to meet the needs of the world's growing population; in particular, technology has promoted unconstrained greed, with capitalism adopting an ideology in which there is no such thing as "enough." Confucius did not provide an answer for how to solve these problems and build a strong system that ensures fair distribution of the social surplus generated by economic and technological development. A related problem is that many rulers have tampered with Confucius' idea of benevolence by perverting its meaning to support their unethical and selfish goals rather than to achieve peace and prosperity; this is the legacy of the *fajia* system.

12.3.1. The Competitive Game Between China and the United States

The state is an institutional innovation that unites a group of individuals to face resource shortages, external threats from competing states, and internal threats from unethical actors (Carneiro, 1970). Unfortunately, the development of states also leads to competition between states, confrontations, and troubles ranging from excessive competition to wars. The leaders of major powers all want to become world leaders, whether for the good of the people they represent or for their own selfish reasons, and this has led to a long history of competition and confrontation between countries. The political collapse of the former Soviet Union left the United States as the last remaining "great power," which feels increasingly threatened by the rapid rise of China. Based on recent events, it appears that a confrontation between China and the United States is inevitable. But unlike the Soviet Union during the Cold War, China has become a market-oriented country, and its competition with the United States has been primarily economic. The confrontation between China and the United States is not an ideological confrontation, but rather a political and economic struggle for dominance of international markets and political discourse in forums such as the United Nations. If such a struggle becomes a fair competition between countries, it will promote technological and institutional innovation, and if it represents mutually beneficial competition ("coopetition") rather than confrontation and conflict, it can promote the transition of humanity to a new, better stage of development – what I have called the *great harmony* in this book. In contrast, if the competition is framed as a zero-sum game, it may lead to warfare and a disaster for all humanity.

China has a long history that the United States lacks. Having learned some lessons from that history, China's leaders have proposed a global community with a shared future for all of humanity; instead, former US President Donald Trump proclaimed an "America First" policy and embarked upon a trade war (Beckwith, 2016). China's exploration of the concept of a global community could lead humanity into a better world, but the Chinese government has not proven to the world that China has abandoned the communist class struggle ideology, nor has it achieved the Confucian *great harmony* that would calm fears that China will fall back into communism's zero-sum ideology. As a result, China has much work ahead of it to gain the trust of the international community.

Although the United States nominally won the Cold War, the human and economic costs were high (including the opportunity costs created by not investing the money wasted on this warfare to improve lives around the world) and it's not clear the net benefit was positive. Similarly, there is unlikely to be a clear winner in the confrontation between the United States and China. At best, there will be high opportunity costs, such as a failure to act together to fight global climate change. After the dissolution of the former Soviet Union in 1991, China successfully purchased the right to manufacture Soviet military technology. Because China has learned the threat of invasion from thousands of years of history, it has invested heavily in this technology to defend itself and became the country with the fastest growth rate of military equipment in the past 30 years. Nonetheless, the United States still has the highest spending on its military of all nations, at three times the Chinese total (Statista, 2022), and this may encourage additional spending by China in an effort to achieve parity. From a socioeconomic perspective, this represents an enormous waste of money that could be better spent on promoting global economic development and improving life for all of humanity.

If China cannot solve its problem of insufficient innovation, it will be unable to compete technologically and economically with the United States, and this will increase the risk of confrontation between the two nations. This risk will be exacerbated if the United States is unwilling to give up its selfish "America First" ideology. Therefore, China needs to build on its successful market-oriented reform to stimulate innovation, promote domestic democracy by finding ways for the people to supervise the government and mitigate or eliminate corruption, and drive development through competition and innovation. In turn, the United States should seek ways to change its role from dominance (oppression of other countries) to leadership (cooperation with other countries and setting a good example for them to follow) so that all nations have basic equality and all nations have their needs addressed. One possibility would be the federation model that I have described in Chapter 4, which would play a crucial political role in moving toward a new development stage for humanity. The American government should remember its experience of building a federal state when the 13 original North American colonies came together to build a new nation; in particular, it should seek ways to negotiate on an equal footing with its allies, transform the current military alliances into a federation of nations, and collectively deal with the various challenges that all members of the federation face. This could be achieved by examining the failures of current federations such as the United Nations to see how these failures could be solved and avoided in the future. This will not be an *easy* problem to solve, but it will be a *necessary* problem to solve.

There's a Chinese saying that while waterbirds and clams compete, fishermen benefit. If China and the United States continue to prioritize a zero-sum game in their relationship, they will damage each other and allow the fisherman – a different nation (a third country) or a different group (such as the BRICS countries) – to achieve dominance. This has happened many times before, including in China. For example, during the Spring and Autumn period and the Warring States period (770–221 BCE), when the countries of what is now eastern China were caught up in disputes among themselves, the Qin people strengthened themselves, and when the other countries had weakened themselves and grown fatigued from seeming endlessly conflicts, the Qin conquered the other countries and unified China.

12.3.2. Sharing Prosperity

Throughout history, famine has forced desperate people to rise up against their leaders, particularly when the situation is exacerbated by a wealth gap that angers the least wealthy individuals. Nearly 2,500 years ago, Confucius noted that a state-owned country will preserve its population but will suffer more from relative poverty than from absolute poverty. Similar results have been obtained in modern society, where wealth inequality has been the main cause of economic crises and social unrest (Chen & Ravallion, 2013; Ravallion, 2001). It is therefore the government's primary responsibility to ensure that the poor benefit from economic growth by ensuring that economic prosperity benefits everyone, not just the rich. The current wealth disparity between the rich and the poor is creating powerful social unrest, which may reinvigorate the world's communist and socialist movements and lead to future revolutions (Chen & Ravallion, 2013).

The Great Depression of the 1930s taught governments that unconstrained capitalism could lead to catastrophic consequences. In the past century, despite the rapid growth of capitalist economies and the disintegration of communist economies such as that of the former Soviet Union, and despite the market-oriented reforms in socialist states such as China, the global wealth gap continues to widen. The *Global Wealth Report* shows that since 2010, 10% of the world's population has come to own more than 80% of global wealth (Credit Suisse, 2022). This has been accompanied by growing economic uncertainty. Since the start of the 21st century, both developed countries and developing countries such as China, which is striving to develop a socialist market economy, have experienced economic slowdowns, stagnation, and even a reversal in economic growth. For example, the GDP growth rates of the United States, Japan, and China have decreased from 2.7%, 4.1%, and 10.6% in 2010 to 2.3%, –0.4%, and 6.0% in 2019, respectively (World Bank, 2020).

Equality for all is a common principle in both democratic and socialist societies. Therefore, shared prosperity should be the fundamental goal of governments. In this context, I interpret "shared prosperity" to mean the use of the benefits from economic growth to increase wealth for the world's impoverished population and gradually narrow the wealth gap. In a society based on shared prosperity, the unfair distribution of wealth gradually disappears, allowing the poor to gain an increasing share of society's growing wealth. However, individual differences in abilities, information asymmetries, variation of geographical characteristics, and other factors (such as government corruption) inevitably lead to inequality. Because society and the economy are complex and interdependent systems, no single approach will solve the problem of unequal distribution of wealth. The world's governments must nonetheless act, even though efforts to improve one inequality index may cause greater inequality based on other indices.

Transfer payments, in which governments reallocate tax income to impoverished citizens, should be supplemented by tax reductions, lower transaction fees, or even direct financial support to reduce economic inequality and achieve shared prosperity. However, different regions have unique characteristics that may lead to different effects of a given policy (see Chapter 6). Solving this problem will require joint efforts by governments and experts such as social scientists and economists to address. Only when the wealth accumulated by society benefits the majority of the people can a government be considered to have achieved shared prosperity. Despite what advocates of *confucian* claim, it is the labor of the people that feeds the government, not the government that feeds the people. In every dynasty of ancient China, those who seized power often had lofty goals at the beginning (e.g., restoring a certain degree of equality) but soon fell into the tradition of plundering and poverty that led to the downfall of previous regimes. Even today, landlords, court officials, government officials, and other politically powerful individuals use information, technology, and power to hoard resources such as land and accumulate wealth, once again leading to a widening wealth gap.

Unfortunately, governments seem unwilling to learn from history, so the cycle of revolution, corruption, and collapse has endlessly repeated. Governments must understand that poverty is first and foremost a political issue and only secondarily an economic one. If a government cannot address inequality through more equitable redistribution of benefits, turbulence and regime change will be inevitable. Modern neoliberal dogma encourages governments to exit the market, but all that this has accomplished in the past is ensuring that those who are already wealthy become wealthier. If we continue to allow the wealth gap to widen, history suggests that this will lead to social disasters. Building a political system that creates the world of the *great harmony* may be the only solution to the eternal issue of inequality between countries and between the rich and the poor.

12.3.3. Achieving the Great Harmony

The risks created by the current global political and economic situation are not restricted to environmental risks. If we continue to follow the zero-sum game promoted by modern capitalism and nationalism, tensions between peoples and nations will increase and may exacerbate the damage that will be caused by global climate change. In particular, this context will make it harder to cooperate in response to global disasters such as warfare and famine. Thus far, we have been fortunate that government leaders have been too wise to use any of the thousands of nuclear weapons that are targeted at large- and medium-sized cities around the world and that there has been no use of the weapons created by the many researchers who are researching and manufacturing biological and chemical weapons. We cannot afford to hope that this wisdom will continue. Instead, we must seek ways to reduce global tensions and promote the *great harmony* so that all of humanity is treated as members of the same family. This will also help governments around the world to improve their ability to predict and respond to natural and anthropogenic disasters so that responses can be faster and more effective.

In 1954, Abraham Maslow (1908–1970) proposed a theory of the hierarchy of human needs (Maslow, 1954), which divided human needs into five categories: the first level is for survival and physiological needs, the second is for safety, the third is for love, the fourth is for respect, and the fifth is for self-actualization. These levels are cumulative and interdependent, with the effects of any given level supporting the other levels. The essence of socioeconomic development should be to meet these needs rather than focusing solely on economic improvement. Despite the enormous economic gains that have been permitted by science and technology, we have made far less progress toward satisfying the five human needs; much work remains to be done to improve our progress. Adopting the *great harmony* concept would be an important and effective way to achieve that improvement. The world of the *great harmony* seems to be within reach, and the main thing that is missing is the awakening of humanity to the need for this new institution.

The *great harmony* proposed by Confucius is a society in which everyone's needs can be met. Its core philosophy is that the world's resources are shared, that the best talents should be rewarded, and other talents should be encouraged to excel, and that society should provide care for those who cannot care for themselves. *The Social Contract* by Jean Jacques Rousseau (1712–1778 CE), which was published in 1762, promoted the idea that there is no divine right for kings and that the people should be sovereigns and control their own fate. Keynesianism advocates government intervention in the economy to benefit a country's citizens, including the development of a welfare society that aims to improve society by providing full employment and stable prices. These two ideas together promote efforts to achieve the *great harmony*. The shared property rights institution I have proposed in this book provides a key component of Confucius' recommendations: it acknowledges the importance of rewarding the great talents while also encouraging them to contribute to the overall health of society.

In a world of shared prosperity, every citizen (regardless of wealth) can enjoy lifelong welfare, ensuring a dignified life without work. This undifferentiated social welfare system can reduce the social cost of identifying wealth disparities. In an ideal society, work will become a recreational activity, and its significance will be reflected in the fact that workers can continue to receive additional income while still receiving welfare payments that can be used to improve their own lives and those of other people, including more than just their family. More importantly, as a social group, working individuals expand their social circle and (ideally) experience some joy in their work. Unlike Marx's ideal country, the world of the *great harmony* would protect individual property as sacred and inviolable, while supporting a society in which multiple property rights coexist. Except for education and safety against both natural and man-made disasters, the government shall not force anyone to participate in most activities. Readers should not worry about people refusing to work; the enthusiasm of people in Nordic countries to work despite the high welfare available to them speaks for itself. Life is so short, and technological progress has made work increasingly easy; the next step will be to make it more enjoyable. Hard work is an important part of the future social life experience.

There is a particular risk that rulers will not make that effort, since many see themselves as prophets and seek to have the people worship them instead of demanding that they serve the people; this adulation is a powerful and intoxicating drug. History has repeatedly proven that selfishness and ignorance can lead to evil acts, and that to prevent these conditions, the power of a government must be constrained by the people's supervision. Governments should remember that the people have raised the government; it's not the government that has raised the people. Two main factors interfere with efforts to achieve the *great harmony*. First, nationalist ideologies promote an "us versus them" attitude rather than the belief that we all belong to the same extended human family. This encourages an approach that goes beyond healthy competition toward a zero-sum game. It also encourages a belief that nationalists who don't care about the harm they do to people from other nations are heroes, not monsters. Second, the ideology of "everyone for themself" ostensibly aims at encouraging self-realization. Instead, this ideology strongly and explicitly discourages collective effort (cooperation) and also promotes an attitude among government officials that they should serve themselves first rather than serving the people.

Because corruption and abuse of public power are prevalent in authoritarian countries, there's a belief that democratic politics aligns more strongly with the people's interests. However, this belief ignores the information asymmetry that lets politicians deceive the people. In each election, politicians use a range of tactics to deceive the people, and candidates who are the best "political performers" often gain power by aiming to please voters rather than dealing with difficult problems or asking people to sacrifice something for the greater good. Even if a politician tries to be fair and just, this can put them at a disadvantage compared to other politicians who gain people's enthusiasm by promising short-term benefits and ignoring long-term consequences. For example, after Russia invaded Ukraine, President Putin's support rapidly increased, and similar short-term, selfish thinking is not uncommon in democratic countries. The greatest ethical tragedy for society that is caused by excessive reliance on the private property institution seems to be how it encourages admiration of those who act selfishly and contempt for those who sacrifice their personal interests to do good. One of Confucius' more powerful insights is that governments should find ways to hire the most excellent individuals – people who can improve the government's performance yet also understand the ethical requirement to serve the people before serving themselves. Governments should also reward individuals who volunteer to share their benefits with others, thereby promoting a society based on mutual dependence. A good suggestion would be to learn from Confucius require a certain amount of experience at one level of government before an employee is allowed to apply for a higher position. In this manner, individuals who lack the necessary understanding of how the system works would have to gain that understanding before they could advance. For example, a person must have experience in low-level work before running for a higher-level position. Of course, corruption may nonetheless arise (in China, perhaps because of the *fajia* legacy), so some means by which the people can supervise the government's behavior is necessary. In Western democracies, this is often accomplished by freedom of speech and through monitoring by a free press.

Science and technology will play an important role in improving the lives of people, but both must be constrained by ethical considerations. For example, research has led to effective means of birth control, but this would be far less meaningful and effective without education and empowerment of women. Long-standing fears of overpopulation have made it ethical to study ways to reduce society's pressure on the environment. But now we are facing a population decrease in many countries that will have serious demographic and economic consequences. It has therefore become ethical to seek ways to motivate more women to have children. Because much warfare arises from conflicts over scarce resources, even today, a decreasing population may become small enough to relieve its pressure on the environment and on natural resources, thereby reducing the need for warfare. Ideological differences have also been a recurring historical cause of warfare, and here, the world can learn from China's tolerance of diversity; if different peoples can learn to accept others with a different philosophy, this removes another cause of conflict. One problem that I mentioned in Chapter 11 is the risk of human diversity being reduced by the extinction of certain cultures or their absorption by a larger or more powerful culture. Finding ways to reward women for being willing to have children, particularly when those women belong to minority groups that need more children to preserve their culture, will be necessary. Increasing societal respect for motherhood (the "filial piety" promoted by Confucius) will help.

The rise of the knowledge economy is changing the course of human social development. After fundamental changes in the socioeconomic landscape, traditional economic principles used to explain industrial development may no longer apply or may apply more weakly than in the past, and new principles will emerge. The economic rules have changed, so it is no longer feasible for economists and politicians to guide future socioeconomic development based only on outdated economic principles. For example, easing monetary policy (i.e., by issuing more of a currency) has been a traditional way to reverse economic contractions or slowdowns, but it's unclear that it is still a good solution. The world is different and operates by different rules. If we cannot recognize and respond to the new rules, a global economic crisis and social unrest will be inevitable. This will be especially true of economic crises that occur simultaneously with natural disasters such as tsunamis and anthropogenic disasters such as climate change. Unfortunately, we have not learned the lessons of history, which concerns me; as George Santayana noted, "those who cannot remember the past are doomed to repeat it." Countries that have already completed their industrial development face a new world, and innovation is the only thing that will help them deal with the new rules. The shared property rights system I have proposed is one approach that will help society enter a new and better stage of civilization.

The path to the great harmony will be long and difficult, but as Westerners say, "the journey of a thousand miles begins with a single step." In this book, I have described many of the steps necessary to complete that journey. I hope that at least one of my ideas will persuade you to take that first step.

References

Abraham, F., & Van Hove, J. (2005). The rise of China: Prospects of regional trade policy. *Review of World Economics*, *141*, 486–509. https://doi.org/10.2139/ssrn.809024

Abramson, D. B. (2019). Ancient and current resilience in the Chengdu Plain: Agropolitan development re-"revisited." *Urban Studies*, *57*(7), 004209801984302. https://doi.org/10.1177/0042098019843020

Acemoglu, D., Egorov, G., & Sonin, K. (2011). Political model of social evolution. *Proceedings of the National Academy of Sciences of the United States of America*, *108*, 21292–21296. https://doi.org/10.1073/pnas.1019454108

Acemoglu, D., Johnson, S., & Robinson, J. A. (2004). *Institutions as a fundamental cause of long-run growth* [Working Paper 10481]. National Bureau of Economic Research. https://doi.org/10.3386/w10481

Achten, S., & Lessmann, C. (2020). Spatial inequality, geography and economic activity. *World Development*, *136*, 105114. https://doi.org/10.1016/j.worlddev.2020.105114

Adsera, A. (2004). Changing fertility rates in developed countries. The impact of labor market institutions. *Journal of Population Economics*, *17*(1), 17–43. https://doi.org/10.1007/s00148-003-0166-x

Ai, B. (2019). Pains and gains of working in Chinese universities: An academic returnee's journey. *Higher Education Research & Development*, *38*, 661–673. https://doi.org/10.1080/07294360.2019.1590320

Ajibade, I., & McBean, G. (2014). Climate extremes and housing rights: A political ecology of impacts, early warning and adaptation constraints in Lagos slum communities. *Geoforum*, *55*, 76–86. https://doi.org/10.1016/j.geoforum.2014.05.005

Alchian, A., & Demsetz, H. (1973). The property right paradigm. *Journal of Economic History*, *33*, 16–27. https://doi.org/10.1017/S0022050700076403

Alderman, H., & Paxson, C. H. (1992). *Do the poor insure? A synthesis of the literature on risk and consumption in developing countries* [Policy Research Working Paper 1008]. World Bank. https://doi.org/10.1007/978-1-349-23458-5_3

Allen, M. G. (2013). Melanesia's violent environments: Towards a political ecology of conflict in the western Pacific. *Geoforum*, *44*, 152–161. https://doi.org/10.1016/j.geoforum.2012.09.015

Amarasekara, C. (2009). The impact of monetary policy on economic growth and inflation in Sri Lanka. *Staff Studies*, *38*(1), 1–44. https://doi.org/10.1016/j.eap.2019.07.002

Angrist, J., & Kugler, A. (2008). Rural windfall or a new resource curse? Coca, income and civil conflict in Columbia. *Review of Economics and Statistics*, *90*(2), 191–215. https://doi.org/10.3386/w11219

Ansar, A., Flyvbjerg, B., Budzier, A., & Lunn, D. (2016). Does infrastructure investment lead to economic growth or economic fragility? Evidence from China. *Oxford Review of Economic Policy*, *32*, 360–390. https://doi.org/10.1093/oxrep/grw022

Aoyama, R. (2016). One belt, one road: China's new global strategy. *Journal of Contemporary East Asia Studies*, *5*, 3–22. https://doi.org/10.1080/24761028.2016.11869094

Aranya, N., Kushnir, T., & Valency, A. (1986). Organizational commitment in a male dominated profession. *Human Relations*, *39*(5), 433–448. https://doi.org/10.1177/001872678603900504

Archer, L. Y., Lay, J., Pauly, T., Graf, P., & Hoppmann, C. (2022). The differential roles of chronic and transient loneliness in daily prosocial behavior. *Psychology and Aging*, *37*(5), 614–625. https://doi.org/10.1037/pag0000681

Arestis, P., & Glickman, M. (2002). Financial crisis in Southeast Asia: Dispelling illusion the Minskyan way. *Cambridge Journal of Economics*, *26*(2), 237–260. https://doi.org/10.1093/cje/26.2.237

Argandoña, A. (2004). Economic ethics and institutional change. *Journal of Business Ethics*, *53*, 191–201. https://doi.org/10.2307/25123292

Ash, R. (2006). The long-term outlook for economic reform in China: Resource constraints, inequalities and sustainability. *Asia and Europe Journal*, *4*, 177–196. https://doi.org/10.1007/s10308-006-0052-8

Audi, M., & Ali, A. (2016). A causality and co-integration analysis of some selected socio-economic determinants of fertility: Empirics from Tunisia. *Bulletin of Business and Economics*, *5*, 20–36. https://doi.org/10.1007/s13132-013-0177-0

Auty, R. M. (1993). *Sustaining development in mineral economies: The resource curse thesis*. Routledge. https://doi.org/10.1016/0301-4207(94)90044-2

Auty, R. M. (2001). The political economy of resource-driven growth. *European Economic Review*, *45*, 839–846. https://doi.org/10.1016/s0014-2921(01)00126-x

Axtell, R. L., Epstein, J. M., Dean, J. S., Gumerman, G. J., Swedlund, A. C., Harburger, J., Chakravarty, S., Hammond, R., Parker, J., & Parker, M. (2002). Population growth and collapse in a multiagent model of the Kayenta Anasazi in Long House Valley. *Proceedings of the National Academy of Sciences of the United States of America*, *99*, 7275–7279. https://doi.org/10.2307/3057853

Azzam, R., & Kong, M. (2021). Correlation of environmental parameters and the water saturation induced deterioration of earthen archaeological sites: The case of world heritage Liangzhu City. *China Heritage*, *4*, 387–400. https://doi.org/10.3390/HERITAGE4010024

Badeeb, R. A., Lean, H. H., & Clark, J. (2017). The evolution of the natural resource curse thesis: A critical literature survey. *Resources Policy*, *51*, 123–134. https://doi.org/10.1016/j.resourpol.2016.10.015

Bai, J. J., Wang, Y., & Sun, W. S. (2022). Exploring the role of agricultural subsidy policies for sustainable agriculture based on Chinese agricultural big data. *Sustainable Energy Technologies and Assessments*, *53*, 102473. https://doi.org/10.1016/j.seta.2022.102473

Bajpai, P. (2022, June 18). *Why China is "the world's factory."* Investopedia. https://www.investopedia.com/articles/investing/102214/why-china-worlds-factory.asp

Baker, S., Bloom, N., Davis, S. J., Kost, K., Sammon, M., & Viratyosin, T. (2020). The unprecedented stock market reaction to COVID-19. *Review of Asset Pricing Studies*, *10*, 742–758. https://doi.org/10.1093/rapstu/raaa008

Balvers, R. J., & McDonald, B. (2021). Designing a global digital currency. *Journal of International Money and Finance*, *111*, 102317. https://doi.org/10.1016/j.jimonfin.2020.102317

Barro, R. J. (2001). Human capital and growth. *American Economic Review*, *91*, 12–17. https://doi.org/10.1257/aer.91.2.12

Bar-Yosef, O. (2000). The impact of radiocarbon dating on old world archaeology: Past achievements and future expectations. *Radiocarbon*, *42*, 23–39. https://doi.org/10.1017/s0033822200053029

Basdevant, Q., & Hall, S. G. (2002). The 1998 Russian crisis: Could the exchange rate volatility have predicted it? *Journal of Policy Modeling*, *24*, 151–168. https://doi.org/10.1016/s0161-8938(02)00103-5

Basten, S., & Jiang, Q. (2014). China's family planning policies: Recent reforms and future prospects. *Studies in Family Planning*, *45*, 493–509. https://doi.org/10.1111/j.1728-4465.2014.00003.x

Bastos, P. (2020). Exposure of belt and road economies to China trade shocks. *Journal of Development Economics*, *145*, 102474. https://doi.org/10.1016/j.jdeveco.2020.102474
Beckwith, R. T. (2016, April 27). Read Donald Trump's 'America First' foreign policy speech. *TIME*. https://time.com/4309786/read-donald-trumps-america-first-foreign-policy-speech/
Beddoe, R., Costanza, R., Farley, J., Garza, E., Kent, J., Kubiszewski, I., Martinez, L., McCowen, T., Murphy, K., Myers, N., Ogden, Z., Stapleton, K., & Woodward, J. (2009). Overcoming systemic roadblocks to sustainability: The evolutionary redesign of worldviews, institutions, and technologies. *Proceedings of the National Academy of Sciences of the United States of America*, *106*, 2483–2489. https://doi.org/10.1073/pnas.0812570106
Bekiros, S., Muzaffar, A. T., Uddin, G. S., & Vidal-García, J. (2017). Money supply and inflation dynamics in the Asia-Pacific economies: A time-frequency approach. *Studies in Nonlinear Dynamics & Econometrics*, *21*(3), 20160051. https://doi.org/10.1515/snde-2016-0051
Bennett, B., Bettis, J., Gopalan, R., & Milbourn, T. (2017). Compensation goals and firm performance. *Journal of Financial Economics*, *124*, 307–330. https://doi.org/10.1016/j.jfineco.2017.01.010
Berger, R., Choi, C. J., & Herstein, R. (2013). China's social market economy: The leverage of economic growth. *International Journal of Asian Business and Information Management*, *4*, 21–30. https://doi.org/10.4018/jabim.2013010103
Berkes, F. (2007). Community-based conservation in a globalized world. *Proceedings of the National Academy of Sciences of the United States of America*, *104*, 15188–15193. https://doi.org/10.1073/pnas.0702098104
Bertram, C. (2004). *Rousseau and the social contract*. Routledge.
Bettencourt, L. M., Lobo, J., Helbing, D., Kühnert, C., & West, G. B. (2007). Growth, innovation, scaling, and the pace of life in cities. *Proceedings of the National Academy of Sciences of the United States of America*, *104*, 7301–7306. https://doi.org/10.1073/pnas.0610172104
Betz, M. R., Partridge, M. D., Farren, M., & Loba, L. (2015). Coal mining, economic development, and the natural resources curse. *Energy Economics*, *50*, 105–116. https://doi.org/10.1016/j.eneco.2015.04.005
Bhattacharjee, Y. (2007). Myanmar's secret history exposed in satellite images. *Science*, *318*, 29. https://doi.org/10.1126/science.318.5847.29
Bildirici, M. E., & Gokmenoglu, S. M. (2019). Does resource curse really exist in precious metal producer countries? *Natural Resources Research*, *28*, 1403–1428.
Bloom, D. E., & Canning, D. (2000). Public health: The health and wealth of nations. *Science*, *287*, 1207–1209. https://doi.org/10.1007/s11053-019-09468-7
Bloom, D. E., & Canning, D. (2003). The health and poverty of nations: From theory to practice. *Journal of Human Development*, *4*, 47–72. https://doi.org/10.1080/1464988032000051487
Blumenthal, D., & Hsiao, W. (2005). Privatization and its discontents – The evolving Chinese health care system. *New England Journal of Medicine*, *353*, 1165–1170. https://doi.org/10.1056/nejmhpr051133
Bongaarts, J. (1998). Global population growth: Demographic consequences of declining fertility. *Science*, *282*, 419–420. https://doi.org/10.1126/science.282.5388.419
Borooah, V. K., Gustafsson, B., & Shi, L. (2006). China and India: Income inequality and poverty north and south of the Himalayas. *Journal of Asian Economics*, *17*, 797–817. https://doi.org/10.1016/j.asieco.2006.08.001
Boserup, E. (1981). *Population and technological change*. University of Chicago Press.
Bowles, S. (2012). Warriors, levelers, and the role of conflict in human social evolution. *Science*, *336*, 876–879. https://doi.org/10.1126/science.1217336

Bridgman, B. (2008). Why are ethnically divided countries poor? *Journal of Macroeconomics*, *30*, 1–18. https://doi.org/10.1016/j.jmacro.2006.08.007

Brodsgaard, K. E. (2010). Governing capacity and institutional change in China in the reform era. *Journal of Asian Study*, *28*, 20–35. https://doi.org/10.22439/CJAS.V28I1.2834

Brodsgaard, K. E. (2017). *Critical readings on the Communist Party of China*. Brill.

Brovkin, V. N. (2003). Corruption in the 20th century Russia. *Crime, Law and Social Change*, *40*, 195–230. https://doi.org/10.1023/A:1025741929051

Brown, P. H., & Park, A. (2002). Education and poverty in rural China. *Economic Education Review*, *21*, 523–541. https://doi.org/10.1016/s0272-7757(01)00040-1

Buchan, N. R., Grimalda, G., Wilson, R., Brewer, M., Fatas, E., & Foddy, M. (2009). Globalization and human cooperation. *Proceedings of the National Academy of Sciences of the United States of America*, *106*, 4138–4142. https://doi.org/10.1073/pnas.0809522106

Burnham, W. D. (1969). The end of American party politics. *Society*, *35*, 12–22. https://doi.org/10.1007/BF02838130

Butzer, K. W. (2000). Ecology: The human role in environmental history. *Science*, *287*, 2427–2428. https://doi.org/10.1126/science.287.5462.2427

Butzer, K. W. (2012). Collapse, environment, and society. *Proceedings of the National Academy of Sciences of the United States of America*, *109*, 3632–3639. https://doi.org/10.1073/pnas.1114845109

Butzer, K. W., & Endfield, G. H. (2012). Critical perspectives on historical collapse. *Proceedings of the National Academy of Sciences of the United States of America*, *109*, 3628–3631. https://doi.org/10.2307/41507010

Buzan, B., & Cox, M. (2013). China and the US: Comparable cases of "peaceful rise"? *Chinese Journal of International Politics*, *6*, 109–132. https://doi.org/10.1093/cjip/pot003

Čadil, J., Petkovová, L., & Blatná, D. (2014). Human capital, economic structure and growth. *Procedia Economics and Finance*, *12*, 85–92. https://doi.org/10.1016/s2212-5671(14)00323-2

Cai, H., & Treisman D. (2006). Did government decentralization cause China's economic miracle? *World Politics*, *58*(4), 505–535. https://doi.org/10.1353/wp.2007.0005

Cai, Y. (2013). China's new demographic reality: Learning from the 2010 census. *Population and Development Review*, *39*, 371–396. https://doi.org/10.2307/23655331

Cai, Z., Liu, Z., Zuo, S., & Cao, S. (2019). Finding a peaceful road to urbanization in China. *Land Use Policy*, *83*, 560–563. https://doi.org/10.1016/j.landusepol.2019.02.042

Cao, C., Baas, J., Wagner, C. S., & Jonkers, K. (2020). Returning scientists and the emergence of China's science system. *Science and Public Policy*, *47*(2), 172–183. https://doi.org/10.1093/scipol/scz056

Cao, G., Feng, C., & Tao, R. (2008). Local "land finance" in China's urban expansion: Challenges and solutions. *China & World Economy*, *16*, 19–30. https://doi.org/10.1111/j.1749-124x.2008.00104.x

Cao, S. (2001). *Mountainous agriculture*. 曹世雄. (2001). 山地农业.中国农业科技出版社, 北京. China Agriculture Science & Technology Press (in Chinese).

Cao, S. (2006). The effect of the Huanghe Valley Civilization by natural environment: The connotation of Yan-Huang and naissance of Chinese civilization. 曹世雄. (2006).自然环境对黄河文明形成的影响 – 炎黄二帝称谓的内涵与中华文明的诞生. 农业考古. Agricultural Archaeology, *1*, 1–7 (in Chinese). https://doi.org/CNKI:SUN:NOSE.0.2006-01-001

Cao, S. (2012a). Socioeconomic value of religion and the impacts of ideological change in China. *Economic Modeling*, *29*, 2621–2626. http://dx.doi.org/10.1016/j.econmod.2012.08.023

Cao, S. (2012b). Why China's approach to institutional change has begun to succeed. *Economic Modeling*, *29*, 679–683. https://doi.org/10.1016/j.econmod.2012.01.012
Cao, S. (2015). Political ecology of national states with examples from Chinese history. *Social Indicators Research*, *124*, 445–462. https://doi.org/10.1007/s11205-014-0800-x
Cao, S. (2016a). Institutional diversity: Why Chinese civilization survives. *Time & Society*, *25*(2), 415–426. https://doi.org/10.1177/0961463X15577270
Cao, S. (2016b). A win–win path for institutional change. *Time & Society*, *25*, 493–512. https://doi.org/10.1177/0961463X15577275
Cao, S. (2017). Evolution of a political industry with examples from Chinese history. *Time & Society*, *26*, 384–398. https://doi.org/10.1177/0961463x15577285
Cao, S., Chen, L., Guan, L., & Wang, G. (2009a). Investigation and analysis of undergraduate students' psychological status in agricultural and forestry universities. 曹世雄, 陈丽, 关立新, 王国升. (2009). 农林院校本科学生心理状态调查分析. 中国林业教育. *Forestry Education in China*, *27*(6), 32–35 (in Chinese).
Cao, S., Chen, L., & Liu, Z. (2007). Disharmony between society and environmental carrying capacity: A historical review, with an emphasis on China. *Ambio*, *36*(4), 409–415. https://doi.org/10.1579/0044-7447(2007)36[409:DBSAEC]2.0.CO;2
Cao, S., Chen, L., Shankman, D., Wang, C., Wang, X., & Zhang, H. (2011). Excessive reliance on afforestation in China's arid and semi-arid regions: Lessons in ecological restoration. *Earth-Science Reviews*, *104*, 240–245. https://doi.org/10.1016/j.earscirev.2010.11.002
Cao, S., Li, S., Ma, H., & Sun, Y. (2015). Escaping the resource curse in China. *Ambio*, *44*, 1–6. https://doi.org/10.1007/s13280-014-0540-9
Cao, S., Liu, Y., & Yu, Z. (2018). China's successes at combating desertification provide roadmap for other nations. *Environment*, *60*, 16–24. https://doi.org/10.1080/00139157.2018.1419002
Cao, S., & Liu, Z. (2020). Avoiding political dangers created when the state is replaced by a government. *Crime, Law and Social Change*, *74*(2), 193–200. https://doi.org/10.1007/s10611-020-09890-6
Cao, S., Liu, Z., Li, W., & Chen, L. (2024). How can governments be motivated to stably and ethically govern a country? Lessons learned from China. *Journal of the Knowledge Economy*, 15, 17579–17597. https://doi.org/10.1007/s13132-024-01835-x
Cao, S., Lv, Y., Zheng, H, & Wang, X. (2014). Challenges facing China's unbalanced urbanization strategy. *Land Use Policy*, *39*, 412–415. https://doi.org/10.1016/j.landusepol.2013.12.004
Cao, S., Lv, Y., Zheng, H., & Wang, X. (2015). Research of the risk factors of China's unsustainable socioeconomic development: Lessons for other nations. *Social Indicators Research*, *123*, 337–347. https://doi.org/10.1007/s11205-014-0740-5
Cao, S., & Ren, Z. (2019). An equilibrium path for institutional change in China. *Time & Society*, *28*, 399–414. https://doi.org/10.1177/0961463X16631766
Cao, S., Tian, T., Qi, F., Ma, L., & Wang, G. (2010). An investigation of women's attitudes towards fertility and China's family planning policy. *Journal of Biosocial Science*, *42*, 359–375. https://doi.org/10.1017/s0021932009990551
Cao, S., & Wang, X. (2009). Dealing with China's future population decline: A proposal for replacing low birth rates with sustainable rates. *Journal of Biosocial Science*, *41*, 693–696. https://doi.org/10.1017/s0021932009003435
Cao, S., Wang, X., & Wang, G. (2009b). Lessons learned from China's fall into the poverty trap. *Journal of Policy Modeling*, *31*, 298–307. https://doi.org/10.1016/j.jpolmod.2008.09.004
Cao, S., Xia, C., & Suo, X. (2022). Is China evolving a new model for civilization? *Futures*, *135*, 102878. https://doi.org/10.1016/j.futures.2021.102878

Cao, S., & Yu, Z. (2019). Seeking the gravediggers of capitalism in China. *Time & Society*, *28*, 1288–1306. https://doi.org/10.1177/0961463X17752285

Cao, S., Zheng, X., & Zhang, J. (2019). Challenge of political globalization. *Time & Society*, *28*, 828–837. https://doi.org/10.1177/0961463X17716550

Cao, Y. (2021, January 29). Lai Xiaomin executed for corruption after review from top court. *China Daily*. www.chinadaily.com.cn/a/202101/29/WS6013df0ea31024ad0baa61d7.html

Carneiro, R. L. (1970). A theory of the origin of the state. *Science*, *169*, 733–738. https://doi.org/10.1126/science.169.3947.733

Carson, R. (1962). *Silent spring*. Houghton Mifflin.

Ceballos, G., & Ehrlich, P. R. (2002). Mammal population losses and the extinction crisis. *Science*, *296*, 904–907. https://doi.org/10.2307/3076641

Cederman, L. (2002). Endogenizing geopolitical boundaries with agent-based modeling. *Proceedings of the National Academy of Sciences of the United States of America*, *99*, 7296–7303. https://doi.org/10.1073/pnas.082081099

CGTN. (2022). *Ukraine conflict day 9: Both sides blame each other for nuclear power plant attack*. https://newseu.cgtn.com/news/2022-03-04/Ukraine-conflict-day-9-Russian-attack-risked-nuclear-disaster-188hciOCLXa/index.html

Chan, K. S., Xu, X., & Gao, Y. (2015). The China growth miracle: The role of the formal and the informal institutions. *The World Economy*, *38*(1), 63–90. https://doi.org/10.1111/twec.12193

Chan, W., & Ngok, K. (2011). Accumulating human capital while increasing educational inequality: A study on higher education policy in China. *Asia Pacific Journal of Education*, *31*, 293–310. https://doi.org/10.1080/02188791.2011.594420

Chapin, F. S., III, Lovecraft, A. L., Zavaleta, E. S., Nelson, J., Robards, M. D., Kofinas, G. P., Trainor, S. F., Peterson, G. D., Huntington, H. P., & Naylor, R. L. (2006). Policy strategies to address sustainability of Alaskan boreal forests in response to a directionally changing climate. *Proceedings of the National Academy of Sciences of the United States of America*, *103*, 16637–16643. https://doi.org/10.1073/pnas.0606955103

Chatterjee, S., & Vogl, T. (2016). *Growth and childbearing in the short- and long-run* [NBER Working Paper No. w23000]. National Bureau of Economic Research. https://doi.org/10.3386/w23000

Chen, G. (2005). A study of healthcare reform in China in light of the USA and Canadian systems. *Chinese Public Administration Review*, *10*(2), 18. https://doi.org/10.22140/cpar.v10i2.203

Chen, G., & Li, Y. (2011). *Blue book of China's economy: Economy of China analysis and forecast*. Social Science Academy Press.

Chen, J. (2007). Rapid urbanization in China: A real challenge to soil protection and food security. *Catena*, *69*, 1–15. https://doi.org/10.1016/j.catena.2006.04.019

Chen, L., & Cao, S. (2013). Lack of integrated solutions hinders environmental recovery in China. *Ecological Engineering*, *54*, 233–235. https://doi.org/10.1016/j.ecoleng.2013.01.015

Chen, S., & Ravallion, M. (2013). More relatively-poor people in a less absolutely-poor world. *Review of Income and Wealth*, *59*, 1–28. https://doi.org/10.1002/qj.2042

Cheng, B., Lv, Y., Zhan, Y., Su, D., & Cao, S. (2015). Constructing China's roads as works of art: A case study of "esthetic greenway" construction in the Shennongjia region of China. *Land Degradation & Development*, *26*, 324–330. https://doi.org/10.1002/ldr.2210

Cheng, L. (2016). Three questions on China's "belt and road initiative." *China Economic Review*, *40*, 309–313. https://doi.org/10.1016/j.chieco.2016.07.008

Cheung, S. (1969). *The theory of share tenancy*. University of Chicago Press.

Chi, M. Q., Muhammad, S., Khan, Z., Ali, S., & Li, R. Y. M. (2021). Is centralization killing innovation? The success story of technological innovation in fiscally decentralized countries. *Technological Forecasting & Social Change*, *168*, 120731. https://doi.org/10.1016/j.techfore.2021.120731

Child Trends Databank. (2015). *Births to unmarried women*. http://www.childtrends.org/?indicators=births-to-unmarried-women

China News. (2013, September 10). *Zhang Shuguang admitted accepting a bribe of over 47.55 million yuan and requesting a bribe for the first time only as a participating academician*. 中国新闻. (2013, September 10). 张曙光承认受贿4755万余元 首次索贿仅为参评院士. 央视网. CCTV Network (in Chinese). news.cntv.cn/2013/09/10/ARTI1378794180970227.shtml

China Statistics Agency. (1952–2023). *China statistical yearbook*. 中国统计. 国家统计年鉴.统计出版社, 北京. China Statistics Press (in Chinese). http://www.stats.gov.cn/sj/ndsj/

Chou, J., Tian, X. Dong, W., & Yuan, X. (2018). Regional temporal and spatial trends in drought and flood disasters in China and assessment of economic losses in recent years. *Sustainability*, *11*, 1–17. https://doi.org/10.20944/preprints201811.0340.v1

Christiansen, T., & Maher, R. (2017). The rise of China – Challenges and opportunities for the European Union. *Asia Europe Journal*, *15*, 121–131. https://doi.org/10.1007/s10308-017-0469-2

Christopherson, S. (2006). Behind the scenes: How transnational firms are constructing a new international division of labor in media work. *Geoforum*, *37*, 739–751. https://doi.org/10.1016/j.geoforum.2006.01.003

Chu, C., & Ching, T. (2001). Ecosystem resilience, specialized adaptation and *population decline*: A modern Malthusian theory. *Journal of Population Economics*, *14*, 7–19. https://doi.org/10.1007/s001480050157

Chua, B. C. (2018, August 20). *Good and evil, and their effects on the body*. Mind & Spirit. https://www.nspirement.com/2018/08/20/good-and-evil-and-their-effects-on-the-body.html

Chused, R. H. (1992, December 31). Married women's property law: 1800–1850. In L. J. Geo (Ed.), *Domestic relations and law*. https://www.degruyterbrill.com/document/doi/10.1515/9783110968941.153/html

Chydenius, A. (1765). *The national gain*. https://www.panarchy.org/chydenius/nationalgain.html

Cline, R. S. (1975). *World power assessment. Center for strategic and international studies*. Georgetown University in Washington.

Coase, R. H. (1959). The federal communications commission. *Journal of Law and Economics*, *2*, 1–40.

Cochran, G., & Harpending, H. (2009). *The 10,000 year explosion: How civilization accelerated human evolution*. Basic Books. https://doi.org/10.1375/twin.12.4.409

Cogorno, M. (2022). In defence of shadows: Legal protection of the dark side of the moon. *Estrema*, *2*, 30–53. https://doi.org/10.51427/com.est.2022.0002

Cohen, J. E. (2003). Human population: The next half century. *Science*, *302*, 1172–1175. https://doi.org/10.1126/science.1088665

Comas, D., Calafell, F., Mateu, E., Pérez-Lezaun, A., Bosch, E., Martínez-Arias, R., Clarimon, J., Facchini, F., Fiori, G., Luiselli, D., Pettener, D., & Bertranpetit, J. (1998). Trading genes along the silk road: MtDNA sequences and the origin of central Asian populations. *American Journal of Human Genetics*, *63*, 1824–1838. https://doi.org/10.1086/302133

Cook, I. G., & Dummer, T. J. B. (2004). Changing health in China: Reevaluating the epidemiological transition model. *Health Policy*, *67*, 329–343. https://doi.org/10.1016/j.healthpol.2003.07.005

Cottee, S., Cushman, T., & Hitchens, C. (2008). *Christopher Hitchens and his critics: Terror, Iraq, and the left*. New York University Press. https://www.jstor.org/stable/j.ctt9qg90t

Credit Suisse. (2022). *Global wealth report 2022*. https://www.credit-suisse.com/media/assets/corporate/docs/about-us/research/publications/global-wealth-report-2022-en.pdf

Crossman, N. D., Burkhard, B., Nedkov, S., Willemen, L., Petz, K., Palomo, I., Drakou, E. G., Martín-Lopez, B., McPhearson, T., Boyanova, K., Alkemade, R., Egoh, B., Dunbar, M. B., & Maes, J. (2013). Blueprint for mapping and modelling ecosystem services. *Ecosystem Services*, *4*, 4–14. https://doi.org/10.1016/j.ecoser.2013.02.001

Crouch, C. (2013). *Europe and problems of marketization: From Polanyi to Scharpf*. Firenze University Press.

Cruces, G., Glüzmann, P., & Lopez Calva, L. F. (2012). Economic crises, maternal and infant mortality, low birth weight and enrollment rates: Evidence from Argentina's downturns. *World Development*, *40*, 303–314. https://doi.org/10.1016/j.worlddev.2011.07.014

Cuenca-García, E., Sánchez, A., & Navarro-Pabsdorf, M. (2019). Assessing the performance of the least developed countries in terms of the millennium development goals. *Evaluation and Program Planning*, *72*, 54–66. https://doi.org/10.1016/j.evalprogplan.2018.09.009

Dalgaard, C. J., & Erickson, L. (2009). Reasonable expectations and the first millennium development goal: How much can aid achieve? *World Development*, *37*, 1170–1181. https://doi.org/10.1016/j.worlddev.2008.11.003

Dasgupta, P. (2004). Environment: How best to face the coming storm. *Science*, *305*, 1716. https://doi.org/10.1126/science.1098546

Dasgupta, P. S., & Ehrlich, P. R. (2013). Pervasive externalities at the population, consumption, and environment nexus. *Science*, *340*, 324–328. https://doi.org/10.1126/science.1224664

Davis, A., & North, D. C. (1971). *American economic growth and institutional change*. Cambridge University Press. https://doi.org/10.2307/133876

Davis, L. J. (2000). The economy of desire in academe. *Chronicle of Higher Education*, *10*, 7–9. https://www.chronicle.com/article/the-economy-of-desire-in-academe/

Davis, L. S. (2010). Institutional flexibility and economic growth. *Journal of Comparative Economics*, *38*, 306–320. https://doi.org/10.1016/j.jce.2010.05.001

Dazzi, C., Papa, G. L., & Poma, I. (2013). Integrating soil survey, land use management and political ecology: A case study in a border area between Peru and Ecuador. *Land Use Policy*, *35*, 302–311. https://doi.org/10.1016/j.landusepol.2013.06.003

de Almeida, A. S., Vieira, I. C. G., & Ferraz S. F. B. (2020). Long-term assessment of oil palm expansion and landscape change in the eastern Brazilian Amazon. *Land Use Policy*, *90*, 104321. https://doi.org/10.1016/j.landusepo1.2019.104321

de Gregorio, J., & Lee, J. W. (2002). Education and income inequality: New evidence from cross-country data. *Review of Income and Wealth*, *48*(3), 395–416. https://doi.org/10.1111/1475-4991.00060

Deininger, K., & Squire, L. (1996). A new data set measuring income inequality. *World Bank Economic Review*, *10*(3), 565–591. https://doi.org/10.2307/3990058

Desai, R. M., Olofsgard, A., & Yousef, T. M. (2003). Democracy, inequality, and inflation. *American Political Science Review*, *97*, 391–406. https://doi.org/10.2139/ssrn.313024

de Secondat, B. C. (1752). *The spirit of laws*. G. Bell & Sons, Ltd.

Diamond, J. (2004). *Collapse: How societies choose to fail or succeed*. Viking.

Dietz, T., Ostrom, E., & Stern, P. C. (2003). The struggle to govern the commons. *Science*, *302*, 1907–1912. https://doi.org/10.4324/9781315092546-4

Dietz, T., & Rosa, E. A. (1997). Effects of population and affluence on CO_2 emissions. *Proceedings of the National Academy of Sciences of the United States of America*, *94*, 175–179. https://doi.org/10.1073/pnas.94.1.175

Dillehay, T. D., & Kolata, A. L. (2004). Long-term human response to uncertain environmental conditions in the Andes. *Proceedings of the National Academy of*

Sciences of the United States of America, 101, 4325–4330. https://doi.org/10.1073/pnas.0400538101

Ding, S., & Knight, J. (2009). Can the augmented Solow model explain China's remarkable economic growth? A cross-country panel data analysis. *Journal of Comparative Economics, 37*, 432–452. 10.1016/j.jce.2009.04.006

Dobbin, F. R. (1993). The social construction of the Great Depression: Industrial policy during the 1930s in the United States, Britain, and France. *Theory and Society, 22*, 1–56. https://doi.org/10.1007/BF00993447

Dong, B., & Torgler, B. (2013). Causes of corruption: Evidence from China. *China Economic Review, 26*, 152–169. https://doi.org/10.1016/j.chieco.2012.09.005

Dong, K. Y., Dou, Y., & Jiang, Q. Z. (2022). Income inequality, energy poverty, and energy efficiency: Who cause who and how? *Technological Forecasting & Social Change, 179*, 121622. https://doi.org/10.1016/j.techfore.2022.121622

Dou, J., Fang, T., & Yang, J. (2015). Technological innovation, population growth and economic growth in China's history. *Journal of World Economy, 38*(7), 143–164.

Dovern, J., & Zuber, C. (2020). How economic crises damage potential output – Evidence from the great recession. *Journal of Macroeconomics, 65*, 103239. https://doi.org/10.1016/j.jmacro.2020.103239

Dugas, M. B. (2016). Baby birds do not always tell the truth. *Proceedings of the National Academy of Sciences of the United States of America, 113*, 13554–13556. https://doi.org/10.1073/pnas.1616640113

Dummer, T. J. B., & Cook, I. G. (2007). Exploring China's rural health crisis: Processes and policy implications. *Health Policy, 83*, 1–16. https://doi.org/10.1016/j.healthpol.2006.12.002

Egorov. B. (2019, January 29). *How the USSR's first McDonald's drove Russians crazy*. Russia Beyond. https://www.rbth.com/history/329911-ussrs-first-mcdonalds

Ehrlich, P. R. (1968). *The population bomb*. Sierra Club/Ballantine Books.

Ehrlich, P. R. (2001). Intervening in evolution: Ethics and actions. *Proceedings of the National Academy of Sciences of the United States of America, 98*, 5477–5480. https://doi.org/10.1073/pnas.091093898

Elvidge, C. D., Baugh, K. E., Kihn, E. A., Kroehl, H. W., Davis, E. R., & Davis, C. W. (1997). Relation between satellite observed visible-near infrared emissions, population, economic activity and electric power consumption. *International Journal of Remote Sensing, 18*, 1373–1379. https://doi.org/10.1080/014311697218485

Engels, F. (1884). *The origin of the family, private property and the state*. Hottingen-Zurich. https://doi.org/10.1089/scc.2022.0029

EPICA. (2004). Eight glacial cycles from an Antarctic ice core. *Nature, 429*, 623–628. https://doi.org/10.1038/nature02599

Essers, D. (2013). Developing country vulnerability in light of the global financial crisis: Shock therapy? *Review of Development Finance, 3*(2), 61–83. https://doi.org/10.1016/j.rdf.2013.02.001

Eyal, G. (2002). Dangerous liaisons between military intelligence and Middle Eastern studies in Israel. *Theory and Society, 31*, 653–693. https://doi.org/10.1023/A:1021302211194

Fafchamps, M. (2011). Development, social norms, and assignment to task. *Proceedings of the National Academy of Sciences of the United States of America, 108*, 21308–21315. https://www.jstor.org/stable/23075607

Fan, Y., Qian D., & Liu X. (2017). Socioeconomic disparities in prevalence, awareness, treatment, and control of hypertension over the life course in China. *International Journal for Equity in Health, 16*(1), 100. https://doi.org/10.1186/s12939-017-0597-8

Fang, C., Zhang, X., & Fan, S. (2002). Emergence of urban poverty and inequality in China: Evidence from household survey. *China Economic Review, 13*, 430–443. https://doi.org/10.1016/s1043-951x(02)00101-3

Fay, M., Leipziger, D., Wodon, Q., & Yepes, T. (2005). Achieving child-health-related millennium development goals: The role of infrastructure. *World Development*, *33*, 1267–1284. https://doi.org/10.1016/j.worlddev.2005.03.001

Fei, W., & Vahid, T. (2023). Impact of technology and economic complexity on environmental pollution and economic growth in developing and developed countries: Using IPAT and STIRPAT models. *Environmental Science and Pollution Research*, *30*, 1–12. 10.1007/s11356-023-27569-y

Felstead, A., Gallie, D., & Green, F. (2002). *Work skills in Britain 1986–2001*. Department for Education and Skills.

Feng, Q., Tian, Y., Yu, T., Yin, Z., & Cao, S. (2019a). Combating desertification through economic development in northwestern China. *Land Degradation & Development*, *30*, 910–917. https://doi.org/10.1002/ldr.3277

Feng, Q., Yang, L., Deo, R. C., AghaKouchak, A., Adamowski, J. F., Stone, R., Yin, Z., Liu, W., Si, J., Wen, X., Zhu, M., & Cao, S. (2019b). Domino effect of climate change over two millennia in ancient China's Hexi Corridor. *Nature Sustainability*, *2*, 957–996. https://doi.org/10.1038/s41893-019-0397-9

Fleisher, B., Li., H., & Zhao, M. Q. (2010). Human capital, economic growth, and regional inequality in China. *Journal of Development Economics*, *92*, 215–231. https://doi.org/10.1016/j.jdeveco.2009.01.010

Flowers, W. L. (2013). Animal frontiers fertility issue: Sex education that everyone needs to understand. *Animal Frontiers*, *9*, 4–5. https://doi.org/10.2527/af.2013-0026

Friedman, M. (1968). The role of monetary policy. *American Economic Review*, *58*, 1–17. https://doi.org/10.4236/jfrm.2014.33007

Fritsch, M. (2017). The theory of economic development: An inquiry into profits, capital, credit, interest, and the business cycle. *Regional Studies*, *51*(4), 654–655. https://doi.org/10.1080/00343404.2017.1278975

Fu, Q., Liu, W., & Li, T. (2015). Spatial distribution of irrigation water use efficiency index system in Heilongjiang Province. 付强, 刘巍, 刘东, 李天霄. (2015). 黑龙江省灌溉用水效率指标体系空间格局研究. 农业机械学报. *Transactions of the Chinese Society for Agricultural Machinery*, *46*(12), 127–132. https://doi.org/10.6041/j.issn.1000-1298.2015.12.018 (in Chinese).

Gallagher, M. E. (2002). Reform and openness: Why China's economic reforms have delayed democracy. *World Politics*, *54*, 338–372. https://doi.org/10.2307/25054191

Ge, X., & Chen, L. (2010). Human capital, population change and economic growth. *Population and Economics*, *2010*(1), 15–20. en.cnki.com.cn/Article_en/CJFDTOTAL-RKJJ201001003.htm

Gérard, R. (2004). Understanding institutional change: Fast-moving and slow-moving institutions. *Studies in Comparative International Development*, *38*(4), 109–131.

Gerland, P., Raftery, A. E., Ševčíková, H., Li, N., Gu, D., Spoorenberg, T., & Bay, G. (2014). World population stabilization unlikely this century. *Science*, *346*, 234–237. https://doi.org/10.1126/science.1257469

Ghijsbrecht, D. (2021). Usufruct in the new Belgian property law. *European Property Law Journal*, *10*(1), 81–96. https://doi.org/10.1515/eplj-2021-0007

Gibney, E. (2016). Chinese satellite is one giant step for the quantum internet. *Nature*, *535*, 478–479. https://doi.org/10.1038/535478a

Giesen, K. (2004). The post-national constellation: Habermas and "the second modernity." *Res Publica*, *10*, 1–13. https://doi.org/10.1023/B:RESP.0000018242.69823.1c

Global Times. (2021a, June 19). 1-billion-ton oil and gas field discovered in Xinjiang's Tarim Basin. *Global Times*. https://www.globaltimes.cn/page/202106/1226540.shtml

Global Times. (2021b, November 7). Jiangsu officials punished after urban management staff snatch elderly street vendor's fruits. *Global Times*. https://www.globaltimes.cn/page/202112/1240905.shtm

Goffin, P., van de Bunt, B., Giovane, M., Leveau, J. H. J., Höppener-Ogawa, S. H., Teusink, B., & Hugenholtz, J. (2010). Understanding the physiology of *Lactobacillus plantarum* at zero growth. *Molecular Systems Biology*, *6*, 413. https://doi.org/10.1038/msb.2010.67

Gohou, G., & Soumare, I. (2012). Does foreign direct investment reduce poverty in Africa and are there regional differences? *World Development*, *40*, 75–95. https://doi.org/10.1016/j.worlddev.2011.05.014

Goldberg, V. P. (1974). Institutional change and the quasi-invisible hand. *Journal of Law and Economics*, *17*, 461–492. https://doi.org/10.1086/466802

Gong, X., & Cortese, C. (2017). A socialist market economy with Chinese characteristics: The accounting annual report of China Mobile. *Accounting Forum*, *41*, 206–220. https://doi.org/10.1016/j.accfor.2017.04.002

Gorodnichenko, Y., & Roland, G. (2011). Individualism, innovation, and long-run growth. *Proceedings of the National Academy of Sciences of the United States of America*, *108*, 21316–21319. https://doi.org/10.2307/23075608

Grabowski, R. (2007). Political development and growth: Japan until World War II. *Journal of Asia Pacific Economics*, *12*, 522–547. https://doi.org/10.1080/13547860701594186

Gradín, C., & Wu, B. B. (2020). Income and consumption inequality in China: A comparative approach with India. *China Economic Review*, *62*, 101463. https://doi.org/10.1016/j.chieco.2020.101463

Grail, T. S. (2009). *Custodial mothers and fathers and their child support: 2007*. U.S. Census Bureau. Report.

Gregory, T., Salomons, A., & Zierahn, U. (2016). *Racing with or against the machine? Evidence from Europe* [Discussion Paper No. 16-053]. Centre for European Economic Research. https://doi.org/10.2139/ssrn.4114211

Grzywacz, A. (2020). Closer to a threat than an opportunity: Polish perception of China's rise and international engagement. *Asia Europe Journal*, *18*, 177–194. https://doi.org/10.1007/s10308-019-00541-7

Guan, L., Sun, G., & Cao, S. (2011). China's bureaucracy hinders environmental recovery. *Ambio*, *40*, 96–99. http://dx.https://doi.org/10.1007/s13280-010-0112-6

Guo, J., Lai, X., Lu, C., & Cao, S. (2022). What has caused China's economic growth. *Economic Systems*, *46*(2), 100892. https://10.1016/j.ecosys.2022.100982

Guo, J., Yu, Z., Ma, Z., Xu, D., & Cao, S. (2021). What factors have driven urbanization in China. *Environment Development and Sustainability*, *24*(3), 6508–6526. https://doi.org/10.1007/s10668-021-01714-4

Gustafsson, B., & Li, S. (2004). Expenditures on education and health care and poverty in rural China. *China Economic Review*, *15*, 292–301. https://doi.org/10.1016/j.chieco.2003.07.004

Gylfason, T. (2001). Natural resources, education, and economic development. *European Economic Review*, *45*, 847–859. https://doi.org/10.1016/s0014-2921(01)00127-1

Haas, P., Keohane, R., & Levy, M. (1993). *Institutions for the Earth: Sources of effective international protection*. MIT Press. https://doi.org/10.2307/2204002

Hachigian, N., & Peng, Y. (2010). The US–China expectations gap: An exchange. *Survival*, *52*, 67–86. https://doi.org/10.1080/00396338.2010.506821

Handl, G. (1972, June 26). *Declaration of the United Nations conference on the human environment*. https://legal.un.org/avl/ha/dunche/dunche.html

Hao, X. (2023). Analysis of the influence factors of social media fatigue among Chinese WeChat Users: A perceived overload perspective. *Communications in Humanities Research*, *7*, 152–158. https://doi.org/10.54254/2753-7064/7/20230857

Hardin, G. (1968). The tragedy of the commons. *Science*, *162*, 1243–1248. https://doi.org/10.1126/science.162.3859.1243

Hasan, I., Wachtel, P., & Zhou, M. (2009). Institutional development, financial deepening and economic growth: Evidence from China. *Journal of Banking and Finance*, *33*, 157–170. https://doi.org/10.1016/j.jbankfin.2007.11.016

Hayami, Y., & Godo, Y. (1998). *Development economics – From the poverty to the wealth of nations*. Oxford University Press. https://doi.org/10.1093/0199272700.001.0001

He, J. (2018). The rules of presumption. In J. He (Ed.), *Methodology of judicial proof and presumption. Masterpieces of contemporary jurisprudents in China* (pp. 217–225). Springer. https://doi.org/10.1007/978-981-10-8025-8_9

Heckscher, E., & Ohlin, B. (1933). *International and inter-regional trade*. Harvard University Press.

Heinemann, F., & Tanz, B. (2008). The impact of trust on reforms. *Journal of Economic Policy Reform, 11*, 173–185. https://doi.org/10.2139/ssrn.1261858

Hellenthal, G., Busby, G. B. J., Band, G., Wilson, J. F., Capelli, C., Falush, D., & Myers, S. (2014). A genetic atlas of human admixture history. *Science, 343*, 747–751. https://doi.org/10.1126/science.1243518

Hendel, I., Shapiro, J., & Willen, P. (2005). Educational opportunity and income inequality. *Journal of Public Economics, 89*, 841–870. https://doi.org/10.3386/w10879

Henri, P. A. O. (2019). Natural resources curse: A reality in Africa. *Resources Policy, 63*, 101406. https://doi.org/10.1016/j.resourpol.2019.101406

Henseke, G. (2011). Demographic change and the economically active populations of OECD countries – Could older workers compensate for the decline? In M. Boppel, S. Boehm, & S. Kunisch (Eds.), *From Gray to Silver. Managing the demographic change successfully* (pp. 29–46). Springer. https://doi.org/10.1007/978-3-642-15594-9_3

Herrmann-Pillath, C. (2006). Cultural species and institutional change in China. *Journal of Economic Issues, 3*, 539–574. https://doi.org/10.1080/00213624.2006.11506935

Heshmati, A. (2007). Global trends in income inequality. *Challenge, 54*(5), 54–75. https://doi.org/10.2753/0577-5132540504

Hibbs, D. A. J., & Olsson, O. (2004). Geography, biogeography, and why some countries are rich and others are poor. *Proceedings of the National Academy of Sciences of the USA, 101*, 3715–3720. https://doi.org/10.1073/pnas.0305531101

Hill, J. (1996). Social isolation and sociocultural diversity. *Journal of Social and Evolutionary Systems, 19*(2), 157–169. http://dx.https://doi.org/10.1016/S1061-7361(96)90023-5

Hilmawan, R., & Clark, J. (2019). An investigation of the resource curse in Indonesia. *Resources Policy, 64*, 101483. https://doi.org/10.1016/j.resourpol.2019.101483

Hoffman, E., McCabe, K., & Smith, V. L. (1996). Social distance and other-regarding behavior in dictator games. *American Economic Review, 86*, 653–660. https://doi.org/10.2307/2118218

Hongyu, L. J. (2022, May 27). Urban greenways across China enrich people's lives. *People's Daily Online*. www.ehangzhou.gov.cn/2022-05/27/c_280623.htm

Horowitz, I. (2006). Privacy, publicity and security: The American context. *EMBO Reports, 7*, S40–S44. https://doi.org/10.1038/sj.embor.7400690

Hou, C. C., & Hou, J. W. 2002). Evolution of economic institutions and China's economic reform. *Social Science Journal, 39*, 363–379. https://doi.org/10.1016/S0362-3319(02)00206-9

Huang, Y. (2016). Understanding China's belt & road initiative: Motivation, framework and assessment. *China Economic Review, 40*, 314–321. https://doi.org/10.1016/j.chieco.2016.07.007

Huisman, J. (2007). Institutional diversity in higher education: A cross-national and longitudinal analysis. *Higher Education Quarterly, 61*, 563–577. http://dx.https://doi.org/10.1111/j.1468-2273.2007.00372.x

Hume, D. (1994). *Hume: Political essays*. Cambridge University Press. https://doi.org/10.1017/CBO9781139170765

Huntington, S. P. (1996). *The clash of civilizations and the remaking of world order*. Simon & Schuster.

Ip, E. C., & Law, M. (2011). Decentralization, agency costs, and the new economic constitution of China. *Constitutional Political Economy, 22*, 355–372. https://doi.org/10.1007/s10602-011-9110-3

Iranpour, R., Stenstrom, M., Tchobanoglous, G., Miller, D., Wright, J., & Vossoughi, M. (1999). Environmental engineering: Energy value of replacing waste disposal with resource recovery. *Science*, *285*, 706–711. https://doi.org/10.1126/science.285.5428.706

IRS. (2022). *Whistleblower office*. U.S. Internal Revenue Service. https://www.irs.gov/compliance/whistleblower-office

Jackson, G., & Deeg, R. (2008). Comparing capitalisms: Understanding institutional diversity and its implications for international business. *Journal of International Business Studies*, *39*, 540–561. https://doi.org/10.1057/palgrave.jibs.8400375

Jarvis, R. G. (2016). The invisible tax: Exploring Black student engagement at historically white institutions. *Berkeley Review of Education*, *6*, 55–78. https://doi.org/10.5070/B86110039

Jefferson, G. H., Rawski, T. G., & Zheng, Y. X. (1992). Growth, efficiency, and convergence in China's state and collective industry. *Economic Development and Cultural Change*, *40*, 239–266. https://doi.org/10.1086/451939

Jensen, T. K., Andersen, A. N., & Skakkebæk, N. E. (2004). Is human fertility declining? *International Congress Series*, *1266*, 32–44.

Ji, K., Magnus, J. R., & Wang, W. (2014). Natural resources, institutional quality, and economic growth in China. *Environmental and Resource Economics*, *57*, 323–343. https://doi.org/10.1007/s10640-013-9673-8

Jiang, C. (2023, June 17). Investigation confirms rat's head in canteen. *China Daily*. https://www.chinadaily.com.cn/a/202306/17/WS648d8dd0a31033ad3f7bcd06.html

Jo, T. (2013). Saving private business enterprises: A heterodox microeconomic approach to market governance and market regulation. *American Journal of Economics & Sociology*, *72*, 447–467. https://doi.org/10.1111/ajes.12009

Joane. (2023, February 6). *China's C919 jetliner allegedly failed its verification test*. Gizmochina. gizmochina.com/2023/02/06/chinas-c919-failed-verification-test/

Jones, R. A. (2005). *The secret of the Totem: Religion and society from McLennan to Freud*. Columbia University Press. https://doi.org/10.7312/jone13438

Jóźwiak, J., & Kotowska, I. E. (2008). Decreasing birth rates in Europe: Reasons and remedies. *European View*, *7*, 225–236. https://doi.org/10.1007/s12290-008-0062-6

Kao, K. C., & Hockham, G. A. (1967). Dielectric fiber surface waveguide for optical frequencies. *Electromagnetic Wave Theory*, *1967*, 441–444. https://doi.org/10.1016/B978-0-08-011921-2.50053-6

Karouni, I. E. (2009). *Institutional change as cultural change*: An illustration by Chinese postsocialist transformation. *International Journal Social Economics*, *36*, 762–772. https://doi.org/10.1108/03068290910963699

Kaspersen, L., & Strandsbjerg, J. (2017). *Does war make states? Investigations of Charles Tilly's historical sociology*. Cambridge University Press. https://doi.org/10.1017/9781316493694

Kates, R. W., Clark, W. C., Corell, R., Hall, J. M., Jaeger, C. C., Lowe, I., McCarthy, J. J., Schellnhuber, H. J., Bolin, B., Dickson, N. M., Faucheux, S., Gallopin, G. C., Grübler, A., Huntley, B., Jäger, J., Jodha, N. S., Kasperson, R. E., Mabogunje, A., Matson, P., … Moore, B. (2001). Environment and development: Sustainability science. *Science*, *292*, 641–642. https://doi.org/10.1126/science.1059386

Katikireddi, S., & Dundas, R. (2017). Relative poverty still matters. *The Lancet Public Health*, *2*(3), e126–e127. https://doi.org/10.1016/S2468-2667(17)30029

Keenan, J. (2017). Comparing Chinese and American managers on whistleblowing. *Employee Responsibilities and Rights Journal*, *192*(2), 85–94. https://doi.org/10.1007/s10672-007-9036-0

Khan, H. (2008). Poverty, environment and economic growth: Exploring the links among three complex issues with specific focus on the Pakistan's case. *Environment, Development and Sustainability*, *10*, 913–929. https://doi.org/10.1007/s10668-007-9092-5

Kiernan, K. (2004). Unmarried cohabitation and parenthood in Britain and Europe. *Law Policy*, *26*, 33–55. https://doi.org/10.1111/j.0265-8240.2004.00162.x
Kim, H. J., Kim, C. J., Ahn, J. A., & Juon, H. S. (2022). Prevalence and correlates of depression among South Korean older adults living in relative poverty. *Archives of Psychiatric Nursing*, *38*, 1–5. https://doi.org/10.1016/j.apnu.2022.01.002
Kissinger, H. (1995). *Diplomacy*. Simon & Schuster.
Knight, J. (2013). The economic causes and consequences of social instability in China. *China Economic Review*, *25*, 17–26. https://doi.org/10.1016/j.chieco.2013.01.001
Kogut, B. M. (2003). *The global internet economy*. MIT Press.
Korey, C. A. (2007). We hold these truths to be self-evident, that all flies and men are created equal: Recent progress on human disease models. *Fly*, *1*(2), 118–122. https://doi.org/10.1016/j.nurpra.2017.03.013
Kornai, J. (2000). What the change of system from socialism to capitalism does and does not mean. *Journal of Economic Perspectives*, *14*, 27–42. https://doi.org/10.1257/jep.14.1.27
Kornhuber, K., Lesk, C., Schleussner, C. F. Jägermeyr, J., Pfleiderer, P., & Horton, R. M. (2023). Risks of synchronized low yields are underestimated in climate and crop model projections. *Nature Communication*, *14*, 3528. https://doi.org/10.1038/s41467-023-38906-7
Kouadio, H. K., & Gakpa, L. L. (2021). Do economic growth and institutional quality reduce poverty and inequality in West Africa? *Journal of Policy Modeling*, *44*(1), 41–63. https://doi.org/10.1016/j.jpolmod.2021.09.010
Krasner, S. D. (2011). Changing state structures: Outside in. *Proceedings of the National Academy of Sciences of the United States of America*, *108*, 21302–21307. https://doi.org/10.1073/pnas.1100244108
Kumar, S., Lim, W. M., Pandey, N., & Westland, J. C. (2021). 20 years of electronic commerce research. *Electronic Commerce Research*, *21*, 1–40. https://doi.org/10.1007/s10660-021-09464-1
Kwon, H. J. (2009). The reform of the developmental welfare state in East Asia. *International Journal of Social Welfare*, *18*, S12–S21. https://doi.org/10.1111/j.1468-2397.2009.00655.x
Lagrotteria, L., & Besescheck, C. (2012). *Higher education in China: Tertiary education in state development*. University of Bridgeport.
Lai Times. (2024, May 13). *Professor Song's suicide after being demoted is really not about Nanlin University! Psychological fragility and lack of ability are the main reasons. Lai Times*. https://www.laitimes.com/en/article/6rcdk_77oo2.html
Lancet Editors. (2009). Melamine and food safety in China. *Lancet*, *373*, 353. https://doi.org/10.1016/S0140-6736(09)60114-8
Lawler, A. (2009). Beyond the Yellow River: How China became China. *Science*, *325*, 930–935. https://doi.org/10.1126/science.325_930
Lee, R. (2011). The outlook for population growth. *Science*, *333*, 569–573. https://doi.org/10.1126/science.1208859
Lenzen, M., & Peters, G. M. (2009). How city dwellers affect their resource hinterland: A spatial impact study of Australian households. *Journal of Industrial Ecology*, *14*, 73–90. https://doi.org/10.1111/j.1530-9290.2009.00190.x
Leung, A. S. M., Liu, X., & Liu, S. (2009). Moral schemas and business practices: The ethics of Guangzhou migrant marketers. *Journal of Business Ethics*, *88*, 11–23. https://doi.org/10.1007/s10551-008-9833-x
Li, L. (1998). Book review: The China miracle: Development strategy and economic reform. *Cato Journal*, *18*, 147–150. https://EconPapers.repec.org/RePEc:cto:journl:v:1:y:1981:i:1:p:147-150
Li, L. (2011). The incentive role of creating "cities" in China. *China Economic Review*, *22*, 172–181. https://doi.org/10.2139/ssrn.1129397

Li, L. (2013). Tantric imagery of two deities in union: Starting with a wood engraving from Dandan Oilik. 李翎. (2013). 密教双身图像研究 – 以丹丹乌里克木板画为引子. 中国国家博物馆. *National Museum of China*, *114*(1), 92–107 (in Chinese).

Li, M., He, B., Guo, R., Li, Y., Chen, Y., & Fan, Y. (2018). Study on population distribution pattern at the county level of China. *Sustainability*, *10*(1), 3598. https://doi.org/10.3390/su10103598

Li, M. Q., & Coxhead, I. (2011). Trade and inequality with limited labor mobility: Theory and evidence from China. *Review of Development Economics*, *15*, 48–65. https://doi.org/10.2139/ssrn.1622552

Li, R. (2021). *China has shut down 3,120 gang-related organizations and 9,888 criminal groups*. 李润发. (2021). 全国已打掉涉黑组织3120个涉恶犯罪集团9888个.政府新闻 2020-5-19. http://www.gov.cn/xinwen/2020-05/19/content_5513085.htm (in Chinese).

Li, S. (2004). Why is property right protection lacking in China: An institutional explanation. *California Management Review*, *46*, 100–115. https://doi.org/10.2307/41166223

Li, S., Du, Y., & Jiao, P. (2022). on the industrial division and coordinated development in the Guangdong–Hong Kong–Macao Greater Bay area. *Contemporary Social Sciences*, *6*, 19–36. https://doi.org/10.19873/j.cnki.2096-0212.2022.06.002

Li, W., Cai, Z., & Cao, S. (2021). What has caused regional income inequality in China? Effects of 10 socioeconomic factors on per capita income. *Environment, Development and Sustainability*, *23*, 13403–13417. https://doi.org/10.1007/s10668-020-01218-7

Li, W., Ma, Z., Guo, J., & Cao, S. (2021). Relationships between resource distribution and socioeconomic development in China. *Journal of Cleaner Production*, *286*, 124975. https://doi.org/10.1016/j.jclepro.2020.124975

Li, Y., Wu, H., Shen, K., Hao, Y., & Zhang, P. (2020). Is environmental pressure distributed equally in China? Empirical evidence from provincial and industrial panel data analysis. *Science of the Total Environment*, *718*, 137363. https://doi.org/10.1016/j.scitotenv.2020.137363

Li, Z., & Yang, B. (2021). Research on the international mobility trends of Chinese researchers. 李子璇, 杨波. (2021). 中国科研人员的国际流动趋势研究.图书情报工作. *Library and Information Work*, *65*(16), 25–34. https://doi.org/10.13266/j.issn.0252-3116.2021.16.003

Liang, X., Silva, D., Tian, N., Béraud-Sudreau, L., & Marksteiner, A. (2021). *Trends in world military expenditure*. Stockholm International Peace Research Institute. https://doi.org/10.55163/DZJD8826

Liao, T. F. (2004). Estimating household structure in ancient China by using historical data: A latent class analysis of partially missing patterns. *Journal of the Royal Statistical Society*, *167*, 125–139. https://doi.org/10.1111/j.1467-985x.2004.00294.x

Lim, M., Metzler, R., & Bar-Yam, Y. (2007). Global pattern formation and ethnic/cultural violence. *Science*, *317*, 1540–1544. https://doi.org/10.1126/science.1142734

Lin, S. C., Kim, D. H., & Wu, Y. C. (2013). Foreign direct investment and income inequality: Human capital matters. *Journal of Regional Science*, *53*(5), 874–896. https://doi.org/10.1111/jors.12077

Lin, Y. (2002). Economic institutional change in post-Mao China. *Chinese Economics*, *35*, 26–51. https://doi.org/10.2753/CES1097-1475350326

Litina, A., Makridis, C. A., & Tsiachtsiras, G. (2021). Do product market reforms raise innovation? Evidence from micro-data across 12 countries. *Technological Forecasting & Social Change*, *169*, 120841. https://doi.org/10.1016/j.techfore.2021.120841

Liu, J. (2010). China's road to sustainability. *Science*, *328*, 50. https://doi.org/10.1126/science.1186234

Liu, J., & Diamond, J. (2005). China's environment in a globalizing world: How China and the rest of the world affect each other. *Nature*, *435*, 1179–1186. https://doi.org/10.1038/4351179a

Liu, L., Chen, C., Zhao, Y., & Zhao, E. (2015). China's carbon-emissions trading: Overview, challenges and future. *Renewable and Sustainable Energy Reviews*, *49*, 254–266. https://doi.org/10.1016/j.rser.2015.04.076

Liu, Q., Yang, Z. F., & Cui, B. S. (2008). Spatial and temporal variability of annual precipitation during 1961–2006 in Yellow River Basin, China. *Journal of Hydrology*, *361*, 330–338. https://doi.org/10.1016/j.jhydrol.2008.08.002

Liu, S., Wu, P., & Huang, C. (2019). The threshold effect of monetary policy on earnings persistence. *Spanish Journal of Finance and Accounting/Revista Española de Financiacióny Contabilidad*, *48*, 68–86. https://doi.org/10.1080/02102412.2018.1461462

Liu, Y., & Xu, Y. (2016). A geographic identification of multidimensional poverty in rural China under the framework of sustainable livelihoods analysis. *Applied Geography*, *73*, 62–76. https://doi.org/10.1016/j.apgeog.2016.06.004

Liu, Y., Zhang, J., & Cao, S. (2016). Institutional change to compensate for low birth rates: The Chinese situation, and comparison with other countries. *Time & Society*, *25*, 406–414. https://doi.org/10.1177/0961463X15591738

Loomis, R. S., & Connor, D. J. (1996). *Productivity and management in agricultural systems*. Cambridge University Press.

Loreau, M., Naeem, S., Inchausti, P., Bengtsson, J., Grime, J. P., Hector, A., Hooper, D. U., Huston, M. A., Raffaelli, D., Schmid, B., Tilman, D., & Wardle, D. A. (2001). Biodiversity and ecosystem functioning: Current knowledge and future challenges. *Science*, *294*, 804–808. https://doi.org/10.2307/3085064

Loyalka, P., Liu, O. L., Li, G., Kardanova, E., Chirikov, I., Hu, S., Yu, N., Ma, L., Guo, F., Beteille, T., Tognatta, N., Gu, L., Ling, G., Federiakin, D., Wang, H., Khanna, S., Bhuradia, A., Shi, Z., & Li, Y. (2021). Skill levels and gains in university STEM education in China, India, Russia and the United States. *Nature Human Behaviour*, *5*, 892–904. https://doi.org/10.1038/s41562-021-01062-3

Lu, Y., Xu, X., Chen, B., Jefferson, T. A., Fearnbach, H., & Yang, G. (2024). Spatiotemporal dynamics of the social structure of Indo-Pacific humpback dolphins (*Sousa chinensis*) in Xiamen waters from 2007 to 2019. *Zoological Research*, *45*(2), 439–450. https://doi.org/10.24272/j.issn.2095-8137.2023.255

Lu, Z., & Deng, X. (2011). *China's western development strategy: Policies, effects and prospects* [Munich Personal RePEc Archive 35201]. https://mpra.ub.uni-muenchen.de/35201/

Lubchenco, J. (1998). Entering the century of the environment: A new social contract for science. *Science*, *279*, 491–497. https://doi.org/10.2307/2894024

Luo, J. (2004). *Over a cup of tea: An introduction to Chinese life and culture*. University Press of America.

Lutz, W., Sanderson, W., & Scherbov, S. (2001). The end of world population growth. *Nature*, *412*, 543–545. https://doi.org/10.1038/35087589

Ma, Z., Li, X., Guo, J., Yang, L., Li, Y., & Cao, S. (2025). Can the New Model of Shared Property Rights Promote Better Corporate Finance in Cahina?. *Financial Innovation*, *11*, 75. https://doi.org/10.1186/s40854-024-00725-0

Mabogunje, A. L. (2000). Institutional radicalization, the state, and the development process in Africa. *Proceedings of the National Academy of Sciences of the United States of America*, *97*, 14007–14014. https://doi.org/10.1073/pnas.200298097

Mallapaty, S. (2024). China conducts first nationwide review of retractions and research misconduct. *Nature*, *626*, 700–701. https://www.nature.com/articles/d41586-024-00397-x

Marginson, S. (2022). All things are in flux: China in global science. *Higher Education*, *83*, 881–910. https://doi.org/10.1007/s10734-021-00712-9

Marquand, D. (2011). Towards a realignment of the mind. *Political Quarterly*, *82*, 140–145. https://doi.org/10.1111/j.1467-923X.2011.02190.x

Marx, K. (1859). *A contribution to the critique of political economy (preface)*. Cambridge University Press. https://doi.org/10.1017/CBO9780511810695.009

Marx, K. (1871). *The civil war in France. Prussian occupation of France*. https://www.marxists.org/archive/marx/works/1871/civil-war-france/index.htm

Maslow, A. H. (1954). *Motivation and personality*. Pearson. https://psycnet.apa.org/record/1955-02233-000

Mauro, L., Pigliaro, F., & Carmeci, G. (2023). Decentralization, social capital, and regional growth: The case of the Italian North–South divide. *European Journal of Political Economy*, *4*, 102363. https://doi.org/10.1016/j.ejpoleco.2023.102363

Mayer, R. (1993). The dictatorship of the proletariat from Plekhanov to Lenin. *Studies in East European Thought*, *45*, 255–280. https://doi.org/10.2307/20099522

McMichael, A. J., Butler, C. D., & Folke, C. (2003). New visions for addressing sustainability. *Science*, *302*, 1919–1920. https://doi.org/10.1126/science.1090001

McMillan, J., & Naughton, B. (1992). How to reform a planned economy: Lessons from China. *Oxford Review of Economic Policy*, *8*, 130–143. https://doi.org/10.1093/oxrep/8.1.130

Mearsheimer, J. (2001). *The tragedy of great power politics*. Norton. https://doi.org/10.2307/3093434

Meinzen-Dick, R. (2007). Beyond panaceas in water institutions. *Proceedings of the National Academy of Sciences of the United States of America*, *104*, 15200–15205. https://doi.org/10.1073/pnas.0702296104

Meon, P., Sekkat, K., & Weill, L. (2009). Institutional change now and benefits tomorrow: How soon is tomorrow? *Economic Politics*, *21*, 319–357. https://doi.org/10.1111/j.1468-0343.2009.00351

Merk, A. (1998). Essays on science and society: The role of science in sustainable development. *Science*, *281*, 336–337. https://doi.org/10.1126/science.281.5375.336

Meyer, B. D., & Sullivan, J. X. (2010). *Further results on measuring the well-being of the poor using income and consumption* [Working Paper w13413]. Harris School of Public Policy Studies. https://doi.org/10.1111/j.1540-5982.2010.01623.x

Mez-Pompa, A. G., & Kaus, A. (1999). From pre-Hispanic to future conservation alternatives: Lessons from Mexico. *Proceedings of the National Academy of Sciences*, *96*(11), 5982–5986. https://doi.org/10.1073/pnas.96.11.5982

Milinski, M., & Rockenbach, B. (2007). Spying on others evolves. *Science*, *317*, 464–465. https://doi.org/10.1126/science.1143918

Miller, F. P., Vandome, A. F., & McBrewster, J. (2010). *Japanese asset price bubble*. Alphascript Publishing. https://ulysseszh.github.io/reveal/japanese_bubble/#/

Montinola, G., Qian, Y., & Weingast, B. (1995). Federalism, Chinese style: The political basis for economic success. *World Politics*, *48*, 50–81. https://doi.org/10.1353/wp.1995.0003

Moore, P. V. (2010). *The international political economy of work and employability*. Palgrave Macmillan. https://doi.org/10.1080/23269995.2011.10707925

Morabia, A. (2009). Historical review epidemic and population patterns in the Chinese Empire (243 B.C.E. to 1911 C.E.): Quantitative analysis of a unique but neglected epidemic catalogue. *Epidemiology and Infection*, *137*(10), 1361–1368. https://doi.org/10.1017/s0950268809990136

Morales, E. (2021, February 1). The U.S.–China brain drain. *Berkeley Political Review*. https://bpr.berkeley.edu/2021/02/01/the-u-s-china-brain-drain

Müller, F. L. (2002). Britain and the German Question: Perceptions of Nationalism and Political Reform, 1830–1863. Palgrave Macmillan. https://doi.org/10.1057/9781403919663_3

Murrell, P. (1993). What is shock therapy? What did it do in Poland and Russia? *Post-Soviet Affairs*, *9*, 111–140. https://doi.org/10.1080/1060586X.1993.10641362

Myers, N. (2000). Sustainable consumption. *Science*, *287*, 2419. https://doi.org/10.1126/science.287.5462.2419

Myerson, R. B. (2011). Toward a theory of leadership and state building. *Proceedings of the National Academy of Sciences of the United States of America*, *108*, 21297–21301. https://doi.org/10.1073/pnas.1019397108

Myrskylä, M., Kohler, H.-P., & Billari, F. C. (2009). Advances in development reverse fertility declines. *Nature*, *460*, 741–743. https://doi.org/10.1038/nature08230

Mzingwane, B., & Plattner, I. E. (2008). Gender differences in the anticipation of difficulties in finding employment among university students: A Botswana study. *Gender & Behaviour*, *6*, 1960–1981. https://doi.org/10.4314/gab.v6i2.23429

New Express. (2014, April 27). *Only 6000 impoverished students with 28000 student loans in Guangdong found jobs*. 新快报. (2014). 广东2.8万名助学贷款贫困生仅6000人找到工作.人民网. *People's Daily*. edu.people.com.cn/n/2014/0427/c1053-24947054.html (in Chinese).

Nguyen, H., Doan, T., & Tran, T. Q. (2020). The effect of various income sources on income inequality: A comparison across ethnic groups in Vietnam. *Environment, Development and Sustainability*, *22*, 813–834. https://doi.org/10.1007/s10668-018-0221-0

Ni, P., Kamiya, M., Li, B., Liu X., & Li, Q. (2020). Technological innovation: A primary driver to promote global urban common prosperity – An analysis of factors influencing the competitiveness of 1,007 cities around the world. *China Economist*, *15*(3), 28–48. https://doi.org/10.19602/j.chinaeconomist.2020.05.03

Nolan, P., & Slater, G. (2003). The labour market: History, structure and prospects. In P. K. Edwards (Ed.), *Industrial relations: Theory and practice* (pp. 58–80). Blackwell.

Normile, D. (2008). China's living laboratory in urbanization. *Science*, *319*, 740–743. https://doi.org/10.1126/science.319.5864.740

Normile, D. (2018). Biologist unveils China's first private research university. *Science*, *359*, 856. https://doi.org/10.1126/science.359.6378.856

North, D. C. (1971). Institutional change and economic development. *Journal of Economic History*, *31*, 118–125. https://www.jstor.org/stable/2117023

North, D. C. (1990). *Institutions, institutional change, and economic performance*. Cambridge University Press. https://doi.org/10.2307/3325144

North, D. C., & Thomas, R. P. (1971). The rise and fall of the manorial system: A theoretical model. *Journal Economic History*, *31*, 777–803. https://doi.org/10.1017/S0022050700074623

Nove, A. (1986). *The Soviet economic system*. Allen & Unwin. https://doi.org/10.2307/2232036

Obach, R. B. B. (2003). *On the edge of scarcity: Environment, resources, population, sustainability, and conflict*. Syracuse University Press. https://doi.org/10.2307/1556667

O'Boyle, E. (2003). Income gap between poor families and others: Signs of individual freedom or proof of social inequality? *Forum for Social Economics*, *32*(2), 57–65. https://doi.org/10.1007/bf02779079

Odum, H. T., & Odum, E. C. (2001). *A prosperous way down: Principles and policies*. University Press of Colorado.

Olson, M. (1993). Dictatorship, democracy, and development. *American Political Science Review*, *87*, 567–576. https://doi.org/10.2307/2938736

Olsson, P., Folke, C., & Hughes, T. P. (2008). Navigating the transition to ecosystem-based management of the Great Barrier Reef, Australia. *Proceedings of the National Academy of Sciences of the United States of America*, *105*, 9489–9494. https://doi.org/10.1073/pnas.0706905105

Oppenheimer, V. K. (2003). Cohabiting and marriage during young men's career-development process. *Demography*, *40*, 127–149. https://doi.org/10.2307/3180815

Oram, D. E., Ashfold, M. J., Laube, J. C., Gooch, L. J., Humphrey, S., Sturges, W. T., Elvidge, E. C. L., Forster, G. L., Harris, N. R. P., Mead, M. I., Samah, A. A., Phang, S. M., Ou-Yang, C.-F., Lin, N.-H., Wang, J.-L., Baker, A. K., Brenninkmeijer, C. A. M., & Sherry, D. (2017). A growing threat to the ozone layer from short-lived anthropogenic chlorocarbons. *Atmospheric Chemistry and Physics*, *17*, 11929–11941. https://doi.org/10.5194/acp-17-11929-2017

Ostrom, E. (2005). *Understanding institutional diversity*. Princeton University Press.

Ostrom, E., Burger, J., Field, C. B., Norgaard, R. B., & Policansky, D. (1999). Revisiting the commons: Local lessons, global challenges. *Science*, *284*, 278–282. http://dx.doi.org/110.1126/science.284.5412.278

Otovescu, C., & Otovescu, A. (2019). The depopulation of Romania – Is it an irreversible process? *Revista de Cercetare Si Intervenţie Socială*, *65*, 370–388. https://doi.org/10.33788/rcis.65.23

Overpeck, J., & Webb, R. (2000). Nonglacial rapid climate events: Past and future. *Proceedings of the National Academy of Sciences of the United States of America*, *97*, 1335–1338. https://doi.org/10.1073/pnas.97.4.1335

Ozili, P. K., & Arun, T. (2020). *Spillover of COVID-19: Impact on the global economy*. University Library of Munich. https://doi.org/10.2139/ssrn.3562570

Papava, V. (1996). The Georgian economy: From 'shock therapy' to 'social promotion'. *Communist Economies & Economic Transformation*, *8*(2), 251–267. https://doi.org/10.1080/14631379608427856

Parcero, O. J., & Papyrikas, E. (2016). Income inequality and the oil resource curse. *Resource and Energy Economics*, *45*, 159–177. https://doi.org/10.1016/j.reseneeco.2016.06.001

Parker, D., Kirkpatrick, C., & Figueira-Theodorakopoulou, C. (2008). Infrastructure regulation and poverty reduction in developing countries: A review of the evidence and a research agenda. *Quarterly Review of Economic Finance*, *48*(2), 177–188. https://doi.org/10.1016/j.qref.2006.12.00

Paulson, M. B. (2018). *Higher education: Handbook of theory and research*. Springer. https://doi.org/10.1007/978-3-319-26829-3

Peng, X. (2011). China's demographic history and future challenges. *Science*, *33*, 581–587. https://doi.org/10.1126/science.1209396

Peters, G., Sacker, D., & Seruga, J. (2016). *A comparative analysis of MOOC – Australia's position in the international education market*. Australasian Conference on Information Systems. https://doi.org/10.48550/arXiv.1606.00885

Petr, J. L. (1986). Comparative analysis of thresholds of non-revolutionary institutional change: China and the United States in the 1980s. *Journal of Economic Issues*, *20*, 561–569. https://doi.org/10.1080/00213624.1986.11504527

Pickering, J., & Peceny, M. (2006). Forging democracy at gunpoint. *International Studies Quarterly*, *50*, 539–559. https://doi.org/10.1111/j.1468-2478.2006.00413.x

Piketty, T. (2007). *Capital in the 21st century*. Harvard University Press.

Pilkey, O. H., & Cooper, J. A. G. 2004). Climate: Society and sea level rise. *Science*, *303*, 1781–1782. https://doi.org/10.1126/science.1093515

Popkin, B. M. (2011). Agricultural policies, food and public health. *EMBO Reports*, *12*, 11–18. https://doi.org/10.1038/embor.2010.200

Porter, M. E. (1991). *Porter on competition and strategy*. Harvard Business School Press.

Prettner, K., Bloom, D. E., & Strulik, H. (2013). Declining fertility and economic wellbeing: Do education and health ride to the rescue? *Labour Economics*, *22*, 70–79. https://doi.org/10.1016/j.labeco.2012.07.001

Pu, X. (2017). Controversial identity of a rising China. *Chinese Journal of International Politics*, *10*, 131–149. https://doi.org/10.1093/cjip/pox004

Qian, Y., & Weingast, B. R. (1997). Federalism as a commitment to preserving market incentives. *Journal of Economic Perspective*, *11*, 83–92. https://doi.org/10.1257/jep.11.4.83

Qiang, J. (2017). Does exports promote the economic growth of China? A long-run view point. *International Journal of Financial Research*, *8*, 64–74. https://doi.org/10.5430/ijfr.v8n2p64

Rands, M. R. W., Adams, W. M., Bennun, L., Butchart, S. H. M., Clements, A., Coomes, D., Entwistle, A., Hodge, I., Kapos, V., Scharlemann, J. P. W., Sutherland, W. J., & Vira, B. (2010). Biodiversity conservation: Challenges beyond 2010. *Science*, *329*, 1298–1303. http://dx.doi.org/10.1126/science.1189138

Ravallion, M. (2001). Growth, inequality and poverty: Looking beyond averages. *World Development*, *29*, 1803–1815. https://doi.org/10.1596/1813-9450-3461

Ravallion, M., & Chen, S. (2007). China's (uneven) progress against poverty. *Journal of Development Economics*, *82*, 1–42. https://doi.org/10.1016/j.jdeveco.2005.07.003

Reher, D. S. (2007). Towards long-term population decline: A discussion of relevant issues. *European Journal of Population*, *23*, 189–207. https://doi.org/10.1007/s10680-007-9120-z

Reynolds, R. H. (1974). *Man, nature and society in selected works of Frederick Philip Grove and Thomas Hardy* [Master of Arts thesis, McMaster University]. http://hdl.handle.net/11375/9721

Ricker, M. (1997). Limits to economic growth as shown by a computable general equilibrium model. *Ecological Economics*, *21*, 141–158. https://doi.org/10.1016/S0921-8009(96)00099-7

Robinson, J. A., Daron, A., & Simon, J. (2005). Institutions as a fundamental cause of long-run growth. *Handbook of Economic Growth*, *1*, 385–472. https://doi.org/10.3386/w10481

Roland, G. (2004). Understanding institutional change: Fast-moving and slow-moving institutions. *Studies in Comparative International Development*, *38*, 109–131. https://doi.org/10.1007/BF02686330

Romer, P. M. (1990). Endogenous technological change. *Journal of Political Economy*, *98*, 71–102. https://doi.org/10.1086/261725

Romm, J., Rosenfeld, A., & Herrmann, S. (1999). *The internet economy and global warming*. Center for Energy and Climate Solutions.

Rosenzweig, M. L. (2001). Loss of speciation rate will impoverish future diversity. *Proceedings of the National Academy of Sciences of the United States of America*, *98*, 5404–5410. https://doi.org/10.1073/pnas.101092798

Ross, R. S. (2012). The problem with the pivot: Obama's new Asia policy is unnecessary and counterproductive. *Foreign Affairs*, *91*(6), 70–82. https://doi.org/10.2307/41720935

Russia Statistics. (2019). *National accounts*. https://eng.rosstat.gov.ru/folder/75924

Ruttan, V. W. (1999). The transition to agricultural sustainability. *Proceedings of the National Academy of Sciences of the United States of America*, *96*, 5961–5967. https://doi.org/10.1073/pnas.96.11.5960

Saboor, A., Sadiq, S., Khan, A. U., & Hameed, G. (2017). Dynamic reflections of crimes, quasi democracy and misery index in Pakistan. *Social Indicators Research*, *133*, 31–45. https://doi.org/10.1007/s11205-016-1348-8

Sachs, J. D. (2002). Rapid population growth saps development. *Science*, *297*, 341. https://doi.org/10.1126/science.1071882

Sachs, J. D. (2004). Sustainable development. *Science*, *304*, 649. https://doi.org/10.1126/science.1071882

Sachs, J. D., & McArthur, J. W. (2005). The millennium project: A plan for meeting the millennium development goals. *The Lancet*, *365*, 347–353. https://doi.org/10.1016/S0140-6736(05)17791-5

Sachs, J. D., & Reid, W. V. (2006). Investments toward sustainable development. *Science*, *312*, 1002. https://doi.org/10.1126/science.1124822

Sachs, J. D., & Warner, A. M. (2001). Natural resources and economic development: The curse of natural resources. *European Economic Review*, *45*, 827–838. https://doi.org/10.1016/S0014-2921(01)00125-8

Salvado, F. P. R. (2017). "España no era Rusia": La revolución española de 1917: Anatomía de un fracas. *Hispania Nova*, *15*, 416–443. https://doi.org/10.20318/hn.2017.3496

San Juan Mesonada, C., & Sunyer Manteiga, C. (2020). Rural depopulation and income convergence. *Economia Agraria y Recursos Naturales*, *19*(2), 29–48. https://doi.org/10.7201/earn.2019.02.02

Sanyou. (2021, May 21). *2020 China patent investigation report released*. Lexology. https://www.lexology.com/library/detail.aspx?g=ac6019e0-311c-4598-8601-649ee1cb930f

Schneiberg, M. (2005). Combining new institutionalisms: Explaining institutional change in American property insurance. *Sociology Forum*, *20*, 93–137. https://doi.org/10.1007/s11206-005-1899-y

Schumpeter, J. A. (1912). *The theory of economic development*. Harvard University Press.

Sen, A. (1981). *Poverty and famines: An essay on entitlement and deprivation*. Clarendon Press. https://doi.org/10.2307/1240373

Serageldin, I. (2002). World poverty and hunger – The challenge for science. *Science*, *296*, 54–58. https://doi.org/10.1126/science.1072035

Seto, K., Sanchez-Rodriguez, R., & Fragkias, M. (2010). The new geography of contemporary urbanization and the environment. *Annual Review Environment and Resources*, *35*, 167–194. https://doi.org/10.1146/annurev-environ-100809-125336

Sevilla, C. (1995). *Explaining the September 1992 ERM crisis: The Maastricht bargain and domestic politics in Germany, France and Great Britain* [Working Paper]. University of Pittsburgh. http://aei.pitt.edu/7014/1/sevilla_christina.pdf

Shang, D., Liu, G., & Cao, S. (2019). Why are Chinese ethics declining? *Time & Society*, *28*, 438–453. https://doi.org/10.1177/0961463X16658803

Sharma, Y. (2021, June 11). *Campus murder highlights stresses on academics to produce*. University World News. http://www.universityworldnews.com/post.php?story=20210611084120155

Shi, F., Lu, H., Guo, Z., Yin, Q., Wu, H., Xu C., Zhang, E., Shi, J., Cheng, J., Xiao, X., & Zhao, C. (2021). The position of the current warm period in the context of the past 2,000 years of summer climate in China. *Geophysical Research Letters*, *48*(5), e2020GL091940. https://doi.org/10.1029/2020GL09194010

Shi, H. (2019). The Chinese mode of supporting social organizations: A new framework. *Humanities and Social Sciences*, *7*(2), 58–66. https://doi.org/10.11648/j.hss.20190702.12

Shi, K., Chang, Z., Chen, Z., Wu, J., & Yu, B. (2020). Identifying and evaluating poverty using multisource remote sensing and point of interest (POI) data: A case study of Chongqing, China. *Journal of Cleaner Production*, *255*, 120245. https://doi.org/10.1016/j.jclepro.2020.120245

Shi, T. (2004). Ecological economics as a policy science: Rhetoric or commitment towards an improved decision-making process on sustainability. *Ecological Economics*, *48*, 23–36. https://doi.org/10.1016/j.ecolecon.2003.08.004

Shi, Y., & Zhang, J. (2008). On high fertility rates in developing countries: Birth limits, birth taxes, or education subsidies? *Journal of Population Economics*, *22*, 603–640. https://doi.org/10.1007/s00148-008-0212-9

Shin, H. B. (2015). Urbanization in China. *International Encyclopedia of the Social & Behavioral Sciences*, *2*, 973–979. https://doi.org/10.1016/B978-0-08-097086-8.72095-2

Si, J. (2005). Attention to poverty and the poor. 司金. 2005. 关注贫困 关注穷人. 老区建设. *Poverty Region Construction*, *7*, 36–37 (in Chinese).

Simonstein, F. (2006). Artificial reproduction technologies (RTs) – All the way to the artificial womb? *Medicine, Health Care and Philosophy*, *9*, 359–365. https://doi.org/10.1007/s11019-006-0005-4

Skousen, M. (1988). Saving the depression: A new look at World War II. *Review of Austrian Economics*, *2*, 211–226. https://doi.org/10.1007/BF01539309

Smith, A. (1776). *An inquiry into the nature and causes of the wealth of nations*. Oxford World's Classics.

Smith, J. (2013). The international political economy of work and employability by Phoebe V. Moore. *Global Discourse*, *2*, 187–189. https://doi.org/10.1080/23269995.2011.10707923

Sobotka, T., & Toulemon, L. (2008). Changing family and partnership behavior: Common trends and persistent diversity across Europe. *Demographic Research*, *19*, 85–138. https://doi.org/10.4054/DEMRES.2008.19.6

Song, Y. (2013). Rising Chinese regional income inequality: The role of fiscal decentralization. *China Economic Review*, *27*, 294–309. https://doi.org/10.1016/j.chieco.2013.02.001

Song, Y., Zhang, Y., Wang, Y., Zhang, B., & Su, J. (2021). The influence of foreign direct investment on the urban–rural income gap: Evidence from China. *Kybernetes*, *51*(1), 466–484. https://doi.org/10.1108/K-07-2020-0488

Song, Z., Storesletten, K., & Zilibott, F. (2011). Growing like China. *American Economic Review*, *101*, 196–233. https://doi.org/10.1257/aer.101.1.196

Spencer, C. S. (2010). Territorial expansion and primary state formation. *Proceedings of the National Academy of Sciences of the United States of America*, *107*, 7119–7126. https://doi.org/10.1073/pnas.1002470107

Statista. (2022). *Countries with the highest military spending worldwide in 2022 (in billion U.S. dollars)*. https://www.statista.com/statistics/262742/countries-with-the-highest-military-spending

Statista. (2023). *Planned financial budget of leading universities in China for 2022*. https://www.statista.com/statistics/1098877/china-financial-budget-of-leading-universities/#:~:text=Budget%20planning%20for%202022%20of%20the%20leading%20universities,for%202022%20amounted%20to%20around%2036.21%20billion%20yuan

Stone, R. (2009). Forensic finds add substance to claims of war atrocities. *Science*, *325*, 374–375. https://doi.org/10.1126/science.325_374

Stovel, K., Golub, B., & Milgrom, E. M. M. (2011). Stabilizing brokerage. *Proceedings of the National Academy of Sciences of the United States of America*, *108*, 21326–21332. https://doi.org/10.1073/pnas.1100920108

Su, C. W., Liu, T. Y., Chang, H. L., & Jiang, X. Z. (2015). Is urbanization narrowing the urban–rural income gap? A cross-regional study of China. *Habitat International*, *48*, 79–86. https://doi.org/10.1016/J.HABITATINT.2015.03.002

Su, W., Zhang, X. D., Wang, Z., Su, X. H., Huang, J. X., Yang, S. Q., Liu, S. C. (2011). 窗体底端 Analyzing disaster-forming environments and the spatial distribution of flood disasters and snow disasters that occurred in China from 1949 to 2000. *Mathematical and Computer Modelling*, *54*, 1069–1078. https://doi.org/10.1016/j.mcm.2010.11.037

Sun, H. P., Sun, W. F., Geng, Y., & Kong, Y. S. (2018). Natural resource dependence, public education investment, and human capital accumulation. *Petroleum Science*, *15*, 657–665. https://doi.org/10.1007/s12182-018-0235-0

Sun, S., Zhai, J., Li, Y., Huang, D., & Wang, G. (2020). Urban waterlogging risk assessment in well-developed region of Eastern China. *Physics and Chemistry of the Earth*, *115*, 102824. https://doi.org/10.1016/j.pce.2019.102824

Suo, X., Yu, Z., & Cao, S. (2023). Utilizing water resources from the Tibetan Plateau: Benefits, risks, and future research requirements. *Catena*, *230*, 107256. https://doi.org/10.1016/j.catena.230.107256

Sutherland, D., & Yao, S. (2011). Income inequality in China over 30 years of reforms. *Cambridge Journal of Regions, Economy and Society*, *4*, 91–105. https://doi.org/10.1093/cjres/rsq036

Syairudin, B., Trisunarno, L., & Gunarta, I. K. (2015). Strategy for achieving the Millennium Development Goals 7–10 through knowledge-based sustainable design approach. *Social and Behavioral Sciences*, *169*, 61–68. https://doi.org/10.1016/j.sbspro.2015.01.286

Taher, S. M. (2020). *Determinants of fertility rate: A regression analysis case of Tunisia*. ScienceOpen Preprints. https://doi.org/10.14293/S2199-1006.1.SOR-.PPUOUNE.v1

Tainter, J. A. (2000). Problem solving: Complexity, history, sustainability. *Population & Environment*, *22*, 3–41. https://doi.org/10.1023/A:1006632214612

Takács-Sánta, A. (2004). The major transitions in the history of human transformation of the biosphere. *Human Ecological Review*, *11*, 51–66. https://www.jstor.org/stable/24707019

Tan, M. (2017). Uneven growth of urban clusters in megaregions and its policy implications for new urbanization in China. *Land Use Policy*, *66*, 72–79. https://doi.org/10.1016/j.landusepol.2017.04.032

Thibodeau, P. (2016, June 20). *China builds world's fastest supercomputer without U.S. chips*. Computerworld. https://www.computerworld.com/article/3085483/china-builds-world-s-fastest-supercomputer-without-u-s-chips.html

Thompson, P. (2007). Adler's theory of the capitalist labour process: A pale(o) imitation. *Organization Studies*, *28*, 1359–1368. https://doi.org/10.1177/0170840607080745

Thompson, P., & Smith, C. (2009). Waving, not drowning: Explaining and exploring the resilience of labor process theory. *Employee Responsibilities and Rights Journal*, *21*, 253–262. https://doi.org/10.1007/s10672-009-9116-4

Tian, X., Hu, Y., Yin, H., Geng, Y., & Bleischwitz, R. (2019). Trade impacts of China's belt and road initiative: From resource and environmental perspectives. *Resources, Conservation and Recycling*, *150*, 104430. https://doi.org/10.1016/j.resconrec.2019.104430

Tilly, C. (1975). *The formation of national states in Western Europe*. Princeton University Press. https://doi.org/10.2307/2064093

Tilly, C. (1990). *Coercion, capital, and European States, AD 990-1990*. Blackwell. https://doi.org/10.2307/2597834

Titcomb, J. (2021, December 3). *China's quantum leap plunges West into a race to protect its secrets*. Aman Tokyo. https://www.telegraph.co.uk/technology/2021/12/03/chinas-quantum-leap-computing-plunges-west-race-protect-secrets/

Towns, A. (1993). *Inside bureaucracy*. Waveland Press.

Tsui, K. Y. (2011). China's infrastructure investment boom and local debt crisis. *Eurasian Geography and Economics*, *52*, 686–711. https://doi.org/10.2747/1539-7216.52.5.686

Turner, J. H. (2003). *Human institutions*. Rowman and Littlefield.

UN-DESA. (1978). *World population prospects 1978*. United Nations Department of Economic and Social Affairs. https://population.un.org/wpp

UN-DESA. (2019). *World population prospects 2019*. United Nations Department of Economic and Social Affairs. https://population.un.org/wpp

United Nations. (1968). *Final act of the international conference on human rights*. https://legal.un.org/avl/pdf/ha/fatchr/Final_Act_of_TehranConf.pdf

United Nations Population Division. (2024). *World population prospects*. United Nations. https://population.un.org/wpp/DefinitionOfRegions

United States Statistics. (1953). *Minerals yearbook 1950 Year 1950 1953*. https://search.library.wisc.edu/digital/A3M2CR4ONJEVFW9A

USA. (1890). *The antitrust laws*. https://en.wikipedia.org/wiki/United_States_antitrust_law

Vahabi, M. (2018). The resource curse literature as seen through the appropriability lens: A critical survey. *Public Choice*, *175*, 393–428. https://doi.org/10.1007/s11127-018-0533-5
Valerio Mendoza, O. M. (2016). Preferential policies and income inequality: Evidence from special economic zones and open cities in China. *China Economic Review*, *40*, 228–240. https://doi.org/10.1016/j.chieco.2016.07.013
Vasil'ev A. M. (2014). Arab revolutions and the protest movement: Causes, driving forces, and results. *Herald of the Russian Academy of Sciences*, *84*, 165–171. https://doi.org/10.1134/S1019331614030113
Verschuren, D., & Cumming, B. F. (2000). Rainfall and drought in equatorial east Africa during the past 1,100 years. *Nature*, *403*, 410–414. https://doi.org/10.1038/35000179
Vlek, C., & Steg, L. (2007). Human behavior and environmental sustainability: Problems, driving forces, and research topics. *Journal of Social Issues*, *63*, 1–19. https://doi.org/10.1111/j.1540-4560.2007.00493.x
von Clausewitz, K. P. J. (1832). *The theory on war* (1989 ed.). Princeton University Press.
Wallerstein, I. (1984). Economic cycles and socialist policies. *Futures*, *16*, 579–585. https://doi.org/10.1016/0016-3287(84)90120-4
Walther, G-R., Post, E., Convey, P., Menze, A., Parmesank, C., Beebee, T. J. C., Fromentin, J.-M., Hoegh-Guldberg, O., & Bairlein, F. (2002). Ecological responses to recent climate change. *Nature*, *416*, 389–395. https://doi.org/10.1038/416389a
Wan, G. H., Hu, X. S., & Liu, W. Q. (2021). China's poverty reduction miracle and relative poverty: Focusing on the roles of growth and inequality. *China Economic Review*, *68*, 101643. https://doi.org/10.1016/j.chieco.202
Wang, B., & Jiang, K. (2006). Scale of China's space exploration program. 汪本强, 江可申. (2006). 中国航空工业产业规模、集中度与绩效的关系研究. 高新技术产业化. *Science and Technology Strategy*, *2006*(1), 75–77 (in Chinese).
Wang, L., & Chen, L. (2016). Spatiotemporal dataset on Chinese population distribution and its driving factors from 1949 to 2013. *Nature Scientific Data*, *3*, 160047. https://doi.org/10.1038/sdata.2016.47
Wang, L., & Potter, C., & Li, Z. (2014). Crisis-induced reform, state–market relations, and entrepreneurial urban growth in China. *Habitat International*, *41*, 50–57. https://doi.org/10.1016/j.habitatint.2013.06.008
Wang, M. (2019). A retrospective and predictive study of fertility rates in China from 2003 to 2018. *Heliyon*, *5*(3), e01460. https://doi.org/10.1016/j.heliyon.2019.e01460
Wang, X. (2006). Income inequality in China and its influencing factors. In G. H. Wan (Ed.), *Inequality and growth in modern China* (pp. 18–32). Oxford Academic. https://doi.org/10.1093/acprof:oso/9780199535194.003.0001
Wang, X., Shao, S., & Li, L. (2019). Agricultural inputs, urbanization, and urban–rural income disparity: Evidence from China. *China Economic Review*, *55*, 67–84. https://doi.org/10.1016/j.chieco.2019.03.009
Wang, X., Wang, Y., Xu, C., Chen, L., & Guo, S. (2016). Convergence of human populations in China: Impact on sustainable development. *Environmental Engineering and Management Journal*, *15*, 2375–2382. https://doi.org/10.30638/eemj.2016.259
Wang, X., Zhang, C., Hasi, E., & Dong, Z. (2010). Has the Three Norths Forest Shelterbelt Program solved the desertification and dust storm problems in arid and semiarid China? *Journal of Arid Environments*, *74*, 13–22. https://doi.org/10.1016/j.jaridenv.2009.08.001
Wang, Z. (2006). The growth of China's private sector: A case study of Zhejiang Province. *China & World Economy*, *14*, 109–120. https://doi.org/10.1111/j.1749-124X.2006.00026.x
Weber, M. (1978). *Economy and society: An outline of interpretive sociology*. University of California Press. https://doi.org/10.17323/1726-3247-2018-3-68-78
Wei, P., Xin, X., Xue, M., Zhang, C., Wang, Y., Zhao, K., Zhou, A., Zhang, S., & Zhu, K. (2023). On the key dynamical processes supporting the 21.7 Zhengzhou

record-breaking hourly rainfall in China. *Advances in Atmospheric Sciences*, *3*, 337–349. https://doi.org/10.1007/s00376-022-2061-y

Wei, Y. Q., & Liu, X. M. (2011). Foreign direct investment in China: Determinants and impact. *China Journal*, *48*, 229–230. http://dx.doi.org/10.2307/3182474

Weinberg, B. A. (2011). Developing science: Scientific performance and brain drains in the developing world. *Journal of Development Economics*, *95*, 95–104. https://doi.org/10.1016/j.jdeveco.2010.05.009

Weingast, B. R. (1995). The economic role of political institutions: Market preserving federalism and economic development. *Journal of Law and Economic Organization*, *11*, 1–31. https://doi.org/10.1093/OXFORDJOURNALS.JLEO.A036861

Weisbrod, S., & Rojas-Suárez, L. (1995). *Financial fragilities in Latin America: The 1980s and 1990s* [Occasional Paper 1995/012]. International Monetary Fund. https://doi.org/10.2139/ssrn.2559972

Weiss, H., & Bradley, R. S. (2001). What drives societal collapse? *Science*, *291*, 609–610. https://doi.org/10.1126/science.1058775

Whalley, J., & Yue, X. (2009). Rural income volatility and inequality in China. *CESifo Economic Studies*, *55*, 648–668. https://doi.org/10.1093/cesifo/ifp014

Whitt, S., & Wilson, R. K. (2007). The dictator game: Fairness and ethnicity in postwar Bosnia. *American Journal of Political Science*, *51*, 655–668. https://doi.org/10.1111/j.1540-5907.2007.00273.x

Whyte, M. K. (2009). Paradoxes of China's economic boom. *Annual Review of Sociology*, *35*, 371–392. https://doi.org/10.1146/annurev-soc-070308-115905

Wilkinson, R. G. (1973). *Poverty and progress: An ecological model of economic development*. Methuen & Co. Ltd. https://doi.org/10.4324/9781003306351

Wilson, C. (2004). Fertility below replacement level. *Science*, *304*, 207–209. https://doi.org/10.1126/science.304.5668.207c

Wilson, W. (1887). The study of administration. *Political Science Quarterly*, *2*, 6. https://doi.org/10.2307/2139277

WIPO. (2019). *World intellectual property indicators 2019*. https://www.wipo.int/publications/en/details.jsp?id=4464&plang=EN

Woodwell, G. M. (2002). The functional integrity of normally forested landscapes: A proposal for an index of environmental capital. *Proceedings of the National Academy of Sciences of the United States of America*, *99*, 13600–13605. https://doi.org/10.1073/pnas.202035299

World Bank. (1958–2023). *World Bank public data*. https://data.worldbank.org.cn

Wu, X. (2010). Qian Xuesen's greatness only owes an apology. 吴晓波. (2010). 钱学森的伟大只欠一个道歉. 新周刊. *New Weekly*, *12*, 1–5 (in Chinese).

Xia, C., Li, X., & Cao, S. (2023). Challenges for the government-controlled higher education system in China. *International Journal of Educational Development*, *97*, 102721. https://doi.org/10.1016/j.ijedudev.2022.102721

Xia, H. (2021). *Population and family planning law of People's Republic of China*. 夏红真. 中华人民共和国人口与计划生育法. September 1, 2002. http://www.npc.gov.cn/npc/c30834/202109/9ab0af08773c465aa91d95648df2a98a.shtml (in Chinese).

Xian, Y., & Zhou, Y. (2014). Income inequality in today's China. *Proceedings of the National Academy of Sciences of the United States of America*, *111*, 6928–6933. https://doi.org/10.1073/PNAS.1403158111

Xing, T. (2020). When the bubble bursts – Recent financial woes of mega rental firm underline the need for reform of the industry. *Beijing Review*, *63*(51), 36–37.

Xinhua. (2016, June 13). The walking marriage of Mosuo ethnic group. *China Daily*. www.chinadaily.com.cn/china/2016-06/13/content_25690011.htm

Xu, C. (2011). The fundamental institutions of China's reforms and development. *Journal of Economic Literature*, *49*, 1076–1151. https://doi.org/10.2307/23071664

Xu, C., Ye, H., & Cao, S. (2011). Constructing China's greenways naturally. *Ecological Engineering*, *37*, 401–406. https://doi.org/10.1016/j.ecoleng.2010.12.009

Xu, X., & Yan, Y. (2014). Does government investment crowd out private investment in China? *Journal of Economic Policy Reform*, *17*, 1–12. https://doi.org/10.1080/17487870.2013.866897

Yang, D. L. (2006). Economic transformation and its political discontents in China: Authoritarianism, unequal growth, and the dilemmas of political development. *Annual Review of Political Science*, *9*, 143–164. https://doi.org/10.1146/annurev.polisci.9.062404.170624

Yang, H. (2004). Land conservation campaign in China: Integrated management, local participation and food supply options. *Geoforum*, *35*, 507–518. https://doi.org/10.1016/j.geoforum.2003.10.002

Yang, J., & Gao, M. (2017). The impact of education expansion on wage inequality. *Applied Economics*, *50*, 1–15. https://doi.org/10.1080/00036846.2017.1361008

Yang, K. (1986). *History of primitive society*. 杨堃. (1986). 原始社会发展史, 北京师范大学出版社,北京. Beijing Normal University Press (in Chinese).

Yang, L., Guo, J., & Cao, S. (2022). What structural factors have held back China's birth rate? *Environment Development and Sustainability*, *26*, 565–578. https://doi.org/10.1007/s10668-022-02723-7

Yang, Z. (2016). Tax reform, fiscal decentralization, and regional economic growth: New evidence from China. *Economic Modelling*, *59*, 520–528. https://doi.org/10.1016/j.econmod.2016.07.020

Yu, X. (1995). Result of geo-environment variance in China in 4000 years. 于希贤. (1995). 近四千年来中国地理环境几次突发变异及其后果的初步研究. 中国历史地理论丛. *China History and Geography Review*, *2*, 45–62 (in Chinese).

Yu, X. (1997). Variance of China geo-environment in 4000 years. 于希贤. (1997). 近几千年来的地理环境灾变. 云南社会科学. *Yunnan Social Science*, *4*, 79–84 (in Chinese).

Yuan, J., Lu, Y., Wang, C., Cao, X., Chen, C., Cui, H., Zhang, M., Wang, C., Li, X., Johnson, A. C., Sweetman, A. J., & Du, D. (2020). Ecology of industrial pollution in China. *Ecosystem Health and Sustainability*, *6*, 1779010. https://doi.org/10.1080/20964129.2020.1779010

Zakaria, M., Fida, B., Janjua, S., & Shahzad, J. (2017). Fertility and financial development in South Asia. *Social Indicators Research*, *133*, 645–668. https://doi.org/10.1007/s11205-016-1382-6

Zastrow, M. (2019). China's tree-planting drive could falter in a warming world. *Nature*, *573*, 474–475. https://doi.org/10.1038/d41586-019-02789-w

Zeng, Y. (2004). Farmland institution reform: Land call up standardization, property right diversity, land construct persistently. 曾业松. 土地制度改革：征地规范化、产权多元化、承包永久化. 中共石家庄市委党校学报. (2004). *Journal of the Party University of Shijiazhuang City Committee of CPC*, *9*, 13–19 (in Chinese).

Zerbo, A., Castro Delgado, R., & González, P. A. (2020). A review of the risk of cholera outbreaks and urbanization in sub-Saharan Africa. *Journal of Biosafety and Biosecurity*, *2*(2), 71–76. https://doi.org/10.1016/j.jobb.2020.11.004

Zhai, Y. (2019). A peaceful prospect or a threat to global order: How Asian youth view a rising China. *International Studies Review*, *21*, 38–56. https://doi.org/10.1093/isr/viy010

Zhang, D. D., Brecke, P., Lee, H. F., He, Y., & Zhang, J. (2007). Global climate change, war, and population decline in recent human history. *Proceedings of the National Academy of Sciences of the United States of America*, *104*, 19214–19219. https://doi.org/10.1073/pnas.0703073104

Zhang, J. (2021). A study on the group of rebel song military generals in the early Jin Dynasty. 张锦涛. 2021.金初叛宋武将群体研究.保定学院学报. *Journal of Baoding University*, *34*(5), 71–77 (in Chinese).

Zhang, M. Y., Zhou, G. S., & Fan, G. (2020). Political control and economic inequality: Evidence from Chinese cities. *China Economic Review*, *61*, 101272. https://doi.org/10.1016/j.chieco.2019.01.011

Zhang, Q., Wu, Z., Guo, G., Zhang, H., & Tarolli, P. (2021). Explicit the urban waterlogging spatial variation and its driving factors: The stepwise cluster analysis model and hierarchical partitioning analysis approach. *Science of the Total Environment*, *763*, 143041. https://doi.org/10.1016/j.scitotenv.2020.143041

Zhang, R., Jiang, D. B., & Zhang, Z. S. (2016). Effects of the uplifts of the main and marginal Tibetan Plateau on the Asian climate under modern and ~30 Ma boundary conditions. *Palaeogeography Palaeoclimatology Palaeoecology*, *510*, 15–25. https://doi.org/10.1016/j.palaeo.2017.12.022

Zhang, W. (2016). The evolution of China's pay inequality from 1987 to 2012. *Journal of Current Chinese Affairs*, *45*(2), 183–217. https://doi.org/10.1177/186810261604500207

Zhang, W. (2017). *The economic system of China*. 张五常. (2017). 中国的经济制度. 中信出版集团, 北京. Zhongxin Press (in Chinese).

Zhang, X. B., Li, X., Fan, S. G., & Luo, X. P. (2008). Resource abundance and regional development in China. *Economics of Transition*, *16*, 7–29. https://doi.org/10.1111/j.1468-0351.2007.00318.x

Zhang, X. H., & Luo, B. (2016). The blocking mechanism in the transmission process of monetary policy – A study on the decline of inflation under accommodative monetary policy. 张兴华,罗彪. (2016).货币政策传导过程中的阻塞机制 – 对宽松货币政策下通货膨胀率下降的研究. 金融论坛. *Financial Forum*, *247*(7), 22–39. https://doi.org/10.16529/j.cnki.11-4613/f.2016.07.004 (in Chinese).

Zhang, Y. (2012). China's evolution toward an authoritarian market economy – A predator–prey evolutionary model with intelligent design. *Public Choice*, *151*, 271–287. https://doi.org/10.1007/s11127-010-9747-x

Zhang, Y., & Wan, G. (2006). The impact of growth and inequality on rural poverty in China. *Journal of Comparative Economics*, *34*, 694–712. https://doi.org/10.1016/j.jce.2006.08.008

Zhao, X. (2006). Competition, public choice, and institutional change: Searching for reasons for improved policy efficiency in institutional reform from "managing large enterprises and cutting small ones loose." *The Chinese Economy*, *39*, 5–73. https://doi.org/10.2753/CES1097-1475390102

Zheng, H., & Cao, S. (2011). The challenge to sustainable development in China revealed by "death villages." *Environmental Science and Technology*, *45*, 9833–9834. https://doi.org/10.1021/es2037977

Zheng, H., Wang, X., & Cao, S. (2014). The land finance model jeopardizes China's sustainable development. *Habitat International*, *44*, 130–136. https://doi.org/10.1016/j.habitatint.2014.05.008

Zheng, J., Bigsten, A., & Hu, A. (2009). Can China's growth be sustained? A productivity perspective. *World Development*, *37*, 874–888. https://doi.org/10.1016/j.worlddev.2008.07.008

Zheng, T. (2023, April 8). *The details of Zhuzhou Public Security Bureau chief and her husband were sacked and "Prince's Milk" collapsed|breaking news*. https://china.postsen.com/celebrities/23454/The-details-of-Zhuzhou-Public-Security-Bureau-chief-and-her-husband-were-sacked-and-Prince%E2%80%99s-Milk-collapsed-Public-Security-Bureau-Ling-Ya-Prince%E2%80%99s-Milk-Group.html

Zhou, L. (2021, May 8). *Most one do not understand the path of innovation at Shenzhen*. 周路明. 2021.大家没读懂的深圳创新路径. 融中财经. Rongzhong Caijing. https://mp.weixin.qq.com/s/raM5zj5H2NSABSbQy9MxnQ (in Chinese).

Zhou, W. (2012). Regulatory models and entrepreneurial growth: Evidence from China's transition economy. *Strategic Change*, *21*, 119–142. https://doi.org/10.1080/08985626.2011.577816

Zhu, B., & Zhang, T. L. (2021). The impact of cross-region industrial structure optimization on economy, carbon emissions and energy consumption: A case of the Yangtze River Delta. *Science of the Total Environment*, *778*, 146089. https://doi.org/10.1016/j.scitotenv.2021.146089

Zhu, X. (2012). Understanding China's growth: Past, present, and future. *Journal of Economic Perspectives*, *26*, 103–124. https://doi.org/10.1257/jep.26.4.103

Zwick, P. (1989). New thinking and new foreign policy under Gorbachev. *Political Science & Politics*, *22*(2), 215–224. https://doi.org/10.2307/419599